A Longma

Emily Brontë's

# WUTHERING HEIGHTS

*Edited by*

**Alison Booth**

University of Virginia

New York   San Francisco   Boston
London   Toronto   Sydney   Tokyo   Singapore   Madrid
Mexico City   Munich   Paris   Cape Town   Hong Kong   Montreal

Vice President and Editor-in-Chief: Joseph P. Terry
Executive Marketing Manager: Joyce Nilsen
Production Coordinator: Scarlett Lindsay
Project Coordination, Text Design, and Electronic Page Makeup:
    Grapevine Publishing Services, Inc.
Cover Designer/Manager: John Callahan
Manufacturing Manager: Mary Fischer
Printer and Binder: R.R. Donnelley / Harrisonburg
Cover Printer: Coral Graphics Services, Inc.

Cover Image: Courtesy of Getty Images, Inc.

Library of Congress Cataloging-in-Publication Data

Brontë, Emily, 1818–1848.
    Emily Bronte's Wuthering Heights / edited by Alison Booth. — A Longman
cultural ed.
        p. cm. — (Longman cultural editions)
    ISBN-13: 978-0-321-21298-6
    ISBN-10: 0-321-21298-3
    1. Triangles (Interpersonal relations)--Fiction. 2. Rejection (Psychology)—Fiction.
3. Yorkshire (England)—Fiction. 4. Rural families—Fiction. 5. Foundlings—Fiction.
6. Psychological fiction. 7. Domestic fiction. I. Booth, Alison. II. Title. III. Title:
Wuthering Heights.

    PR4172.W7 2008
    823'.8—dc22
                                                                    2007047394

Copyright © 2009 by Pearson Education, Inc.

All rights reserved. No part of this publication may be reproduced, stored in a
retrieval system, or transmitted, in any form or by any means, electronic, mechanical, photocopying, recording, or otherwise, without the prior written permission of
the publisher. Printed in the United States.

Please visit our Web site at www.ablongman.com

ISBN-13: 978-0-321-21298-6
ISBN-10:   0-321-21298-3

3 4 5 6 7 8 9 10—DOH—11 10 09 08

# Contents

# List of Illustrations

# *About Longman Cultural Editions*

Reading always seems to vibrate with the transformation of the day—now, yesterday, and centuries ago, when the presses first put printed language into wide circulation. Correspondingly, literary culture has always been a matter of change: of new practices confronting established traditions; of texts transforming under the pressure of new techniques of reading and new perspectives of understanding; of canons shifting and expanding; of informing traditions getting reviewed and renewed, recast and reformed by emerging cultural interests and concerns; of culture, too, as a variable "text"—a reading. Inspired by the innovative *Longman Anthology of British Literature*, Longman Cultural Editions respond creatively to the changes, past and recent, by presenting key texts in contexts that illuminate the lively intersections of literature, tradition, and culture. A principal work is made more interesting by materials that place it in relation to its past, present, and future, enabling us to see how it may be reworking traditional debates and practices, how it appears amid the conversations and controversies of its own historical moment, how it gains new significances in subsequent eras of reading and reaction. Readers new to the work will discover attractive paths for exploration, while those more experienced will encounter fresh perspectives and provocative juxtapositions.

Longman Cultural Editions serve not only several kinds of readers but also (appropriately) their several contexts, from various courses of study to independent adventure. Handsomely produced and affordably priced, our volumes offer appealing companions to *The Longman Anthology of British Literature*, in some cases enriching and expanding units originally developed for the *Anthology*, and in other cases presenting this wealth for the first time. The logic and composition of the contexts vary across the series. The constants are the complete text of an important literary work, reliably edited, headed by an inviting introduction, and supplemented by helpful annotation; a table of dates to track its composition, publication, and public reception in relation to biographical, cultural, and historical events; and a guide for further inquiry and study. With these common measures and uncommon assets, Longman Cultural Editions encourage your literary pleasures with resources for lively reflection and adventurous inquiry.

SUSAN J. WOLFSON
General Editor
Professor of English
Princeton University

# About This Edition

One of the most famous novels of all time, *Wuthering Heights* has attracted generations of avid readers, fans, collectors, and critics from around the world. Yet in Emily Brontë's short, obscure life, she published only a few poems and this single novel, and she left behind only a few letters and short diary papers, some artworks, and various artifacts. With so little evidence of what she was really like, biographical interest has centered on the Brontë family or on Emily's sister Charlotte Brontë, author of *Jane Eyre* and other novels. It was Charlotte who began the posthumous mythmaking about her sister novelists Emily and Anne in the 1850 edition of *Wuthering Heights* (see pp. 320–38). And it was Elizabeth Gaskell's authorized biography, *The Life of Charlotte Brontë*, published ten years after *Wuthering Heights* first appeared (see pp. 308–12, 375–77; referred to throughout this volume as LCB), that put Haworth on the tourists' beaten track along with such pilgrimage sites as Stratford-upon-Avon (Shakespeare's birthplace). The short, brilliant lives of the Brontë children became the stuff of legend before the last person who actually knew them had died.

Unlike many episodes of celebrity, fascination with the Brontës has never faded. The Brontë Society, reputed to be the oldest literary society in the world, was founded in 1893, and two years later it launched a journal that has outlasted most other journals of literary studies.[1] Editions of *Wuthering Heights*, biographical studies and personal responses, criticism, and educational guides have appeared unabated. *WorldCat/OCLC*, an online database combining the cat-

---

[1]*Transactions of the Brontë Society* came out annually under different titles through 1987, semi-annually from 1988, and since 2002, *Brontë Studies* has appeared three times a year.

alogues of libraries around the world, shows over 2,300 items.[2] The novel has been translated into European, Asian, and Middle Eastern languages, and over twenty novels relate the Brontës' lives or extrapolate from *Wuthering Heights*. Numerous adaptations for the stage, including dance and music, as well as sound recordings are based on Emily Brontë's work. Films, as early as 1920 and as late as 2007, include Luis Buñuel's *Abismos de pasion*, produced in Mexico in 1953. Monty Python's Flying Circus produced "The Semaphore Version of *Wuthering Heights*," and Kate Bush had a hit song, "Wuthering Heights," in 1978. Until 2006, more than 80,000 people annually visited the Brontë Parsonage Museum and "Brontë Country."[3] *Wuthering Heights* has entered not only literary tradition but also popular culture; the character of Heathcliff is almost as familiar and imitable as that of Frankenstein's Monster or Dracula.

This edition of *Wuthering Heights* offers perspectives on how a single novel by a Yorkshire clergyman's daughter came to such international prominence. These perspectives encompass the historical contexts of Emily Brontë's life (1818–48), of her novel (1757–1803), and of critical and popular responses since the first publication in 1847. We offer an accurate and readable text of the novel that closely follows this first edition, the only one that Emily Brontë oversaw. Although this edition is marred by publisher Thomas Newby's unreliable printing, it conveys Brontë's prose style, at once economical and pulsing with dashes and exclamation points—combining the enthusiasm of a country teenager with the sophistication of a cosmopolitan adult. This edition also adheres more closely to Brontë's representation of Yorkshire dialect than the 1850 edition that Charlotte supervised. To establish a correct text, we substantially revised the University of Virginia Etext Center's Online Book Initiative digital file of *Wuthering Heights* with reference to other editorial works, in particular the meticulous scholarly edition by Hilda Marsden and

[2]*WorldCat/OCLC* includes media; of 1,845 books, 572 are in languages other than English. The search result numbers may include repetitions and extraneous materials. Books related to a title search "Wuthering Heights" appear most often in Chinese (87), German (85), Spanish (77), French (59), Dutch (45), Korean (27), Japanese (25), Polish (23), and Italian (15); sixteen other languages are also listed (in September 2007). The 1939 film by William Wyler was presented in Chinese (*Pao xiao shan zhuang*) in 1997; the 1992 film directed by Peter Kominsky appeared as *Les Hauts de Hurlevent* (the longstanding French title of *Wuthering Heights*) in 1997.

[3]In July 2007, the seven millionth visitor came to the Brontë Parsonage Museum since it opened in 1928 (Brontë Society).

Ian Jack (Oxford: Clarendon, 1976), to whom any editor of *Wuthering Heights* is indebted. My edition retains Brontë's almost tactile response to varieties of spoken or "diary" English, though I silently modernize punctuation. Throughout this edition, we adhere to the original text of the selected readings, in particular the British spellings, but we follow American rules for quotation marks.

My annotations assist readers who are not professional Brontë scholars. I translate Joseph's dialect, but I advise you that if you read his speeches aloud, you'll begin to catch on to the sounds: The consonants are usually the same as standard English, while the vowels have been pushed forward or stretched. (For a Victorian study of Yorkshire dialect, see pp. 377–80.)

The contextual materials expand prevailing interpretations of *Wuthering Heights* in both time and space. A range of readings substantiate Emily Brontë's life and context, along the main themes of responses to the novel. Speculation on her character, experience, relationships, and authorship; on her home in Haworth and the sources of her writing in Ireland or Yorkshire—all have preoccupied reviews, tourism, adaptations, and literary criticism, early and late.

Along with texts that situate the novel in the customs, laws, and ideology of Victorian society, there are readings on matters often neglected in earlier studies: spaces, houses, economic and material conditions, and the effects of regional locale.

Victorian perspectives on the legal status and education of women, domestic management and design, and the role of servants all illuminate the many ways that *Wuthering Heights* speaks to concerns of our own day. These more private concerns extend to the public realm of regions and nations. A novel set in Yorkshire by the daughter of an Irishman, *Wuthering Heights* assembles a mélange of cultures, races, and nationalities. From folklore to family legend to regional landscape, readings in this edition substantiate the setting of Wuthering Heights, a milieu to which readers and critics have been irresistibly drawn.

Popular responses and scholarly studies of *Wuthering Heights* illuminate each other; curious readers will find ample resources to pursue these in Further Reading.[4]

---

[4]Sources are cited by author's last name; when two or more sources by the same author are listed, a short title is noted in the text. Elizabeth Gaskell's *The Life of Charlotte Brontë* is cited as LCB. Juliet Barker's *The Brontës: A Life in Letters* is cited as *Letters*, to distinguish it from Barker's definitive biography, cited as *Brontës*.

I wish to thank my research assistants: Kathryn McCann, for gathering resources on Brontë studies and adaptations; Kristin Gilger, for help in shaping an accurate text of the novel; Kiera Allison, for assistance with illustrations, bibliographies, the map, and other materials; and Jessica Swope, for proofreading. This volume is much the better for Susan Wolfson's expert and astute editing; she is the best of collaborative general editors. I gladly thank Dianne Hall and Chrysta Meadowbrooke for their enthusiasm, efficiency, and keen-eyed expertise in editorial production and copyediting; it has been a pleasure to work things up for this first ideal audience.

I am grateful for permission to use the University of Virginia Etext Center's Online Book Initiative digital file of *Wuthering Heights* as the basis for this edition of the novel. The frontispiece of Volume II of Gaskell's *The Life of Charlotte Brontë* appears courtesy of Special Collections, University of Virginia Library. Excerpts from Ellen Nussey's "Reminiscences of Charlotte Brontë" appear courtesy of Cornell University Library, Making of America Digital Collection. I extend grateful acknowledgment to Stephen Thomas of the University of Adelaide Library for the digital edition of Isabella Beeton's *Book of Household Management* (eBooks@Adelaide). I have been fortunate to immerse myself in Brontëana in Charlottesville, Virginia, as well as in Haworth, Yorkshire: The University of Virginia has supported my work on this edition through a research travel grant, a Sesquicentennial sabbatical fellowship, research assistants, and not least, the extraordinary resources and staff of the University of Virginia Library.

ALISON BOOTH
University of Virginia

# Introduction

## Who Was Emily Brontë?

In her lifetime, Emily Brontë had no public face. Some thought that "Ellis Bell," the author of *Wuthering Heights*, was just a second pseudonym for "Currer Bell," the author of *Jane Eyre*. Yet half a century later, critics were comparing her to Shakespeare. Before she died at age thirty, her sister Charlotte read to her a review—a scene Charlotte described in a letter:

> What a bad set the Bells must be! What appalling books they write! To-day, as Emily appeared a little easier, I thought the 'Review' would amuse her, so I read it aloud to her and Anne. As I sat between them at our . . . fireside, I studied the two ferocious authors. Ellis, the "man of un-common talents, but dogged, brutal, and morose," sat lean-ing back in his easy-chair, drawing his impeded breath as he best could, and looking, alas! piteously pale and wasted; it is not his wont to laugh, but he smiled, half amused and half in scorn, as he listened. (Barker, *Letters*, 213)

The difference between the now frail, unmarried young woman and the brutal masculine genius supposed to have written *Wuthering Heights* has fascinated readers ever since the identity of Emily Brontë became widely known in 1850. What a combination of fame and artistic triumph, on the one hand, and obscure, morbid suffering on the other. It has the air of a Gothic tale, and like so many Gothic fic-tions of tyrannical patriarchs, haunted houses, dangerous weather, and captive heroines, it is gendered. Had Ellis Bell indeed been a man of the world or had lived to write other novels, *Wuthering Heights* would be no less haunting and magnificent, but it stands out as the singular—and sole—novel by a woman. In November 2007, a first edition of *Wuthering Heights* (1847) sold at auction for £114,000, or about $230,000, as much as four times the predicted price.

Emily Brontë comes across as a genuine heroic force: a fearless woman who, when bitten by a possibly rabid dog, took a hot iron and seared her wound to cauterize it, keeping the incident secret till the danger passed; a tall young Victorian lady with beautiful eyes and hair, and no patience for small talk or fashion, who kept a pet hawk, who tramped the moors by herself and knew how to handle a gun, and who, when dying of tuberculosis, refused to go to bed or see a doctor. And at the same time she was brilliant—knew Latin, German, and French; was exceptionally accomplished in music and art—and while managing the household with efficient skill, she wrote thrilling poetry and fiction. She was a perfect modern heroine.

Biographies and other studies have probed the secrets of this self-sufficient being, her publications, and her lost manuscripts. Along with Charlotte, Emily Brontë is that rare woman writer who has never fallen into obscurity. She made a rough first impression. Although it is not true that early reviews of *Wuthering Heights* entirely condemned it, reviewers were dismayed by the blunt language and violent scenes, the evil of Heathcliff and the conduct of the Catherines. It was all the more dismaying to find that a tale of adulterous love and bitter revenge came from a woman's hands. The earliest biographical sketches gave Emily Brontë an androgynous character that, combined with the signals of unorthodoxy and determined will, repelled many Victorians. In marked contrast, Charlotte Brontë by 1860 was widely admired as a great writer who was also a good, self-sacrificing, domestic woman.[1]

The tide began to turn toward Emily in 1883 with the first full-length biography, by a poet who had much in common with Emily Brontë, Mary Robinson. The following decades brought a series of "fact and fiction" revelations, as well as the recovery of more manuscripts. In 1912, May Sinclair spoke for those who revered Emily Brontë as supreme poet and pagan visionary—infinitely Charlotte Brontë's superior. In the twentieth century, *Wuthering Heights* was read, variously, as a timeless myth of Oedipal proportions, as a bold experiment in narrative point of view and form, as a Romantic tragedy

---

[1]A sample survey of the subjects in British and American collective biographies of women 1850–1930 lists 27 short "lives" of Charlotte (a top score near Queen Victoria's), whereas Emily appears only 5 times (Booth 394–95).

(the Hollywood preference), as existentialist philosophy, and as a work of feminist imagination—but always, too, a Victorian novel.

## The Ghosts of the Brontës

In 1891, Harriet Prescott Spofford, whose work appeared regularly in leading literary journals in the United States, published a poem about the sisters:[2] "Brontë." "There are two ghosts upon the stair!" it intones through eleven nine-line stanzas reminiscent of ballads and poems by Tennyson and Poe. The two are Anne, "so slender and so fair," and Emily (as described in the second stanza), who haunt a still-living Charlotte in and around the parsonage:

> There are two ghosts without the door,—
> One lofty as when first she wore
> The purple of her youth, and bore
> Her state like some young queen. Full white
> And icy as the northern light
> The death-mask on her face. And see,
> A cold flame where her heart should be!
> Calm, bitter calm, and fair and frore,[3]
> There are two ghosts without the door. (lines 10–18)

This is the Emily Brontë that possessed many hearts: tall, majestic, young, heartlessly cold and remote—like the ghost of Cathy at the beginning of *Wuthering Heights.*

"Brontë" tracks a series of encounters with the ghosts about the house and across the landscape in winter and summer. "Woe to that house of gloom and dearth, / There are two ghosts beside the hearth!" Melodramatic though the idiom may be, it conveys what Charlotte, suddenly forlorn of all her siblings, might have felt:

> Sometimes at night about her bed
> The moonlight, in a glamour[4] shed,

---

[2]Published in *Century* (43 [November 1891]: 59–60), reprinted in Spofford's *In Titian's Garden, and Other Poems* (1897, 39–42) and online at http://moa.cit.cornell.edu. When Patrick Brunty or Prunty changed his name at Cambridge University, he may have had in mind Admiral Horatio Nelson (1758–1805), who in 1799 became Duke of Bronte (a town in Sicily). *Bronte* means thunder in Greek.

[3]Frosty, frozen (see Milton's *Paradise Lost* 2.595).

[4]Magic spell (not our modern sense of celebrity-aura).

Puts on the likeness of the dead.
The glamour creeps along the wall,
Far off soft voices seem to fall,
Soft footsteps falter through the room,
She cries, and reaches in the gloom,
And life, and light, and joy are fled,—
There are two ghosts about her bed.

The gentle cunning fails her hand,
Here where they woke, they wrought, they planned,
While day slides o'er the lonesome land,
The needle poised, the pencil prone,—
Pale fingers moving with her own,—
The book, that once strange witchery threw,
Forgotten slipt,—they read it, too,—
Awake, asleep, astir, at stand,
There are two ghosts at her right hand. (lines 64–81)

By the poem's final lines, Charlotte has found fame and love, and "life was dear"; yet, like Heathcliff, she is called to join the ghosts:

Out, to the open, and away!
Oh, love past death and death's despair,
There are three ghosts upon the stair! (lines 97–99)

Spofford's poem was published at a time when educated people attended séances and communed with dead authors. In many ways, the Brontës dwell in our imaginations both as living ghosts of their fictional worlds and as all-too-material presences in the Brontë industry that has survived them. Today there are three very solid Brontë sisters upon the grass beyond the window of the Brontë Parsonage Museum Shop. Emily stands tall, the dominant figure, far-sighted, with long neck and enormous hands, looking as if she were about to sing. Anne looks down at the earth, Charlotte looks up to heaven. This bronze statue—perhaps intentionally painful?—is expressionistic and stylized in the modern way of 1951; it won a prize for the sculptor, Jocelyn Horner (1902–73).[5]

[5]Designed for the planned memorial chapel in Haworth Church, it was placed in the Leeds Art Gallery until moved to Haworth in 1990; it won the 1951 Leeds Gold Medal (*Brontë Society Transactions* 12:63 [1953]: 222). Portrait statues of women other than queens and saints are extremely rare.

## Location, Location, Location

*Wuthering Heights* conveys a palpable sense of space and location. Lockwood arrives as a kind of tourist in the North of England and records his observations of Heathcliff and his house. Brontë readers and pilgrims ever since have been fascinated by the supposed original places, much as people today revisit film locations (Rachel Williams). Haworth, in Yorkshire, where Emily Brontë lived between the ages of three and thirty, beckons as a gateway to *Wuthering Heights* and intimacy with the Brontë family. Devotees can gaze at the horsehair sofa where Emily is said to have died and locate the plaque above her burial site in the church beyond the graveyard, with its flat gravestones that seem to crowd the very doorstep of the parsonage.[6] Those who can escape the tour bus may follow in Emily Brontë's footsteps to "the Brontë waterfall," across the rebuilt "Brontë bridge," up a steep, long rise to Top Withens, the wind-exposed stone farm house, now a roofless ruin often referred to as "Wuthering Heights." Haworth itself has been seen through a gloomy lens, both treasured and deplored as the dungeon of genius, the unhealthy cause of the Brontës' early deaths. Visitors from Matthew Arnold to Virginia Woolf to Sylvia Plath have been haunted by the ghostly allure of Brontë Country.

*Wuthering Heights* instigates such morbid, such ecstatic curiosity. The very real estate can make or break a person. An entire social history is given concrete form in the two houses, Wuthering Heights and Thrushcross Grange, similarly difficult to escape or to enter. The characters seem to move backward temporally and psychologically as they approach the Heights, built around 1500. Life there in 1801 (when Lockwood arrives) seems to take place in the harsher conditions of the eighteenth-century yeomanry, with pewter rather than china, dip candles rather than wax, only basic food, shared living space, few servants, and scarce distinction among ranks. There is a primitive authenticity, in this setting, but all the women in *Wuthering Heights* prefer Thrushcross Grange, with its beautiful drawing room, plentiful candles, fireplaces, and servants. The Heights is a man's world, where the master may

[6]The parsonage museum in 2007 exhibited a prop from Paramount's *Wuthering Heights* (1992), a grave marker: "Here Lieth the Body of Catherine Earnshaw Linton, wife of Edgar Linton, who died March 20 1784." Unearthly thresholds preoccupy the novel and its fans.

drink and gamble as he likes, where a lady won't last long, and where Heathcliff thrives.

## Heathcliff

Many readers feel the force of Isabella's warning to Nelly that Heathcliff is "a lying fiend, a monster, and not a human being!" Nelly herself wonders, "Is he a ghoul, or a vampire?" He is the driving power of the novel. His single name speaks of untamed wilderness, and he bears traits of folklore and fairy tales: Is he a changeling? a foundling? a prince in disguise? Whatever he is, he is a reviled outsider: dark, speaking gibberish, perhaps a gypsy thief. Did Mr. Earnshaw really find him on the streets of Liverpool? Or does his affection for the urchin, and naming him after a dead son, suggest an illegitimate child? If so, the intimacy with Cathy becomes even more charged. With her he finds a primordial love, as if they were born of one flesh or spirit ("I am Heathcliff"). Cathy might marry Heathcliff just as her daughter might legitimately marry her first cousins. Kinship and love in this novel are tight and gothically twisted.

Heathcliff is more than a menace at the erotic center of the novel. Cruel as he is, he is also a victim. Like millions of children in workhouses, factories, or farms, he is abused and exploited. Some critics, noting the Brontës' Irish background, propose that the Liverpool vagrant boy might be an Irish immigrant; others, citing Liverpool as a major port in the slave trade, wonder if his descent is African. Whatever his obscure origins, he turns the tables on his oppressors as a self-made man—hence as a stand-in for manufacturers and plantation owners rather than workers or slaves. He has a penchant, moreover, for wielding his new power over women and children.

## Catherines I and II

If Heathcliff provokes comparisons to vampires or demons, the young women, including Isabella, attract epithets that suggest witchery, sexual impropriety, or worthlessness. As a child, the first Catherine is hardly evil or bad; she is willful and rebellious, but she is clever with words, loves stories, nature, and Heathcliff, and shares his erotic and heroic intensity. Nelly chastises her for choosing Edgar for his status and property, but her only other choice—in the novel's restricted world—would be to languish at the Heights or be "degraded" to Heathcliff's level. It is only at the brink of death that she may cross the threshold to the undomesticated freedom before she became a woman.

The experiences of the women in the novel reflect transitions in gender and class ideologies in the era of the Brontës' childhood. With rising standards of living and manufacturing, many women who would formerly have been active producers of household goods could aspire to be ladies who commanded servants, as do Catherine and Isabella at Thrushcross Grange. Yet, married women still could not own property or have a claim, even, to any earnings from their skills. Although the younger Catherine enjoys a brighter outlook—an indulgent, loving father who educates her and provides lots of books and comforts—she is still a domestic darling, immured in a garden with a chaperone.

But change was in the air. In 1848, the year of Emily Brontë's death, groups organized to improve female education and the training and support for governesses, followed in 1859 by the Society for Promoting the Employment of Women. The laws that make the young Catherine and all her belongings legally the property of Linton Heathcliff when they marry took a long time to change, but not for lack of trying. Charlotte Brontë's school friend Mary Taylor (Emily also knew her) was outspoken on careers for women, and Charlotte's literary friends Elizabeth Gaskell and Harriet Martineau were among the 3,000 who signed a petition for legal reform, allowing married women the right to their property and earnings. Although the bill failed in 1857, the Married Women's Property Act was finally passed in 1882.[7]

Although novels by Charlotte and Anne address "the woman question" and related political issues, there is no such polemic in *Wuthering Heights*. Yet the female characters, including Nelly, defy the advice books on feminine conduct. Catherine I breaks every rule for young ladies and household managers. She never forfeits

[7]From 1865, Mary Taylor contributed to *Victoria Magazine* a series of articles on the theme of expanding paid occupations for women. Barbara Bodichon and Emily Davies collaborated with the group that helped produce *Victoria*. Thus there were only a few degrees of separation between the Brontës and the reformers who by 1865 were organizing campaigns for women's suffrage and women's higher education.

anything she wants to do to spare others' feelings; she gives no thought to the well-being of the household; though clever, she rarely uses her reason. Both she and Cathy II are snobs who scorn poor and dirty admirers, and Cathy I is not shy about manipulating and abusing her husband, her sister-in-law, and the servants. Young Catherine is a slight improvement: She tries to spare her father, to please her peevish husband and nurse him in illness, and eventually to make the Heights a more harmonious place. Gradually, in accord with the civilizing function with which Victorians invested female domesticity, she learns her own power of influence in teaching Hareton to read.

### Nelly Dean and Joseph: Literacy and Religion

Because education can transform lives, it is a central theme in the Victorian novel. Books, reading, and literacy are important in *Wuthering Heights*, which is infused with Nelly's education, Joseph's scriptural literacy, and, at last, Hareton's learning to read. The Heights is virtually anti-literate, lacking books, paper, reading-light, and places to read; Hindley and Heathcliff refuse to educate the household's children, whose only encounters with books are Joseph's lessons from the Bible and Methodist tracts on sin and damnation. At Thrushcross Grange, books are liberally available. Nelly as well as Lockwood and young Catherine freely browse its library, which includes classics in Greek, Latin, and French, as well as English. Young Catherine imports books to the Heights to entertain Linton and eventually to educate Hareton, whose literacy heralds the new era, when innovations in printing and transportation, along with access to education, made a small private library—and gentility—within the means of middle-class landowners and manufacturers.[8]

In the 1840s, as literacy spread rapidly to growing populations of industrial and domestic workers, Yorkshire lagged behind. One of the few indices of literacy in previous centuries is the rate of signature in a parish register upon marriage; those who could not sign their names

---

[8]The rise of literacy is usually associated with the rise of the novel around 1750, but male literacy was already widespread by 1675 and at times declined after that (Hunter 67). Squires like the Earnshaws would have been able to read for generations. Female literacy rates were always lower (about 40% of women in England could read in 1750, as compared to 60% of men; Hunter 72).

made a mark instead. In 1856, by this measure, almost half of the men and women in the Keighley and Bradford areas of the West Riding were illiterate, above the national average (Stephens 97). Only by the end of the century were there any regions where female literacy was greater than male; boys were more likely to be sent to school than girls. In the West Riding, both male and female literacy remained low, as the population was too dispersed to support schools, and fewer women were employed in domestic service (19, 21).

In *Wuthering Heights*, Nelly and Joseph reveal different effects of literacy. Nelly is a housekeeper, raised as if she were Hindley's sister, and has made the most of her ability to read. She identifies with her employers and speaks the King's English. Unlike Zillah and Joseph at the Heights, who attend the chapel, she is an Anglican like her employers. Yet this may be in name only: The kirk or church has no incumbent and the building is decaying, and Nelly is also well versed in folk beliefs. She has two ghostly visions—of the white, moving shape in the night when Isabella elopes and of the child image of Hindley at the crossroads. Moreover, her head is filled with balladry, an indigenous literacy. The servants (along with the two Catherines) reveal an uneasy fascination with fairy and folklore.

Joseph's literacy is indistinguishable from his religion; he has learned to read in order to read the Bible. He is a Dissenter, probably Methodist, and makes the most of that movement's authorization of grassroots preaching, as well as Calvinist doctrines of original sin and eternal damnation.[9] In Lockwood's dream, Joseph brings him to hear "the Pious Discourse delivered by the Reverend Jabes Branderham, in the Chapel of Gimmerden Sough," and attacks him for his supposed unrepentant sin. His extreme piety thinly covers his ignorance and vindictiveness. He is cowed by superstitious threats, such as Catherine's pretended witchcraft. Joseph is a satire of Christian hypocrisy, while his speeches also resemble a nonsense ballad refrain.

---

[9]Methodism was founded by John Wesley (1703–91), a famous minister in the Church of England, as an evangelical, missionary, and social reform movement that enfranchised popular preachers and individual response to the teachings of Christ. After his death, Jabez Bunting (1779–1858) led Wesleyan Methodism for about 50 years, as it became a more formal denomination with its own clergy and chapels competing with the government's church (Cracknell and White 33). There were many splinter groups by 1801. Branderham, in Lockwood's dream, caricatures Bunting.

Through these key portraits of literate servants, we glimpse perspectives on the culture of the Brontë parsonage. The family was immersed in folklore and balladry not only through the servants but also through literary magazines, the works of Sir Walter Scott, and other publications. Commonly, regional stereotyping of the "stage Yorkshireman" or the "stage Irishman" cohabits with a Romantic and antiquarian respect for folk ways. Yorkshire, with its disregard for rank, can be hard to read for an outsider. Servants mix with the family, and a bit of superstition is quite rational. After all, isn't Catherine's ghost real?

Even Joseph's fiery Methodism would have its positive side in Emily Brontë's perspective. The family collaborated with the various religious groups in Haworth, and Aunt Branwell's Methodism profoundly influenced Anne Brontë. Religious reform had not only helped to foster workers' education but also their campaigns for other reforms. But Methodist discipline could be applied hypocritically to others, as Rev. Carus Wilson enforced Spartan living at the Clergy Daughters' School at Cowan Bridge when Emily attended it. By the 1830s, Methodism gradually had the effect of stamping out regional customs and pastimes—overtly, in the name of religious prohibition but, more covertly, in the interests of a disciplined work force (Thompson 406–9). Joseph as a voice of Methodism delivered in local dialect is a fascinating contradiction: Entitled by the new faith, he supports a movement that would eventually repress folk ways.

In her *Life of Charlotte Brontë*, Elizabeth Gaskell expresses grudging admiration for age-old Yorkshire culture. Haworth had had its religious revival around 1750 with the evangelical ministry of Rev. William Grimshaw, a preacher who, writes Gaskell, "built a chapel for the Wesleyan Methodists, and not very long after the Baptists established themselves in a place of worship." Before and after Grimshaw's chastening influence, however,

> the code of morals seemed to be formed upon that of their Norse ancestors. . . . A great capability for drinking, without the head being affected, was considered as one of the manly virtues. The games of foot-ball on Sundays, with the challenges to the neighbouring parishes . . . [brought] riotous strangers to fill the public-houses. . . . The sexton,

> standing at the foot of the open grave, announced that the "arvill" [wake] would be held at the Black Bull, or whatever public-house might be fixed upon. . . . As few "shirked their liquor," there were very frequently "up-and-down fights" before the close of the day; sometimes with the horrid additions of "pawsing" and "gouging," and biting. (LCB 23–26).

To understand the Brontës, we need to learn the language—harsh as its "pawsing" may be—of a wild culture.

At the beginning of the second volume of *Wuthering Heights*, Lockwood records a change in the plan of narration. During the week, Nelly has sat with him at different times and told him the story of Heathcliff. Lockwood is well enough to sit up and continue writing, but now, "I'll continue it in her own words, only a little condensed. She is, on the whole, a very fair narrator and I don't think I could improve her style." Such moments in the novel alert the reader to the process of telling and recording, and hence to the responsibility of reading. The way the novel is narrated—generations of family history "condensed" by one of the witnesses for a stranger, who reports it—is ingenious, not to say tricky. Nelly is a "very fair," that is, good narrator, but she also considers herself to be "fair" in her decisions to help, hinder, or fail to act. Lockwood, even more, considers himself to be impartial, resisting the urge to improve on a poor man's daughter's speech, but from the very start showing misjudgment. Learning how to read the information before us is one of the challenges and fascinations of *Wuthering Heights*. Here, let Emily Brontë take over in her own—or rather, in her narrators'—words. The very first pages confront us with a scene of "reading" or misreading that can lead to comedy or to haunting nightmare.

# Table of Dates:
# The Life of Emily Brontë

1776    The Declaration of Independence is written; American colonies are at war with Britain.

1789    The French Revolution starts.

1802    The Napoleonic Wars begin. Harriet Martineau, friend of Charlotte Brontë, is born.

1807    The British slave trade is abolished.

1810    Elizabeth Gaskell is born.

1811–12  Luddites riot in Yorkshire.

1815    Irish-born Arthur Wellesley, First Duke of Wellington, the model for heroes in the Brontës' childhood sagas, defeats Napoleon at the Battle of Waterloo.

1816    Charlotte Brontë is born (third daughter of Patrick and Maria Brontë).

1817    Patrick Branwell Brontë is born.

1818    Emily Jane Brontë is born on July 30 in Thornton, the fifth child.

1819    Queen Victoria and John Ruskin are born.

1820    Anne Brontë is born. The Brontës settle in Haworth.

1821    Maria Branwell Brontë dies; Aunt Elizabeth Branwell arrives to help care for the young children.

| | |
|---|---|
| 1824 | Emily joins her three sisters Maria, Elizabeth, and Charlotte at the Clergy Daughters' School. |
| 1825 | Maria and Elizabeth return from school to die. Charlotte and Emily are withdrawn from school. |
| 1826 | Patrick gives Branwell toy soldiers that inspire tales and dramas created by the four surviving children. |
| 1829 | The Catholic Emancipation Bill is enacted. |
| 1831 | Emily's and Anne's Kingdom of Gondal separates from Charlotte and Branwell's Kingdom of Angria. |
| 1832 | The First Reform Bill extends the franchise in the middle classes and in industrial districts. |
| 1833 | Slavery is abolished in all British colonies; the Factory Act regulates working hours and requires inspections. |
| 1835 | Emily attends Roe Head School, where Charlotte serves as teacher, assistant to Miss Wooler. Emily becomes so ill that she returns to Haworth. |
| 1837 | Queen Victoria ascends the throne. |
| 1838 | Emily teaches at Law Hill School near Halifax for six months. |
| 1839 | Sarah Ellis publishes *The Women of England.* |
| | Chartist petition to Parliament (Chartist Movement 1838–48) seeks rights for workers. Infant Custody Act grants mothers custody of children under the age of seven. |
| 1842 | Emily and Charlotte attend the Pensionnat Heger in Brussels to prepare themselves to open their own school in England. At the school, Emily writes essays in French, studies German, and teaches piano. Less than a year later, they return due to Aunt Branwell's death. Charlotte returns to Brussels, but Emily stays at home. |
| 1845–49 | Potato famine occurs in Ireland, leading to massive emigration and starvation. |

| | |
|---|---|
| 1846 | *Poems* by Currer, Ellis, and Acton Bell is published. |
| 1847 | *Jane Eyre*, *Wuthering Heights*, and *Agnes Grey* are published. |
| 1848 | A new edition of *Poems* is issued by Smith, Elder. Confusion over the pseudonyms leads Charlotte and Anne to travel to London to prove their identities. |
| | September 24: Branwell dies. |
| | December 19: Emily dies of tuberculosis. |
| | Revolutions take place in several European capitals. Queen's College for women is founded in London. |
| 1849 | May 28: Anne dies in Scarborough. |
| 1850 | A new edition of *Wuthering Heights* (and of *Agnes Grey*) appears with Charlotte's biographical notice and preface. Charlotte meets Elizabeth Gaskell and visits Harriet Martineau in the Lake District (Matthew Arnold saw them together there). |
| 1851 | The Great Exhibition takes place in London. |
| 1854 | Charlotte Brontë marries Arthur Bell Nicholls, her father's curate. Barbara Leigh Smith Bodichon publishes *A Brief Summary, in Plain Language, of the Most Important Laws Concerning Women*. |
| 1854–56 | The Crimean War and Florence Nightingale's campaign there challenge the military establishment and launch professional nursing. |
| 1855 | Charlotte dies March 31. |
| 1857 | Elizabeth Gaskell publishes *The Life of Charlotte Brontë*. |
| | Matrimonial Causes Act addresses legal rights of women in marriage. |
| 1859 | Charles Darwin publishes *The Origin of Species*. Samuel Smiles publishes *Self-Help*. |
| 1861 | Patrick Brontë dies. Henry Mayhew's *London Labour and the London Poor* and Isabella Beeton's *Book of Household Management* are published. |

1865        Elizabeth Gaskell dies.

           Civil War ends in United States.

1867       Second Reform Bill extends the franchise, with proposals of suffrage for women.

1870       Elementary Education Act increases access to schooling for all classes. First college for women opens at Cambridge University.

1876       Harriet Martineau dies.

1877       Mary Robinson publishes first biography of Emily Brontë.

1881       Married Women's Property Act is passed.

1893       The Brontë Society is founded. William Wright's *The Brontës in Ireland* is published.

1895       First Brontë Museum opens, and *Transactions* of the Brontë Society begins publication.

1900       Mary A. Ward's Haworth edition of the Brontë novels is published.

1901       Queen Victoria dies.

1906       Arthur Bell Nicholls dies, having sold Brontë manuscripts and other remains to Clement Shorter in 1895.

1910       Clement Shorter publishes *The Complete Poems of Emily Jane Brontë*.

1914–18    World War I.

1918       Women's suffrage is won (with restrictions); equal voting rights are gained by 1928.

1923       C. W. Hatfield publishes a revised *Complete Poems of Emily Jane Brontë*.

1928       The Brontë Parsonage Museum opens.

# *The Chronology of* Wuthering Heights

At once mythic and calendrically precise, the events of *Wuthering Heights* have prompted chronological tabulation, first by C. P. Sanger in 1926, then refined by A. Stuart Daley in 1974.

1757  Hindley Earnshaw is born.

1762  Edgar Linton is born.

c. 1764 Heathcliff is born.

1765  Summer: Catherine Earnshaw is born.

    Late in year: Isabella Linton is born.

1771  Mr. Earnshaw returns from Liverpool with Heathcliff.

1773  Spring or summer: Mrs. Earnshaw dies.

1777  October: Mr. Earnshaw dies.

    Hindley returns from college with a wife, Frances.

    November: Catherine and Heathcliff spy on the Lintons; injured, Catherine stays at Thrushcross Grange.

1778  June: Hareton Earnshaw is born.

1778–79 Frances Earnshaw dies; Hindley takes to drink.

1780  Summer: Edgar Linton visits and proposes.

    Heathcliff disappears.

    Mr. and Mrs. Linton catch the fever from Catherine, who is staying at the Grange; they die in autumn.

1783    Spring: Catherine marries Edgar; Nelly moves to the Grange.

        September: Heathcliff returns; lives at Heights.

1784    January: Heathcliff marries Isabella.

        March 20: Catherine (Edgar's daughter) is born.

        March 21: Catherine (Edgar's wife) dies; Isabella escapes to South of England four days later.

        September: Linton Heathcliff (Isabella's son) is born. Hindley Earnshaw dies; Heathcliff claims the Heights.

1797    Isabella Heathcliff dies; Linton arrives at the Grange, and Heathcliff takes him to the Heights in August.

1801    August: Catherine Linton marries Linton Heathcliff.

        September: Edgar Linton dies.

        Autumn: Linton Heathcliff dies; Lockwood rents Thrushcross Grange.

        November: Lockwood visits the Heights. Nelly Dean tells Lockwood the story during his illness.

1802    January: Lockwood leaves, and Nelly moves to the Heights at the end of the month.

        April: Heathcliff dies.

        September: Lockwood returns.

1803    January 1: Hareton Earnshaw and Catherine Linton to marry.

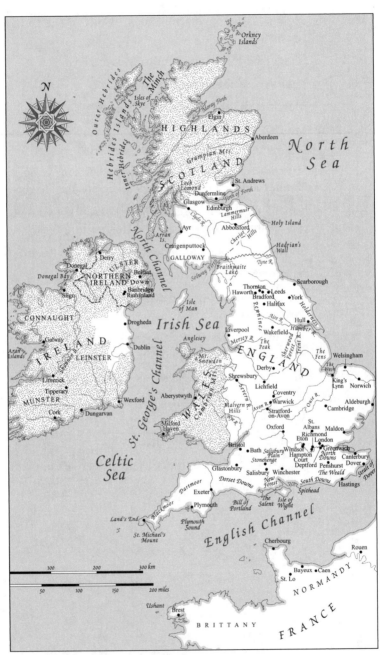

Map of Britain with Brontë "homelands."

# Wuthering Heights

Emily Brontë

1847

# WUTHERING HEIGHTS

## A NOVEL,

BY

## ELLIS BELL,

IN THREE VOLUMES.

### VOL. I.

### LONDON:

THOMAS CAUTLEY NEWBY, PUBLISHER,
72, MORTIMER St., CAVENDISH Sq.

1847.

Title page of the first edition (Anne Brontë's *Agnes Grey* in third volume.)

# Volume 1

## Chapter 1

1801——I have just returned from a visit to my landlord—the solitary neighbour that I shall be troubled with. This is certainly a beautiful country![1] In all England, I do not believe that I could have fixed on a situation so completely removed from the stir of society. A perfect misanthropist's Heaven—and Mr. Heathcliff and I are such a suitable pair to divide the desolation between us. A capital fellow! He little imagined how my heart warmed towards him when I beheld his black eyes withdraw so suspiciously under their brows, as I rode up, and when his fingers sheltered themselves, with a jealous resolution, still further in his waistcoat, as I announced my name.

"Mr. Heathcliff?" I said.

A nod was the answer.

"Mr. Lockwood, your new tenant, sir. I do myself the honour of calling as soon as possible after my arrival, to express the hope that I have not inconvenienced you by my perseverance in soliciting the occupation of Thrushcross Grange: I heard, yesterday, you had had some thoughts—"

"Thrushcross Grange is my own, sir," he interrupted, wincing, "I should not allow any one to inconvenience me, if I could hinder it—walk in!"

The "walk in" was uttered with closed teeth, and expressed the sentiment, "Go to the Deuce!"[2] Even the gate over which he leant manifested no sympathizing movement to the words; and I think that circumstance determined me to accept the invitation: I felt interested in a man who seemed more exaggeratedly reserved than myself.

When he saw my horse's breast fairly pushing the barrier, he did pull out his hand to unchain it, and then sullenly preceded me up the causeway, calling, as we entered the court:

"Joseph, take Mr. Lockwood's horse; and bring up some wine."

"Here we have the whole establishment of domestics, I suppose," was the reflection, suggested by this compound order. "No

[1]Region, district.
[2]Go to the devil.

wonder the grass grows up between the flags, and cattle are the only hedge-cutters."[3]

Joseph was an elderly, nay, an old man: very old, perhaps, though hale and sinewy.

"The Lord help us!" he soliloquised in an undertone of peevish displeasure, while relieving me of my horse: looking, meantime, in my face so sourly that I charitably conjectured he must have need of divine aid to digest his dinner, and his pious ejaculation had no reference to my unexpected advent.

Wuthering Heights is the name of Mr. Heathcliff's dwelling, "Wuthering" being a significant provincial adjective, descriptive of the atmospheric tumult to which its station is exposed in stormy weather. Pure, bracing ventilation they must have up there, at all times, indeed: one may guess the power of the north wind, blowing over the edge, by the excessive slant of a few stunted firs at the end of the house; and by a range of gaunt thorns all stretching their limbs one way, as if craving alms of the sun. Happily, the architect had foresight to build it strong: the narrow windows are deeply set in the wall, and the corners defended with large jutting stones.

Before passing the threshold, I paused to admire a quantity of grotesque carving lavished over the front, and especially about the principal door, above which, among a wilderness of crumbling griffins and shameless little boys, I detected the date "1500" and the name "Hareton Earnshaw." I would have made a few comments, and requested a short history of the place from the surly owner, but his attitude at the door appeared to demand my speedy entrance or complete departure, and I had no desire to aggravate his impatience, previous to inspecting the penetralium.[4]

One step brought us into the family sitting-room, without any introductory lobby or passage: they call it here "the house" preeminently. It includes kitchen and parlour, generally, but I believe, at Wuthering Heights the kitchen is forced to retreat altogether into another quarter—at least I distinguished a chatter of tongues and a clatter of culinary utensils, deep within; and I observed no signs of roasting, boiling, or baking, about the huge fire-place; nor any glit-

---

[3]Lockwood concludes that one servant, Joseph, performs the functions of a groom and a butler, and that there is no gardener to mow between the flagstones or to trim the hedges, which the farm animals eat unrestrained.

[4]Interior [of the building].

ter of copper saucepans and tin cullenders on the walls. One end, indeed, reflected splendidly both light and heat from ranks of immense pewter dishes, interspersed with silver jugs and tankards, towering row after row, in a vast oak dresser, to the very roof. The latter had never been underdrawn:[5] its entire anatomy lay bare to an inquiring eye, except where a frame of wood laden with oatcakes and clusters of legs of beef, mutton, and ham, concealed it. Above the chimney were sundry villainous old guns, and a couple of horse-pistols, and, by way of ornament, three gaudily painted canisters disposed along its ledge. The floor was of smooth, white stone; the chairs, high-backed, primitive structures painted green, one or two heavy black ones lurking in the shade. In an arch under the dresser, reposed a huge, liver-coloured bitch pointer, surrounded by a swarm of squealing puppies, and other dogs haunted other recesses.

The apartment and furniture would have been nothing extraordinary as belonging to a homely, northern farmer with a stubborn countenance and stalwart limbs set out to advantage in knee-breeches and gaiters. Such an individual, seated in his arm-chair, his mug of ale frothing on the round table before him, is to be seen in any circuit of five or six miles among these hills, if you go at the right time, after dinner. But Mr. Heathcliff forms a singular contrast to his abode and style of living. He is a dark-skinned gipsy in aspect, in dress and manners a gentleman—that is, as much a gentleman as many a country squire: rather slovenly, perhaps, yet not looking amiss with his negligence, because he has an erect and handsome figure—and rather morose. Possibly some people might suspect him of a degree of under-bred pride; I have a sympathetic chord within that tells me it is nothing of the sort; I know, by instinct, his reserve springs from an aversion to showy displays of feeling—to manifestations of mutual kindliness. He'll love and hate, equally under cover, and esteem it a species of impertinence to be loved or hated again—No, I'm running on too fast—I bestow my own attributes over-liberally on him. Mr. Heathcliff may have entirely dissimilar reasons for keeping his hand out of the way when he meets a would-be acquaintance, to those which actuate me. Let me hope my constitution is almost peculiar: my dear

---

[5]No boards or plaster ceiling had ever covered it.

mother used to say I should never have a comfortable home, and only last summer I proved myself perfectly unworthy of one.

While enjoying a month of fine weather at the sea-coast, I was thrown into the company of a most fascinating creature, a real goddess in my eyes, as long as she took no notice of me. I "never told my love"[6] vocally; still, if looks have language, the merest idiot might have guessed I was over head and ears. She understood me at last, and looked a return—the sweetest of all imaginable looks. And what did I do? I confess it with shame—shrank icily into myself, like a snail, at every glance retired colder and farther; till, finally, the poor innocent was led to doubt her own senses, and, overwhelmed with confusion at her supposed mistake, persuaded her mamma to decamp.

By this curious turn of disposition I have gained the reputation of deliberate heartlessness, how undeserved, I alone can appreciate.

I took a seat at the end of the hearthstone opposite that towards which my landlord advanced, and filled up an interval of silence by attempting to caress the canine mother, who had left her nursery, and was sneaking wolfishly to the back of my legs, her lip curled up, and her white teeth watering for a snatch.

My caress provoked a long, guttural gnarl.

"You'd better let the dog alone," growled Mr. Heathcliff, in unison, checking fiercer demonstrations with a punch of his foot. "She's not accustomed to be spoiled—not kept for a pet."

Then, striding to a side-door, he shouted again.

"Joseph!"

Joseph mumbled indistinctly in the depths of the cellar, but gave no intimation of ascending; so his master dived down to him, leaving me *vis-à-vis* the ruffianly bitch and a pair of grim, shaggy sheep dogs, who shared with her a jealous guardianship over all my movements.

Not anxious to come in contact with their fangs, I sat still—but, imagining they would scarcely understand tacit insults, I unfortunately indulged in winking and making faces at the trio, and some turn of my physiognomy so irritated madam, that she suddenly broke into a fury, and leapt on my knees. I flung her back, and hastened to interpose the table between us. This proceeding

---

[6]William Shakespeare, *Twelfth Night* 2.4.109. Viola, disguised as a young man, indirectly confesses her love to Orsino by telling a tale of her sister, who "never told her love, / But let concealment, like a worm i' the bud, / Feed on her."

roused the whole hive. Half-a-dozen four-footed fiends, of various sizes and ages, issued from hidden dens to the common centre. I felt my heels and coat-laps peculiar subjects of assault; and, parrying off the larger combatants as effectually as I could with the poker, I was constrained to demand, aloud, assistance from some of the household in re-establishing peace.

Mr. Heathcliff and his man climbed the cellar steps with vexatious phlegm. I don't think they moved one second faster than usual, though the hearth was an absolute tempest of worrying and yelping.

Happily, an inhabitant of the kitchen made more dispatch; a lusty dame, with tucked-up gown, bare arms, and fire-flushed cheeks, rushed into the midst of us flourishing a frying-pan; and used that weapon, and her tongue, to such purpose, that the storm subsided magically, and she only remained, heaving like a sea after a high wind, when her master entered on the scene.

"What the devil is the matter?" he asked, eyeing me in a manner that I could ill endure after this inhospitable treatment.

"What the devil, indeed!" I muttered. "The herd of possessed swine[7] could have had no worse spirits in them than those animals of yours, sir. You might as well leave a stranger with a brood of tigers!"

"They won't meddle with persons who touch nothing," he remarked, putting the bottle before me, and restoring the displaced table. "The dogs do right to be vigilant. Take a glass of wine?"

"No, thank you."

"Not bitten, are you?"

"If I had been, I would have set my signet on the biter."[8]

Heathcliff's countenance relaxed into a grin.

"Come, come," he said, "you are flurried, Mr. Lockwood. Here, take a little wine. Guests are so exceedingly rare in this house that I and my dogs, I am willing to own, hardly know how to receive them. Your health, sir!"

I bowed and returned the pledge, beginning to perceive that it would be foolish to sit sulking for the misbehaviour of a pack of

---

[7]Referring to the cure of the man possessed by demons in Luke 8.33: "Then went the devils out of the man, and entered into the swine: and the herd ran violently down a steep place into the lake, and were choked" (King James translation).

[8]I would have struck the dog with my fist (as if marking it with a signet ring).

curs; besides, I felt loath to yield the fellow further amusement, at my expense, since his humour took that turn.

He—probably swayed by prudential consideration of the folly of offending a good tenant—relaxed a little, in the laconic style of chipping off his pronouns and auxiliary verbs, and introduced what he supposed would be a subject of interest to me, a discourse on the advantages and disadvantages of my present place of retirement.

I found him very intelligent on the topics we touched; and, before I went home, I was encouraged so far as to volunteer another visit, to-morrow.

He evidently wished no repetition of my intrusion. I shall go, notwithstanding. It is astonishing how sociable I feel myself compared with him.

## Chapter 2

Yesterday afternoon set in misty and cold. I had half a mind to spend it by my study fire, instead of wading through heath and mud to Wuthering Heights.

On coming up from dinner, however, (N.B. I dine between twelve and one o'clock; the housekeeper, a matronly lady taken as a fixture along with the house, could not, or would not comprehend my request that I might be served at five),[1] on mounting the stairs with this lazy intention, and stepping into the room, I saw a servant-girl on her knees, surrounded by brushes and coal-scuttles, and raising an infernal dust as she extinguished the flames with heaps of cinders. This spectacle drove me back immediately; I took my hat, and, after a four miles walk, arrived at Heathcliff's garden gate just in time to escape the first feathery flakes of a snow shower.

On that bleak hill top the earth was hard with a black frost, and the air made me shiver through every limb. Being unable to remove the chain, I jumped over, and, running up the flagged causeway bordered with straggling gooseberry bushes, knocked vainly for admittance, till my knuckles tingled and the dogs howled.

---

[1]Customary hours for meals varied by class and region. In London around 1800, Lockwood or other fashionable people would be likely to dine at 6 p.m., and an hour earlier in the country. Nelly Dean is enforcing the sort of schedule followed even by well-off provincial households at that time.

"Wretched inmates!" I ejaculated, mentally, "you deserve perpetual isolation from your species for your churlish inhospitality. At least, I would not keep my doors barred in the day time—I don't care—I will get in!"

So resolved, I grasped the latch, and shook it vehemently. Vinegar-faced Joseph projected his head from a round window of the barn.

"Whet are ye for?" he shouted. "T' maister's dahn i' t' fowld. Goa rahnd by th' end ut' laith, if yah went tuh spake tull him."[2]

"Is there nobody inside to open the door?" I hallooed responsively.

"They's nobbut t' missis, and shoo'll not oppen't an ye mak yer flaysome dins till neeght."[3]

"Why? Cannot you tell her who I am, eh, Joseph?"

"Nor-ne me! I'll hae noa hend wi't,"[4] muttered the head, vanishing.

The snow began to drive thickly. I seized the handle to essay another trial, when a young man, without coat, and shouldering a pitchfork, appeared in the yard behind. He hailed me to follow him, and, after marching through a wash-house, and a paved area containing a coal-shed, pump, and pigeon cote, we at length arrived in the large, warm, cheerful apartment where I was formerly received.

It glowed delightfully in the radiance of an immense fire, compounded of coal, peat, and wood; and near the table, laid for a plentiful evening meal, I was pleased to observe the "missis," an individual whose existence I had never previously suspected.

I bowed and waited, thinking she would bid me take a seat. She looked at me, leaning back in her chair, and remained motionless and mute.

"Rough weather!" I remarked. "I'm afraid, Mrs. Heathcliff, the door must bear the consequence of your servants' leisure attendance: I had hard work to make them hear me!"

---

[2]"What do you want? The master's down at the fold. Go round by the end of the barn, if you want to speak to him." On Yorkshire dialect, see "Dialect," pp. 377–80.

[3]"There's only the Missus, and she won't open even if you make your awful noise until night." Most of Joseph's words, like *shoo* (she) and *neeght* (night) have the consonants of Standard English with different vowel sounds, or are recognizable.

[4]"Not I! I'll have no hand in it."

She never opened her mouth. I stared—she stared also. At any rate, she kept her eyes on me, in a cool, regardless manner, exceedingly embarrassing and disagreeable.

"Sit down," said the young man, gruffly. "He'll be in soon."

I obeyed; and hemmed, and called the villain Juno, who deigned, at this second interview, to move the extreme tip of her tail, in token of owning my acquaintance.

"A beautiful animal!" I commenced again. "Do you intend parting with the little ones, madam?"

"They are not mine," said the amiable hostess, more repellingly than Heathcliff himself could have replied.

"Ah, your favourites are among these!" I continued, turning to an obscure cushion full of something like cats.

"A strange choice of favourites," she observed scornfully.

Unluckily, it was a heap of dead rabbits—I hemmed once more, and drew closer to the hearth, repeating my comment on the wildness of the evening.

"You should not have come out," she said, rising and reaching from the chimney piece two of the painted canisters.

Her position before was sheltered from the light; now, I had a distinct view of her whole figure and countenance. She was slender, and apparently scarcely past girlhood: an admirable form, and the most exquisite little face that I have ever had the pleasure of beholding; small features, very fair; flaxen ringlets, or rather golden, hanging loose on her delicate neck; and eyes—had they been agreeable in expression, they would have been irresistible. Fortunately for my susceptible heart, the only sentiment they evinced hovered between scorn and a kind of desperation, singularly unnatural to be detected there.

The canisters were almost out of her reach; I made a motion to aid her; she turned upon me as a miser might turn, if any one attempted to assist him in counting his gold.

"I don't want your help," she snapped, "I can get them for myself."

"I beg your pardon," I hastened to reply.

"Were you asked to tea?" she demanded, tying an apron over her neat black frock, and standing with a spoonful of the leaf poised over the pot.

"I shall be glad to have a cup," I answered.

"Were you asked?" she repeated.

"No," I said, half smiling. "You are the proper person to ask me."

She flung the tea back, spoon and all, and resumed her chair in a pet,[5] her forehead corrugated, and her red under-lip pushed out, like a child's, ready to cry.

Meanwhile, the young man had slung onto his person a decidedly shabby upper garment, and, erecting himself before the blaze, looked down on me from the corner of his eyes, for all the world as if there were some mortal feud unavenged between us. I began to doubt whether he were a servant or not; his dress and speech were both rude, entirely devoid of the superiority observable in Mr. and Mrs. Heathcliff; his thick brown curls were rough and uncultivated, his whiskers encroached bearishly over his cheeks, and his hands were embrowned like those of a common labourer. Still his bearing was free, almost haughty, and he showed none of a domestic's assiduity in attending on the lady of the house.

In the absence of clear proofs of his condition, I deemed it best to abstain from noticing his curious conduct, and, five minutes afterwards, the entrance of Heathcliff relieved me, in some measure, from my uncomfortable state.

"You see, sir, I am come according to promise!" I exclaimed, assuming the cheerful; "and I fear I shall be weather-bound for half an hour, if you can afford me shelter during that space."

"Half an hour?" he said, shaking the white flakes from his clothes; "I wonder you should select the thick of a snow-storm to ramble about in. Do you know that you run a risk of being lost in the marshes? People familiar with these moors often miss their road on such evenings, and, I can tell you, there is no chance of a change at present."

"Perhaps I can get a guide among your lads, and he might stay at the Grange till morning—could you spare me one?"

"No, I could not."

"Oh, indeed! Well, then, I must trust to my own sagacity."

"Umph!"

"Are you going to mak' th' tea?" demanded he of the shabby coat, shifting his ferocious gaze from me to the young lady.

"Is *he* to have any?" she asked, appealing to Heathcliff.

[5]Sulking.

"Get it ready, will you?" was the answer, uttered so savagely that I started. The tone in which the words were said revealed a genuine bad nature. I no longer felt inclined to call Heathcliff a capital fellow.

When the preparations were finished, he invited me with—

"Now, sir, bring forward your chair." And we all, including the rustic youth, drew round the table, an austere silence prevailing while we discussed our meal.[6]

I thought, if I had caused the cloud, it was my duty to make an effort to dispel it. They could not every day sit so grim and taciturn, and it was impossible, however ill-tempered they might be, that the universal scowl they wore was their every day countenance.

"It is strange," I began, in the interval of swallowing one cup of tea and receiving another, "it is strange how custom can mould our tastes and ideas; many could not imagine the existence of happiness in a life of such complete exile from the world as you spend, Mr. Heathcliff; yet, I'll venture to say, that surrounded by your family, and with your amiable lady as the presiding genius over your home and heart—"

"My amiable lady!" he interrupted, with an almost diabolical sneer on his face. "Where is she—my amiable lady?"

"Mrs. Heathcliff, your wife, I mean."

"Well, yes—Oh! you would intimate that her spirit has taken the post of ministering angel, and guards the fortunes of Wuthering Heights, even when her body is gone. Is that it?"

Perceiving myself in a blunder, I attempted to correct it. I might have seen there was too great a disparity between the ages of the parties to make it likely that they were man and wife. One was about forty, a period of mental vigour at which men seldom cherish the delusion of being married for love, by girls; that dream is reserved for the solace of our declining years. The other did not look seventeen.

Then it flashed upon me—"The clown at my elbow, who is drinking his tea out of a basin and eating his bread with unwashed hands, may be her husband: Heathcliff junior, of course. Here is the consequence of being buried alive: she has thrown herself away upon that boor, from sheer ignorance that better individuals existed! A sad pity—I must beware how I cause her to regret her choice."

---

[6]A slightly amusing expression for the process of dining (not speaking).

The last reflection may seem conceited; it was not. My neighbour struck me as bordering on repulsive. I knew, through experience, that I was tolerably attractive.

"Mrs. Heathcliff is my daughter-in-law," said Heathcliff, corroborating my surmise. He turned, as he spoke, a peculiar look in her direction, a look of hatred—unless he has a most perverse set of facial muscles that will not, like those of other people, interpret the language of his soul.

"Ah, certainly—I see now; you are the favoured possessor of the beneficent fairy," I remarked, turning to my neighbour.

This was worse than before: the youth grew crimson, and clenched his fist with every appearance of a meditated assault. But he seemed to recollect himself, presently, and smothered the storm in a brutal curse, muttered on my behalf, which, however, I took care not to notice.

"Unhappy in your conjectures, sir!" observed my host; "we neither of us have the privilege of owning your good fairy; her mate is dead. I said she was my daughter-in-law, therefore, she must have married my son."

"And this young man is—"

"Not my son, assuredly!"

Heathcliff smiled again, as if it were rather too bold a jest to attribute the paternity of that bear to him.

"My name is Hareton Earnshaw," growled the other; "and I'd counsel you to respect it!"

"I've shown no disrespect," was my reply, laughing internally at the dignity with which he announced himself.

He fixed his eye on me longer than I cared to return the stare, for fear I might be tempted either to box his ears or render my hilarity audible. I began to feel unmistakably out of place in that pleasant family circle. The dismal spiritual atmosphere overcame, and more than neutralized the glowing physical comforts round me; and I resolved to be cautious how I ventured under those rafters a third time.

The business of eating being concluded, and no one uttering a word of sociable conversation, I approached a window to examine the weather.

A sorrowful sight I saw: dark night coming down prematurely, and sky and hills mingled in one bitter whirl of wind and suffocating snow.

"I don't think it possible for me to get home now, without a guide," I could not help exclaiming. "The roads will be buried already; and, if they were bare, I could scarcely distinguish a foot in advance."

"Hareton, drive those dozen sheep into the barn porch. They'll be covered if left in the fold all night; and put a plank before them," said Heathcliff.

"How must I do?" I continued, with rising irritation.

There was no reply to my question; and, on looking round, I saw only Joseph bringing in a pail of porridge for the dogs, and Mrs. Heathcliff leaning over the fire, diverting herself with burning a bundle of matches which had fallen from the chimney-piece as she restored the tea-canister to its place.

The former, when he had deposited his burden, took a critical survey of the room, and, in cracked tones, grated out:

"Aw woonder hagh yah can faishion tuh stand thear i' idleness un war, when all on 'em's goan aght! Bud yah're a nowt, and it's noa use talking—yah'll niver mend uh yer ill ways, bud goa raight tuh t' divil, like yer mother afore ye!"[7]

I imagined, for a moment, that this piece of eloquence was addressed to me; and, sufficiently enraged, stepped towards the aged rascal with an intention of kicking him out of the door.

Mrs. Heathcliff, however, checked me by her answer.

"You scandalous old hypocrite!" she replied. "Are you not afraid of being carried away bodily, whenever you mention the devil's name? I warn you to refrain from provoking me, or I'll ask your abduction as a special favour. Stop, look here, Joseph," she continued, taking a long, dark book from a shelf. "I'll show you how far I've progressed in the Black Art[8]—I shall soon be competent to make a clear house of it. The red cow didn't die by chance; and your rheumatism can hardly be reckoned among providential visitations!"

"Oh, wicked, wicked!" gasped the elder, "may the Lord deliver us from evil!"

---

[7]"I wonder how you can fashion to [bring yourself to] stand there in idleness and worse, when all of them have gone out! But you're a nothing, and there's no use talking—you'll never mend your bad ways; but go right to the devil, like your mother before you!"

[8]Magic that draws on evil spirits to cause harm to enemies. Catherine here and following mocks Joseph's prophesy that she will go to the devil by pretending to be a genuine "little witch," as Lockwood describes her.

"No, reprobate! you are a castaway—be off, or I'll hurt you seriously! I'll have you all modelled in wax and clay; and the first who passes the limits I fix, shall—I'll not say what he shall be done to—but you'll see! Go! I'm looking at you!"

The little witch put a mock malignity into her beautiful eyes, and Joseph, trembling with sincere horror, hurried out praying and ejaculating "wicked" as he went.

I thought her conduct must be prompted by a species of dreary fun; and, now that we were alone, I endeavoured to interest her in my distress.

"Mrs. Heathcliff," I said, earnestly, "you must excuse me for troubling you—I presume, because, with that face, I'm sure you cannot help being good-hearted. Do point out some landmarks by which I may know my way home—I have no more idea how to get there than you would have how to get to London!"

"Take the road you came," she answered, ensconcing herself in a chair, with a candle, and the long book open before her. "It is brief advice, but as sound as I can give."

"Then, if you hear of me being discovered dead in a bog or a pit full of snow, your conscience won't whisper that it is partly your fault?"

"How so? I cannot escort you. They wouldn't let me go to the end of the garden-wall."

"*You!* I should be sorry to ask you to cross the threshold, for my convenience, on such a night," I cried. "I want you to *tell* me my way, not to *show* it; or else to persuade Mr. Heathcliff to give me a guide."

"Who? There is himself, Earnshaw, Zillah, Joseph, and I. Which would you have?"

"Are there no boys at the farm?"

"No, those are all."

"Then, it follows that I am compelled to stay."

"That you may settle with your host. I have nothing to do with it."

"I hope it will be a lesson to you, to make no more rash journeys on these hills," cried Heathcliff's stern voice from the kitchen entrance. "As to staying here, I don't keep accommodations for visitors; you must share a bed with Hareton or Joseph, if you do."

"I can sleep on a chair in this room," I replied.

"No, no! A stranger is a stranger, be he rich or poor—it will not suit me to permit any one the range of the place while I am off guard!" said the unmannerly wretch.

With this insult my patience was at an end. I uttered an expression of disgust, and pushed past him into the yard, running against Earnshaw in my haste. It was so dark that I could not see the means of exit, and, as I wandered round, I heard another specimen of their civil behaviour amongst each other.

At first, the young man appeared about to befriend me.

"I'll go with him as far as the park," he said.

"You'll go with him to hell!" exclaimed his master, or whatever relation he bore. "And who is to look after the horses, eh?"

"A man's life is of more consequence than one evening's neglect of the horses; somebody must go," murmured Mrs. Heathcliff, more kindly than I expected.

"Not at your command!" retorted Hareton. "If you set store on him, you'd better be quiet."

"Then I hope his ghost will haunt you; and I hope Mr. Heathcliff will never get another tenant till the Grange is a ruin!" she answered sharply.

"Hearken, hearken; shoo's cursing on 'em!" muttered Joseph, towards whom I had been steering.

He sat within earshot, milking the cows by the aid of a lantern, which I seized unceremoniously, and calling out that I would send it back on the morrow, rushed to the nearest postern.

"Maister, maister, he's staling t' lantern!" shouted the ancient, pursuing my retreat. "Hey, Gnasher! Hey, dog! Hey, Wolf, holld him, holld him!"

On opening the little door, two hairy monsters flew at my throat, bearing me down and extinguishing the light; while a mingled guffaw, from Heathcliff and Hareton, put the copestone[9] on my rage and humiliation.

Fortunately, the beasts seemed more bent on stretching their paws, and yawning, and flourishing their tails, than devouring me alive; but they would suffer no resurrection, and I was forced to lie till their malignant masters pleased to deliver me. Then, hatless and trembling with wrath, I ordered the miscreants to let me out—on

---

[9]Topped off or pushed to the limit.

their peril to keep me one minute longer—with several incoherent threats of retaliation that, in their indefinite depth of virulency, smacked of King Lear.[10]

The vehemence of my agitation brought on a copious bleeding at the nose, and still Heathcliff laughed, and still I scolded. I don't know what would have concluded the scene had there not been one person at hand rather more rational than myself and more benevolent than my entertainer. This was Zillah, the stout housewife, who at length issued forth to inquire into the nature of the uproar. She thought that some of them had been laying violent hands on me; and, not daring to attack her master, she turned her vocal artillery against the younger scoundrel.

"Well, Mr. Earnshaw," she cried, "I wonder what you'll have agait[11] next! Are we going to murder folk on our very door-stones? I see this house will never do for me—look at t' poor lad, he's fair choking! Wisht, wisht! you munn't[12] go on so—come in, and I'll cure that. There now, hold ye still."

With these words she suddenly splashed a pint of icy water down my neck, and pulled me into the kitchen. Mr. Heathcliff followed, his accidental merriment expiring quickly in his habitual moroseness.

I was sick exceedingly, and dizzy and faint; and thus compelled, perforce, to accept lodgings under his roof. He told Zillah to give me a glass of brandy, and then passed on to the inner room, while she condoled with me on my sorry predicament, and having obeyed his orders, whereby I was somewhat revived, ushered me to bed.

## Chapter 3

While leading the way upstairs, she recommended that I should hide the candle, and not make a noise; for her master had an odd notion about the chamber she would put me in, and never let anybody lodge there willingly.

I asked the reason.

---

[10]Lear vows to commit "the terrors of the earth" in vengeance (*King Lear* 2.4.280–83).

[11]"You'll be up to."

[12]"Hush! you mustn't."

She did not know, she answered; she had only lived there a year or two; and they had so many queer goings on, she could not begin to be curious.

Too stupified to be curious myself, I fastened my door and glanced round for the bed. The whole furniture consisted of a chair, a clothes-press,[1] and a large oak case, with squares cut out near the top resembling coach windows.

Having approached this structure, I looked inside, and perceived it to be a singular sort of old-fashioned couch, very conveniently designed to obviate the necessity for every member of the family having a room to himself. In fact, it formed a little closet, and the ledge of a window, which it enclosed, served as a table.

I slid back the panelled sides, got in with my light, pulled them together again, and felt secure against the vigilance of Heathcliff, and every one else.

The ledge, where I placed my candle, had a few mildewed books piled up in one corner; and it was covered with writing scratched on the paint. This writing, however, was nothing but a name repeated in all kinds of characters, large and small—*Catherine Earnshaw*, here and there varied to *Catherine Heathcliff*, and then again to *Catherine Linton*.

In vapid listlessness I leant my head against the window, and continued spelling over Catherine Earnshaw—Heathcliff—Linton, till my eyes closed; but they had not rested five minutes when a glare of white letters started from the dark, as vivid as spectres— the air swarmed with Catherines; and rousing myself to dispel the obtrusive name, I discovered my candle wick reclining on one of the antique volumes, and perfuming the place with an odour of roasted calf-skin.

I snuffed it off, and, very ill at ease under the influence of cold and lingering nausea, sat up, and spread open the injured tome on my knee. It was a Testament, in lean type, and smelling dreadfully musty: a fly-leaf bore the inscription—"Catherine Earnshaw, her book," and a date some quarter of a century back.

I shut it, and took up another, and another, till I had examined all. Catherine's library was select, and its state of dilapidation

---

[1]A cupboard with shelves, used before wardrobes and closets became common; like the box-bed that Lockwood describes below as a "closet" or little room, it is part of the old-fashioned furnishing of Wuthering Heights.

proved it to have been well used, though not altogether for a legitimate purpose; scarcely one chapter had escaped a pen-and-ink commentary—at least, the appearance of one—covering every morsel of blank that the printer had left.

Some were detached sentences; other parts took the form of a regular diary, scrawled in an unformed, childish hand. At the top of an extra page, quite a treasure probably when first lighted on, I was greatly amused to behold an excellent caricature of my friend Joseph, rudely yet powerfully sketched.

An immediate interest kindled within me for the unknown Catherine, and I began, forthwith, to decypher her faded hieroglyphics.

"An awful Sunday!" commenced the paragraph beneath. "I wish my father were back again. Hindley is a detestable substitute—his conduct to Heathcliff is atrocious—H. and I are going to rebel—we took our initiatory step this evening.

"All day had been flooding with rain; we could not go to church, so Joseph must needs get up a congregation in the garret; and, while Hindley and his wife basked downstairs before a comfortable fire—doing anything but reading their Bibles, I'll answer for it—Heathcliff, myself, and the unhappy plough-boy were commanded to take our Prayer-books and mount. We were ranged in a row, on a sack of corn, groaning and shivering, and hoping that Joseph would shiver too, so that he might give us a short homily for his own sake. A vain idea! The service lasted precisely three hours; and yet my brother had the face to exclaim, when he saw us descending,

"'What! done already?'

"On Sunday evenings we used to be permitted to play, if we did not make much noise; now a mere titter is sufficient to send us into corners!

"'You forget you have a master here,' says the tyrant. 'I'll demolish the first who puts me out of temper! I insist on perfect sobriety and silence. Oh, boy! was that you? Frances, darling, pull his hair as you go by; I heard him snap his fingers.'

"Frances pulled his hair heartily, and then went and seated herself on her husband's knee; and there they were, like two babies, kissing and talking nonsense by the hour—foolish palaver that we should be ashamed of.

"We made ourselves as snug as our means allowed in the arch of the dresser. I had just fastened our pinafores together, and hung them up for a curtain, when in comes Joseph, on an errand from the stables. He tears down my handywork, boxes my ears, and croaks:

"'T' maister nobbut just buried, and Sabbath nut o'ered, und t' sahnd uh t' gospel still i' yer lugs, and yah darr be laiking! shame on ye! Sit ye down, ill childer; they's good books eneugh if ye'll read 'em; sit ye dahn, and think uh yer sowls!'[2]

"Saying this, he compelled us so to square our positions that we might receive, from the far-off fire, a dull ray to show us the text of the lumber he thrust upon us.

"I could not bear the employment. I took my dingy volume by the scroop,[3] and hurled it into the dog-kennel, vowing I hated a good book.

"Heathcliff kicked his to the same place.

"Then there was a hubbub!

"'Maister Hindley!' shouted our chaplain. 'Maister, coom hither! Miss Cathy's riven th' back off "Th' Helmet uh' Salvation," un' Heathcliff's pawsed his fit intuh t' first part uh "T' Brooad Way to Destruction!" It's fair flaysome ut yuh let 'em goa on this gait. Ech! th' owd man ud uh laced 'em properly—bud he's goan!'[4]

"Hindley hurried up from his paradise on the hearth, and seizing one of us by the collar, and the other by the arm, hurled both into the back-kitchen, where, Joseph asseverated, 'owd Nick' would fetch us as sure as we were living; and, so comforted, we each sought a separate nook to await his advent.

"I reached this book, and a pot of ink from a shelf, and pushed the house-door ajar to give me light, and I have got the time on with writing for twenty minutes; but my companion is impatient and proposes that we should appropriate the dairy woman's cloak, and have a scamper on the moors, under its shelter. A pleasant suggestion—and then, if the surly old man come

[2]"The master only just buried, and Sabbath not over, and the sound of the gospel still in your ears, and you dare to be playing! Shame on you! Sit you down, bad children! There's good books enough if you'll read them; sit down, and think of your souls!"
[3]Back or spine of a book.
[4]"Torn the back off . . . kicked his feet into the first part of . . . It's just awful that you let them go on in this way. Oh, the old man would have whipped them properly—but he's gone!" Joseph gives imaginary titles of admonitory tracts considered to be Sunday reading material for Methodists or other Dissenters at that period. He warns in the next paragraph that the devil ("old Nick") will get them.

in, he may believe his prophesy verified—we cannot be damper, or colder, in the rain than we are here."

\* \* \* \* \*

I suppose Catherine fulfilled her project, for the next sentence took up another subject; she waxed lachrymose.

"How little did I dream that Hindley would ever make me cry so!" she wrote. "My head aches, till I cannot keep it on the pillow; and still I can't give over. Poor Heathcliff! Hindley calls him a vagabond, and won't let him sit with us, nor eat with us any more; and, he says, he and I must not play together, and threatens to turn him out of the house if we break his orders.

"He has been blaming our father (how dared he?) for treating H. too liberally; and swears he will reduce him to his right place—"

\* \* \* \* \*

I began to nod drowsily over the dim page; my eye wandered from manuscript to print. I saw a red ornamented title—"Seventy Times Seven,[5] and the First of the Seventy-First. A Pious Discourse delivered by the Reverend Jabes Branderham, in the Chapel of Gimmerden Sough." And while I was, half consciously, worrying my brain to guess what Jabes Branderham would make of his subject, I sank back in bed, and fell asleep.

Alas, for the effects of bad tea and bad temper! what else could it be that made me pass such a terrible night? I don't remember another that I can at all compare with it since I was capable of suffering.

I began to dream, almost before I ceased to be sensible of my locality. I thought it was morning; and I had set out on my way home, with Joseph for a guide. The snow lay yards deep in our road; and, as we floundered on, my companion wearied me with constant reproaches that I had not brought a pilgrim's staff, telling me I could never get into the house without one, and boastfully flourishing a heavy-headed cudgel, which I understood to be so denominated.

For a moment I considered it absurd that I should need such a weapon to gain admittance into my own residence. Then, a new

---

[5]See Matthew 18.21–35; Jesus's reply when asked how many times someone should be forgiven before being punished. Branderham speaks of the unforgivable sin, "the first of the seventy-first," that justifies retribution. The imaginary Jabes Branderham suggests the Methodist leader Jabez Bunting (1779–1858). The Chapel of Gimmerden Sough has been compared to Chapel-le-Breer near Southowram, not far from where Emily Brontë served as a teacher.

idea flashed across me. I was not going there; we were journeying to hear the famous Jabes Branderham preach from the text—"Seventy Times Seven," and either Joseph, the preacher, or I had committed the "First of the Seventy-First," and were to be publicly exposed and excommunicated.

We came to the chapel—I have passed it really in my walks twice or thrice: it lies in a hollow between two hills—an elevated hollow—near a swamp whose peaty moisture is said to answer all the purposes of embalming on the few corpses deposited there. The roof has been kept whole hitherto, but as the clergyman's stipend[6] is only twenty pounds per annum, and a house with two rooms threatening speedily to determine into one,[7] no clergyman will undertake the duties of pastor, especially as it is currently reported that his flock would rather let him starve than increase the living by one penny from their own pockets. However, in my dream, Jabes had a full and attentive congregation, and he preached—good God! what a sermon: divided into *four hundred and ninety* parts—each fully equal to an ordinary address from the pulpit—and each discussing a separate sin! Where he searched for them, I cannot tell; he had his private manner of interpreting the phrase, and it seemed necessary the brother should sin different sins on every occasion.

They were of the most curious character—odd transgressions that I never imagined previously.

Oh, how weary I grew! How I writhed, and yawned, and nodded, and revived! How I pinched, and pricked myself, and rubbed my eyes, and stood up, and sat down again, and nudged Joseph to inform me if he would *ever* have done!

I was condemned to hear all out—finally, he reached the "*First of the Seventy-First.*" At that crisis, a sudden inspiration descended on me; I was moved to rise and denounce Jabes Branderham as the sinner of the sin that no Christian need pardon.

---

[6]In many rural parishes the income from taxes and tithes and the housing were inadequate to hire a clergyman, who was expected to maintain a gentleman's household.

[7]The two rooms will become one when the walls collapse. Patrick Brontë struggled to make ends meet for a family of two adults and four to six children, plus servants, on an income about six times as large as "twenty pounds per annum." During Emily's lifetime there were disputes in Haworth about the church income and expenses; many residents like Joseph were Dissenters and objected to supporting the established Church of England.

"Sir," I exclaimed, "sitting here within these four walls, at one stretch, I have endured and forgiven the four hundred and ninety heads of your discourse. Seventy times seven times have I plucked up my hat and been about to depart—seventy times seven times have you preposterously forced me to resume my seat. The four hundred and ninety-first is too much. Fellow-martyrs, have at him! Drag him down, and crush him to atoms, that the place[8] which knows him may know him no more!"

"*Thou art the Man!*"[9] cried Jabes, after a solemn pause, leaning over his cushion. "Seventy times seven times didst thou gapingly contort thy visage—seventy times seven did I take counsel with my soul—Lo, this is human weakness; this also may be absolved! The First of the Seventy-First is come. Brethren, execute upon him the judgment written![10] Such honour have all His saints!"

With that concluding word, the whole assembly, exalting their pilgrim's staves, rushed round me in a body, and I, having no weapon to raise in self-defence, commenced grappling with Joseph, my nearest and most ferocious assailant, for his. In the confluence of the multitude, several clubs crossed; blows, aimed at me, fell on other sconces. Presently the whole chapel resounded with rappings and counter-rappings. Every man's hand was against his neighbour;[11] and Branderham, unwilling to remain idle, poured forth his zeal in a shower of loud taps on the boards of the pulpit, which responded so smartly that, at last, to my unspeakable relief, they woke me.

And what was it that had suggested the tremendous tumult, what had played Jabes's part in the row? Merely the branch of a fir-tree that touched my lattice, as the blast wailed by, and rattled its dry cones against the panes!

I listened doubtingly an instant; detected the disturber, then turned and dozed, and dreamt again; if possible, still more disagreeably than before.

This time, I remembered I was lying in the oak closet, and I heard distinctly the gusty wind and the driving of the snow; I

---

[8]Job 7.10: "neither shall his place know him any more."

[9]2 Samuel 12.7.

[10]Psalm 149.9: "To execute upon them the judgment written: this honour have all his saints."

[11]See Genesis 16.12; Isaiah 19.2; Zechariah 8.10.

heard, also, the fir-bough repeat its teasing sound, and ascribed it to the right cause. But it annoyed me so much that I resolved to silence it, if possible; and, I thought, I rose and endeavoured to unhasp the casement. The hook was soldered into the staple, a circumstance observed by me when awake, but forgotten.

"I must stop it, nevertheless!" I muttered, knocking my knuckles through the glass, and stretching an arm out to seize the importunate branch; instead of which, my fingers closed on the fingers of a little, ice-cold hand!

The intense horror of nightmare came over me. I tried to draw back my arm, but the hand clung to it, and a most melancholy voice sobbed,

"Let me in—let me in!"

"Who are you?" I asked, struggling, meanwhile, to disengage myself.

"Catherine Linton," it replied, shiveringly. (Why did I think of *Linton*? I had read *Earnshaw* twenty times for Linton.) "I'm come home, I'd lost my way on the moor!"

As it spoke, I discerned, obscurely, a child's face looking through the window. Terror made me cruel; and, finding it useless to attempt shaking the creature off, I pulled its wrist on to the broken pane, and rubbed it to and fro till the blood ran down and soaked the bed-clothes. Still it wailed, "Let me in!" and maintained its tenacious gripe, almost maddening me with fear.

"How can I?" I said at length. "Let *me* go, if you want me to let you in!"

The fingers relaxed, I snatched mine through the hole, hurriedly piled the books up in a pyramid against it, and stopped my ears to exclude the lamentable prayer.

I seemed to keep them closed above a quarter of an hour, yet the instant I listened again, there was the doleful cry moaning on!

"Begone!" I shouted, "I'll never let you in, not if you beg for twenty years."

"It's twenty years," mourned the voice, "twenty years, I've been a waif for twenty years!"

Thereat began a feeble scratching outside, and the pile of books moved as if thrust forward.

I tried to jump up, but could not stir a limb; and so yelled aloud, in a frenzy of fright.

To my confusion, I discovered the yell was not ideal.[12] Hasty footsteps approached my chamber door: somebody pushed it open, with a vigorous hand, and a light glimmered through the squares at the top of the bed. I sat shuddering yet, and wiping the perspiration from my forehead: the intruder appeared to hesitate, and muttered to himself.

At last, he said in a half-whisper, plainly not expecting an answer, "Is any one here?"

I considered it best to confess my presence, for I knew Heathcliff's accents, and feared he might search further, if I kept quiet.

With this intention, I turned and opened the panels—I shall not soon forget the effect my action produced.

Heathcliff stood near the entrance, in his shirt and trousers; with a candle dripping over his fingers, and his face as white as the wall behind him. The first creak of the oak startled him like an electric shock. The light leaped from his hold to a distance of some feet, and his agitation was so extreme that he could hardly pick it up.

"It is only your guest, sir," I called out, desirous to spare him the humiliation of exposing his cowardice further. "I had the misfortune to scream in my sleep, owing to a frightful nightmare. I'm sorry I disturbed you."

"Oh, God confound you, Mr. Lockwood! I wish you were at the—" commenced my host, setting the candle on a chair, because he found it impossible to hold it steady.

"And who showed you up into this room?" he continued, crushing his nails into his palms, and grinding his teeth to subdue the maxillary convulsions. "Who was it? I've a good mind to turn them out of the house this moment!"

"It was your servant, Zillah," I replied, flinging myself on to the floor, and rapidly resuming my garments. "I should not care if you did, Mr. Heathcliff; she richly deserves it. I suppose that she wanted to get another proof that the place was haunted, at my expense. Well, it is—swarming with ghosts and goblins! You have reason in shutting it up, I assure you. No one will thank you for a doze in such a den!"

"What do you mean?" asked Heathcliff, "and what are you doing? Lie down and finish out the night, since you *are* here; but, for Heaven's sake! don't repeat that horrid noise. Nothing could excuse it, unless you were having your throat cut!"

[12]Imaginary (an idea only).

"If the little fiend had got in at the window, she probably would have strangled me!" I returned. "I'm not going to endure the persecutions of your hospitable ancestors again. Was not the Reverend Jabes Branderham akin to you on the mother's side? And that minx, Catherine Linton, or Earnshaw, or however she was called— she must have been a changeling—wicked little soul! She told me she had been walking the earth those twenty years: a just punishment for her mortal transgressions, I've no doubt!"

Scarcely were these words uttered, when I recollected the association of Heathcliff's with Catherine's name in the book, which had completely slipped from my memory till thus awakened. I blushed at my inconsideration; but without showing further consciousness of the offence, I hastened to add,

"The truth is, sir, I passed the first part of the night in—" Here, I stopped afresh. I was about to say "perusing those old volumes;" then it would have revealed my knowledge of their written, as well as their printed contents; so, correcting myself, I went on,

"In spelling over the name scratched on that window-ledge— a monotonous occupation, calculated to set me asleep, like counting, or—"

"What *can* you mean by talking in this way to *me*!" thundered Heathcliff, with savage vehemence. "How—how *dare* you, under my roof?—God! he's mad to speak so!" And he struck his forehead with rage.

I did not know whether to resent this language, or pursue my explanation; but he seemed so powerfully affected that I took pity and proceeded with my dreams; affirming I had never heard the appellation of "Catherine Linton" before, but reading it often over produced an impression which personified itself when I had no longer my imagination under control.

Heathcliff gradually fell back into the shelter of the bed as I spoke, finally sitting down almost concealed behind it. I guessed, however, by his irregular and intercepted breathing, that he struggled to vanquish an excess of violent emotion.

Not liking to show him that I had heard the conflict, I continued my toilette rather noisily, looked at my watch, and soliloquized on the length of the night:

"Not three o'clock yet! I could have taken oath it had been six— time stagnates here—we must surely have retired to rest at eight!"

"Always at nine in winter, and always rise at four," said my host, suppressing a groan; and, as I fancied, by the motion of his shadow's arm, dashing a tear from his eyes.

"Mr. Lockwood," he added, "you may go into my room. You'll only be in the way, coming down stairs so early; and your childish outcry has sent sleep to the devil for me."

"And for me too," I replied. "I'll walk in the yard till daylight, and then I'll be off; and you need not dread a repetition of my intrusion. I'm now quite cured of seeking pleasure in society, be it country or town. A sensible man ought to find sufficient company in himself."

"Delightful company!" muttered Heathcliff. "Take the candle, and go where you please. I shall join you directly. Keep out of the yard, though, the dogs are unchained; and the house—Juno mounts sentinel there, and—nay, you can only ramble about the steps and passages. But away with you! I'll come in two minutes!"

I obeyed, so far as to quit the chamber; when, ignorant where the narrow lobbies led, I stood still, and was witness, involuntarily, to a piece of superstition on the part of my landlord, which belied oddly his apparent sense.

He got on to the bed, and wrenched open the lattice, bursting, as he pulled at it, into an uncontrollable passion of tears.

"Come in! come in!" he sobbed. "Cathy, do come! Oh, do—*once* more! Oh! my heart's darling, hear me *this* time—Catherine, at last!"

The spectre showed a spectre's ordinary caprice; it gave no sign of being; but the snow and wind whirled wildly through, even reaching my station, and blowing out the light.

There was such anguish in the gush of grief that accompanied this raving that my compassion made me overlook its folly, and I drew off, half angry to have listened at all, and vexed at having related my ridiculous nightmare, since it produced that agony; though *why* was beyond my comprehension.

I descended cautiously to the lower regions and landed in the back-kitchen, where a gleam of fire, raked compactly together, enabled me to rekindle my candle.

Nothing was stirring except a brindled, grey cat,[13] which crept from the ashes, and saluted me with a querulous mew.

[13]See *Macbeth* 4.1.1 and 1.1.9.

Two benches, shaped in sections of a circle, nearly enclosed the hearth. On one of these I stretched myself, and Grimalkin[14] mounted the other. We were both of us nodding, ere any one invaded our retreat; and then it was Joseph, shuffling down a wooden ladder that vanished in the roof, through a trap: the ascent to his garret, I suppose.

He cast a sinister look at the little flame which I had enticed to play between the ribs, swept the cat from its elevation, and bestowing himself in the vacancy, commenced the operation of stuffing a three-inch pipe with tobacco. My presence in his sanctum was evidently esteemed a piece of impudence too shameful for remark. He silently applied the tube to his lips, folded his arms, and puffed away.

I let him enjoy the luxury unannoyed; and after sucking out his last wreath, and heaving a profound sigh, he got up, and departed as solemnly as he came.

A more elastic footstep entered next, and now I opened my mouth for a "good-morning," but closed it again, the salutation unachieved; for Hareton Earnshaw was performing his orisons, *sotto voce*,[15] in a series of curses directed against every object he touched, while he rummaged a corner for a spade or shovel to dig through the drifts. He glanced over the back of the bench, dilating his nostrils, and thought as little of exchanging civilities with me as with my companion, the cat.

I guessed by his preparations that egress was allowed, and leaving my hard couch, made a movement to follow him. He noticed this, and thrust at an inner door with the end of his spade, intimating by an inarticulate sound, that there was the place where I must go, if I changed my locality.

It opened into the house, where the females were already astir: Zillah urging flakes of flame up the chimney with a colossal bellows, and Mrs. Heathcliff, kneeling on the hearth, reading a book by the aid of the blaze.

She held her hand interposed between the furnace-heat and her eyes, and seemed absorbed in her occupation, desisting from it only to chide the servant for covering her with sparks, or to push away a dog, now and then, that snoozled its nose over-forwardly into her face.

---

[14]An old female cat or, metaphorically, a hostile old woman (i.e., associated with witchlike powers).

[15]Lockwood doesn't utter his greeting because Hareton is muttering curses, which Lockwood sarcastically describes as prayers in a low voice (Italian).

I was surprised to see Heathcliff there also. He stood by the fire, his back towards me, just finishing a stormy scene to poor Zillah, who ever and anon interrupted her labour to pluck up the corner of her apron, and heave an indignant groan.

"And you, you worthless—" he broke out as I entered, turning to his daughter-in-law, and employing an epithet as harmless as duck, or sheep, but generally represented by a dash.

"There you are at your idle tricks again! The rest of them do earn their bread—you live on my charity! Put your trash away, and find something to do. You shall pay me for the plague of having you eternally in my sight—do you hear, damnable jade?"

"I'll put my trash away, because you can make me, if I refuse," answered the young lady, closing her book and throwing it on a chair. "But I'll not do anything, though you should swear your tongue out, except what I please!"

Heathcliff lifted his hand, and the speaker sprang to a safer distance, obviously acquainted with its weight.

Having no desire to be entertained by a cat-and-dog combat, I stepped forward briskly, as if eager to partake the warmth of the hearth, and innocent of any knowledge of the interrupted dispute. Each had enough decorum to suspend further hostilities. Heathcliff placed his fists, out of temptation, in his pockets; Mrs. Heathcliff curled her lip, and walked to a seat far off, where she kept her word by playing the part of a statue during the remainder of my stay.

That was not long. I declined joining their breakfast, and at the first gleam of dawn took an opportunity of escaping into the free air, now clear, and still, and cold as impalpable ice.

My landlord hallooed for me to stop ere I reached the bottom of the garden, and offered to accompany me across the moor. It was well he did, for the whole hill-back was one billowy, white ocean, the swells and falls not indicating corresponding rises and depressions in the ground. Many pits, at least, were filled to a level, and entire ranges of mounds, the refuse of the quarries, blotted from the chart which my yesterday's walk left pictured in my mind.

I had remarked on one side of the road, at intervals of six or seven yards, a line of upright stones, continued through the whole length of the barren.[16] These were erected, and daubed with lime

---

[16]Uncultivated land, often marshy.

on purpose to serve as guides in the dark, and also when a fall, like the present, confounded the deep swamps on either hand with the firmer path; but, excepting a dirty dot pointing up here and there, all traces of their existence had vanished, and my companion found it necessary to warn me frequently to steer to the right or left, when I imagined I was following correctly the windings of the road.

We exchanged little conversation, and he halted at the entrance of Thrushcross park, saying I could make no error there. Our adieux were limited to a hasty bow, and then I pushed forward, trusting to my own resources, for the porter's lodge is untenanted as yet.

The distance from the gate to the Grange is two miles; I believe I managed to make it four, what with losing myself among the trees, and sinking up to the neck in snow, a predicament which only those who have experienced it can appreciate. At any rate, whatever were my wanderings, the clock chimed twelve as I entered the house, and that gave exactly an hour for every mile of the usual way from Wuthering Heights.

My human fixture and her satellites rushed to welcome me; exclaiming, tumultuously, they had completely given me up. Everybody conjectured that I perished last night, and they were wondering how they must set about the search for my remains.

I bid them be quiet, now that they saw me returned, and, benumbed to my very heart, I dragged upstairs, whence, after putting on dry clothes, and pacing to and fro thirty or forty minutes, to restore the animal heat, I am adjourned to my study, feeble as a kitten, almost too much so to enjoy the cheerful fire and smoking coffee which the servant has prepared for my refreshment.

## Chapter 4

What vain weather-cocks we are! I, who had determined to hold myself independent of all social intercourse, and thanked my stars that, at length, I had lighted on a spot where it was next to impracticable—I, weak wretch, after maintaining till dusk a struggle with low spirits and solitude, was finally compelled to strike my colours; and, under pretence of gaining information concerning the necessities of my establishment, I desired Mrs. Dean, when she brought in supper, to sit down while I ate it, hoping sincerely she would prove a regular gossip, and either rouse me to animation or lull me to sleep by her talk.

"You have lived here a considerable time," I commenced; "did you not say sixteen years?"

"Eighteen, sir; I came, when the mistress was married, to wait on her; after she died, the master retained me for his housekeeper."

"Indeed."

There ensued a pause. She was not a gossip, I feared, unless about her own affairs, and those could hardly interest me.

However, having studied for an interval, with a fist on either knee, and a cloud of meditation over her ruddy countenance, she ejaculated—

"Ah, times are greatly changed since then!"

"Yes," I remarked, "you've seen a good many alterations, I suppose?"

"I have; and troubles too," she said.

"Oh, I'll turn the talk on my landlord's family!" I thought to myself. "A good subject to start—and that pretty girl-widow, I should like to know her history; whether she be a native of the country, or, as is more probable, an exotic that the surly indigenae[1] will not recognise for kin."

With this intention I asked Mrs. Dean why Heathcliff let Thrushcross Grange, and preferred living in a situation and residence so much inferior.

"Is he not rich enough to keep the estate in good order?" I enquired.

"Rich, sir!" she returned. "He has, nobody knows what money, and every year it increases. Yes, yes, he's rich enough to live in a finer house than this; but he's very near—close-handed; and, if he had meant to flit to Thrushcross Grange, as soon as he heard of a good tenant, he could not have borne to miss the chance of getting a few hundreds more. It is strange people should be so greedy, when they are alone in the world!"

"He had a son, it seems?"

"Yes, he had one—he is dead."

"And that young lady, Mrs. Heathcliff, is his widow?"

"Yes."

[1]Natives.

"Where did she come from originally?"

"Why, sir, she is my late master's daughter; Catherine Linton was her maiden name. I nursed her, poor thing! I did wish Mr. Heathcliff would remove here, and then we might have been together again."

"What, Catherine Linton!" I exclaimed, astonished. But a minute's reflection convinced me it was not my ghostly Catherine. "Then," I continued, "my predecessor's name was Linton?"

"It was."

"And who is that Earnshaw, Hareton Earnshaw, who lives with Mr. Heathcliff? are they relations?"

"No; he is the late Mrs. Linton's nephew."

"The young lady's cousin, then?"

"Yes; and her husband was her cousin also—one, on the mother's—the other on the father's side—Heathcliff married Mr. Linton's sister."

"I see the house at Wuthering Heights has 'Earnshaw' carved over the front door. Are they an old family?"

"Very old, sir; and Hareton is the last of them, as our Miss Cathy is of us—I mean, of the Lintons. Have you been to Wuthering Heights? I beg pardon for asking; but I should like to hear how she is."

"Mrs. Heathcliff? she looked very well, and very handsome; yet, I think, not very happy."

"Oh dear, I don't wonder! And how did you like the master?"

"A rough fellow, rather, Mrs. Dean. Is not that his character?"

"Rough as a saw-edge, and hard as whinstone! The less you meddle with him the better."

"He must have had some ups and downs in life to make him such a churl. Do you know anything of his history?"

"It's a cuckoo's, sir—I know all about it; except where he was born, and who were his parents, and how he got his money, at first. And Hareton has been cast out like an unfledged dunnock.[2] The unfortunate lad is the only one, in all this parish, that does not guess how he has been cheated!"

---

[2]Cuckoos replace the eggs in other birds' nests with their own; when hatched, the young cuckoos are larger than the roosting birds' natural offspring, and usurp the care and feeding in that nest. The dunnock or hedge-sparrow is one of the small birds exploited by the cuckoo. Heathcliff's role as the adopted interloper who takes over has been linked to the Brontë family history in Ireland or to the first owner of Law Hill, the school at which Emily Brontë taught.

"Well, Mrs. Dean, it will be a charitable deed to tell me something of my neighbours—I feel I shall not rest, if I go to bed; so be good enough to sit and chat an hour."

"Oh, certainly, sir! I'll just fetch a little sewing, and then I'll sit as long as you please; but you've caught cold, I saw you shivering; and you must have some gruel to drive it out."

The worthy woman bustled off, and I crouched nearer the fire. My head felt hot, and the rest of me chill; moreover I was excited, almost to a pitch of foolishness, through my nerves and brain. This caused me to feel, not uncomfortable, but rather fearful, as I am still, of serious effects from the incidents of to-day and yesterday.

She returned presently, bringing a smoking basin and a basket of work; and, having placed the former on the hob, drew in her seat, evidently pleased to find me so companionable.

Before I came to live here, she commenced,[3] waiting no further invitation to her story, I was almost always at Wuthering Heights; because my mother had nursed Mr. Hindley Earnshaw, that was Hareton's father, and I got used to playing with the children. I ran errands too, and helped to make hay, and hung about the farm ready for anything that anybody would set me to.

One fine summer morning—it was the beginning of harvest, I remember—Mr. Earnshaw, the old master, came down stairs, dressed for a journey; and, after he had told Joseph what was to be done during the day, he turned to Hindley, and Cathy, and me—for I sat eating my porridge with them—and he said, speaking to his son,

"Now, my bonny man, I'm going to Liverpool, to-day . . . What shall I bring you? You may choose what you like; only let it be little, for I shall walk there and back; sixty miles each way, that is a long spell!"

Hindley named a fiddle, and then he asked Miss Cathy; she was hardly six years old, but she could ride any horse in the stable, and she chose a whip.

He did not forget me, for he had a kind heart, though he was rather severe, sometimes. He promised to bring me a pocketful of apples and pears, and then he kissed his children good-bye, and set off.

[3]Nelly Dean takes over the narration and continues through vol. 2, ch. 16, as if she were speaking to Lockwood.

It seemed a long while to us all—the three days of his absence—and often did little Cathy ask when he would be home. Mrs. Earnshaw expected him by supper-time, on the third evening; and she put the meal off hour after hour. There were no signs of his coming, however, and at last the children got tired of running down to the gate to look. Then it grew dark, she would have had them to bed, but they begged sadly to be allowed to stay up; and, just about eleven o'clock, the door-latch was raised quietly and in stept the master. He threw himself into a chair, laughing and groaning, and bid them all stand off, for he was nearly killed—he would not have such another walk for the three kingdoms.

"And at the end of it, to be flighted[4] to death!" he said, opening his great-coat, which he held bundled up in his arms, "See here, wife; I was never so beaten[5] with anything in my life; but you must e'en take it as a gift of God, though it's as dark almost as if it came from the devil."

We crowded round, and, over Miss Cathy's head, I had a peep at a dirty, ragged, black-haired child; big enough both to walk and talk—indeed, its face looked older than Catherine's—yet, when it was set on its feet, it only stared round, and repeated over and over again some gibberish that nobody could understand. I was frightened, and Mrs. Earnshaw was ready to fling it out of doors. She did fly up—asking how he could fashion to bring that gipsy brat[6] into the house, when they had their own bairns to feed, and fend for? What he meant to do with it, and whether he were mad?

The master tried to explain the matter; but he was really half dead with fatigue, and all that I could make out, amongst her scolding, was a tale of his seeing it starving, and houseless, and as good as dumb, in the streets of Liverpool[7] where he picked it up and inquired for its owner. Not a soul knew to whom it belonged, he said, and his money and time being both limited, he thought it better to take it home with him at once, than run into vain expenses there; because he was determined he would not leave it as he found it.

[4]Flayed.

[5]Exhausted.

[6]The gypsies or Roma, falsely thought to come from Egypt, have been nomadic presences in Britain and Europe for many centuries.

[7]A port city, Liverpool had many homeless, hungry people and orphans, both at the time that Nelly Dean recalls (1770s) and at the time that Brontë was writing (1840s). See pp. 339 and p. 367.

Well, the conclusion was that my mistress grumbled herself calm; and Mr. Earnshaw told me to wash it, and give it clean things, and let it sleep with the children.

Hindley and Cathy contented themselves with looking and listening till peace was restored; then, both began searching their father's pockets for the presents he had promised them. The former was a boy of fourteen, but when he drew out what had been a fiddle, crushed to morsels in the great-coat, he blubbered aloud, and Cathy, when she learnt the master had lost her whip in attending on the stranger, showed her humour[8] by grinning and spitting at the stupid little thing, earning for her pains a sound blow from her father to teach her cleaner manners.

They entirely refused to have it in bed with them, or even in their room, and I had no more sense, so I put it on the landing of the stairs, hoping it might be gone on the morrow. By chance, or else attracted by hearing his voice, it crept to Mr. Earnshaw's door and there he found it on quitting his chamber. Inquiries were made as to how it got there; I was obliged to confess, and in recompense for my cowardice and inhumanity was sent out of the house.

This was Heathcliff's first introduction to the family. On coming back a few days afterwards, for I did not consider my banishment perpetual, I found they had christened him "Heathcliff"; it was the name of a son who died in childhood, and it has served him ever since, both for Christian and surname.

Miss Cathy and he were now very thick; but Hindley hated him, and to say the truth I did the same; and we plagued and went on with him shamefully, for I wasn't reasonable enough to feel my injustice, and the mistress never put in a word on his behalf, when she saw him wronged.

He seemed a sullen, patient child; hardened, perhaps, to ill-treatment. He would stand Hindley's blows without winking or shedding a tear, and my pinches moved him only to draw in a breath and open his eyes, as if he had hurt himself by accident and nobody was to blame.

This endurance made old Earnshaw furious when he discovered his son persecuting the poor, fatherless child, as he called him. He took to Heathcliff strangely, believing all he said (for that

---

[8]Ill temper (from the medieval theory that emotions derived from bodily "humors"—spirits or fluids).

matter, he said precious little, and generally the truth,) and pet-
ting him up far above Cathy, who was too mischievous and wayward for a favourite.

So, from the very beginning, he bred bad feeling in the house;
and at Mrs. Earnshaw's death, which happened in less than two
years after, the young master had learnt to regard his father as an
oppressor rather than a friend, and Heathcliff as a usurper of his
parent's affections and his privileges, and he grew bitter with
brooding over these injuries.

I sympathised a while, but, when the children fell ill of the
measles and I had to tend them, and take on me the cares of a
woman at once, I changed my ideas. Heathcliff was dangerously
sick, and while he lay at the worst he would have me constantly by
his pillow; I suppose he felt I did a good deal for him, and he had-
n't wit to guess that I was compelled to do it. However, I will say
this, he was the quietest child that ever nurse watched over. The
difference between him and the others forced me to be less partial:
Cathy and her brother harassed me terribly; *he* was as uncom-
plaining as a lamb; though hardness, not gentleness, made him
give little trouble.

He got through, and the doctor affirmed it was in a great measure owing to me, and praised me for my care. I was vain of his
commendations, and softened towards the being by whose means I
earned them, and thus Hindley lost his last ally; still I couldn't dote
on Heathcliff, and I wondered often what my master saw to admire
so much in the sullen boy who never, to my recollection, repaid his
indulgence by any sign of gratitude. He was not insolent to his
benefactor; he was simply insensible, though knowing perfectly the
hold he had on his heart, and conscious he had only to speak and
all the house would be obliged to bend to his wishes.

As an instance, I remember Mr. Earnshaw once bought a couple
of colts at the parish fair, and gave the lads each one. Heathcliff
took the handsomest, but it soon fell lame, and when he discovered
it, he said to Hindley,

"You must exchange horses with me; I don't like mine, and if
you won't I shall tell your father of the three thrashings you've
given me this week, and show him my arm, which is black to the
shoulder."

Hindley put out his tongue, and cuffed him over the ears.

"You'd better do it at once," he persisted, escaping to the porch (they were in the stable): "you will have to, and if I speak of these blows, you'll get them again with interest."

"Off, dog!" cried Hindley, threatening him with an iron weight, used for weighing potatoes and hay.

"Throw it," he replied, standing still, "and then I'll tell how you boasted that you would turn me out of doors as soon as he died, and see whether he will not turn you out directly."

Hindley threw it, hitting him on the breast, and down he fell, but staggered up immediately, breathless and white, and had not I prevented it he would have gone just so to the master, and got full revenge by letting his condition plead for him, intimating who had caused it.

"Take my colt, gipsy, then!" said young Earnshaw, "And I pray that he may break your neck; take him, and be damned, you beggarly interloper! and wheedle my father out of all he has—only, afterwards, show him what you are, imp of Satan—And take that, I hope he'll kick out your brains!"

Heathcliff had gone to loose the beast, and shift it to his own stall—He was passing behind it, when Hindley finished his speech by knocking him under its feet, and without stopping to examine whether his hopes were fulfilled, ran away as fast as he could.

I was surprised to witness how coolly the child gathered himself up, and went on with his intention, exchanging saddles and all, and then sitting down on a bundle of hay to overcome the qualm which the violent blow occasioned, before he entered the house.

I persuaded him easily to let me lay the blame of his bruises on the horse; he minded little what tale was told since he had what he wanted. He complained so seldom, indeed, of such stirs as these, that I really thought him not vindictive—I was deceived, completely, as you will hear.

## Chapter 5

In the course of time, Mr. Earnshaw began to fail. He had been active and healthy, yet his strength left him suddenly; and when he was confined to the chimney-corner he grew grievously irritable. A nothing vexed him, and suspected slights of his authority nearly threw him into fits.

This was especially to be remarked if any one attempted to impose upon, or domineer over, his favourite: he was painfully jealous lest a word should be spoken amiss to him, seeming to have got into his head the notion that, because he liked Heathcliff, all hated, and longed to do him an ill-turn.

It was a disadvantage to the lad, for the kinder among us did not wish to fret the master, so we humoured his partiality; and that humouring was rich nourishment to the child's pride and black tempers. Still it became in a manner necessary; twice, or thrice, Hindley's manifestations of scorn, while his father was near, roused the old man to a fury. He seized his stick to strike him, and shook with rage that he could not do it.

At last, our curate (we had a curate then who made the living answer[1] by teaching the little Lintons and Earnshaws, and farming his bit of land himself)—he advised that the young man should be sent to college, and Mr. Earnshaw agreed, though with a heavy spirit, for he said—

"Hindley was naught, and would never thrive as where[2] he wandered."

I hoped heartily we should have peace now. It hurt me to think the master should be made uncomfortable by his own good deed. I fancied the discontent of age and disease arose from his family disagreements, as he would have it that it did—really, you know, sir, it was in his sinking frame.

We might have got on tolerably, notwithstanding, but for two people, Miss Cathy, and Joseph the servant; you saw him, I dare say, up yonder. He was, and is yet, most likely, the wearisomest, self-righteous pharisee that ever ransacked a Bible to rake the promises to himself and fling the curses to his neighbours. By his knack of sermonizing and pious discoursing, he contrived to make a great impression on Mr. Earnshaw, and the more feeble the master became, the more influence he gained.

He was relentless in worrying him about his soul's concerns, and about ruling his children rigidly. He encouraged him to regard

---

[1]Made it "pay" or offer enough support. A curate is an ordained minister of the Church of England and is employed by a parish rector or clergyman who might be absentee or who might need an assistant. Patrick Brontë, a perpetual curate, employed a series of curates to assist him later in life.

[2]No matter where.

Hindley as a reprobate; and, night after night, he regularly grumbled out a long string of tales against Heathcliff and Catherine; always minding to flatter Earnshaw's weakness by heaping the heaviest blame on the last.

Certainly, she had ways with her such as I never saw a child take up before; and she put all of us past our patience fifty times and oftener in a day. From the hour she came down stairs till the hour she went to bed, we had not a minute's security that she wouldn't be in mischief. Her spirits were always at high-water mark, her tongue always going—singing, laughing, and plaguing everybody who would not do the same. A wild, wick slip[3] she was—but she had the bonniest eye, and sweetest smile, and lightest foot in the parish; and, after all, I believe she meant no harm; for when once she made you cry in good earnest, it seldom happened that she would not keep you company, and oblige you to be quiet, that you might comfort her.

She was much too fond of Heathcliff. The greatest punishment we could invent for her was to keep her separate from him; yet she got chided more than any of us on his account.

In play, she liked, exceedingly, to act the little mistress; using her hands freely, and commanding her companions. She did so to me, but I would not bear slapping and ordering; and so I let her know.

Now, Mr. Earnshaw did not understand jokes from his children. He had always been strict and grave with them; and Catherine, on her part, had no idea why her father should be crosser and less patient in his ailing condition than he was in his prime.

His peevish reproofs wakened in her a naughty delight to provoke him; she was never so happy as when we were all scolding her at once, and she defying us with her bold, saucy look and her ready words; turning Joseph's religious curses into ridicule, baiting me, and doing just what her father hated most, showing how her pretended insolence, which he thought real, had more power over Heathcliff than his kindness; how the boy would do *her* bidding in anything, and *his* only when it suited his own inclination.

After behaving as badly as possible all day, she sometimes came fondling to make it up at night.

---

[3]Lively or "quick" little thing; rascal. The two Catherines have "wicked," witchlike charms to different degrees.

"Nay, Cathy," the old man would say, "I cannot love thee; thou'rt worse than thy brother. Go, say thy prayers, child, and ask God's pardon. I doubt thy mother and I must rue that we ever reared thee!"

That made her cry, at first; and then, being repulsed continually hardened her, and she laughed if I told her to say she was sorry for her faults, and beg to be forgiven.

But the hour came, at last that ended Mr. Earnshaw's troubles on earth. He died quietly in his chair one October evening, seated by the fire-side.

A high wind blustered round the house, and roared in the chimney. It sounded wild and stormy, yet it was not cold, and we were all together—I, a little removed from the hearth, busy at my knitting, and Joseph reading his Bible near the table (for the servants generally sat in the house then, after their work was done). Miss Cathy had been sick, and that made her still; she leant against her father's knee, and Heathcliff was lying on the floor with his head in her lap.

I remember the master, before he fell into a doze, stroking her bonny hair—it pleased him rarely to see her gentle—and saying—

"Why canst thou not always be a good lass, Cathy?"

And she turned her face up to his, and laughed, and answered,

"Why cannot you always be a good man, father?"

But as soon as she saw him vexed again, she kissed his hand, and said she would sing him to sleep. She began singing very low, till his fingers dropped from hers, and his head sank on his breast. Then I told her to hush, and not stir, for fear she should wake him. We all kept as mute as mice a full half-hour, and should have done longer, only Joseph, having finished his chapter, got up and said that he must rouse the master for prayers and bed. He stepped forward, and called him by name, and touched his shoulder, but he would not move—so he took the candle and looked at him.

I thought there was something wrong as he set down the light; and seizing the children each by an arm, whispered them to "frame upstairs, and make little din[4]—they might pray alone that evening—he had summut to do."

"I shall bid father good-night first," said Catherine, putting her arms round his neck, before we could hinder her.

[4]"Get going [scoot] upstairs, and be quiet."

The poor thing discovered her loss directly—she screamed out—
"Oh, he's dead, Heathcliff! he's dead!"

And they both set up a heart-breaking cry.

I joined my wail to theirs, loud and bitter; but Joseph asked what we could be thinking of to roar in that way over a saint in Heaven.

He told me to put on my cloak and run to Gimmerton for the doctor and the parson. I could not guess the use that either would be of, then. However, I went, through wind and rain, and brought one, the doctor, back with me; the other said he would come in the morning.

Leaving Joseph to explain matters, I ran to the children's room; their door was ajar, I saw they had never laid down, though it was past midnight; but they were calmer, and did not need me to console them. The little souls were comforting each other with better thoughts than I could have hit on; no parson in the world ever pictured Heaven so beautifully as they did, in their innocent talk; and, while I sobbed, and listened, I could not help wishing we were all there safe together.

## Chapter 6

Mr. Hindley came home to the funeral; and—a thing that amazed us, and set the neighbours gossiping right and left—he brought a wife with him.

What she was, and where she was born, he never informed us; probably, she had neither money nor name to recommend her, or he would scarcely have kept the union from his father.

She was not one that would have disturbed the house much on her own account. Every object she saw, the moment she crossed the threshold, appeared to delight her; and every circumstance that took place about her, except the preparing for the burial, and the presence of the mourners.

I thought she was half silly, from her behaviour while that went on; she ran into her chamber, and made me come with her, though I should have been dressing the children; and there she sat shivering and clasping her hands, and asking repeatedly—

"Are they gone yet?"

Then she began describing with hysterical emotion the effect it produced on her to see black; and started, and trembled, and, at last, fell a weeping—and when I asked what was the matter? answered, she didn't know; but she felt so afraid of dying!

I imagined her as little likely to die as myself. She was rather thin, but young, and fresh complexioned, and her eyes sparkled as bright as diamonds. I did remark, to be sure, that mounting the stairs made her breathe very quick, that the least sudden noise set her all in a quiver, and that she coughed troublesomely sometimes: but I knew nothing of what these symptoms portended, and had no impulse to sympathize with her. We don't in general take to foreigners[1] here, Mr. Lockwood, unless they take to us first.

Young Earnshaw was altered considerably in the three years of his absence. He had grown sparer, and lost his colour, and spoke and dressed quite differently; and, on the very day of his return, he told Joseph and me we must thenceforth quarter ourselves in the back-kitchen, and leave the house for him. Indeed he would have carpeted and papered a small spare room for a parlour; but his wife expressed such pleasure at the white floor, and huge glowing fire-place, at the pewter dishes, and delf-case,[2] and dog-kennel, and the wide space there was to move about in, where they usually sat, that he thought it unnecessary to her comfort, and so dropped the intention.

She expressed pleasure, too, at finding a sister among her new acquaintance, and she prattled to Catherine, and kissed her, and ran about with her, and gave her quantities of presents, at the beginning. Her affection tired very soon, however, and when she grew peevish, Hindley became tyrannical. A few words from her, evincing a dislike to Heathcliff, were enough to rouse in him all his old hatred of the boy. He drove him from their company to the servants, deprived him of the instructions of the curate, and insisted that he should labour out of doors instead, compelling him to do so as hard as any other lad on the farm.

He bore his degradation pretty well at first, because Cathy taught him what she learnt, and worked or played with him in the

---

[1]Strangers.

[2]Dresser or cupboard for dishes (delf is glazed earthenware, made at Delft in Holland, imitated in England). Hindley Earnshaw has acquired modern ideas about rank (separation from servants, a parlor) and décor (wallpaper, carpets, and perhaps china and glass), but his wife admires the pre-industrial style of the yeomanry that persists at Wuthering Heights when Lockwood arrives in 1801. See "A Tale of Two Houses," p. 357.

fields. They both promised fair to grow up as rude as savages, the young master being entirely negligent how they behaved, and what they did, so they kept clear of him. He would not even have seen after their going to church on Sundays, only Joseph and the curate reprimanded his carelessness when they absented themselves, and that reminded him to order Heathcliff a flogging, and Catherine a fast from dinner or supper.

But it was one of their chief amusements to run away to the moors in the morning and remain there all day, and the after punishment grew a mere thing to laugh at. The curate might set as many chapters as he pleased for Catherine to get by heart, and Joseph might thrash Heathcliff till his arm ached; they forgot everything the minute they were together again, at least the minute they contrived some naughty plan of revenge; and many a time I've cried to myself to watch them growing more reckless daily, and I not daring to speak a syllable for fear of losing the small power I still retained over the unfriended creatures.

One Sunday evening, it chanced that they were banished from the sitting-room, for making a noise, or a light offence of the kind, and when I went to call them to supper, I could discover them nowhere.

We searched the house, above and below, and the yard and stables; they were invisible; and, at last, Hindley in a passion told us to bolt the doors, and swore nobody should let them in that night.

The household went to bed; and I, too anxious to lie down, opened my lattice and put my head out to hearken, though it rained, determined to admit them in spite of the prohibition, should they return.

In a while, I distinguished steps coming up the road, and the light of a lantern glimmered through the gate.

I threw a shawl over my head and ran to prevent them from waking Mr. Earnshaw by knocking. There was Heathcliff, by himself; it gave me a start to see him alone.

"Where is Miss Catherine?" I cried hurriedly. "No accident, I hope?"

"At Thrushcross Grange," he answered, "and I would have been there too, but they had not the manners to ask me to stay."

"Well, you will catch it!" I said, "you'll never be content till you're sent about your business. What in the world led you wandering to Thrushcross Grange?"

"Let me get off my wet clothes, and I'll tell you all about it, Nelly," he replied.

I bid him beware of rousing the master, and while he undressed and I waited to put out the candle, he continued—

"Cathy and I escaped from the wash-house to have a ramble at liberty, and getting a glimpse of the Grange lights, we thought we would just go and see whether the Lintons passed their Sunday evenings standing shivering in corners, while their father and mother sat eating and drinking, and singing and laughing, and burning their eyes out before the fire. Do you think they do? Or reading sermons, and being catechised by their man-servant, and set to learn a column of Scripture names, if they don't answer properly?"

"Probably not," I responded. "They are good children, no doubt, and don't deserve the treatment you receive, for your bad conduct."

"Don't you cant,[3] Nelly," he said. "Nonsense! We ran from the top of the Heights to the park, without stopping—Catherine completely beaten in the race, because she was barefoot. You'll have to seek for her shoes in the bog to-morrow. We crept through a broken hedge, groped our way up the path, and planted ourselves on a flower-plot under the drawing-room window. The light came from thence; they had not put up the shutters, and the curtains were only half closed. Both of us were able to look in by standing on the basement,[4] and clinging to the ledge,[5] and we saw—ah! it was beautiful—a splendid place carpeted with crimson, and crimson-covered chairs and tables, and a pure white ceiling bordered by gold, a shower of glass-drops hanging in silver chains from the centre, and shimmering with little soft tapers. Old Mr. and Mrs. Linton were not there. Edgar and his sister had it entirely to themselves; shouldn't they have been happy? We should have thought ourselves in heaven! And now, guess what your good children were doing? Isabella—I believe she is eleven, a year younger than Cathy—lay screaming at the farther end of the room, shrieking as if witches were running red hot needles into her. Edgar stood on the hearth

---

[3]"Cant" has a wide range of meanings, here most relevantly an auctioneer's, beggar's, or thief's patter or verbal routine. "Cant" is an adjective of praise for Nelly, see p. 50. See also "Dialect," p. 380.

[4]A rim of stonework surrounding the foundation of the house.

[5]Here, the windowsill.

weeping silently, and in the middle of the table sat a little dog, shaking its paw and yelping, which, from their mutual accusations, we understood they had nearly pulled in two between them. The idiots! That was their pleasure! to quarrel who should hold a heap of warm hair, and each begin to cry because both, after struggling to get it, refused to take it. We laughed outright at the petted things, we did despise them! When would you catch me wishing to have what Catherine wanted? or find us by ourselves, seeking entertainment in yelling, and sobbing, and rolling on the ground, divided by the whole room? I'd not exchange, for a thousand lives, my condition here, for Edgar Linton's at Thrushcross Grange—not if I might have the privilege of flinging Joseph off the highest gable, and painting the house-front with Hindley's blood!"

"Hush, hush!" I interrupted. "Still you have not told me, Heathcliff, how Catherine is left behind?"

"I told you we laughed," he answered. "The Lintons heard us, and with one accord, they shot like arrows to the door; there was silence, and then a cry, 'O, mamma, mamma! Oh, papa! Oh, mamma, come here. Oh, papa, oh!' They really did howl out, something in that way. We made frightful noises to terrify them still more, and then we dropped off the ledge, because somebody was drawing the bars, and we felt we had better flee. I had Cathy by the hand, and was urging her on, when all at once she fell down.

"'Run, Heathcliff, run!' she whispered. 'They have let the bulldog loose, and he holds me!'

"The devil had seized her ankle, Nelly; I heard his abominable snorting. She did not yell out—no! She would have scorned to do it, if she had been spitted on the horns of a mad cow. I did, though: I vociferated curses enough to annihilate any fiend in Christendom, and I got a stone and thrust it between his jaws, and tried with all my might to cram it down his throat. A beast of a servant came up with a lantern, at last, shouting—

"'Keep fast, Skulker, keep fast!'

"He changed his note, however, when he saw Skulker's game.[6] The dog was throttled off, his huge, purple tongue hanging half a foot out of his mouth, and his pendent lips streaming with bloody slaver.

[6]Prey.

"The man took Cathy up; she was sick; not from fear, I'm certain, but from pain. He carried her in; I followed, grumbling execrations and vengeance.

"'What prey, Robert?' hallooed Linton from the entrance.

"'Skulker has caught a little girl, sir,' he replied, 'and there's a lad here,' he added, making a clutch at me, 'who looks an out-and-outer![7] Very like, the robbers were for putting them through the window, to open the doors to the gang after all were asleep, that they might murder us at their ease. Hold your tongue, you foul-mouthed thief, you! you shall go to the gallows for this—Mr. Linton, sir, don't lay by your gun!'

"'No, no, Robert,' said the old fool. 'The rascals knew that yesterday was my rent day; they thought to have me cleverly. Come in; I'll furnish them a reception. There, John, fasten the chain. Give Skulker some water, Jenny. To beard a magistrate in his stronghold, and on the Sabbath, too! Where will their insolence stop? Oh, my dear Mary, look here! Don't be afraid, it is but a boy—yet the villain scowls so plainly in his face, would it not be a kindness to the country to hang him at once, before he shows his nature in acts as well as features?'

"He pulled me under the chandelier, and Mrs. Linton placed her spectacles on her nose and raised her hands in horror. The cowardly children crept nearer also, Isabella lisping—

"'Frightful thing! Put him in the cellar, papa. He's exactly like the son of the fortune-teller, that stole my tame pheasant. Isn't he, Edgar?'

"While they examined me, Cathy came round; she heard the last speech, and laughed. Edgar Linton, after an inquisitive stare, collected sufficient wit to recognise her. They see us at church, you know, though we seldom meet them elsewhere.

"'That's Miss Earnshaw!' he whispered to his mother, 'and look how Skulker has bitten her—how her foot bleeds!'

"'Miss Earnshaw? Nonsense!' cried the dame; 'Miss Earnshaw scouring the country with a gipsy! And yet, my dear, the child is in mourning—surely it is—and she may be lamed for life!'

"'What culpable carelessness in her brother!' exclaimed Mr. Linton, turning from me to Catherine. 'I've understood from

[7]A total ruffian or scoundrel. The Lintons' fear of murderers and burglars is realistic, as is the likelihood that Heathcliff could be hanged for a small theft; the landowner, as magistrate, could largely determine the conviction and punishment.

Shielders'" (that was the curate, sir) "'that he lets her grow up in absolute heathenism. But who is this? Where did she pick up this companion? Oho! I declare he is that strange acquisition my late neighbour made in his journey to Liverpool—a little Lascar, or an American or Spanish castaway.'[8]

"'A wicked boy, at all events,' remarked the old lady, 'and quite unfit for a decent house! Did you notice his language, Linton? I'm shocked that my children should have heard it.'

"I recommenced cursing—don't be angry, Nelly—and so Robert was ordered to take me off—I refused to go without Cathy—he dragged me into the garden, pushed the lantern into my hand, assured me that Mr. Earnshaw should be informed of my behaviour, and bidding me march, directly, secured the door again.

"The curtains were still looped up at one corner, and I resumed my station as spy; because, if Catherine had wished to return, I intended shattering their great glass panes to a million fragments, unless they let her out.

"She sat on the sofa[9] quietly. Mrs. Linton took off the grey cloak of the dairy maid which we had borrowed for our excursion, shaking her head, and expostulating with her, I suppose; she was a young lady and they made a distinction between her treatment and mine. Then the woman-servant brought a basin of warm water, and washed her feet; and Mr. Linton mixed a tumbler of negus, and Isabella emptied a plateful of cakes into her lap, and Edgar stood gaping at a distance. Afterwards, they dried and combed her beautiful hair, and gave her a pair of enormous slippers, and wheeled her to the fire, and I left her, as merry as she could be, dividing her food between the little dog and Skulker, whose nose she pinched as he ate; and kindling a spark of spirit in the vacant blue eyes of the Lintons—a dim reflection from her own enchanting face—I saw they were full of stupid admiration; she is so immeasurably superior to them—to everybody on earth, is she not, Nelly?"

"There will more come of this business than you reckon on," I answered, covering him up and extinguishing the light. "You are

[8]A "Lascar" was a sailor from South Asia, a "castaway" could be the survivor of a shipwreck or an outcast; that is, Heathcliff appears to be a racially obscure refugee from overseas.

[9]A word unknown in English until 1717; it comes from the Arabic for the raised, cushioned area for seating honored guests in council. The sofa is in keeping with the more modern décor at the Grange.

incurable, Heathcliff, and Mr. Hindley will have to proceed to extremities, see if he won't."

My words came truer than I desired. The luckless adventure made Earnshaw furious—And then, Mr. Linton, to mend matters, paid us a visit himself on the morrow; and read the young master such a lecture on the road he guided his family, that he was stirred to look about him, in earnest.

Heathcliff received no flogging, but he was told that the first word he spoke to Miss Catherine should ensure a dismissal; and Mrs. Earnshaw undertook to keep her sister-in-law in due restraint, when she returned home; employing art, not force—with force she would have found it impossible.

## Chapter 7

Cathy stayed at Thrushcross Grange five weeks, till Christmas. By that time her ankle was thoroughly cured, and her manners much improved. The mistress visited her often, in the interval, and commenced her plan of reform by trying to raise her self-respect with fine clothes and flattery, which she took readily: so that, instead of a wild, hatless little savage jumping into the house, and rushing to squeeze us all breathless, there lighted from a handsome black pony a very dignified person, with brown ringlets falling from the cover of a feathered beaver, and a long cloth habit[1] which she was obliged to hold up with both hands that she might sail in.

Hindley lifted her from her horse, exclaiming delightedly,

"Why, Cathy, you are quite a beauty! I should scarcely have known you—you look like a lady now—Isabella Linton is not to be compared with her, is she, Frances?"

"Isabella has not her natural advantages," replied his wife, "but she must mind and not grow wild again here. Ellen, help Miss Catherine off with her things—Stay, dear, you will disarrange your curls—let me untie your hat."

I removed the habit, and there shone forth beneath, a grand plaid silk frock, white trousers, and burnished shoes; and, while her eyes sparkled joyfully when the dogs came bounding up to wel-

[1]The riding habit.

come her, she dare hardly touch them lest they should fawn upon her splendid garments.

She kissed me gently—I was all flour making the Christmas cake, and it would not have done to give me a hug—and then she looked round for Heathcliff. Mr. and Mrs. Earnshaw watched anxiously their meeting, thinking it would enable them to judge, in some measure, what grounds they had for hoping to succeed in separating the two friends.

Heathcliff was hard to discover, at first. If he were careless and uncared for, before Catherine's absence, he had been ten times more so, since.

Nobody but I even did him the kindness to call him a dirty boy, and bid him wash himself, once a week; and children of his age seldom have a natural pleasure in soap and water. Therefore, not to mention his clothes, which had seen three months' service in mire and dust, and his thick uncombed hair, the surface of his face and hands was dismally beclouded. He might well skulk behind the settle, on beholding such a bright, graceful damsel enter the house, instead of a rough-headed counterpart of himself, as he expected.

"Is Heathcliff not here?" she demanded, pulling off her gloves, and displaying fingers wonderfully whitened with doing nothing, and staying indoors.

"Heathcliff, you may come forward," cried Mr. Hindley, enjoying his discomfiture and gratified to see what a forbidding young blackguard he would be compelled to present himself. "You may come and wish Miss Catherine welcome, like the other servants."

Cathy, catching a glimpse of her friend in his concealment, flew to embrace him; she bestowed seven or eight kisses on his cheek within the second, and then stopped, and drawing back, burst into a laugh, exclaiming,

"Why, how very black and cross you look! and how—how funny and grim! But that's because I'm used to Edgar and Isabella Linton. Well, Heathcliff, have you forgotten me?"

She had some reason to put the question, for shame and pride threw double gloom over his countenance, and kept him immovable.

"Shake hands, Heathcliff," said Mr. Earnshaw, condescendingly; "once in a way, that is permitted."

"I shall not!" replied the boy, finding his tongue at last, "I shall not stand to be laughed at, I shall not bear it!"

And he would have broken from the circle, but Miss Cathy seized him again.

"I did not mean to laugh at you," she said, "I could not hinder myself. Heathcliff, shake hands, at least! What are you sulky for? It was only that you looked odd—If you wash your face and brush your hair, it will be all right. But you are so dirty!"

She gazed concernedly at the dusky fingers she held in her own, and also at her dress, which she feared had gained no embellishment from its contact with his.

"You needn't have touched me!" he answered, following her eye and snatching away his hand. "I shall be as dirty as I please, and I like to be dirty, and I will be dirty."

With that he dashed head foremost out of the room, amid the merriment of the master and mistress, and to the serious disturbance of Catherine, who could not comprehend how her remarks should have produced such an exhibition of bad temper.

After playing lady's maid to the newcomer, and putting my cakes in the oven, and making the house and kitchen cheerful with great fires befitting Christmas Eve, I prepared to sit down and amuse myself by singing carols, all alone; regardless of Joseph's affirmations that he considered the merry tunes I chose as next door to songs.

He had retired to private prayer in his chamber, and Mr. and Mrs. Earnshaw were engaging Missy's attention by sundry gay trifles bought for her to present to the little Lintons, as an acknowledgment of their kindness.

They had invited them to spend the morrow at Wuthering Heights, and the invitation had been accepted, on one condition: Mrs. Linton begged that her darlings might be kept carefully apart from that "naughty, swearing boy."

Under these circumstances I remained solitary. I smelt the rich scent of the heating spices; and admired the shining kitchen utensils, the polished clock, decked in holly, the silver mugs ranged on a tray ready to be filled with mulled ale for supper; and, above all, the speckless purity of my particular care—the scoured and well-swept floor.

I gave due inward applause to every object, and then I remembered how old Earnshaw used to come in when all was tidied, and call me a cant lass,[2] and slip a shilling into my hand as a Christmas

---

[2]Lively, handy. See "Dialect," p. 380.

box; and from that I went on to think of his fondness for Heathcliff, and his dread lest he should suffer neglect after death had removed him; and that naturally led me to consider the poor lad's situation now, and from singing I changed my mind to crying. It struck me soon, however, there would be more sense in endeavouring to repair some of his wrongs than shedding tears over them—I got up and walked into the court to seek him.

He was not far; I found him smoothing the glossy coat of the new pony in the stable, and feeding the other beasts, according to custom.

"Make haste, Heathcliff!" I said, "the kitchen is so comfortable—and Joseph is upstairs; make haste, and let me dress you smart before Miss Cathy comes out—and then you can sit together, with the whole hearth to yourselves, and have a long chatter till bedtime."

He proceeded with his task and never turned his head towards me.

"Come—are you coming?" I continued. "There's a little cake for each of you, nearly enough; and you'll need half an hour's donning."[3]

I waited five minutes, but getting no answer left him . . . Catherine supped with her brother and sister-in-law: Joseph and I joined at an unsociable meal, seasoned with reproofs on one side and sauciness on the other. His cake and cheese remained on the table all night, for the fairies. He managed to continue work till nine o'clock, and then marched dumb and dour to his chamber.

Cathy sat up late, having a world of things to order for the reception of her new friends. She came into the kitchen, once, to speak to her old one, but he was gone, and she only staid to ask what was the matter with him, and then went back.

In the morning, he rose early; and, as it was a holiday, carried his ill-humour onto the moors; not re-appearing till the family were departed for church. Fasting and reflection seemed to have brought him to a better spirit. He hung about me for a while, and having screwed up his courage, exclaimed abruptly,

"Nelly, make me decent, I'm going to be good."

"High time, Heathcliff," I said, "you *have* grieved Catherine; she's sorry she ever came home, I dare say! It looks as if you envied her, because she is more thought of than you."

[3]Dressing.

The notion of *envying* Catherine was incomprehensible to him, but the notion of grieving her he understood clearly enough.

"Did she say she was grieved?" he inquired, looking very serious.

"She cried when I told her you were off again this morning."

"Well, *I* cried last night," he returned, "and I had more reason to cry than she."

"Yes, you had the reason of going to bed with a proud heart and an empty stomach," said I. "Proud people breed sad sorrows for themselves—But, if you be ashamed of your touchiness, you must ask pardon, mind, when she comes in. You must go up and offer to kiss her, and say—you know best what to say—only, do it heartily, and not as if you thought her converted into a stranger by her grand dress. And now, though I have dinner to get ready, I'll steal time to arrange you so that Edgar Linton shall look quite a doll beside you; and that he does. You are younger, and yet, I'll be bound, you are taller and twice as broad across the shoulders—you could knock him down in a twinkling; don't you feel that you could?"

Heathcliff's face brightened a moment; then it was overcast afresh, and he sighed.

"But, Nelly, if I knocked him down twenty times, that wouldn't make him less handsome or me more so. I wish I had light hair and a fair skin, and was dressed and behaved as well, and had a chance of being as rich as he will be!"

"And cried for mamma, at every turn—" I added, "and trembled if a country lad heaved his fist against you, and sat at home all day for a shower of rain.—O, Heathcliff, you are showing a poor spirit! Come to the glass, and I'll let you see what you should wish. Do you mark those two lines between your eyes; and those thick brows that, instead of rising arched, sink in the middle; and that couple of black fiends, so deeply buried, who never open their windows boldly, but lurk glinting under them, like devil's spies? Wish and learn to smooth away the surly wrinkles, to raise your lids frankly, and change the fiends to confident, innocent angels, suspecting and doubting nothing, and always seeing friends where they are not sure of foes—Don't get the expression of a vicious cur that appears to know the kicks it gets are its desert, and yet hates all the world, as well as the kicker, for what it suffers."

"In other words, I must wish for Edgar Linton's great blue eyes and even forehead," he replied. "I do—and that won't help me to them."

"A good heart will help you to a bonny face, my lad," I continued, "if you were a regular black; and a bad one will turn the bonniest into something worse than ugly. And now that we've done washing, and combing, and sulking—tell me whether you don't think yourself rather handsome? I'll tell you, I do. You're fit for a prince in disguise. Who knows, but your father was Emperor of China, and your mother an Indian queen, each of them able to buy up, with one week's income, Wuthering Heights and Thrushcross Grange together? And you were kidnapped by wicked sailors, and brought to England. Were I in your place, I would frame[4] high notions of my birth; and the thoughts of what I was should give me courage and dignity to support the oppressions of a little farmer!"

So I chattered on; and Heathcliff gradually lost his frown, and began to look quite pleasant; when, all at once, our conversation was interrupted by a rumbling sound moving up the road and entering the court. He ran to the window, and I to the door, just in time to behold the two Lintons descend from the family carriage, smothered in cloaks and furs, and the Earnshaws dismount from their horses—they often rode to church in winter. Catherine took a hand of each of the children, and brought them into the house and set them before the fire, which quickly put colour into their white faces.

I urged my companion to hasten now, and show his amiable humour; and he willingly obeyed. But ill luck would have it that, as he opened the door leading from the kitchen on one side, Hindley opened it on the other; they met, and the master, irritated at seeing him clean and cheerful, or, perhaps, eager to keep his promise to Mrs. Linton, shoved him back with a sudden thrust, and angrily bade Joseph "keep the fellow out of the room—send him into the garret till dinner is over. He'll be cramming his fingers in the tarts, and stealing the fruit, if left alone with them a minute."

"Nay, sir," I could not avoid answering, "he'll touch nothing, not he—and, I suppose, he must have his share of the dainties as well as we."

"He shall have his share of my hand, if I catch him downstairs till dark," cried Hindley. "Begone, you vagabond! What, you are

---

[4]Imagine, conjure up. Heathcliff's seeming exotic origins extend here to the fairy-tale secret of lofty birth.

attempting the coxcomb,[5] are you? Wait till I get hold of those elegant locks—see if I won't pull them a bit longer!"

"They are long enough already," observed Master Linton, peeping from the door-way; "I wonder they don't make his head ache. It's like a colt's mane over his eyes!"

He ventured this remark without any intention to insult; but Heathcliff's violent nature was not prepared to endure the appearance of impertinence from one whom he seemed to hate, even then, as a rival. He seized a tureen of hot apple-sauce, the first thing that came under his gripe, and dashed it full against the speaker's face and neck—who instantly commenced a lament that brought Isabella and Catherine hurrying to the place.

Mr. Earnshaw snatched up the culprit directly and conveyed him to his chamber, where, doubtless, he administered a rough remedy to cool the fit of passion, for he reappeared red and breathless. I got the dish-cloth, and rather spitefully, scrubbed Edgar's nose and mouth, affirming it served him right for meddling. His sister began weeping to go home, and Cathy stood by confounded, blushing for all.

"You should not have spoken to him!" she expostulated with Master Linton. "He was in a bad temper, and now you've spoilt your visit, and he'll be flogged—I hate him to be flogged! I can't eat my dinner. Why did you speak to him, Edgar?"

"I didn't," sobbed the youth, escaping from my hands, and finishing the remainder of the purification with his cambric pocket-handkerchief. "I promised mamma that I wouldn't say one word to him, and I didn't!"

"Well, don't cry!" replied Catherine, contemptuously. "You're not killed—don't make more mischief—my brother is coming—be quiet! Give over, Isabella! Has any body hurt *you*?"

"There, there, children—to your seats!" cried Hindley, bustling in. "That brute of a lad has warmed me nicely. Next time, Master Edgar, take the law into your own fists—it will give you an appetite!"

The little party recovered its equanimity at sight of the fragrant feast. They were hungry after their ride, and easily consoled, since no real harm had befallen them.

Mr. Earnshaw carved bountiful platefuls; and the mistress made them merry with lively talk. I waited behind her chair, and

[5]Trying to show off or put on a foolish display of fashion (like the comb of a rooster); "coxcomb" can also mean "head."

was pained to behold Catherine, with dry eyes and an indifferent air, commence cutting up the wing of a goose before her.

"An unfeeling child," I thought to myself, "how lightly she dismisses her old playmate's troubles. I could not have imagined her to be so selfish."

She lifted a mouthful to her lips; then, she set it down again: her cheeks flushed, and the tears gushed over them. She slipped her fork to the floor, and hastily dived under the cloth to conceal her emotion. I did not call her unfeeling long, for I perceived she was in purgatory throughout the day, and wearying to find an opportunity of getting by herself, or paying a visit to Heathcliff, who had been locked up by the master, as I discovered, on endeavouring to introduce to him a private mess of victuals.[6]

In the evening we had a dance. Cathy begged that he might be liberated then, as Isabella Linton had no partner; her entreaties were vain, and I was appointed to supply the deficiency.

We got rid of all gloom in the excitement of the exercise, and our pleasure was increased by the arrival of the Gimmerton band, mustering fifteen strong; a trumpet, a trombone, clarionets, bassoons, French horns, and a bass viol, besides singers. They go the rounds of all the respectable houses, and receive contributions every Christmas, and we esteemed it a first-rate treat to hear them.

After the usual carols had been sung, we set them to songs and glees. Mrs. Earnshaw loved the music, and so they gave us plenty.

Catherine loved it too; but she said it sounded sweetest at the top of the steps, and she went up in the dark; I followed. They shut the house door below, never noting our absence, it was so full of people. She made no stay at the stairs' head, but mounted farther, to the garret where Heathcliff was confined, and called him. He stubbornly declined answering for a while—she persevered, and finally persuaded him to hold communion with her through the boards.

I let the poor things converse unmolested, till I supposed the songs were going to cease, and the singers to get some refreshment; then, I clambered up the ladder to warn her.

Instead of finding her outside, I heard her voice within. The little monkey had crept by the skylight of one garret, along the roof, into the skylight of the other, and it was with the utmost difficulty I could coax her out again.

[6]A "mess" is a portion of food, therefore his own meal.

When she did come, Heathcliff came with her; and she insisted that I should take him into the kitchen, as my fellow-servant had gone to a neighbour's to be removed from the sound of our "devil's psalmody," as it pleased him to call it.

I told them I intended, by no means; to encourage their tricks; but as the prisoner had never broken his fast since yesterday's dinner, I would wink at his cheating Mr. Hindley that once.

He went down; I set him a stool by the fire, and offered him a quantity of good things; but he was sick and could eat little, and my attempts to entertain him were thrown away. He leant his two elbows on his knees, and his chin on his hands, and remained wrapt in dumb meditation. On my inquiring the subject of his thoughts, he answered gravely,—

"I'm trying to settle how I shall pay Hindley back. I don't care how long I wait, if I can only do it, at last. I hope he will not die before I do!"

"For shame, Heathcliff!" said I. "It is for God to punish wicked people; we should learn to forgive."

"No, God won't have the satisfaction that I shall," he returned. "I only wish I knew the best way! Let me alone, and I'll plan it out: while I'm thinking of that, I don't feel pain."

But, Mr. Lockwood, I forget these tales cannot divert you. I'm annoyed how I should dream of chattering on at such a rate; and your gruel cold, and you nodding for bed! I could have told Heathcliff's history, all that you need hear, in half-a-dozen words.

Thus interrupting herself, the housekeeper rose, and proceeded to lay aside her sewing; but I felt incapable of moving from the hearth, and I was very far from nodding.

"Sit still, Mrs. Dean," I cried, "do sit still, another half hour! You've done just right to tell the story leisurely. That is the method I like; and you must finish it in the same style. I am interested in every character you have mentioned, more or less."

"The clock is on the stroke of eleven, sir."

"No matter—I'm not accustomed to go to bed in the long hours.[7] One or two is early enough for a person who lies till ten."

[7]Just before 12 (vs. "small hours," 1 or 2 o'clock).

"You shouldn't lie till ten. There's the very prime of the morning gone long before that time. A person who has not done one half his day's work by ten o'clock, runs a chance of leaving the other half undone."

"Nevertheless, Mrs. Dean, resume your chair; because to-morrow I intend lengthening the night till afternoon. I prognosticate for myself an obstinate cold, at least."

"I hope not, sir. Well, you must allow me to leap over some three years; during that space, Mrs. Earnshaw—"

"No, no, I'll allow nothing of the sort! Are you acquainted with the mood of mind in which, if you were seated alone, and the cat licking its kitten on the rug before you, you would watch the operation so intently that puss's neglect of one ear would put you seriously out of temper?"

"A terribly lazy mood, I should say."

"On the contrary, a tiresomely active one. It is mine at present, and, therefore, continue minutely. I perceive that people in these regions acquire over people in towns the value that a spider in a dungeon does over a spider in a cottage, to their various occupants; and yet the deepened attraction is not entirely owing to the situation of the looker-on. They *do* live more in earnest, more in themselves, and less in surface change, and frivolous external things. I could fancy a love for life here almost possible; and I was a fixed unbeliever in any love of a year's standing—one state resembles setting a hungry man down to a single dish on which he may concentrate his entire appetite, and do it justice—the other, introducing him to a table laid out by French cooks; he can perhaps extract as much enjoyment from the whole, but each part is a mere atom in his regard and remembrance."

"Oh! here we are the same as anywhere else, when you get to know us," observed Mrs. Dean, somewhat puzzled at my speech.

"Excuse me," I responded, "you, my good friend, are a striking evidence against that assertion. Excepting a few provincialisms of slight consequence, you have no marks of the manners that I am habituated to consider as peculiar to your class. I am sure you have thought a great deal more than the generality of servants think. You have been compelled to cultivate your reflective faculties, for want of occasions for frittering your life away in silly trifles."

Mrs. Dean laughed.

"I certainly esteem myself a steady, reasonable kind of body," she said, "not exactly from living among the hills, and seeing one set of faces, and one series of actions, from year's end to year's end; but I have undergone sharp discipline which has taught me wisdom; and then, I have read more than you would fancy, Mr. Lockwood. You could not open a book in this library that I have not looked into, and got something out of also; unless it be that range of Greek and Latin, and that of French—and those I know one from another; it is as much as you can expect of a poor man's daughter."

"However, if I am to follow my story in true gossip's fashion,[8] I had better go on; and instead of leaping three years, I will be content to pass to the next summer—the summer of 1778, that is nearly twenty-three years ago."

## Chapter 8

On the morning of a fine June day, my first bonny little nursling, and the last of the ancient Earnshaw stock, was born.

We were busy with the hay in a far away field, when the girl that usually brought our breakfasts came running, an hour too soon, across the meadow and up the lane, calling me as she ran.

"Oh, such a grand bairn!" she panted out. "The finest lad that ever breathed! But the doctor says missis must go; he says she's been in a consumption these many months. I heard him tell Mr. Hindley—and now she has nothing to keep her, and she'll be dead before winter. You must come home directly. You're to nurse it, Nelly—to feed it with sugar and milk, and take care of it, day and night—I wish I were you, because it will be all yours when there is no missis!"

"But is she very ill?" I asked, flinging down my rake, and tying my bonnet.

"I guess she is; yet she looks bravely," replied the girl, "and she talks as if she thought of living to see it grow a man. She's out of her head for joy, it's such a beauty! If I were her I'm certain I should not die. I should get better at the bare sight of it, in spite of Ken-

---

[8]The leisurely, chatty style of a female companion's storytelling. In earlier senses, a "gossip" was a godparent or a friendly companion such as a nurse; it took on the meaning Nelly applies here before it narrowed to mean a tattle-tale or the secrets and criticism shared about others (especially between women).

neth. I was fairly mad at him. Dame Archer brought the cherub down to master, in the house, and his face just began to light up, then the old croaker steps forward, and, says he:—'Earnshaw, it's a blessing your wife has been spared to leave you this son. When she came, I felt convinced we shouldn't keep her long; and now, I must tell you, the winter will probably finish her. Don't take on, and fret about it too much, it can't be helped. And besides, you should have known better than to choose such a rush of a lass!'"[1]

"And what did the master answer?" I enquired.

"I think he swore—but I didn't mind him, I was straining to see the bairn," and she began again to describe it rapturously. I, as zealous as herself, hurried eagerly home to admire, on my part, though I was very sad for Hindley's sake; he had room in his heart only for two idols—his wife and himself—he doted on both, and adored one, and I couldn't conceive how he would bear the loss.

When we got to Wuthering Heights, there he stood at the front door; and, as I passed in, I asked, how was the baby?

"Nearly ready to run about, Nell!" he replied, putting on a cheerful smile.

"And the mistress?" I ventured to inquire; "the doctor says she's—"

"Damn the doctor!" he interrupted, reddening. "Frances is quite right—she'll be perfectly well by this time next week. Are you going upstairs? will you tell her that I'll come, if she'll promise not to talk. I left her because she would not hold her tongue; and she must—tell her Mr. Kenneth says she must be quiet."

I delivered this message to Mrs. Earnshaw; she seemed in flighty spirits, and replied merrily—

"I hardly spoke a word, Ellen, and there he has gone out twice, crying. Well, say I promise I won't speak; but that does not bind me not to laugh at him!"

Poor soul! Till within a week of her death that gay heart never failed her; and her husband persisted doggedly, nay, furiously, in affirming her health improved every day. When Kenneth warned him that his medicines were useless at that stage of the malady, and he needn't put him to further expense by attending her, he retorted—

"I know you need not—she's well—she does not want any more attendance from you! She never was in a consumption. It was

---

[1] A frail girl, slender as a reed.

a fever; and it is gone—her pulse is as slow as mine now, and her cheek as cool."

He told his wife the same story, and she seemed to believe him; but one night, while leaning on his shoulder, in the act of saying she thought she should be able to get up to-morrow, a fit of coughing took her—a very slight one—he raised her in his arms; she put her two hands about his neck, her face changed, and she was dead.

As the girl had anticipated, the child Hareton fell wholly into my hands. Mr. Earnshaw, provided he saw him healthy, and never heard him cry, was contented, as far as regarded him. For himself, he grew desperate; his sorrow was of that kind that will not lament; he neither wept nor prayed—he cursed and defied—execrated God and man, and gave himself up to reckless dissipation.

The servants could not bear his tyrannical and evil conduct long; Joseph and I were the only two that would stay. I had not the heart to leave my charge; and besides, you know, I had been his foster sister, and excused his behaviour more readily than a stranger would.

Joseph remained to hector over tenants and labourers; and because it was his vocation to be where he had plenty of wickedness to reprove.

The master's bad ways and bad companions formed a pretty example for Catherine and Heathcliff. His treatment of the latter was enough to make a fiend of a saint. And, truly, it appeared as if the lad *were* possessed of something diabolical at that period. He delighted to witness Hindley degrading himself past redemption; and became daily more notable for savage sullenness and ferocity.

I could not half tell what an infernal house we had. The curate dropped calling, and nobody decent came near us, at last; unless Edgar Linton's visits to Miss Cathy might be an exception. At fifteen she was the queen of the country-side; she had no peer: and she did turn out a haughty, headstrong creature! I own I did not like her, after her infancy was past; and I vexed her frequently by trying to bring down her arrogance; she never took an aversion to me, though. She had a wondrous constancy to old attachments; even Heathcliff kept his hold on her affections unalterably, and young Linton, with all his superiority, found it difficult to make an equally deep impression.

He was my late master; that is his portrait over the fireplace. It used to hang on one side, and his wife's on the other; but hers has been removed, or else you might see something of what she was. Can you make that out?

Mrs. Dean raised the candle, and I discerned a soft-featured face, exceedingly resembling the young lady at the Heights, but more pensive and amiable in expression. It formed a sweet picture. The long light hair curled slightly on the temples; the eyes were large and serious; the figure almost too graceful. I did not marvel how Catherine Earnshaw could forget her first friend for such an individual. I marvelled much how he, with a mind to correspond with his person, could fancy my idea of Catherine Earnshaw.

"A very agreeable portrait," I observed to the housekeeper. "Is it like?"

"Yes," she answered; "but he looked better when he was animated; that is his every day countenance; he wanted spirit in general."

Catherine had kept up her acquaintance with the Lintons since her five weeks' residence among them; and as she had no temptation to show her rough side in their company, and had the sense to be ashamed of being rude where she experienced such invariable courtesy, she imposed unwittingly on the old lady and gentleman, by her ingenuous cordiality; gained the admiration of Isabella, and the heart and soul of her brother—acquisitions that flattered her from the first, for she was full of ambition—and led her to adopt a double character without exactly intending to deceive any one.

In the place where she heard Heathcliff termed a "vulgar young ruffian," and "worse than a brute," she took care not to act like him; but at home she had small inclination to practise politeness that would only be laughed at, and restrain an unruly nature when it would bring her neither credit nor praise.

Mr. Edgar seldom mustered courage to visit Wuthering Heights openly. He had a terror of Earnshaw's reputation, and shrunk from encountering him, and yet, he was always received with our best attempts at civility: the master himself avoided offending him—knowing why he came—and if he could not be gracious, kept out of the way. I rather think his appearance there was distasteful to Catherine; she was not artful, never played the coquette, and had evidently an objection to her two friends meeting at all; for when Heathcliff expressed contempt of Linton, in his presence, she could not half coincide, as she did in his absence; and when Linton evinced disgust and antipathy to Heathcliff, she dare not treat his sentiments with indifference, as if depreciation of her playmate were of scarcely any consequence to her.

I've had many a laugh at her perplexities and untold troubles, which she vainly strove to hide from my mockery. That sounds ill-natured—but she was so proud, it became really impossible to pity her distresses, till she should be chastened into more humility.

She did bring herself, finally, to confess, and to confide in me. There was not a soul else that she might fashion into an adviser.

Mr. Hindley had gone from home, one afternoon; and Heathcliff presumed to give himself a holiday on the strength of it. He had reached the age of sixteen then, I think, and without having bad features or being deficient in intellect, he contrived to convey an impression of inward and outward repulsiveness that his present aspect retains no traces of.

In the first place, he had, by that time, lost the benefit of his early education; continual hard work, begun soon and concluded late, had extinguished any curiosity he once possessed in pursuit of knowledge, and any love for books or learning. His childhood's sense of superiority, instilled into him by the favours of old Mr. Earnshaw, was faded away. He struggled long to keep up an equality with Catherine in her studies, and yielded with poignant though silent regret; but, he yielded completely; and there was no prevailing on him to take a step in the way of moving upward, when he found he must, necessarily, sink beneath his former level. Then personal appearance sympathised with mental deterioration; he acquired a slouching gait, and ignoble look; his naturally reserved disposition was exaggerated into an almost idiotic excess of unsociable moroseness; and he took a grim pleasure, apparently, in exciting the aversion rather than the esteem of his few acquaintance.

Catherine and he were constant companions still, at his seasons of respite from labour; but he had ceased to express his fondness for her in words, and recoiled with angry suspicion from her girlish caresses, as if conscious there could be no gratification in lavishing such marks of affection on him. On the before-named occasion he came into the house to announce his intention of doing nothing, while I was assisting Miss Cathy to arrange her dress—she had not reckoned on his taking it into his head to be idle, and imagining she would have the whole place to herself, she managed, by some means, to inform Mr. Edgar of her brother's absence, and was then preparing to receive him.

"Cathy, are you busy, this afternoon?" asked Heathcliff. "Are you going anywhere?"

"No, it is raining," she answered.

"Why have you that silk frock on, then?" he said. "Nobody coming here, I hope?"

"Not that I know of," stammered Miss; "but you should be in the field now, Heathcliff. It is an hour past dinner time; I thought you were gone."

"Hindley does not often free us from his accursed presence," observed the boy; "I'll not work any more to-day, I'll stay with you."

"O, but Joseph will tell," she suggested; "you'd better go!"

"Joseph is loading lime on the farther side of Pennistow Crag;[2] it will take him till dark, and he'll never know."

So saying, he lounged to the fire, and sat down. Catherine reflected an instant, with knitted brows—she found it needful to smooth the way for an intrusion.

"Isabella and Edgar Linton talked of calling this afternoon," she said, at the conclusion of a minute's silence. "As it rains, I hardly expect them; but they may come, and if they do, you run the risk of being scolded for no good."

"Order Ellen to say you are engaged, Cathy," he persisted. "Don't turn me out for those pitiful, silly friends of yours! I'm on the point, sometimes, of complaining that they—but I'll not—"

"That they what?" cried Catherine, gazing at him with a troubled countenance. "Oh, Nelly!" she added petulantly, jerking her head away from my hands, "you've combed my hair quite out of curl! That's enough, let me alone. What are you on the point of complaining about, Heathcliff?"

"Nothing—only look at the almanack on that wall." He pointed to a framed sheet hanging near the window, and continued;

"The crosses are for the evenings you have spent with the Lintons, the dots for those spent with me—Do you see, I've marked every day?"

---

[2]Digging lime in the hills to use as fertilizer—one of many details that may be read as connecting *Wuthering Heights* to the Brontës' region. Many have identified a high rock ledge, Ponden Kirk, as the original of Pennistone or Pennistow Crag.

"Yes—very foolish; as if I took notice!" replied Catherine, in a peevish tone. "And where is the sense of that?"

"To show that I *do* take notice," said Heathcliff.

"And should I always be sitting with you," she demanded, growing more irritated. "What good do I get—What do you talk about? You might be dumb or a baby for anything you say to amuse me, or for anything you do, either!"

"You never told me before that I talked too little, or that you disliked my company, Cathy!" exclaimed Heathcliff in much agitation.

"It is no company at all, when people know nothing and say nothing," she muttered.

Her companion rose up, but he hadn't time to express his feelings further, for a horse's feet were heard on the flags, and, having knocked gently, young Linton entered, his face brilliant with delight at the unexpected summons he had received.

Doubtless Catherine marked the difference between her friends as one came in, and the other went out. The contrast resembled what you see in exchanging a bleak, hilly, coal country for a beautiful fertile valley; and his voice and greeting were as opposite as his aspect—He had a sweet, low manner of speaking, and pronounced his words as you do: that's less gruff than we talk here, and softer.

"I'm not come too soon, am I?" he said, casting a look at me. I had begun to wipe the plate, and tidy some drawers at the far end in the dresser.

"No," answered Catherine. "What are you doing there, Nelly?"

"My work, Miss," I replied. (Mr. Hindley had given me directions to make a third party in any private visits Linton chose to pay.)

She stepped behind me and whispered crossly, "Take yourself and your dusters off! When company are in the house, servants don't commence scouring and cleaning in the room where they are!"

"It's a good opportunity, now that master is away," I answered aloud; "he hates me to be fidgeting over these things in his presence—I'm sure Mr. Edgar will excuse me."

"I hate you to be fidgeting in *my* presence," exclaimed the young lady imperiously, not allowing her guest time to speak—she had failed to recover her equanimity since the little dispute with Heathcliff.

"I'm sorry for it, Miss Catherine!" was my response; and I proceeded assiduously with my occupation.

She, supposing Edgar could not see her, snatched the cloth from my hand, and pinched me, with a prolonged wrench, very spitefully on the arm.

I've said I did not love her, and rather relished mortifying her vanity, now and then; besides, she hurt me extremely, so I started up from my knees, and screamed out.

"O, Miss, that's a nasty trick! You have no right to nip me, and I'm not going to bear it!"

"I didn't touch you, you lying creature!" cried she, her fingers tingling to repeat the act, and her ears red with rage. She never had power to conceal her passion, it always set her whole complexion in a blaze.

"What's that, then?" I retorted, showing a decided purple witness to refute her.

She stamped her foot, wavered a moment, and then, irresistibly impelled by the naughty spirit within her, slapped me on the cheek a stinging blow that filled both eyes with water.

"Catherine, love! Catherine!" interposed Linton, greatly shocked at the double fault of falsehood and violence which his idol had committed.

"Leave the room, Ellen!" she repeated, trembling all over.

Little Hareton, who followed me everywhere, and was sitting near me on the floor, at seeing my tears commenced crying himself, and sobbed out complaints against "wicked aunt Cathy," which drew her fury on to his unlucky head. She seized his shoulders, and shook him till the poor child waxed livid, and Edgar thoughtlessly laid hold of her hands to deliver him. In an instant one was wrung free, and the astonished young man felt it applied over his own ear in a way that could not be mistaken for jest.

He drew back in consternation—I lifted Hareton in my arms, and walked off to the kitchen with him, leaving the door of communication open, for I was curious to watch how they would settle their disagreement.

The insulted visitor moved to the spot where he had laid his hat, pale and with a quivering lip.

"That's right!" I said to myself. "Take warning and begone! It's a kindness to let you have a glimpse of her genuine disposition."

"Where are you going?" demanded Catherine, advancing to the door.

He swerved aside and attempted to pass.

"You must not go!" she exclaimed energetically.

"I must and shall!" he replied in a subdued voice.

"No," she persisted, grasping the handle; "not yet, Edgar Linton—sit down, you shall not leave me in that temper. I should be miserable all night, and I won't be miserable for you!"

"Can I stay after you have struck me?" asked Linton.

Catherine was mute.

"You've made me afraid, and ashamed of you," he continued; "I'll not come here again!"

Her eyes began to glisten and her lids to twinkle.

"And you told a deliberate untruth!" he said.

"I didn't!" she cried, recovering her speech. "I did nothing deliberately—Well, go, if you please—get away! And now I'll cry—I'll cry myself sick!"

She dropped down on her knees by a chair and set to weeping in serious earnest.

Edgar persevered in his resolution as far as the court; there, he lingered. I resolved to encourage him.

"Miss is dreadfully wayward, sir!" I called out. "As bad as any marred[3] child—you'd better be riding home, or else she will be sick, only to grieve us."

The soft thing looked askance through the window—he possessed the power to depart, as much as a cat possesses the power to leave a mouse half killed, or a bird half eaten—

Ah, I thought, there will be no saving him—He's doomed, and flies to his fate!

And, so it was; he turned abruptly, hastened into the house again, shut the door behind him; and, when I went in a while after to inform them that Earnshaw had come home rabid drunk, ready to pull the old place about our ears (his ordinary frame of mind in that condition), I saw the quarrel had merely effected a closer intimacy—had broken the outworks of youthful timidity, and enabled them to forsake the disguise of friendship, and confess themselves lovers.

Intelligence of Mr. Hindley's arrival drove Linton speedily to his horse, and Catherine to her chamber. I went to hide little Hare-

[3]Spoiled.

ton, and to take the shot out of the master's fowling-piece, which he was fond of playing with in his insane excitement, to the hazard of the lives of any who provoked, or even attracted his notice too much; and I had hit upon the plan of removing it, that he might do less mischief, if he did go the length of firing the gun.

## Chapter 9

He entered, vociferating oaths dreadful to hear; and caught me in the act of stowing his son away in the kitchen cupboard. Hareton was impressed with a wholesome terror of encountering either his wild-beast's fondness or his madman's rage—for in one he ran a chance of being squeezed and kissed to death, and in the other of being flung into the fire, or dashed against the wall—and the poor thing remained perfectly quiet wherever I chose to put him.

"There, I've found it out at last!" cried Hindley, pulling me back by the skin of the neck, like a dog. "By Heaven and Hell, you've sworn between you to murder that child! I know how it is, now, that he is always out of my way. But, with the help of Satan, I shall make you swallow the carving knife, Nelly! You needn't laugh; for I've just crammed Kenneth, head-downmost, in the Blackhorse marsh; and two is the same as one—and I want to kill some of you, I shall have no rest till I do!"

"But I don't like the carving knife, Mr. Hindley," I answered; "it has been cutting red herrings—I'd rather be shot, if you please."

"You'd rather be damned!" he said, "and so you shall—No law in England can hinder a man from keeping his house decent, and mine's abominable! open your mouth."

He held the knife in his hand, and pushed its point between my teeth; but, for my part, I was never much afraid of his vagaries. I spat out, and affirmed it tasted detestably—I would not take it on any account.

"Oh!" said he, releasing me, "I see that hideous little villain is not Hareton—I beg your pardon, Nell—if it be, he deserves flaying alive for not running to welcome me, and for screaming as if I were a goblin. Unnatural cub, come hither! I'll teach thee to impose on a good-hearted, deluded father—Now, don't you think the lad would be handsomer cropped? It makes a dog fiercer, and I love some-thing fierce—Get me a scissors—something fierce and trim! Besides, it's infernal affectation—devilish conceit it is—to cherish our ears—we're asses enough without them. Hush, child, hush! well then, it is my darling! wisht, dry thy eyes—there's a joy; kiss me; what! it won't? Kiss me, Hareton! Damn thee, kiss me! By God, as if I would rear such a monster! As sure as I'm living, I'll break the brat's neck."

Poor Hareton was squalling and kicking in his father's arms with all his might, and redoubled his yells when he carried him upstairs and lifted him over the bannister. I cried out that he would frighten the child into fits, and ran to rescue him.

As I reached them, Hindley leant forward on the rails to listen to a noise below, almost forgetting what he had in his hands.

"Who is that?" he asked, hearing some one approaching the stair's-foot.

I leant forward, also, for the purpose of signing to Heathcliff, whose step I recognized, not to come further; and, at the instant when my eye quitted Hareton, he gave a sudden spring, delivered himself from the careless grasp that held him, and fell.

There was scarcely time to experience a thrill of horror before we saw that the little wretch was safe. Heathcliff arrived underneath just at the critical moment; by a natural impulse, he arrested his descent, and setting him on his feet, looked up to discover the author of the accident.

A miser who has parted with a lucky lottery ticket for five shillings and finds next day he has lost in the bargain five thousand pounds, could not show a blanker countenance than he did on beholding the figure of Mr. Earnshaw above—It expressed, plainer than words could do, the intensest anguish at having made himself the instrument of thwarting his own revenge. Had it been dark, I dare say, he would have tried to remedy the mistake by smashing Hareton's skull on the steps; but, we witnessed his salvation; and I was presently below with my precious charge pressed to my heart.

Hindley descended more leisurely, sobered and abashed.

"It is your fault, Ellen," he said, "you should have kept him out of sight; you should have taken him from me! Is he injured anywhere?"

"Injured!" I cried angrily, "If he's not killed, he'll be an idiot! Oh! I wonder his mother does not rise from her grave to see how you use him. You're worse than a heathen—treating your own flesh and blood in that manner!"

He attempted to touch the child, who, on finding himself with me, sobbed off his terror directly. At the first finger his father laid on him, however, he shrieked again louder than before, and struggled as if he would go into convulsions.

"You shall not meddle with him!" I continued, "He hates you—they all hate you—that's the truth! A happy family you have; and a pretty state you're come to!"

"I shall come to a prettier yet, Nelly!" laughed the misguided man, recovering his hardness. "At present, convey yourself and him away—And, hark you, Heathcliff! clear you too,[1] quite from my reach and hearing . . . I wouldn't murder you to-night, unless, perhaps, I set the house on fire; but that's as my fancy goes—"

While saying this he took a pint bottle of brandy from the dresser, and poured some into a tumbler.

"Nay don't!" I entreated, "Mr. Hindley, do take warning. Have mercy on this unfortunate boy, if you care nothing for yourself!"

"Any one will do better for him than I shall," he answered.

"Have mercy on your own soul!" I said, endeavouring to snatch the glass from his hand.

"Not I! on the contrary, I shall have great pleasure in sending it to perdition, to punish its maker," exclaimed the blasphemer. "Here's to its hearty damnation!"

He drank the spirits, and impatiently bade us go; terminating his command with a sequel of horrid imprecations, too bad to repeat, or remember.

"It's a pity he cannot kill himself with drink," observed Heathcliff, muttering an echo of curses back when the door was shut. "He's doing his very utmost; but his constitution defies him—Mr. Kenneth says he would wager his mare, that he'll outlive any man on this side Gimmerton, and go to the grave a hoary sinner; unless some happy chance out of the common course befall him."

I went into the kitchen and sat down to lull my little lamb to sleep. Heathcliff, as I thought, walked through to the barn. It turned out, afterwards, that he only got as far as the other side the settle, when he flung himself on a bench by the wall, removed from the fire, and remained silent.

[1]You clear off too.

I was rocking Hareton on my knee, and humming a song that began;

> "It was far in the night,[2] and the bairnies grat,
> The mither beneath the mools heard that"—

when Miss Cathy, who had listened to the hubbub from her room, put her head in, and whispered,
"Are you alone, Nelly?"
"Yes, Miss," I replied.
She entered and approached the hearth. I, supposing she was going to say something, looked up. The expression of her face seemed disturbed and anxious. Her lips were half asunder as if she meant to speak; and she drew a breath; but it escaped in a sigh, instead of a sentence.
I resumed my song, not having forgotten her recent behaviour.
"Where's Heathcliff?" she said, interrupting me.
"About his work in the stable," was my answer.
He did not contradict me; perhaps he had fallen into a doze.
There followed another long pause, during which I perceived a drop or two trickle from Catherine's cheek to the flags.
Is she sorry for her shameful conduct? I asked myself. That will be a novelty, but she may come to the point as she will—I shan't help her!
No, she felt small trouble regarding any subject, save her own concerns.
"Oh, dear!" she cried at last, "I'm very unhappy!"
"A pity," observed I, "you're hard to please—so many friends and so few cares, and can't make yourself content!"
"Nelly, will you keep a secret for me?" she pursued, kneeling down by me, and lifting her winsome eyes to my face with that sort of look which turns off bad temper, even when one has all the right in the world to indulge it.
"Is it worth keeping?" I inquired less sulkily.

---

[2] A slight variation on a translation of a Danish ballad, "The Ghaist's Warning," found in Walter Scott's *The Lady of the Lake*, Notes to Canto IV (243–46). "It was late in the night, and the little ones wept, / The mother in the grave heard that." The ballad relates to the folk belief that a dead mother returns to nurse her babies. See "Ballads," p. 383.

"Yes, and it worries me, and I must let it out! I want to know what I should do—To-day, Edgar Linton has asked me to marry him, and I've given him an answer—Now, before I tell you whether it was a consent, or denial—you tell me which it ought to have been."

"Really, Miss Catherine, how can I know?" I replied. "To be sure, considering the exhibition you performed in his presence this afternoon, I might say it would be wise to refuse him—since he asked you after that, he must either be hopelessly stupid, or a venturesome fool."

"If you talk so, I won't tell you any more," she returned peevishly, rising to her feet. "I accepted him, Nelly; be quick, and say whether I was wrong!"

"You accepted him? Then, what good is it discussing the matter? You have pledged your word, and cannot retract."

"But, say whether I should have done so—do!" she exclaimed in an irritated tone; chafing her hands together, and frowning.

"There are many things to be considered before that question can be answered properly," I said sententiously. "First and foremost, do you love Mr. Edgar?"

"Who can help it? Of course I do," she answered.

Then I put her through the following catechism—for a girl of twenty-two it was not injudicious.

"Why do you love him, Miss Cathy?"

"Nonsense, I do—that's sufficient."

"By no means; you must say why?"

"Well, because he is handsome, and pleasant to be with."

"Bad," was my commentary.

"And because he is young and cheerful."

"Bad, still."

"And, because he loves me."

"Indifferent, coming there."

"And he will be rich, and I shall like to be the greatest woman of the neighbourhood, and I shall be proud of having such a husband."

"Worst of all! And now, say how you love him?"

"As every body loves—You're silly, Nelly."

"Not at all—Answer."

"I love the ground under his feet, and the air over his head, and everything he touches, and every word he says—I love all his looks, and all his actions, and him entirely, and altogether. There now!"

"And why?"

"Nay—you are making a jest of it; it is exceedingly ill-natured! It's no jest to me!" said the young lady, scowling, and turning her face to the fire.

"I'm very far from jesting, Miss Catherine," I replied, "you love Mr. Edgar, because he is handsome, and young, and cheerful, and rich, and loves you. The last, however, goes for nothing—You would love him without that, probably; and with it you wouldn't, unless he possessed the four former attractions."

"No, to be sure not—I should only pity him—hate him, perhaps, if he were ugly, and a clown."

"But there are several other handsome, rich young men in the world; handsomer, possibly, and richer than he is—What should hinder you from loving them?"

"If there be any, they are out of my way—I've seen none like Edgar."

"You may see some; and he won't always be handsome, and young, and may not always be rich."

"He is now; and I have only to do with the present—I wish you would speak rationally."

"Well, that settles it—if you have only to do with the present, marry Mr. Linton."

"I don't want your permission for that—I *shall* marry him; and yet, you have not told me whether I'm right."

"Perfectly right; if people be right to marry only for the present. And now, let us hear what you are unhappy about. Your brother will be pleased . . . The old lady and gentleman will not object, I think—you will escape from a disorderly, comfortless home into a wealthy respectable one; and you love Edgar, and Edgar loves you. All seems smooth and easy—where is the obstacle?"

"*Here!* and *here!*" replied Catherine, striking one hand on her forehead, and the other on her breast. "In whichever place the soul lives—in my soul, and in my heart, I'm convinced I'm wrong!"

"That's very strange! I cannot make it out."

"It's my secret; but if you will not mock at me, I'll explain it; I can't do it distinctly—but I'll give you a feeling of how I feel."

She seated herself by me again; her countenance grew sadder and graver, and her clasped hands trembled.

"Nelly, do you never dream queer dreams?" she said, suddenly, after some minutes' reflection.

"Yes, now and then," I answered.

"And so do I. I've dreamt in my life dreams that have stayed with me ever after, and changed my ideas; they've gone through and through me, like wine through water, and altered the colour of my mind. And this is one—I'm going to tell it—but take care not to smile at any part of it."

"Oh! don't, Miss Catherine!" I cried. "We're dismal enough without conjuring up ghosts and visions to perplex us. Come, come, be merry, and like yourself! Look at little Hareton—*he's* dreaming nothing dreary. How sweetly he smiles in his sleep!"

"Yes; and how sweetly his father curses in his solitude! You remember him, I dare say, when he was just such another as that chubby thing—nearly as young and innocent. However, Nelly, I shall oblige you to listen—it's not long, and I've no power to be merry tonight."

"I won't hear it, I won't hear it!" I repeated, hastily.

I was superstitious about dreams then, and am still; and Catherine had an unusual gloom in her aspect, that made me dread something from which I might shape a prophecy, and foresee a fearful catastrophe.

She was vexed, but she did not proceed. Apparently taking up another subject, she re-commenced in a short time.

"If I were in heaven, Nelly, I should be extremely miserable."

"Because you are not fit to go there," I answered. "All sinners would be miserable in heaven."

"But it is not for that. I dreamt, once, that I was there."

"I tell you I won't hearken to your dreams, Miss Catherine! I'll go to bed," I interrupted again.

She laughed, and held me down, for I made a motion to leave my chair.

"This is nothing," cried she; "I was only going to say that heaven did not seem to be my home; and I broke my heart with weeping to come back to earth; and the angels were so angry that they flung me out, into the middle of the heath on the top of Wuthering Heights; where I woke sobbing for joy. That will do to explain my secret, as well as the other. I've no more business to marry Edgar Linton than I have to be in heaven; and if the wicked man in there had not brought Heathcliff so low, I shouldn't have thought of it. It would degrade me to marry Heathcliff, now; so he shall never know how I love him; and that, not because he's handsome, Nelly, but because he's more myself than I am. Whatever our souls are made of, his and mine are the same, and Linton's is as different as a moonbeam from lightning, or frost from fire."

Ere this speech ended I became sensible of Heathcliff's presence. Having noticed a slight movement, I turned my head, and saw him rise from the bench, and steal out, noiselessly. He had listened till he heard Catherine say it would degrade her to marry him, and then he stayed to hear no farther.

My companion, sitting on the ground, was prevented by the back of the settle from remarking his presence or departure; but I started, and bade her hush!

"Why?" she asked, gazing nervously round.

"Joseph is here," I answered, catching, opportunely, the roll of his cartwheels up the road; "and Heathcliff will come in with him. I'm not sure whether he were not at the door this moment."

"Oh, he couldn't overhear me at the door!" said she. "Give me Hareton, while you get the supper, and when it is ready ask me to sup with you. I want to cheat my uncomfortable conscience, and be convinced that Heathcliff has no notion of these things—he has not, has he? He does not know what being in love is?"

"I see no reason that he should not know, as well as you," I returned; "and if *you* are his choice, he'll be the most unfortunate creature that ever was born! As soon as you become Mrs. Linton, he loses friend, and love, and all! Have you considered how you'll bear the separation, and how he'll bear to be quite deserted in the world? Because, Miss Catherine—"

"He quite deserted! we separated!" she exclaimed, with an accent of indignation. "Who is to separate us, pray? They'll meet the fate of Milo![3] Not as long as I live, Ellen—for no mortal creature. Every Linton on the face of the earth might melt into nothing, before I could consent to forsake Heathcliff. Oh, that's not what I intend—that's not what I mean! I shouldn't be Mrs. Linton were such a price demanded! He'll be as much to me as he has been all his lifetime. Edgar must shake off his antipathy, and tolerate him, at least. He will when he learns my true feelings towards him. Nelly, I see

---

[3]In the classical fable, Milo, an athlete, tried to pull a tree up by the roots, but the tree seized his hands and held him as wild beasts devoured him.

now, you think me a selfish wretch, but did it never strike you that if Heathcliff and I married, we should be beggars? whereas, if I marry Linton, I can aid Heathcliff to rise, and place him out of my brother's power."

"With your husband's money, Miss Catherine?" I asked. "You'll find him not so pliable as you calculate upon; and, though I'm hardly a judge, I think that's the worst motive you've given yet for being the wife of young Linton."

"It is not," retorted she, "it is the best! The others were the satisfaction of my whims; and for Edgar's sake, too, to satisfy him. This is for the sake of one who comprehends in his person my feelings to Edgar and myself. I cannot express it; but surely you and every body have a notion that there is, or should be, an existence of yours beyond you. What were the use of my creation if I were entirely contained here? My great miseries in this world have been Heathcliff's miseries, and I watched and felt each from the beginning; my great thought in living is himself. If all else perished, and *he* remained, I should still continue to be; and, if all else remained, and he were annihilated, the Universe would turn to a mighty stranger. I should not seem a part of it. My love for Linton is like the foliage in the woods. Time will change it, I'm well aware, as winter changes the trees—my love for Heathcliff resembles the eternal rocks beneath—a source of little visible delight, but necessary. Nelly, I *am* Heathcliff—he's always, always in my mind—not as a pleasure, any more than I am always a pleasure to myself—but, as my own being—so, don't talk of our separation again—it is impracticable; and—"

She paused, and hid her face in the folds of my gown; but I jerked it forcibly away. I was out of patience with her folly!

"If I can make any sense of your nonsense, Miss," I said, "it only goes to convince me that you are ignorant of the duties you undertake in marrying; or else, that you are a wicked, unprincipled girl. But trouble me with no more secrets. I'll not promise to keep them."

"You'll keep that?" she asked, eagerly.

"No, I'll not promise," I repeated.

She was about to insist, when the entrance of Joseph finished our conversation; and Catherine removed her seat to a corner, and nursed Hareton, while I made the supper.

After it was cooked, my fellow servant and I began to quarrel who should carry some to Mr. Hindley; and we didn't settle it till all was nearly cold. Then we came to the agreement that we would let him ask, if he wanted any, for we feared particularly to go into his presence when he had been some time alone.

"Und hah isn't that nowt comed in frough' th' field, be this time? What is he abaht? girt idle seeght!"[4] demanded the old man, looking round for Heathcliff.

"I'll call him," I replied. "He's in the barn, I've no doubt."

I went and called, but got no answer. On returning, I whispered to Catherine that he had heard a good part of what she said, I was sure; and told how I saw him quit the kitchen just as she complained of her brother's conduct regarding him.

She jumped up in a fine fright—flung Hareton on to the settle, and ran to seek for her friend herself, not taking leisure to consider why she was so flurried, or how her talk would have affected him.

She was absent such a while that Joseph proposed we should wait no longer. He cunningly conjectured they were staying away in order to avoid hearing his protracted blessing. They were "ill eneugh for ony fahl manners,"[5] he affirmed. And, on their behalf, he added that night a special prayer to the usual quarter of an hour's supplication before meat, and would have tacked another to the end of the grace, had not his young mistress broken in upon him with a hurried command that he must run down the road, and, wherever Heathcliff had rambled, find and make him re-enter directly!

"I want to speak to him, and I *must*, before I go upstairs," she said. "And the gate is open, he is somewhere out of hearing; for he would not reply, though I shouted at the top of the fold as loud as I could."

Joseph objected at first; she was too much in earnest, however, to suffer contradiction; and, at last, he placed his hat on his head, and walked grumbling forth.

Meantime, Catherine paced up and down the floor, exclaiming,—

"I wonder where he is—I wonder where he *can* be! What did I say, Nelly? I've forgotten. Was he vexed at my bad humour this af-

---

[4]"Why hasn't that nothing [good-for-nothing] come in from the field, by this time? What's he up to, the great idle sight?"

[5]They were "bad enough for any foul manners."

ternoon? Dear! tell me what I've said to grieve him? I do wish he'd come. I do wish he would!"

"What a noise for nothing!" I cried, though rather uneasy myself. "What a trifle scares you! It's surely no great cause of alarm that Heathcliff should take a moonlight saunter on the moors, or even lie, too sulky to speak to us, in the hay-loft. I'll engage he's lurking there. See if I don't ferret him out!"

I departed to renew my search; its result was disappointment, and Joseph's quest ended in the same.

"Yon lad gets war un' war!" observed he on re-entering. "He's left th' yate ut t' full swing, and miss's pony has trodden dahn two rigs uh corn, un plottered through, raight o'er intuh t' meadow! Hahsomdiver, t' maister 'ull play t' divil to-morn, and he'll do weel. He's patience itsseln wi' sich careless, offald craters—patience itsseln he is! Bud he'll nut be soa allus—yah's see, all on ye! Yah munn't drive him out of his heead fur nowt!"[6]

"Have you found Heathcliff, you ass?" interrupted Catherine. "Have you been looking for him, as I ordered?"

"Aw sud more likker look for th' horse," he replied. "It 'ud be tuh more sense. Bud, Aw can look for norther horse nur man uf a neeght loike this—as black as t' chimbley! und Heathcliff's noan t' chap to coom ut *maw* whistle—happen he'll be less hard uh hearing wi' *ye*!"[7]

It *was* a very dark evening for summer; the clouds appeared inclined to thunder, and I said we had better all sit down; the approaching rain would be certain to bring him home without further trouble.

However, Catherine would not be persuaded into tranquillity. She kept wandering to and fro, from the gate to the door, in a state of agitation which permitted no repose, and at length took up a permanent situation on one side of the wall, near the road; where, heedless of my expostulations, and the growling thunder, and the great drops that began to plash around her, she remained, calling at intervals, and then listening, and then crying outright. She beat Hareton, or any child, at a good, passionate fit of crying.

[6]"worse and worse. . . . He's left the gate swinging wide open, and Miss's pony has trodden down two rows of corn [wheat], and scrambled . . . into the meadow! However, the master will play the devil tomorrow morning, . . . careless, worthless creatures—patience itself he is! . . . You mustn't drive him out his head for nothing!"

[7]It would make more sense to look for the horse; "neither horse nor man on a night like this—as black as the chimney!" Heathcliff won't "come at my whistle," etc.

About midnight, while we still sat up, the storm came rattling over the Heights in full fury. There was a violent wind, as well as thunder, and either one or the other split a tree off at the corner of the building; a huge bough fell across the roof, and knocked down a portion of the east chimney-stack, sending a clatter of stones and soot into the kitchen fire.

We thought a bolt had fallen in the middle of us, and Joseph swung onto his knees, beseeching the Lord to remember the Patriarchs Noah and Lot; and, as in former times, spare the righteous,[8] though he smote the ungodly. I felt some sentiment that it must be a judgment on us also. The Jonah, in my mind, was Mr. Earnshaw, and I shook the handle of his den that I might ascertain if he were yet living. He replied audibly enough, in a fashion which made my companion vociferate more clamorously than before, that a wide distinction might be drawn between saints like himself and sinners like his master. But the uproar passed away in twenty minutes, leaving us all unharmed, excepting Cathy, who got thoroughly drenched for her obstinacy in refusing to take shelter, and standing bonnetless and shawl-less to catch as much water as she could with her hair and clothes.

She came in and lay down on the settle, all soaked as she was, turning her face to the back, and putting her hands before it.

"Well, Miss!" I exclaimed, touching her shoulder. "You are not bent on getting your death, are you? Do you know what o'clock it is? Half-past twelve. Come! come to bed; there's no use waiting longer on that foolish boy—he'll be gone to Gimmerton, and he'll stay there now. He guesses we shouldn't wake for him till this late hour; at least, he guesses that only Mr. Hindley would be up; and he'd rather avoid having the door opened by the master."

"Nay, nay; he's noan at Gimmerton!" said Joseph. "Aw's niver wonder, bud he's at t' bothom uf a bog-hoile. This visitation worn't for nowt, und Aw wod hev ye tuh look aht, Miss,—yah muh be t' next. Thank Hivin for all! All warks togither for gooid tuh them as

---

[8]See 2 Peter 2.5 and 7. Noah and Lot are righteous men who escape a civilization's destruction by flood or fire, respectively. For once, Nelly shares Joseph's tendency to read events as divine judgment. Characteristically she is more hopeful of foregiveness. Mr. Earnshaw resembles Jonah when he at first runs away on a ship and endangers the lives of everyone on board. When Jonah finally accepts his duty to preach in Nineveh, the city repents and is spared.

is chozzen, and piked aht froo' th' rubbidge! Yah knaw whet t' Scripture ses—"[9]

And he began quoting several texts; referring us to chapters and verses where we might find them.

I, having vainly begged the wilful girl to rise and remove her wet things, left him preaching and her shivering, and betook myself to bed with little Hareton, who slept as fast as if every one had been sleeping round him.

I heard Joseph read on a while afterwards; then, I distinguished his slow step on the ladder, and then I dropt asleep.

Coming down somewhat later than usual, I saw, by the sunbeams piercing the chinks of the shutters, Miss Catherine still seated near the fire-place. The house door was ajar, too; light entered from its unclosed windows; Hindley had come out, and stood on the kitchen hearth, haggard and drowsy.

"What ails you, Cathy?" he was saying when I entered. "You look as dismal as a drowned whelp—Why are you so damp and pale, child?"

"I've been wet!" she answered reluctantly, "and I'm cold, that's all."

"Oh, she is naughty!" I cried, perceiving the master to be tolerably sober. "She got steeped in the shower of yesterday evening, and there she has sat, the night through, and I couldn't prevail on her to stir."

Mr. Earnshaw stared at us in surprise. "The night through," he repeated. "What kept her up, not fear of the thunder, surely? That was over, hours since."

Neither of us wished to mention Heathcliff's absence, as long as we could conceal it; so I replied, I didn't know how she took it into her head to sit up; and she said nothing.

The morning was fresh and cool; I threw back the lattice, and presently the room filled with sweet scents from the garden; but Catherine called peevishly to me.

"Ellen, shut the window. I'm starving!"[10] And her teeth chattered as she shrunk closer to the almost extinguished embers.

---

[9]"No, no; he's not at Gimmerton! . . . I shouldn't wonder if he's at the bottom of a bog-hole. This visitation [heavenly sign] wasn't for nothing, and I would have you look out, Miss—you may be the next. Thank Heaven for all! All works together for good to them as are chosen, and picked out from the rubbish. You know what the Scripture says" (Romans 8.28).

[10]Freezing.

"She's ill—" said Hindley, taking her wrist; "I suppose that's the reason she would not go to bed—Damn it! I don't want to be troubled with more sickness here—What took you into the rain?"

"Running after t' lads, as usuald!" croaked Joseph, catching an opportunity, from our hesitation, to thrust in his evil tongue. "If Aw wur yah, maister, Aw'd just slam t' boards i' their faces all on 'em, gentle and simple! Never a day ut yah're off, but yon cat uh Linton comes sneaking hither—and Miss Nelly, shoo's a fine lass! shoo sits watching for ye i' t' kitchen; and as yah're in at one door, he's aht at t'other—Und, then, wer grand lady goes a-coorting of her side! It's bonny behaviour, lurking amang t' fields after twelve ut' night, wi' that fahl, flaysome divil uf a gipsy, Heathcliff! They think *Aw'm* blind; but Aw'm noan, nowt ut t' soart! Aw seed young Linton, boath coming and going, and Aw seed *yah*" (directing his discourse to me), "yah gooid fur nowt, slattenly witch! nip up and bolt intuh th' hahs, t' minute yah heard t' maister's horse fit clatter up t' road."[11]

"Silence, eavesdropper!" cried Catherine, "None of your insolence, before me! Edgar Linton came yesterday, by chance, Hindley; and it was *I* who told him to be off, because I knew you would not like to have met him as you were."

"You lie, Cathy, no doubt," answered her brother, "and you are a confounded simpleton! But never mind Linton, at present—Tell me, were you not with Heathcliff last night? Speak the truth, now. You need not be afraid of harming him—Though I hate him as much as ever, he did me a good turn, a short time since, that will make my conscience tender of breaking his neck. To prevent it, I shall send him about his business, this very morning; and after he's gone, I'd advise you all to look sharp, I shall only have the more humour for you!"

"I never saw Heathcliff last night," answered Catherine, beginning to sob bitterly: "and if you do turn him out of doors, I'll go with him. But perhaps you'll never have an opportunity—perhaps

---

[11]"If I were you, I'd just slam the doors in their faces, all of them, gentle and simple [of any rank]. Never a day that you're away but that cat Linton comes sneaking here, and Miss Nelly she's a fine lass! She sits watching for you in the kitchen, and while you're in at one door, he's out at the other; and then, our grand lady goes on her side [in her turn]! It's great behavior, lurking among the fields with that foul, dreadful devil of a gipsy, Heathcliff! They think I'm blind; but I'm not, nothing of the sort! I saw young Linton, both coming and going, and I saw you . . . you good for nothing, slatternly witch! Jump and bolt into the house, the minute you heard the master's horse's feet clatter up the road."

he's gone." Here she burst into uncontrollable grief, and the remainder of her words were inarticulate.

Hindley lavished on her a torrent of scornful abuse, and bid her get to her room immediately, or she shouldn't cry for nothing! I obliged her to obey; and I shall never forget what a scene she acted, when we reached her chamber. It terrified me—I thought she was going mad, and I begged Joseph to run for the doctor.

It proved the commencement of delirium; Mr. Kenneth, as soon as he saw her, pronounced her dangerously ill; she had a fever.

He bled her, and he told me to let her live on whey and water gruel; and take care she did not throw herself down stairs, or out of the window; and then he left, for he had enough to do in the parish, where two or three miles was the ordinary distance between cottage and cottage.

Though I cannot say I made a gentle nurse, and Joseph and the master were no better; and though our patient was as wearisome and headstrong as a patient could be, she weathered it through.

Old Mrs. Linton paid us several visits, to be sure, and set things to rights, and scolded and ordered us all; and when Catherine was convalescent, she insisted on conveying her to Thrushcross Grange; for which deliverance we were very grateful. But the poor dame had reason to repent of her kindness; she and her husband both took the fever, and died within a few days of each other.

Our young lady returned to us, saucier, and more passionate, and haughtier than ever. Heathcliff had never been heard of since the evening of the thunder-storm, and, one day, I had the misfortune, when she had provoked me exceedingly, to lay the blame of his disappearance on her (where indeed it belonged, as she well knew). From that period, for several months, she ceased to hold any communication with me, save in the relation of a mere servant. Joseph fell under a ban also; he *would* speak his mind, and lecture her all the same as if she were a little girl; and she esteemed herself a woman, and our mistress, and thought that her recent illness gave her a claim to be treated with consideration. Then the doctor had said that she would not bear crossing much, she ought to have her own way; and it was nothing less than murder, in her eyes, for any one to presume to stand up and contradict her.

From Mr. Earnshaw and his companions she kept aloof; and tutored by Kenneth, and serious threats of a fit that often attended her rages, her brother allowed her whatever she pleased to demand, and generally avoided aggravating her fiery temper. He was rather *too* indulgent in humouring her caprices; not from affection, but from pride; he wished earnestly to see her bring honour to the family by an alliance with the Lintons, and, as long as she let him alone, she might trample on us like slaves for aught he cared!

Edgar Linton, as multitudes have been before and will be after him, was infatuated; and believed himself the happiest man alive on the day he led her to Gimmerton chapel, three years subsequent to his father's death.

Much against my inclination, I was persuaded to leave Wuthering Heights and accompany her here. Little Hareton was nearly five years old, and I had just begun to teach him his letters. We made a sad parting, but Catherine's tears were more powerful than ours— When I refused to go, and when she found her entreaties did not move me, she went lamenting to her husband and brother. The former offered me munificent wages; the latter ordered me to pack up—he wanted no women in the house, he said, now that there was no mistress; and as to Hareton, the curate should take him in hand by and bye. And so, I had but one choice left, to do as I was ordered—I told the master he got rid of all decent people only to run to ruin a little faster; I kissed Hareton good bye; and, since then, he has been a stranger, and it's very queer to think it, but I've no doubt he has completely forgotten all about Ellen Dean and that he was ever more than all the world to her, and she to him!

At this point of the housekeeper's story she chanced to glance towards the time-piece over the chimney; and was in amazement on seeing the minute-hand measure half past one. She would not hear of staying a second longer—In truth, I felt rather disposed to defer the sequel of her narrative, myself: and now that she is vanished to her rest, and I have meditated for another hour or two, I shall summon courage to go, also, in spite of aching laziness of head and limbs.

## Chapter 10

A charming introduction to a hermit's life! Four weeks' torture, tossing and sickness! Oh, these bleak winds and bitter, northern skies, and impassable roads, and dilatory country surgeons! And, oh, this dearth of the human physiognomy, and, worse than all, the terrible intimation of Kenneth that I need not expect to be out of doors till spring!

Mr. Heathcliff has just honoured me with a call. About seven days ago he sent me a brace of grouse—the last of the season. Scoundrel! He is not altogether guiltless in this illness of mine; and that I had a great mind to tell him. But, alas! how could I offend a man who was charitable enough to sit at my bedside a good hour, and talk on some other subject than pills and draughts, blisters and leeches?

This is quite an easy interval. I am too weak to read, yet I feel as if I could enjoy something interesting. Why not have up Mrs. Dean to finish her tale? I can recollect its chief incidents, as far as she had gone. Yes, I remember her hero had run off, and never been heard of for three years: and the heroine was married. I'll ring; she'll be delighted to find me capable of talking cheerfully.

Mrs. Dean came.

"It wants twenty minutes, sir, to taking the medicine," she commenced.

"Away, away with it!" I replied; "I desire to have—"

"The doctor says you must drop the powders."

"With all my heart! Don't interrupt me. Come and take your seat here. Keep your fingers from that bitter phalanx of vials. Draw your knitting out of your pocket—that will do—now continue the history of Mr. Heathcliff, from where you left off, to the present day. Did he finish his education on the Continent, and come back a gentleman? or did he get a sizer's place at college?[1] or escape to America, and earn honours by drawing blood from his foster country? or make a fortune more promptly, on the English highways?"

"He may have done a little in all these vocations, Mr. Lockwood; but I couldn't give my word for any. I stated before that I didn't know how he gained his money; neither am I aware of the means he took to raise his mind from the savage ignorance into which it was sunk; but,

---

[1]A sizar was an impoverished scholarship student. While university education and continental travel would have been beyond Heathcliff's means, a sizar could become a gentleman: Emily Brontë's Irish father Patrick, from a very modest background, was a sizar at St. John's College, Cambridge. Lockwood suggests Heathcliff could have joined the colonial side in the War of Independence 1776–83, thus attacking the fatherland (Earnshaw's England) that had adopted him, or he could have become the highway robber the Lintons thought he would grow up to be when they caught him outside Thrushcross Grange. This is a humorous list, probable and improbable, decent and illegal, of ways to beat the enormous odds against a farm boy becoming a gentleman.

with your leave, I'll proceed in my own fashion, if you think it will amuse and not weary you. Are you feeling better this morning?"

"Much."

"That's good news."

I got Miss Catherine and myself to Thrushcross Grange: and to my agreeable disappointment, she behaved infinitely better than I dared to expect. She seemed almost over fond of Mr. Linton; and even to his sister, she showed plenty of affection. They were both very attentive to her comfort, certainly. It was not the thorn bending to the honeysuckles, but the honeysuckles embracing the thorn. There were no mutual concessions; one stood erect, and the others yielded; and who *can* be ill-natured and bad-tempered, when they encounter neither opposition nor indifference?

I observed that Mr. Edgar had a deep-rooted fear of ruffling her humour. He concealed it from her; but if ever he heard me answer sharply, or saw any other servant grow cloudy at some imperious order of hers, he would show his trouble by a frown of displeasure that never darkened on his own account. He, many a time, spoke sternly to me about my pertness; and averred that the stab of a knife could not inflict a worse pang than he suffered at seeing his lady vexed.

Not to grieve a kind master I learnt to be less touchy; and, for the space of half a year, the gunpowder lay as harmless as sand, because no fire came near to explode it. Catherine had seasons of gloom and silence, now and then: they were respected with sympathizing silence by her husband, who ascribed them to an alteration in her constitution, produced by her perilous illness, as she was never subject to depression of spirits before. The return of sunshine was welcomed by answering sunshine from him. I believe I may assert that they were really in possession of deep and growing happiness.

It ended. Well, we *must* be for ourselves in the long run; the mild and generous are only more justly selfish than the domineering— and it ended when circumstances caused each to feel that the one's interest was not the chief consideration in the other's thoughts.

On a mellow evening in September, I was coming from the garden with a heavy basket of apples which I had been gathering. It had got dusk, and the moon looked over the high wall of the court, causing undefined shadows to lurk in the corners of the numerous projecting portions of the building. I set my burden on the house steps by the kitchen door, and lingered to rest and draw in a few more breaths of the soft, sweet air; my eyes were on the moon, and my back to the entrance, when I heard a voice behind me say—

"Nelly, is that you?"

It was a deep voice, and foreign in tone; yet, there was something in the manner of pronouncing my name which made it sound familiar. I turned about to discover who spoke, fearfully, for the doors were shut, and I had seen nobody on approaching the steps.

Something stirred in the porch; and moving nearer, I distinguished a tall man dressed in dark clothes, with dark face and hair. He leant against the side, and held his fingers on the latch, as if intending to open for himself.

"Who can it be?" I thought. "Mr. Earnshaw? Oh no! The voice has no resemblance to his."

"I have waited here an hour," he resumed, while I continued staring; "and the whole of that time all round has been as still as death. I dared not enter. You do not know me? Look, I'm not a stranger!"

A ray fell on his features; the cheeks were sallow, and half covered with black whiskers; the brows lowering, the eyes deep-set and singular. I remembered the eyes.

"What!" I cried, uncertain whether to regard him as a worldly visiter, and I raised my hands in amazement. "What! you come back? Is it really you? Is it?"

"Yes, Heathcliff," he replied, glancing from me up to the windows, which reflected a score of glittering moons, but showed no lights from within. "Are they at home—where is she? Nelly, you are not glad—you needn't be so disturbed. Is she here? Speak! I want to have one word with her—your mistress. Go, and say some person from Gimmerton desires to see her."

"How will she take it?" I exclaimed, "what will she do? The surprise bewilders me—it will put her out of her head! And you *are* Heathcliff? But altered! Nay, there's no comprehending it. Have you been for a soldier?"

"Go, and carry my message," he interrupted impatiently; "I'm in hell till you do!"

He lifted the latch, and I entered; but when I got to the parlour where Mr. and Mrs. Linton were, I could not persuade myself to proceed.

At length, I resolved on making an excuse to ask if they would have the candles lighted, and I opened the door.

They sat together in a window whose lattice lay back against the wall, and displayed, beyond the garden trees and the wild green park, the valley of Gimmerton, with a long line of mist winding nearly to its top (for very soon after you pass the chapel, as you may have noticed, the sough[2] that runs from the marshes joins a beck[3] which follows the bend of the glen). Wuthering Heights rose above this silvery vapour; but our old house was invisible—it rather dips down on the other side.

Both the room, and its occupants, and the scene they gazed on, looked wondrously peaceful. I shrank reluctantly from performing my errand, and was actually going away, leaving it unsaid, after having put my question about the candles, when a sense of my folly compelled me to return, and mutter:

"A person from Gimmerton wishes to see you, ma'am."

"What does he want?" asked Mrs. Linton.

"I did not question him," I answered.

"Well, close the curtains, Nelly," she said; "and bring up tea. I'll be back again directly."

She quitted the apartment; Mr. Edgar inquired carelessly, who it was?

"Some one mistress does not expect," I replied. "That Heathcliff, you recollect him, sir, who used to live at Mr. Earnshaw's."

"What, the gipsy—the plough-boy?" he cried. "Why did you not say so to Catherine?"

"Hush! you must not call him by those names, master," I said. "She'd be sadly grieved to hear you. She was nearly heartbroken when he ran off; I guess his return will make a jubilee[4] to her."

Mr. Linton walked to a window on the other side of the room that overlooked the court. He unfastened it, and leant out. I suppose they were below, for he exclaimed, quickly:—

"Don't stand there, love! Bring the person in, if it be any one particular."

[2]The ditch.

[3]A brook or stream.

[4]A celebration, based on the ancient Hebrew festival every 50 years (Leviticus 25), in which slaves were freed and property released.

Ere long, I heard the click of the latch, and Catherine flew upstairs, breathless and wild, too excited to show gladness; indeed, by her face, you would rather have surmised an awful calamity.

"Oh, Edgar, Edgar!" she panted, flinging her arms round his neck. "Oh, Edgar, darling! Heathcliff's come back—he is!" And she tightened her embrace to a squeeze.

"Well, well," cried her husband, crossly, "don't strangle me for that! He never struck me as such a marvellous treasure. There is no need to be frantic!"

"I know you didn't like him," she answered, repressing a little the intensity of her delight. "Yet for my sake, you must be friends now. Shall I tell him to come up?"

"Here," he said, "into the parlour?"

"Where else?" she asked.

He looked vexed, and suggested the kitchen as a more suitable place for him.

Mrs. Linton eyed him with a droll expression—half angry, half laughing, at his fastidiousness.

"No," she added, after a while; "I cannot sit in the kitchen. Set two tables here, Ellen; one for your master and Miss Isabella, being gentry; the other for Heathcliff and myself, being of the lower orders. Will that please you, dear? Or must I have a fire lighted elsewhere? If so, give directions. I'll run down and secure my guest. I'm afraid the joy is too great to be real!"

She was about to dart off again; but Edgar arrested her.

"*You* bid him step up," he said, addressing me; "and, Catherine, try to be glad without being absurd! The whole household need not witness the sight of your welcoming a runaway servant as a brother."

I descended and found Heathcliff waiting under the porch, evidently anticipating an invitation to enter. He followed my guidance without waste of words, and I ushered him into the presence of the master and mistress, whose flushed cheeks betrayed signs of warm talking. But the lady's glowed with another feeling when her friend appeared at the door; she sprang forward, took both his hands, and led him to Linton; and then she seized Linton's reluctant fingers and crushed them into his.

Now fully revealed by the fire and candlelight, I was amazed, more than ever, to behold the transformation of Heathcliff. He had grown a tall, athletic, well-formed man, beside whom my master seemed quite slender and youth-like. His upright carriage suggested the idea of his having been in the army. His countenance was much older in expression and decision of feature than Mr. Linton's; it looked intelligent, and retained no marks of former degradation. A half-civilized ferocity lurked yet in the depressed brows and eyes full of black fire, but it was subdued; and his manner was even dignified, quite divested of roughness though too stern for grace.

My master's surprise equalled or exceeded mine: he remained for a minute at a loss how to address the ploughboy, as he had called him; Heathcliff dropped his slight hand, and stood looking at him coolly till he chose to speak.

"Sit down, sir," he said, at length. "Mrs. Linton, recalling old times, would have me give you a cordial reception, and, of course, I am gratified when anything occurs to please her."

"And I also," answered Heathcliff, "especially if it be anything in which I have a part. I shall stay an hour or two willingly."

He took a seat opposite Catherine, who kept her gaze fixed on him as if she feared he would vanish were she to remove it. He did not raise his to her often; a quick glance now and then sufficed; but it flashed back, each time more confidently, the undisguised delight he drank from hers.

They were too much absorbed in their mutual joy to suffer embarrassment. Not so Mr. Edgar: he grew pale with pure annoyance, a feeling that reached its climax when his lady rose—and stepping across the rug, seized Heathcliff's hands again, and laughed like one beside herself.

"I shall think it a dream to-morrow!" she cried. "I shall not be able to believe that I have seen, and touched, and spoken to you once more—and yet, cruel Heathcliff! you don't deserve this welcome. To be absent and silent for three years, and never to think of me!"

"A little more than you have thought of me!" he murmured. "I heard of your marriage, Cathy, not long since; and, while waiting in the yard below, I meditated this plan—just to have one glimpse of your face—a stare of surprise, perhaps, and pretended pleasure; afterwards settle my score with Hindley; and then prevent the law by doing execution on myself. Your welcome has put these ideas out of my mind; but beware of meeting me with another aspect next time! Nay, you'll not drive me off again—you were really sorry for me, were you? Well, there was cause. I've fought through a bitter life since I last heard your voice, and you must forgive me, for I struggled only for you!"

"Catherine, unless we are to have cold tea, please to come to the table," interrupted Linton, striving to preserve his ordinary tone, and a due measure of politeness. "Mr. Heathcliff will have a long walk, wherever he may lodge to-night; and I'm thirsty."

She took her post before the urn; and Miss Isabella came, summoned by the bell; then, having handed their chairs forward, I left the room.

The meal hardly endured ten minutes—Catherine's cup was never filled, she could neither eat nor drink. Edgar had made a slop in his saucer, and scarcely swallowed a mouthful.

Their guest did not protract his stay, that evening, above an hour longer. I asked, as he departed, if he went to Gimmerton?

"No, to Wuthering Heights," he answered, "Mr. Earnshaw invited me when I called this morning."

Mr. Earnshaw invited *him*! and *he* called on Mr. Earnshaw! I pondered this sentence painfully, after he was gone. Is he turning out a bit of a hypocrite, and coming into the country to work mischief under a cloak? I mused—I had a presentiment, in the bottom of my heart, that he had better have remained away.

About the middle of the night, I was wakened from my first nap by Mrs. Linton gliding into my chamber, taking a seat on my bedside, and pulling me by the hair to rouse me.

"I cannot rest, Ellen," she said by way of apology. "And I want some living creature to keep me company in my happiness! Edgar is sulky, because I'm glad of a thing that does not interest him—He refuses to open his mouth, except to utter pettish, silly speeches; and he affirmed I was cruel and selfish for wishing to talk when he was so sick and sleepy. He always contrives to be sick at the least cross! I gave a few sentences of commendation to Heathcliff, and he, either for a head-ache or a pang of envy, began to cry; so I got up and left him."

"What use is it praising Heathcliff to him?" I answered. "As lads they had an aversion to each other, and Heathcliff would hate just as much to hear him praised—it's human nature. Let Mr. Linton alone about him, unless you would like an open quarrel between them."

"But does it not show great weakness?" pursued she. "I'm not envious—I never feel hurt at the brightness of Isabella's yellow hair, and the whiteness of her skin; at her dainty elegance, and the fondness all the family exhibit for her. Even you, Nelly, if we have a dispute sometimes, you back Isabella, at once; and I yield like a foolish mother—I call her a darling, and flatter her into a good temper. It pleases her brother to see us cordial, and that pleases me. But they are very much alike: they are spoiled children, and fancy the world was made for their accommodation; and, though I humour both, I think a smart chastisement might improve them, all the same."

"You're mistaken, Mrs. Linton," said I, "They humour you—I know what there would be to do if they did not! You can well afford to indulge their passing whims, as long as their business is to anticipate all your desires—You may, however, fall out, at last, over something of equal consequence to both sides; and then those you term weak are very capable of being as obstinate as you!"

"And then we shall fight to the death, shan't we, Nelly?" she returned, laughing. "No! I tell you, I have such faith in Linton's love that I believe I might kill him, and he wouldn't wish to retaliate."

I advised her to value him the more for his affection.

"I do," she answered, "but he needn't resort to whining for trifles. It is childish; and, instead of melting into tears because I said that Heathcliff was now worthy of any one's regard, and it would honour the first gentleman in the country to be his friend, he ought to have said it for me, and been delighted from sympathy—He must get accustomed to him, and he may as well like him—considering how Heathcliff has reason to object to him, I'm sure he behaved excellently!"

"What do you think of his going to Wuthering Heights?" I inquired. "He is reformed in every respect, apparently—quite a Christian—offering the right hand of fellowship to his enemies all round!"

"He explained it," she replied. "I wondered as much as you— He said he called to gather information concerning me from you, supposing you resided there still; and Joseph told Hindley, who came out and fell to questioning him of what he had been doing, and how he had been living, and finally desired him to walk in— There were some persons sitting at cards—Heathcliff joined them; my brother lost some money to him; and, finding him plentifully supplied, he requested that he would come again in the evening, to which he consented. Hindley is too reckless to select his acquaintance prudently; he doesn't trouble himself to reflect on the causes he might have for mistrusting one whom he has basely injured—But Heathcliff affirms his principal reason for resuming a connection with his ancient persecutor is a wish to install himself in quarters at walking distance from the Grange, and an attachment to the house where we lived together, and likewise a hope that I shall have more opportunities of seeing him there than I could have if he settled in Gimmerton. He means to offer liberal payment for permission to lodge at the Heights; and doubtless my brother's covetousness will prompt him to accept the terms; he was always greedy, though what he grasps with one hand, he flings away with the other."

"It's a nice place for a young man to fix his dwelling in!" said I. "Have you no fear of the consequences, Mrs. Linton?"

"None for my friend," she replied, "his strong head will keep him from danger—a little for Hindley, but he can't be made morally worse than he is; and I stand between him and bodily harm—The event of this evening reconciled me to God and humanity! I had risen in angry rebellion against providence—Oh, I've endured very, very bitter misery, Nelly! If that creature knew how bitter, he'd be ashamed to cloud its removal with idle petulance—It was kindness for him which induced me to bear it alone; had I expressed the agony I frequently felt, he would have been taught to long for its alleviation as ardently as I—However, it's over, and I'll take no revenge on his folly—I can afford to suffer anything, hereafter! Should the meanest thing alive slap me on the cheek, I'd not only turn the other, but I'd ask pardon for provoking it—and, as a proof, I'll go make my peace with Edgar instantly—Good night— I'm an angel!"

In this self-complacent conviction she departed; and the success of her fulfilled resolution was obvious on the morrow—Mr. Linton had not only abjured his peevishness (though his spirits seemed still subdued by Catherine's exuberance of vivacity) but he ventured no objection to her taking Isabella with her to Wuthering Heights in the afternoon; and she rewarded him with such a summer of sweetness and affection, in return, as made the house a paradise for several days; both master and servants profiting from the perpetual sunshine.

Heathcliff—Mr. Heathcliff I should say in future—used the liberty of visiting at Thrushcross Grange cautiously, at first: he seemed estimating how far its owner would bear his intrusion. Catherine, also, deemed it judicious to moderate her expressions of pleasure in receiving him; and he gradually established his right to be expected. He retained a great deal of the reserve for which his boyhood was remarkable, and that served to repress all startling demonstrations of feeling. My master's uneasiness experienced a lull, and further circumstances diverted it into another channel for a space.

His new source of trouble sprang from the not anticipated misfortune of Isabella Linton evincing a sudden and irresistible attraction towards the tolerated guest—She was at that time a charming young lady of eighteen; infantile in manners, though possessed of keen wit, keen feelings, and a keen temper, too, if irritated. Her brother, who loved her tenderly, was appalled at this fantastic preference. Leaving aside the degradation of an alliance with a nameless man, and the possible fact that his property, in default of heirs male, might pass into such a one's power, he had sense to comprehend Heathcliff's disposition—to know that, though his exterior was altered, his mind was unchangeable, and unchanged. And he dreaded that mind; it revolted him; he shrank forebodingly from the idea of committing Isabella to its keeping.

He would have recoiled still more had he been aware that her attachment rose unsolicited, and was bestowed where it awakened no reciprocation of sentiment; for the minute he discovered its existence, he laid the blame on Heathcliff's deliberate designing.

We had all remarked, during some time, that Miss Linton fretted and pined over something. She grew cross and wearisome, snapping at and teazing Catherine continually, at the imminent risk of exhausting her limited patience. We excused her to a certain extent, on the plea of ill health—she was dwindling and fading before our eyes—But, one day when she had been peculiarly wayward, rejecting her breakfast, complaining that the servants did not do what she told them; that the mistress would allow her to be nothing in the house, and Edgar neglected her; that she had caught a cold with the doors being left open, and we let the parlour fire go out on purpose to vex her; with a hundred yet more frivolous accusations—Mrs. Linton peremptorily insisted that she should get to bed; and, having scolded her heartily, threatened to send for the doctor.

Mention of Kenneth caused her to exclaim, instantly, that her health was perfect, and it was only Catherine's harshness which made her unhappy.

"How can you say I am harsh, you naughty fondling?" cried the mistress, amazed at the unreasonable assertion. "You are surely losing your reason. When have I been harsh, tell me?"

"Yesterday," sobbed Isabella, "and now!"

"Yesterday!" said her sister-in-law. "On what occasion?"

"In our walk along the moor; you told me to ramble where I pleased, while you sauntered on with Mr. Heathcliff!"

"And that's your notion of harshness?" said Catherine, laughing. "It was no hint that your company was superfluous; we didn't care whether you kept with us or not; I merely thought Heathcliff's talk would have nothing entertaining for your ears."

"Oh, no," wept the young lady, "you wished me away, because you knew I liked to be there!"

"Is she sane?" asked Mrs. Linton, appealing to me. "I'll repeat our conversation, word for word, Isabella; and you point out any charm it could have had for you."

"I don't mind the conversation," she answered: "I wanted to be with—"

"Well!" said Catherine, perceiving her hesitate to complete the sentence.

"With him; and I won't be always sent off!" she continued, kindling up. "You are a dog in the manger, Cathy, and desire no one to be loved but yourself!"

"You are an impertinent little monkey!" exclaimed Mrs. Linton, in surprise. "But I'll not believe this idiocy! It is impossible that you can covet the admiration of Heathcliff—that you consider him an agreeable person! I hope I have misunderstood you, Isabella?"

"No, you have not," said the infatuated girl. "I love him more than ever you loved Edgar; and he might love me, if you would let him!"

"I wouldn't be you for a kingdom, then!" Catherine declared, emphatically—and she seemed to speak sincerely. "Nelly, help me to convince her of her madness. Tell her what Heathcliff is—an unreclaimed creature, without refinement—without cultivation; an arid wilderness of furze and whinstone. I'd as soon put that little canary into the park on a winter's day as recommend you to bestow your heart on him! It is deplorable ignorance of his character, child, and nothing else, which makes that dream enter your head. Pray don't imagine that he conceals depths of benevolence and affection beneath a stern exterior! He's not a rough diamond—a pearl-containing oyster of a rustic; he's a fierce, pitiless, wolfish man. I never say to him 'let this or that enemy alone, because it would be ungenerous or cruel to harm them,' I say, 'let them alone, because *I* should hate them to be wronged': and he'd crush you, like a sparrow's egg, Isabella, if he found you a troublesome charge. I know he couldn't love a Linton; and yet he'd be quite capable of marrying your fortune and expectations. Avarice is growing with him a besetting sin. There's my picture; and I'm his friend—so much so, that had he thought seriously to catch you, I should, perhaps, have held my tongue, and let you fall into his trap."

Miss Linton regarded her sister-in-law with indignation.

"For shame! for shame!" she repeated, angrily. "You are worse than twenty foes, you poisonous friend!"

"Ah! You won't believe me, then?" said Catherine. "You think I speak from wicked selfishness?"

"I'm certain you do," retorted Isabella; "and I shudder at you!"

"Good!" cried the other. "Try for yourself, if that be your spirit; I have done, and yield the argument to your saucy insolence."

"And I must suffer for her egotism!" she sobbed, as Mrs. Linton left the room. "All, all is against me; she has blighted my single consolation. But she uttered falsehoods, didn't she? Mr. Heathcliff is not a fiend; he has an honourable soul, and a true one, or how could he remember her?"

"Banish him from your thoughts, miss," I said. "He's a bird of bad omen; no mate for you. Mrs. Linton spoke strongly, and yet, I can't contradict her. She is better acquainted with his heart than I, or any one besides; and she never would represent him as worse than he is. Honest people don't hide their deeds. How has he been living? how has he got rich? why is he staying at Wuthering Heights, the house of a man whom he abhors? They say Mr. Earnshaw is worse and worse since he came. They sit up all night together continually; and Hindley has been borrowing money on his land, and does nothing but play and drink, I heard only a week ago; it was Joseph who told me—I met him at Gimmerton."

"'Nelly,' he said, 'we's hae a Crahnr's 'quest enah, at ahr folks. One on 'em's a'most getten his finger cut off wi' hauding t'other froo' sticking hisseln loike a cawlf. That's maister, yah knaw, ut's soa up o' going tuh t' grand 'sizes. He's noan feard uh t' Bench uh judges, norther Paul, nur Peter, nur John, nur Matthew, nor noan on 'em, nut he. He fair likes, he langs to set his brazened face agean 'em! And yon bonny lad Heathcliff, yah mind, he's a rare un! He can girn a laugh as weel's onybody at a raight divil's jest. Does he niver say nowt of his fine living amang us, when he goes tuh t' Grange? This is t' way on't—up at sun-dahn; dice, brandy, cloised shutters, und can'le leeght till next day, at nooin—then, t' fooil gangs banning un' raving tuh his cham'er, makking dacent fowks dig thur fingers i' thur lugs fur varry shaume; un' the knave, wah, he can cahnt his brass, un' ate, un' sleep, un' off tuh his neighbour's tuh gossip wi' t' wife. I' course, he tells Dame Catherine hah hor fathur's goold runs intuh his pocket, and her fathur's son gallops dahn t' broad road, while he flees afore to oppen t' pikes.'[5] Now, Miss Linton, Joseph is an old rascal, but no liar; and, if his account of Heathcliff's conduct be true, you would never think of desiring such a husband, would you?"

"You are leagued with the rest, Ellen!" she replied. "I'll not listen to your slanders. What malevolence you must have to wish to convince me that there is no happiness in the world!"

Whether she would have got over this fancy if left to herself, or persevered in nursing it perpetually, I cannot say; she had little time

---

[5] "We shall have a Coroner's inquest [soon] enough, at our house. One of them almost had his finger cut off from holding the other from sticking himself like a calf. That's master, you know, that's so up on going to the grand assizes [he wants to take Heathcliff to court]. He's not afraid of the Bench of judges, neither Paul, nor Peter, nor John, nor Matthew, nor any of them, not he. He actually likes, he longs to set his brazened face against them [the judges of the Gospels]! And that fine fellow Heathcliff, mind you, he's a rare one! He can bare his teeth laughing as well as anybody [can] at a true devil's jest. Does he never say anything about his fine living among us, when he goes to the Grange? This is how it goes: up at sundown; dice, brandy, closed shutters, and candle light till next day, at noon. Then, the fool goes cursing and raving to his chamber, making decent folks dig their fingers in their ears for very shame. And the knave, well, he can count his money, and eat, and sleep, and go off to his neighbors to gossip with the wife. Of course, he tells Mistress Catherine how her father's gold runs into his pocket, and [how] her father's son gallops down the broad road [to destruction], while he runs ahead to open the toll gates [to let Hindley rush to ruin]." Referring to the biblical quote "For wide is the gate, and broad is the way, that leadeth to destruction . . .": Matthew 7.13.

to reflect. The day after, there was a justice-meeting at the next town; my master was obliged to attend; and Mr. Heathcliff, aware of his absence, called rather earlier than usual.

Catherine and Isabella were sitting in the library, on hostile terms, but silent: the latter alarmed at her recent indiscretion, and the disclosure she had made of her secret feelings in a transient fit of passion; the former, on mature consideration, really offended with her companion; and, if she laughed again at her pertness, inclined to make it no laughing matter to *her*.

She did laugh as she saw Heathcliff pass the window. I was sweeping the hearth, and I noticed a mischievous smile on her lips. Isabella, absorbed in her meditations, or a book, remained till the door opened, and it was too late to attempt an escape, which she would gladly have done had it been practicable.

"Come in, that's right!" exclaimed the mistress, gaily, pulling a chair to the fire. "Here are two people sadly in need of a third to thaw the ice between them; and you are the very one we should both of us choose. Heathcliff, I'm proud to show you, at last, somebody that dotes on you more than myself. I expect you to feel flattered—nay, it's not Nelly; don't look at her! My poor little sister-in-law is breaking her heart by mere contemplation of your physical and moral beauty. It lies in your own power to be Edgar's brother! No, no, Isabella; you sha'n't run off," she continued, arresting, with feigned playfulness, the confounded girl, who had risen indignantly. "We were quarrelling like cats about you, Heathcliff; and I was fairly beaten in protestations of devotion and admiration; and, moreover, I was informed that if I would but have the manners to stand aside, my rival, as she will have herself to be, would shoot a shaft into your soul that would fix you for ever, and send my image into eternal oblivion!"

"Catherine," said Isabella, calling up her dignity, and disdaining to struggle from the tight grasp that held her, "I'd thank you to adhere to the truth and not slander me, even in joke! Mr. Heathcliff, be kind enough to bid this friend of yours release me—she forgets that you and I are not intimate acquaintances, and what amuses her is painful to me beyond expression."

As the guest answered nothing, but took his seat, and looked thoroughly indifferent what sentiments she cherished concerning him, she turned, and whispered an earnest appeal for liberty to her tormenter.

"By no means!" cried Mrs. Linton in answer. "I won't be named a dog in the manger again. You *shall* stay, now then! Heathcliff, why don't you evince satisfaction at my pleasant news? Isabella swears that the love Edgar has for me is nothing to that she entertains for you. I'm sure she made some speech of the kind, did she not, Ellen? And she has fasted ever since the day before yesterday's walk, from sorrow and rage that I despatched her out of your society, under the idea of its being unacceptable."

"I think you belie her," said Heathcliff, twisting his chair to face them. "She wishes to be out of my society now, at any rate!"

And he stared hard at the object of discourse, as one might do at a strange repulsive animal, a centipede from the Indies,[6] for instance, which curiosity leads one to examine in spite of the aversion it raises.

The poor thing couldn't bear that; she grew white and red in rapid succession, and, while tears beaded her lashes, bent the strength of her small fingers to loosen the firm clutch of Catherine, and perceiving that as fast as she raised one finger off her arm, another closed down, and she could not remove the whole together, she began to make use of her nails, and their sharpness presently ornamented the detainer's with crescents of red.

"There's a tigress!" exclaimed Mrs. Linton, setting her free, and shaking her hand with pain. "Begone, for God's sake, and hide your vixen face! How foolish to reveal those talons to *him*. Can't you fancy the conclusions he'll draw? Look, Heathcliff! they are instruments that will do execution—you must beware of your eyes."

"I'd wrench them off her fingers, if they ever menaced me," he answered, brutally, when the door had closed after her. "But what did you mean by teasing the creature in that manner, Cathy? You were not speaking the truth, were you?"

"I assure you I was," she returned. "She has been pining for your sake several weeks; and raving about you this morning, and pouring forth a deluge of abuse, because I represented your failings in a plain light for the purpose of mitigating her adoration. But don't notice it further. I wished to punish her sauciness, that's all— I like her too well, my dear Heathcliff, to let you absolutely seize and devour her up."

---

[6]A Caribbean centipede is very poisonous.

"And I like her too ill to attempt it," said he, "except in a very ghoulish fashion. You'd hear of odd things if I lived alone with that mawkish, waxen face; the most ordinary would be painting on its white the colours of the rainbow, and turning the blue eyes black, every day or two; they detestably resemble Linton's."

"Delectably," observed Catherine. "They are dove's eyes—angel's!"

"She's her brother's heir,[7] is she not?" he asked, after a brief silence.

"I should be sorry to think so," returned his companion. "Half-a-dozen nephews shall erase her title, please Heaven! Abstract your mind from the subject, at present—you are too prone to covet your neighbour's goods: remember *this* neighbour's goods are mine."

"If they were *mine*, they would be none the less that," said Heathcliff, "but though Isabella Linton may be silly, she is scarcely mad; and—in short, we'll dismiss the matter, as you advise."

From their tongues, they did dismiss it; and Catherine, probably, from her thoughts. The other, I felt certain, recalled it often in the course of the evening; I saw him smile to himself—grin rather—and lapse into ominous musing whenever Mrs. Linton had occasion to be absent from the apartment.

I determined to watch his movements. My heart invariably cleaved to the master's, in preference to Catherine's side; with reason, I imagined, for he was kind, and trustful, and honourable; and she—she could not be called the *opposite*, yet she seemed to allow herself such wide latitude, that I had little faith in her principles, and still less sympathy for her feelings. I wanted something to happen which might have the effect of freeing both Wuthering Heights and the Grange of Mr. Heathcliff, quietly, leaving us as we had been prior to his advent. His visits were a continual nightmare to me; and, I suspected, to my master also. His abode at the

[7]The elder Mr. Linton's will named his son Edgar as heir and upon the latter's death the estate would pass "in tail" to any of his sons (the "half-a-dozen nephews" of Isabella that Catherine predicts in the next speech). Isabella, the Linton's daughter, would be next in line if Edgar had no sons, and in turn Isabella's male offspring would be next. No daughters can be heirs to Thrushcross Grange, though the second Cathy does have some personal property that Heathcliff later prevents Edgar from putting in trust before she marries (a woman's property in default of a settlement or trust belonged to her husband at this time in English law). See "Wills, Women, and Property," p. 355.

Heights was an oppression past explaining. I felt that God had forsaken the stray sheep there to its own wicked wanderings, and an evil beast prowled between it and the fold, waiting his time to spring and destroy.

## Chapter 11

Sometimes, while meditating on these things in solitude, I've got up in a sudden terror, and put on my bonnet to go see how all was at the farm; I've persuaded my conscience that it was a duty to warn him how people talked regarding his ways; and then I've recollected his confirmed bad habits, and, hopeless of benefiting him, have flinched from re-entering the dismal house, doubting if I could bear to be taken at my word.

One time, I passed the old gate, going out of my way, on a journey to Gimmerton. It was about the period that my narrative has reached—a bright, frosty afternoon; the ground bare, and the road hard and dry.

I came to a stone where the highway branches off on to the moor at your left hand; a rough sand-pillar, with the letters W. H. cut on its north side, on the east, G., and on the south-west, T. G. It serves as guide-post to the Grange, and Heights, and village.

The sun shone yellow on its grey head, reminding me of summer; and I cannot say why, but all at once, a gush of child's sensations flowed into my heart. Hindley and I held it a favourite spot twenty years before.

I gazed long at the weather-worn block; and, stooping down, perceived a hole near the bottom still full of snail-shells and pebbles which we were fond of storing there with more perishable things—and, as fresh as reality, it appeared that I beheld my early playmate seated on the withered turf, his dark, square head bent forward, and his little hand scooping out the earth with a piece of slate.

"Poor Hindley!" I exclaimed, involuntarily.

I started—my bodily eye was cheated into a momentary belief that the child lifted its face and stared straight into mine! It vanished in a twinkling; but, immediately, I felt an irresistible yearning to be at the Heights. Superstition urged me to comply with this impulse—supposing he should be dead! I thought—or should die soon!—supposing it were a sign of death!

The nearer I got to the house the more agitated I grew; and on catching sight of it, I trembled every limb. The apparition had outstripped me; it stood looking through the gate. That was my first idea on observing an elf-locked, brown-eyed boy setting his ruddy countenance against the bars. Further reflection suggested this must be Hareton, *my* Hareton, not altered greatly since I left him, ten months since.

"God bless thee, darling!" I cried, forgetting instantaneously my foolish fears. "Hareton, it's Nelly—Nelly, thy nurse."

He retreated out of arm's length, and picked up a large flint.

"I am come to see thy father, Hareton," I added, guessing from the action that Nelly, if she lived in his memory at all, was not recognized as one with me.

He raised his missile to hurl it; I commenced a soothing speech, but could not stay his hand. The stone struck my bonnet, and then ensued, from the stammering lips of the little fellow, a string of curses which, whether he comprehended them or not, were delivered with practised emphasis, and distorted his baby features into a shocking expression of malignity.

You may be certain this grieved more than angered me. Fit to cry, I took an orange from my pocket, and offered it to propitiate him.

He hesitated, and then snatched it from my hold, as if he fancied I only intended to tempt and disappoint him.

I showed another, keeping it out of his reach.

"Who has taught you those fine words, my barn,"[1] I inquired. "The curate?"

"Damn the curate, and thee! Gie me that," he replied.

"Tell us where you got your lessons, and you shall have it," said I. "Who's your master?"

"Devil daddy," was his answer.

"And what do you learn from daddy?" I continued.

He jumped at the fruit; I raised it higher. "What does he teach you?" I asked.

"Naught," said he, "but to keep out of his gait[2]—Daddy cannot bide me, because I swear at him."

"Ah! and the devil teaches you to swear at daddy?" I observed.

[1]Bairn, child.
[2]Way.

"Ay—nay," he drawled.

"Who, then?"

"Heathcliff."

I asked if he liked Mr. Heathcliff?

"Ay!" he answered again.

Desiring to have his reasons for liking him, I could only gather the sentences—"I known't—he pays dad back what he gies to me—he curses daddy for cursing me—He says I mun do as I will."

"And the curate does not teach you to read and write, then?" I pursued.

"No, I was told the curate should have his —— teeth dashed down his —— throat, if he stepped over the threshold—Heathcliff had promised that!"

I put the orange in his hand, and bade him tell his father that a woman called Nelly Dean was waiting to speak with him, by the garden gate.

He went up the walk, and entered the house; but, instead of Hindley, Heathcliff appeared on the door stones, and I turned directly and ran down the road as hard as ever I could race, making no halt till I gained the guide post, and feeling as scared as if I had raised a goblin.

This is not much connected with Miss Isabella's affair; except that it urged me to resolve further on mounting vigilant guard, and doing my utmost to check the spread of such bad influence at the Grange, even though I should wake a domestic storm by thwarting Mrs. Linton's pleasure.

The next time Heathcliff came, my young lady chanced to be feeding some pigeons in the court. She had never spoken a word to her sister-in-law for three days; but she had likewise dropped her fretful complaining, and we found it a great comfort.

Heathcliff had not the habit of bestowing a single unnecessary civility on Miss Linton, I knew. Now, as soon as he beheld her, his first precaution was to take a sweeping survey of the housefront. I was standing by the kitchen window, but I drew out of sight. He then stept across the pavement to her, and said something: she seemed embarrassed, and desirous of getting away; to prevent it, he laid his hand on her arm. She averted her face; he apparently put some question which she had no mind to answer. There was another rapid glance at the house, and supposing himself unseen, the scoundrel had the impudence to embrace her.

"Judas! Traitor!" I ejaculated. "You are a hypocrite too, are you? A deliberate deceiver."

"Who is, Nelly?" said Catherine's voice at my elbow—I had been over-intent on watching the pair outside to mark her entrance.

"Your worthless friend!" I answered warmly, "the sneaking rascal yonder—Ah, he has caught a glimpse of us—he is coming in! I wonder will he have the heart to find a plausible excuse for making love to Miss, when he told you he hated her?"

Mrs. Linton saw Isabella tear herself free, and run into the garden; and a minute after, Heathcliff opened the door.

I couldn't withhold giving some loose to my indignation; but Catherine angrily insisted on silence, and threatened to order me out of the kitchen, if I dared be so presumptuous as to put in my insolent tongue.

"To hear you, people might think *you* were the mistress!" she cried. "You want setting down in your right place! Heathcliff, what are you about, raising this stir? I said you must let Isabella alone!— I beg you will, unless you are tired of being received here, and wish Linton to draw the bolts against you!"

"God forbid that he should try!" answered the black villain—I detested him just then. "God keep him meek and patient! Every day I grow madder after sending him to heaven!"

"Hush!" said Catherine, shutting the inner door. "Don't vex me. Why have you disregarded my request? Did she come across you on purpose?"

"What is it to you?" he growled, "I have a right to kiss her, if she chooses, and you have no right to object—I am not *your* husband, *you* needn't be jealous of me!"

"I'm not jealous of you," replied the mistress; "I'm jealous for you. Clear your face, you shan't scowl at me! If you like Isabella, you shall marry her. But, do you like her, tell the truth, Heathcliff? There, you won't answer. I'm certain you don't!"

"And would Mr. Linton approve of his sister marrying that man?" I inquired.

"Mr. Linton should approve," returned my lady decisively.

"He might spare himself the trouble," said Heathcliff, "I could do as well without his approbation—And, as to you, Catherine, I have a mind to speak a few words, now, while we are at it—I want you to be aware that I *know* you have treated me infernally—infernally!

Do you hear? And, if you flatter yourself that I don't perceive it you are a fool—and if you think I can be consoled by sweet words, you are an idiot—and if you fancy I'll suffer unrevenged, I'll convince you of the contrary, in a very little while! Meantime, thank you for telling me your sister-in-law's secret—I swear I'll make the most of it—and stand you aside!"

"What new phase of his character is this?" exclaimed Mrs. Linton, in amazement. "I've treated you infernally—and you'll take your revenge! How will you take it, ungrateful brute? How have I treated you infernally?"

"I seek no revenge on you," replied Heathcliff less vehemently. "That's not the plan—The tyrant grinds down his slaves and they don't turn against him, they crush those beneath them—You are welcome to torture me to death for your amusement, only allow me to amuse myself a little in the same style—And refrain from insult, as much as you are able. Having levelled my palace, don't erect a hovel and complacently admire your own charity in giving me that for a home. If I imagined you really wished me to marry Isabella, I'd cut my throat!"

"Oh, the evil is that I am *not* jealous, is it?" cried Catherine. "Well, I won't repeat my offer of a wife—It is as bad as offering Satan a lost soul—Your bliss lies, like his, in inflicting misery— You prove it—Edgar is restored from the ill-temper he gave way to at your coming; I begin to be secure and tranquil; and you, restless to know us at peace, appear resolved on exciting a quarrel—quarrel with Edgar, if you please, Heathcliff, and deceive his sister; you'll hit on exactly the most efficient method of revenging yourself on me."

The conversation ceased—Mrs. Linton sat down by the fire, flushed and gloomy. The spirit which served her was growing intractable; she could neither lay nor control it. He stood on the hearth with folded arms, brooding on his evil thoughts; and in this position I left them to seek the master, who was wondering what kept Catherine below so long.

"Ellen," said he, when I entered, "have you seen your mistress?"

"Yes, she's in the kitchen, sir," I answered. "She's sadly put out by Mr. Heathcliff's behaviour; and, indeed, I do think it's time to arrange his visits on another footing. There's harm in being too soft, and now it's come to this—." And I related the scene in the court, and, as near as I dared, the whole subsequent dispute. I fancied it could not be very prejudicial to Mrs. Linton, unless she made it so, afterwards, by assuming the defensive for her guest.

Edgar Linton had difficulty in hearing me to the close—His first words revealed that he did not clear his wife of blame.

"This is insufferable!" he exclaimed. "It is disgraceful that she should own him for a friend, and force his company on me! Call me two men out of the hall, Ellen—Catherine shall linger no longer to argue with the low ruffian—I have humoured her enough."

He descended, and bidding the servants wait in the passage went, followed by me, to the kitchen. Its occupants had recommenced their angry discussion; Mrs. Linton, at least, was scolding with renewed vigour; Heathcliff had moved to the window, and hung his head, somewhat cowed by her violent rating, apparently.

He saw the master first, and made a hasty motion that she should be silent; which she obeyed, abruptly, on discovering the reason of his intimation.

"How is this?" said Linton, addressing her; "what notion of propriety must you have to remain here, after the language which has been held to you by that blackguard? I suppose, because it is his ordinary talk, you think nothing of it—you are habituated to his baseness, and, perhaps, imagine I can get used to it too!"

"Have you been listening at the door, Edgar?" asked the mistress, in a tone particularly calculated to provoke her husband, implying both carelessness and contempt of his irritation.

Heathcliff, who had raised his eyes at the former speech, gave a sneering laugh at the latter, on purpose, it seemed, to draw Mr. Linton's attention to him.

He succeeded; but Edgar did not mean to entertain him with any high flights of passion.

"I have been so far forbearing with you, sir," he said quietly; "not that I was ignorant of your miserable, degraded character, but I felt you were only partly responsible for that; and Catherine wishing to keep up your acquaintance, I acquiesced—foolishly. Your presence is a moral poison that would contaminate the most virtuous—for that cause, and to prevent worse consequences, I shall deny you, hereafter, admission into this house, and give notice, now, that I require your instant departure. Three minutes' delay will render it involuntary and ignominious."

Heathcliff measured the height and breadth of the speaker with an eye full of derision.

"Cathy, this lamb of yours threatens like a bull!" he said. "It is in danger of splitting its skull against my knuckles. By God, Mr. Linton, I'm mortally sorry that you are not worth knocking down!"

My master glanced towards the passage, and signed me to fetch the men—he had no intention of hazarding a personal encounter.

I obeyed the hint; but Mrs. Linton, suspecting something, followed, and when I attempted to call them, she pulled me back, slammed the door to, and locked it.

"Fair means!" she said, in answer to her husband's look of angry surprise. "If you have not the courage to attack him, make an apology, or allow yourself to be beaten. It will correct you of feigning more valour than you possess. No, I'll swallow the key before you shall get it! I'm delightfully rewarded for my kindness to each! After constant indulgence of one's weak nature, and the other's bad one, I earn, for thanks, two samples of blind ingratitude, stupid to absurdity! Edgar, I was defending you, and yours; and I wish Heathcliff may flog you sick, for daring to think an evil thought of me!"

It did not need the medium of a flogging to produce that effect on the master. He tried to wrest the key from Catherine's grasp; and for safety she flung it into the hottest part of the fire; whereupon Mr. Edgar was taken with a nervous trembling, and his countenance grew deadly pale. For his life he could not avert that access of emotion—mingled anguish and humiliation overcame him completely. He leant on the back of a chair, and covered his face.

"Oh! Heavens! In old days this would win you knighthood!" exclaimed Mrs. Linton. "We are vanquished! we are vanquished! Heathcliff would as soon lift a finger at you as a king would march his army against a colony of mice. Cheer up, you sha'n't be hurt! Your type is not a lamb, it's a sucking leveret."[3]

"I wish you joy of the milk-blooded coward, Cathy!" said her friend. "I compliment you on your taste: and that is the slavering, shivering thing you preferred to me! I would not strike him with

---

[3]Catherine refers to Heathcliff's comparison of Edgar to a lamb, above; his animal "type" is more pathetic, a baby hare, still nursing. "Leveret" implies effeminate, dependent softness: a mistress, or as Heathcliff soon translates, a "milk-blooded coward."

my fist, but I'd kick him with my foot, and experience considerable satisfaction. Is he weeping, or is he going to faint for fear?"

The fellow approached and gave the chair on which Linton rested a push. He'd better have kept his distance: my master quickly sprang erect, and struck him full on the throat a blow that would have levelled a slighter man.

It took his breath for a minute; and, while he choked, Mr. Linton walked out by the back door into the yard, and from thence, to the front entrance.

"There! you've done with coming here," cried Catherine. "Get away, now—he'll return with a brace of pistols, and half-a-dozen assistants. If he did overhear us, of course, he'd never forgive you. You've played me an ill turn, Heathcliff! But, go—make haste! I'd rather see Edgar at bay than you."

"Do you suppose I'm going with that blow burning in my gullet?" he thundered. "By Hell, no! I'll crush his ribs in like a rotten hazel-nut, before I cross the threshold! If I don't floor him now, I shall murder him some time, so, as you value his existence, let me get at him!"

"He is not coming," I interposed, framing a bit of a lie. "There's the coachman, and the two gardeners; you'll surely not wait to be thrust into the road by them! Each has a bludgeon, and master will, very likely, be watching from the parlour windows, to see that they fulfil his orders."

The gardeners and coachman *were* there; but Linton was with them. They had already entered the court—Heathcliff, on second thoughts, resolved to avoid a struggle against the three underlings; he seized the poker, smashed the lock from the inner door, and made his escape as they tramped in.

Mrs. Linton, who was very much excited, bid me accompany her upstairs. She did not know my share in contributing to the disturbance, and I was anxious to keep her in ignorance.

"I'm nearly distracted, Nelly!" she exclaimed, throwing herself on the sofa. "A thousand smiths' hammers are beating in my head! Tell Isabella to shun me—this uproar is owing to her; and should she or any one else aggravate my anger at present, I shall get wild. And, Nelly, say to Edgar, if you see him again to-night, that I'm in danger of being seriously ill—I wish it may prove true. He has startled and distressed me shockingly! I want to frighten him. Besides,

he might come and begin a string of abuse, or complainings; I'm
certain I should recriminate, and God knows where we should end!
Will you do so, my good Nelly? You are aware that I am no way
blamable in this matter. What possessed him to turn listener?
Heathcliff's talk was outrageous, after you left us; but I could soon
have diverted him from Isabella, and the rest meant nothing. Now,
all is dashed wrong by the fool's-craving to hear evil of self that
haunts some people like a demon! Had Edgar never gathered our
conversation, he would never have been the worse for it. Really,
when he opened on me in that unreasonable tone of displeasure, after I had scolded Heathcliff till I was hoarse for *him*, I did not care,
hardly, what they did to each other; especially as I felt that, however the scene closed, we should all be driven asunder for nobody
knows how long! Well, if I cannot keep Heathcliff for my friend—
if Edgar will be mean and jealous—I'll try to break their hearts by
breaking my own. That will be a prompt way of finishing all, when
I am pushed to extremity! But it's a deed to be reserved for a forlorn hope—I'd not take Linton by surprise with it. To this point he
has been discreet in dreading to provoke me; you must represent
the peril of quitting that policy, and remind him of my passionate
temper, verging, when kindled, on frenzy—I wish you could dismiss
that apathy out of your countenance, and look rather more anxious about me."

The stolidity with which I received these instructions was, no
doubt, rather exasperating, for they were delivered in perfect sincerity; but I believed a person who could plan the turning of her fits
of passion to account, beforehand, might, by exerting her will,
manage to control herself tolerably even while under their influence; and I did not wish to "frighten" her husband, as she said, and
multiply his annoyances for the purpose of serving her selfishness.

Therefore I said nothing when I met the master coming towards
the parlour; but I took the liberty of turning back to listen whether
they would resume their quarrel together.

He began to speak first.

"Remain where you are, Catherine," he said, without any
anger in his voice, but with much sorrowful despondency. "I shall
not stay. I am neither come to wrangle, nor be reconciled: but I
wish just to learn whether, after this evening's events, you intend to
continue your intimacy with—"

"Oh, for mercy's sake," interrupted the mistress, stamping her foot, "for mercy's sake, let us hear no more of it now! Your cold blood cannot be worked into a fever—your veins are full of ice-water—but mine are boiling, and the sight of such chillness makes them dance."

"To get rid of me—answer my question," persevered Mr. Linton. "You *must* answer it; and that violence does not alarm me. I have found that you can be as stoical as any one, when you please. Will you give up Heathcliff hereafter, or will you give up me? It is impossible for you to be *my* friend and *his* at the same time; and I absolutely *require* to know which you choose."

"I require to be let alone!" exclaimed Catherine, furiously. "I demand it! Don't you see I can scarcely stand? Edgar, you—you leave me!"

She rung the bell till it broke with a twang; I entered leisurely. It was enough to try the temper of a saint, such senseless, wicked rages! There she lay dashing her head against the arm of the sofa, and grinding her teeth, so that you might fancy she would crash them to splinters!

Mr. Linton stood looking at her in sudden compunction and fear. He told me to fetch some water. She had no breath for speaking.

I brought a glass full; and, as she would not drink, I sprinkled it on her face. In a few seconds she stretched herself out stiff, and turned up her eyes, while her cheeks, at once blanched and livid, assumed the aspect of death.

Linton looked terrified.

"There is nothing in the world the matter," I whispered. I did not want him to yield, though I could not help being afraid in my heart.

"She has blood on her lips!" he said, shuddering.

"Never mind!" I answered, tartly. And I told him how she had resolved, previous to his coming, on exhibiting a fit of frenzy.

I incautiously gave the account aloud, and she heard me, for she started up—her hair flying over her shoulders, her eyes flashing, the muscles of her neck and arms standing out preternaturally. I made up my mind for broken bones, at least; but she only glared about her for an instant, and then rushed from the room.

The master directed me to follow; I did, to her chamber door; she hindered me from going farther by securing it against me.

As she never offered to descend to breakfast next morning, I went to ask whether she would have some carried up.

"No!" she replied, peremptorily.

The same question was repeated at dinner and tea; and again on the morrow after, and received the same answer. Mr. Linton, on his part, spent his time in the library, and did not inquire concerning his wife's occupations. Isabella and he had had an hour's interview, during which he tried to elicit from her some sentiment of proper horror for Heathcliff's advances; but he could make nothing of her evasive replies, and was obliged to close the examination unsatisfactorily; adding, however, a solemn warning, that if she were so insane as to encourage that worthless suitor, it would dissolve all bonds of relationship between herself and him.

## Chapter 12

While Miss Linton moped about the park and garden, always silent, and almost always in tears; and her brother shut himself up among books that he never opened—wearying, I guessed, with a continual vague expectation that Catherine, repenting her conduct, would come of her own accord to ask pardon, and seek a reconciliation; and *she* fasted pertinaciously, under the idea, probably, that at every meal, Edgar was ready to choke for her absence, and pride alone held him from running to cast himself at her feet; I went about my household duties, convinced that the Grange had but one sensible soul in its walls, and that lodged in my body.

I wasted no condolences on miss, nor any expostulations on my mistress, nor did I pay attention to the sighs of my master, who yearned to hear his lady's name, since he might not hear her voice.

I determined they should come about as they pleased for me; and though it was a tiresomely slow process, I began to rejoice at length in a faint dawn of its progress, as I thought at first.

Mrs. Linton, on the third day, unbarred her door; and having finished the water in her pitcher and decanter, desired a renewed supply, and a basin of gruel, for she believed she was dying. That I set down as a speech meant for Edgar's ears; I believed no such thing, so I kept it to myself, and brought her some tea and dry toast.

She ate and drank eagerly; and sank back on her pillow again, clenching her hands and groaning.

"Oh, I will die," she exclaimed, "since no one cares anything about me. I wish I had not taken that."

Then a good while after I heard her murmur,

"No, I'll not die—he'd be glad—he does not love me at all—he would never miss me!"

"Did you want anything, ma'am?" I enquired, still preserving my external composure, in spite of her ghastly countenance and strange exaggerated manner.

"What is that apathetic being doing?" she demanded, pushing the thick entangled locks from her wasted face. "Has he fallen into a lethargy, or is he dead?"

"Neither," replied I; "if you mean Mr. Linton. He's tolerably well, I think, though his studies occupy him rather more than they ought; he is continually among his books, since he has no other society."

I should not have spoken so, if I had known her true condition, but I could not get rid of the notion that she acted a part of her disorder.

"Among his books!" she cried, confounded. "And I dying! I on the brink of the grave! My God! does he know how I'm altered?" continued she, staring at her reflection in a mirror, hanging against the opposite wall. "Is that Catherine Linton? He imagines me in a pet—in play, perhaps. Cannot you inform him that it is frightful earnest? Nelly, if it be not too late, as soon as I learn how he feels, I'll choose between these two—either to starve, at once, that would be no punishment unless he had a heart—or to recover and leave the country. Are you speaking the truth about him now? Take care. Is he actually so utterly indifferent for my life?"

"Why, ma'am," I answered, "the master has no idea of your being deranged; and, of course, he does not fear that you will let yourself die of hunger."

"You think not? Cannot you tell him I will?" she returned; "persuade him—speak of your own mind—say you are certain I will!"

"No, you forget, Mrs. Linton," I suggested, "that you have eaten some food with a relish this evening, and to-morrow you will perceive its good effects."

"If I were only sure it would kill him," she interrupted, "I'd kill myself directly! These three awful nights, I've never closed my lids—and oh, I've been tormented! I've been haunted, Nelly! But I begin to fancy you don't like me. How strange! I thought, though everybody hated and despised each other, they could not avoid loving me—and they have all turned to enemies in a few hours. *They* have, I'm positive; the people *here*. How dreary to meet death, surrounded by their cold faces! Isabella, terrified and repelled, afraid to enter the room, it would be so dreadful to watch Catherine go. And Edgar standing solemnly by to see it over; then offering prayers of thanks to God for restoring peace to his house, and going back to his *books*! What in the name of all that feels, has he to do with *books*, when I am dying?"

She could not bear the notion which I had put into her head of Mr. Linton's philosophical resignation. Tossing about, she increased her feverish bewilderment to madness, and tore the pillow with her teeth; then raising herself up all burning, desired that I would open the window. We were in the middle of winter, the wind blew strong from the north-east, and I objected.

Both the expressions flitting over her face, and the changes of her moods, began to alarm me terribly; and brought to my recollection her former illness, and the doctor's injunction that she should not be crossed.

A minute previously she was violent; now, supported on one arm, and not noticing my refusal to obey her, she seemed to find childish diversion in pulling the feathers from the rents she had just made, and ranging them on the sheet according to their different species: her mind had strayed to other associations.

"That's a turkey's,"[1] she murmured to herself; "and this is a wild duck's; and this is a pigeon's. Ah, they put pigeons' feathers in the pillows—no wonder I couldn't die! Let me take care to throw it on the floor when I lie down. And here is a moor-cock's; and this— I should know it among a thousand—it's a lapwing's. Bonny bird; wheeling over our heads in the middle of the moor. It wanted to get to its nest, for the clouds had touched the swells,[2] and it felt rain coming. This feather was picked up from the heath, the bird was not shot—we saw its nest in the winter, full of little skeletons. Heathcliff set a trap over it, and the old ones dare not come. I made him promise he'd never shoot a lapwing, after that, and he didn't.

[1] In *Hamlet*, 4.5, especially ll. 169–75, Ophelia's "distraction" or madness induces a similar chanting list of kinds of flowers with medicinal and symbolic associations. Here, the birds suggest Catherine's memories of childhood rambles on the moors. Northern English folklore held that pigeons' feathers or a feather bed created restlessness, or prevented the soul from leaving the body; death might be delayed by placing a bag of pigeon feathers under the dying person.

[2] The uplands.

Yes, here are more! Did he shoot my lapwings, Nelly? Are they red, any of them? Let me look."

"Give over with that baby-work!" I interrupted, dragging the pillow away, and turning the holes towards the mattress, for she was removing its contents by handfuls. "Lie down and shut your eyes, you're wandering. There's a mess! The down is flying about like snow!"

I went here and there collecting it.

"I see in you, Nelly," she continued, dreamily, "an aged woman—you have grey hair, and bent shoulders. This bed is the fairy cave under Peniston Crag,[3] and you are gathering elf-bolts to hurt our heifers; pretending, while I am near, that they are only locks of wool. That's what you'll come to fifty years hence; I know you are not so now. I'm not wandering, you're mistaken, or else I should believe you really *were* that withered hag, and I should think I *was* under Penistone Crag, and I'm conscious it's night, and there are two candles on the table making the black press shine like jet."

"The black press? where is that?" I asked. "You are talking in your sleep!"

"It's against the wall, as it always is," she replied. "It *does* appear odd—I see a face in it!"

"There's no press in the room, and never was," said I, resuming my seat, and looping up the curtain that I might watch her.

"Don't *you* see that face?" she enquired, gazing earnestly at the mirror.

And say what I could, I was incapable of making her comprehend it to be her own; so I rose and covered it with a shawl.

"It's behind there still!" she pursued, anxiously. "And it stirred. Who is it? I hope it will not come out when you are gone! Oh! Nelly, the room is haunted! I'm afraid of being alone!"

I took her hand in mine, and bid her be composed, for a succession of shudders convulsed her frame, and she *would* keep straining her gaze towards the glass.

"There's nobody here!" I insisted. "It was *yourself*, Mrs. Linton; you knew it a while since."

---

[3]Peniston Quarry was near Haworth. Caves were commonly assumed to house fairies. Elves supposedly fired shots at herds, harming the cattle. Catherine's reality, with candles shining on the wood of the cabinet for storing clothes, is a memory of old-fashioned Wuthering Heights (see ch. 3, n. 1).

"Myself," she gasped, "and the clock is striking twelve! It's true, then; that's dreadful!"

Her fingers clutched the clothes, and gathered them over her eyes. I attempted to steal to the door with an intention of calling her husband; but I was summoned back by a piercing shriek. The shawl had dropped from the frame.

"Why, what *is* the matter?" cried I. "Who is coward now? Wake up! That is the glass—the mirror, Mrs. Linton; and you see yourself in it, and there am I, too, by your side."

Trembling and bewildered, she held me fast, but the horror gradually passed from her countenance; its paleness gave place to a glow of shame.

"Oh, dear! I thought I was at home," she sighed. "I thought I was lying in my chamber at Wuthering Heights. Because I'm weak, my brain got confused, and I screamed unconsciously. Don't say anything; but stay with me. I dread sleeping, my dreams appall me."

"A sound sleep would do you good, ma'am," I answered; "and I hope this suffering will prevent your trying starving again."

"Oh, if I were but in my own bed in the old house!" she went on bitterly, wringing her hands. "And that wind sounding in the firs by the lattice. Do let me feel it—it comes straight down the moor—do let me have one breath!"

To pacify her, I held the casement ajar, a few seconds. A cold blast rushed through; I closed it, and returned to my post.

She lay still, now; her face bathed in tears—Exhaustion of body had entirely subdued her spirit; our fiery Catherine was no better than a wailing child!

"How long is it since I shut myself in here?" she asked, suddenly reviving.

"It was Monday evening," I replied, "and this is Thursday night, or rather Friday morning, at present."

"What! of the same week?" she exclaimed. "Only that brief time?"

"Long enough to live on nothing but cold water and ill-temper," observed I.

"Well, it seems a weary number of hours," she muttered doubtfully, "it must be more—I remember being in the parlour, after they had quarreled; and Edgar being cruelly provoking, and me running into this room desperate—As soon as ever I had barred the door, utter blackness overwhelmed me, and I fell on the floor—I couldn't explain to Edgar how certain I felt of having a fit, or going raging mad, if he persisted in teasing me! I had no command of tongue, or brain, and he did not guess my agony, perhaps; it barely left me sense to try to escape from him and his voice—Before I recovered sufficiently to see and hear, it began to be dawn; and Nelly, I'll tell you what I thought, and what has kept recurring and recurring till I feared for my reason—I thought as I lay there with my head against that table leg, and my eyes dimly discerning the grey square of the window, that I was enclosed in the oak-panelled bed at home; and my heart ached with some great grief which, just waking, I could not recollect—I pondered, and worried myself to discover what it could be; and most strangely, the whole last seven years of my life grew a blank! I did not recall that they had been at all. I was a child; my father was just buried, and my misery arose from the separation that Hindley had ordered between me and Heathcliff—I was laid alone, for the first time, and rousing from a dismal doze after a night of weeping—I lifted my hand to push the panels aside, it struck the table-top! I swept it along the carpet, and then, memory burst in—my late anguish was swallowed in a paroxysm of despair—I cannot say why I felt so wildly wretched—it must have been temporary derangement, for there is scarcely cause—But supposing at twelve years old I had been wrenched from the Heights, and every early association, and my all in all, as Heathcliff was at that time, and been converted at a stroke into Mrs. Linton, the lady of Thrushcross Grange, and the wife of a stranger; an exile, and outcast, thenceforth, from what had been my world—You may fancy a glimpse of the abyss where I grovelled! Shake your head as you will, Nelly, *you* have helped to unsettle me! You should have spoken to Edgar, indeed you should, and compelled him to leave me quiet! Oh, I'm burning! I wish I were out of doors—I wish I were a girl again, half savage and hardy, and free . . . and laughing at injuries, not maddening under them! Why am I so changed? why does my blood rush into a hell of tumult at a few words? I'm sure I should be myself were I once among the heather on those hills . . . Open the window again wide, fasten it open! Quick, why don't you move?"

"Because I won't give you your death of cold," I answered.

"You won't give me a chance of life, you mean," she said sullenly. "However, I'm not helpless yet, I'll open it myself."

And sliding from the bed before I could hinder her, she crossed the room, walking very uncertainly, threw it back, and bent out, careless of the frosty air that cut about her shoulders as keen as a knife.

I entreated, and finally attempted to force her to retire. But I soon found her delirious strength much surpassed mine (she *was* delirious, I became convinced by her subsequent actions and ravings).

There was no moon, and every thing beneath lay in misty darkness; not a light gleamed from any house, far or near; all had been extinguished long ago; and those at Wuthering Heights were never visible . . . still she asserted she caught their shining.

"Look!" she cried eagerly, "that's my room with the candle in it, and the tree swaying before it . . . and the other candle is in Joseph's garret . . . Joseph sits up late, doesn't he? He's waiting till I come home that he may lock the gate . . . Well, he'll wait a while yet. It's a rough journey, and a sad heart to travel it; and we must pass by Gimmerton Kirk, to go that journey! We've braved its ghosts often together, and dared each other to stand among the graves and ask them to come . . . But Heathcliff, if I dare you now, will you venture? If you do, I'll keep you. I'll not lie there by myself; they may bury me twelve feet deep, and throw the church down over me, but I won't rest till you are with me . . . I never will!"

She paused, and resumed with a strange smile, "He's considering . . . he'd rather I'd come to him! Find a way, then! not through that Kirkyard . . . You are slow! Be content, you always followed me!"

Perceiving it vain to argue against her insanity, I was planning how I could reach something to wrap about her, without quitting my hold of herself, for I could not trust her alone by the gaping lattice; when, to my consternation, I heard the rattle of the door-handle, and Mr. Linton entered. He had only then come from the library; and, in passing through the lobby, had noticed our talking and been attracted by curiosity, or fear, to examine what it signified, at that late hour.

"Oh, sir!" I cried, checking the exclamation risen to his lips at the sight which met him, and the bleak atmosphere of the chamber. "My poor mistress is ill, and she quite masters me; I cannot manage her at all; pray, come and persuade her to go to bed. Forget your anger, for she's hard to guide any way but her own."

"Catherine ill?" he said, hastening to us. "Shut the window, Ellen! Catherine! why . . ."

He was silent; the haggardness of Mrs. Linton's appearance smote him speechless, and he could only glance from her to me in horrified astonishment.

"She's been fretting here," I continued, "and eating scarcely anything, and never complaining: she would admit none of us till this evening, and so we couldn't inform you of her state, as we were not aware of it ourselves, but it is nothing."

I felt I uttered my explanations awkwardly; the master frowned. "It is nothing, is it, Ellen Dean?" he said sternly. "You shall account more clearly for keeping me ignorant of this!" And he took his wife in his arms, and looked at her with anguish.

At first she gave him no glance of recognition . . . he was invisible to her abstracted gaze. The delirium was not fixed, however; having weaned her eyes from contemplating the outer darkness, by degrees she centred her attention on him, and discovered who it was that held her.

"Ah! you are come, are you, Edgar Linton?" she said with angry animation . . . "You are one of those things that are ever found when least wanted, and when you are wanted, never! I suppose we shall have plenty of lamentations, now . . . I see we shall . . . but they can't keep me from my narrow home out yonder—my resting-place, where I'm bound before Spring is over! There it is, not among the Lintons, mind, under the chapel-roof, but in the open air, with a head-stone; and you may please yourself, whether you go to them, or come to me!"

"Catherine, what have you done?" commenced the master. "Am I nothing to you, any more? Do you love that wretch Heath——"

"Hush!" cried Mrs. Linton. "Hush, this moment! You mention that name, and I end the matter, instantly, by a spring from the window! What you touch at present you may have; but my soul will be on that hill-top before you lay hands on me again. I don't want you, Edgar; I'm past wanting you . . . Return to your books . . . I'm glad you possess a consolation, for all you had in me is gone."

"Her mind wanders, sir," I interposed. "She has been talking nonsense the whole evening; but, let her have quiet and proper attendance, and she'll rally . . . Hereafter, we must be cautious how we vex her."

"I desire no further advice from you," answered Mr. Linton. "You knew your mistress's nature, and you encouraged me to harass her. And not to give me one hint of how she has been these three days! It was heartless! Months of sickness could not cause such a change!"

I began to defend myself, thinking it too bad to be blamed for another's wicked waywardness!

"I knew Mrs. Linton's nature to be headstrong and domineering," cried I; "but I didn't know that you wished to foster her fierce temper! I didn't know that, to humour her, I should wink at Mr. Heathcliff. I performed the duty of a faithful servant in telling you, and I have got a faithful servant's wages! Well, it will teach me to be careful next time. Next time you may gather intelligence for yourself!"

"The next time you bring a tale to me, you shall quit my service, Ellen Dean," he replied.

"You'd rather hear nothing about it, I suppose, then, Mr. Linton?" said I. "Heathcliff has your permission to come a courting to Miss and to drop in at every opportunity your absence offers, on purpose to poison the mistress against you?"

Confused as Catherine was, her wits were alert at applying our conversation.

"Ah! Nelly has played traitor!" she exclaimed passionately. "Nelly is my hidden enemy—you witch! So you do seek elf-bolts to hurt us! Let me go, and I'll make her rue! I'll make her howl a recantation!"

A maniac's fury kindled under her brows; she struggled desperately to disengage herself from Linton's arms. I felt no inclination to tarry the event; and resolving to seek medical aid on my own responsibility, I quitted the chamber.

In passing the garden to reach the road, at a place where a bridle hook is driven into the wall, I saw something white moved irregularly, evidently by another agent than the wind. Notwithstanding my hurry, I staid to examine it, lest ever after I should have the conviction impressed on my imagination that it was a creature of the other world.

My surprise and perplexity were great to discover, by touch more than vision, Miss Isabella's springer, Fanny, suspended by a handkerchief, and nearly at its last gasp.

I quickly released the animal, and lifted it into the garden. I had seen it follow its mistress upstairs, when she went to bed, and wondered much how it could have got out there, and what mischievous person had treated it so.

While untying the knot round the hook, it seemed to me that I repeatedly caught the beat of horses' feet galloping at some distance; but there were such a number of things to occupy my reflections that I hardly gave the circumstance a thought, though it was a strange sound, in that place, at two o'clock in the morning.

Mr. Kenneth was fortunately just issuing from his house to see a patient in the village as I came up the street; and my account of Catherine Linton's malady induced him to accompany me back immediately.

He was a plain, rough man; and he made no scruple to speak his doubts of her surviving this second attack; unless she were more submissive to his directions than she had shown herself before.

"Nelly Dean," said he, "I can't help fancying there's an extra cause for this. What has there been to do at the Grange? We've odd reports up here. A stout, hearty lass like Catherine does not fall ill for a trifle; and that sort of people should not either. It's hard work bringing them through fevers, and such things. How did it begin?"

"The master will inform you," I answered; "but you are acquainted with the Earnshaws' violent dispositions, and Mrs. Linton caps them all. I may say this; it commenced in a quarrel. She was struck during a tempest of passion with a kind of fit. That's her account, at least; for she flew off in the height of it, and locked herself up. Afterwards, she refused to eat, and now she alternately raves and remains in a half dream, knowing those about her, but having her mind filled with all sorts of strange ideas and illusions."

"Mr. Linton will be sorry?" observed Kenneth, interrogatively.

"Sorry? he'll break his heart should anything happen!" I replied. "Don't alarm him more than necessary."

"Well, I told him to beware," said my companion, "and he must bide the consequences of neglecting my warning. Hasn't he been thick with Mr. Heathcliff lately?"

"Heathcliff frequently visits at the Grange," answered I, "though more on the strength of the mistress having known him when a boy, than because the master likes his company. At present, he's discharged from the trouble of calling; owing to some presumptuous aspirations after Miss Linton which he manifested. I hardly think he'll be taken in again."

"And does Miss Linton turn a cold shoulder on him?" was the doctor's next question.

"I'm not in her confidence," returned I, reluctant to continue the subject.

"No, she's a sly one," he remarked, shaking his head. "She keeps her own counsel! But she's a real little fool. I have it from good authority that last night—and a pretty night it was!—she and Heathcliff were walking in the plantation at the back of your house, above two hours; and he pressed her not to go in again, but just mount his horse and away with him! My informant said she could only put him off by pledging her word of honour to be prepared on their first meeting after that: when it was to be, he didn't hear, but you urge Mr. Linton to look sharp!"

This news filled me with fresh fears; I outstripped Kenneth, and ran most of the way back. The little dog was yelping in the garden yet. I spared a minute to open the gate for it, but instead of going to the house door, it coursed up and down snuffing the grass, and would have escaped to the road, had I not seized and conveyed it in with me.

On ascending to Isabella's room, my suspicions were confirmed; it was empty. Had I been a few hours sooner, Mrs. Linton's illness might have arrested her rash step. But what could be done now? There was a bare possibility of overtaking them if pursued instantly. *I* could not pursue them, however; and I dare not rouse the family, and fill the place with confusion; still less unfold the business to my master, absorbed as he was in his present calamity, and having no heart to spare for a second grief!

I saw nothing for it but to hold my tongue, and suffer matters to take their course; and Kenneth being arrived, I went with a badly composed countenance to announce him.

Catherine lay in a troubled sleep; her husband had succeeded in soothing the excess of frenzy; he now hung over her pillow, watching every shade, and every change of her painfully expressive features.

The doctor, on examining the case for himself, spoke hopefully to him of its having a favourable termination, if we could only preserve around her perfect and constant tranquillity. To me, he signified the threatening danger was not so much death, as permanent alienation of intellect.

I did not close my eyes that night, nor did Mr. Linton; indeed, we never went to bed; and the servants were all up long before the usual hour, moving through the house with stealthy tread, and exchanging whispers as they encountered each other in their vocations. Every one was active, but Miss Isabella; and they began to remark how sound she slept—her brother too asked if she had risen, and seemed impatient for her presence, and hurt that she showed so little anxiety for her sister-in-law.

I trembled lest he should send me to call her; but I was spared the pain of being the first proclaimant of her flight. One of the maids, a thoughtless girl, who had been on an early errand to Gimmerton, came panting upstairs, open-mouthed, and dashed into the chamber, crying.

"Oh, dear, dear! What mun[4] we have next? Master, master, our young lady——"

"Hold your noise!" cried I hastily, enraged at her clamorous manner.

"Speak lower, Mary—What is the matter?" said Mr. Linton. "What ails your young lady?"

"She's gone, she's gone! Yon Heathcliff's run off wi' her!" gasped the girl.

"That is not true!" exclaimed Linton, rising in agitation. "It cannot be—how has the idea entered your head? Ellen Dean, go and seek her—it is incredible—it cannot be."

As he spoke he took the servant to the door, and then repeated his demand to know her reasons for such an assertion.

"Why, I met on the road a lad that fetches milk here," she stammered, "and he asked whether we weren't in trouble at the Grange— I thought he meant for Missis's sickness, so I answered, yes. Then says he, 'they's somebody gone after 'em, I guess?' I stared. He saw I knew naught about it, and he told how a gentleman and lady had stopped to have a horse's shoe fastened at a blacksmith's shop, two miles out of Gimmerton, not very long after midnight! and how the blacksmith's lass had got up to spy who they were; she knew them both directly—And she noticed the man—Heathcliff it was, she felt certain, nob'dy could mistake him, besides—put a sovereign in her father's hand for payment. The lady had a cloak about her face; but having desired a sup of water, while she drank, it fell back, and she saw her very plain—Heathcliff held both bridles as they rode on, and

---

[4]Must.

they set their faces from the village, and went as fast as the rough roads would let them. The lass said nothing to her father, but she told it all over Gimmerton this morning."

I ran and peeped, for form's sake, into Isabella's room; confirming, when I returned, the servant's statement—Mr. Linton had resumed his seat by the bed; on my re-entrance, he raised his eyes, read the meaning of my blank aspect, and dropped them without giving an order, or uttering a word.

"Are we to try any measures for overtaking and bringing her back," I inquired. "How should we do?"

"She went of her own accord," answered the master; "she had a right to go if she pleased—Trouble me no more about her— Hereafter she is only my sister in name; not because I disown her, but because she has disowned me."

And that was all he said on the subject; he did not make a single inquiry further, or mention her in any way, except directing me to send what property she had in the house to her fresh home, wherever it was, when I knew it.

## Chapter 13

For two months the fugitives remained absent; in those two months, Mrs. Linton encountered and conquered the worst shock of what was denominated a brain fever. No mother could have nursed an only child more devotedly than Edgar tended her. Day and night he was watching, and patiently enduring all the annoyances that irritable nerves and a shaken reason could inflict: and, though Kenneth remarked that what he saved from the grave would only recompense his care by forming the source of constant future anxiety—in fact, that his health and strength were being sacrificed to preserve a mere ruin of humanity—he knew no limits in gratitude and joy, when Catherine's life was declared out of danger; and hour after hour he would sit beside her, tracing the gradual return to bodily health, and flattering his too sanguine hopes with the illusion that her mind would settle back to its right balance also, and she would soon be entirely her former self.

The first time she left her chamber, was at the commencement of the following March. Mr. Linton had put on her pillow, in the morning, a handful of golden crocuses; her eye, long stranger to any gleam of pleasure, caught them in waking, and shone delighted as she gathered them eagerly together.

"These are the earliest flowers at the Heights!" she exclaimed. "They remind me of soft thaw winds, and warm sunshine, and nearly melted snow—Edgar, is there not a south wind, and is not the snow almost gone?"

"The snow is quite gone down here, darling!" replied her husband, "and I only see two white spots on the whole range of moors— The sky is blue, and the larks are singing, and the becks and brooks are all brim full. Catherine, last spring at this time, I was longing to have you under this roof—now, I wish you were a mile or two up those hills; the air blows so sweetly, I feel that it would cure you."

"I shall never be there, but once more!" said the invalid; "and then you'll leave me, and I shall remain, for ever. Next spring you'll long again to have me under this roof, and you'll look back and think you were happy to-day."

Linton lavished on her the kindest caresses, and tried to cheer her by the fondest words; but, vaguely regarding the flowers, she let the tears collect on her lashes and stream down her cheeks unheeding.

We knew she was really better, and, therefore, decided that long confinement to a single place produced much of this despondency, and it might be partially removed by a change of scene.

The master told me to light a fire in the many-weeks-deserted parlour, and to set an easy-chair in the sunshine by the window; and then he brought her down, and she sat a long while enjoying the genial heat, and, as we expected, revived by the objects round her, which, though familiar, were free from the dreary associations investing her hated sick chamber. By evening, she seemed greatly exhausted; yet no arguments could persuade her to return to that apartment, and I had to arrange the parlour sofa for her bed, till another room could be prepared.

To obviate the fatigue of mounting and descending the stairs, we fitted up this, where you lie at present, on the same floor with the parlour: and she was soon strong enough to move from one to the other, leaning on Edgar's arm.

Ah, I thought myself, she might recover, so waited on as she was. And there was double cause to desire it, for on her existence depended that of another; we cherished the hope that in a little while, Mr. Linton's heart would be gladdened, and his lands secured from a stranger's gripe, by the birth of an heir.

I should mention that Isabella sent to her brother, some six weeks from her departure, a short note announcing her marriage with Heathcliff. It appeared dry and cold; but at the bottom was dotted in with pencil an obscure apology, and an entreaty for kind remembrance, and reconciliation, if her proceeding had offended him; asserting that she could not help it then, and being done, she had now no power to repeal it.

Linton did not reply to this, I believe; and, in a fortnight more I got a long letter which I considered odd coming from the pen of a bride just out of the honeymoon. I'll read it, for I keep it yet. Any relic of the dead is precious, if they were valued living.

DEAR ELLEN, it begins.

I came last night to Wuthering Heights, and heard, for the first time that Catherine has been, and is yet, very ill. I must not write to her, I suppose, and my brother is either too angry or too distressed to answer what I sent him. Still, I must write to somebody, and the only choice left me is you.

Inform Edgar that I'd give the world to see his face again—that my heart returned to Thrushcross Grange in twenty-four hours after I left it, and is there at this moment, full of warm feelings for him, and Catherine! *I can't follow it, though*—(those words are underlined)—they need not expect me, and they may draw what conclusions they please; taking care, however, to lay nothing at the door of my weak will, or deficient affection.

The remainder of the letter is for yourself, alone. I want to ask you two questions: the first is,

How did you contrive to preserve the common sympathies of human nature when you resided here? I cannot recognise any sentiment which those around share with me.

The second question, I have great interest in; it is this—

Is Mr. Heathcliff a man? If so, is he mad? And if not, is he a devil? I shan't tell my reasons for making this inquiry; but I beseech you to explain, if you can, what I have married—that is, when you call to see me; and you must call, Ellen, very soon. Don't write, but come, and bring me something from Edgar.

Now, you shall hear how I have been received in my new home, as I am led to imagine the Heights will be. It is to amuse myself that I dwell on such subjects as the lack of external comforts; they never occupy my thoughts, except at the moment when I miss them—I should laugh and dance for joy, if I found their absence was the total of my miseries, and the rest was an unnatural dream!

The sun set behind the Grange, as we turned on to the moors; by that, I judged it to be six o'clock; and my companion halted half-an-hour, to inspect the park, and the gardens, and, probably, the place itself, as well as he could; so it was dark when we dismounted in the paved yard of the farm-house, and your old fellow-servant, Joseph, issued out to receive us by the light of a dip candle.[1] He did it with a courtesy that redounded to his credit. His first act was to elevate his torch to a level with my face, squint malignantly, project his under lip, and turn away.

Then he took the two horses, and led them into the stables; reappearing for the purpose of locking the outer gate, as if we lived in an ancient castle.

Heathcliff stayed to speak to him, and I entered the kitchen—a dingy, untidy hole; I dare say you would not know it, it is so changed since it was in your charge.

By the fire stood a ruffianly child, strong in limb and dirty in garb, with a look of Catherine in his eyes and about his mouth.

"This is Edgar's legal nephew," I reflected—"mine in a manner; I must shake hands, and—yes—I must kiss him. It is right to establish a good understanding at the beginning."

I approached, and, attempting to take his chubby fist, said—

"How do you do, my dear?"

He replied in a jargon I did not comprehend.

"Shall you and I be friends, Hareton?" was my next essay at conversation.

An oath, and a threat to set Throttler on me if I did not "frame off,"[2] rewarded my perseverance.

"Hey, Throttler, lad!" whispered the little wretch, rousing a half-bred bull-dog from its lair in a corner. "Now, wilt tuh be ganging?"[3] he asked authoritatively.

Love for my life urged a compliance; I stepped over the threshold to wait till the others should enter. Mr. Heathcliff was nowhere

[1] A cheap, smelly candle made of animal fat, befitting Joseph's *dis*creditable welcome.

[2] Get lost, leave.

[3] "Will you be going?"

visible; and Joseph, whom I followed to the stables, and requested to accompany me in, after staring and muttering to himself, screwed up his nose and replied—

"Mim! mim! mim! Did iver Christian body hear owt like it? Minching un' munching! Hah can Aw tell whet ye say?"[4]

"I say, I wish you to come with me into the house!" I cried, thinking him deaf, yet highly disgusted at his rudeness.

"Nor nuh me![5] Aw getten summut else to do,"[6] he answered, and continued his work, moving his lantern jaws meanwhile, and surveying my dress and countenance (the former a great deal too fine, but the latter, I'm sure, as sad[7] as he could desire) with sovereign contempt.

I walked round the yard, and through a wicket, to another door, at which I took the liberty of knocking, in hopes some more civil servant might shew himself.

After a short suspense it was opened by a tall, gaunt man, without neckerchief, and otherwise extremely slovenly; his features were lost in masses of shaggy hair that hung on his shoulders; and *his* eyes, too, were like a ghostly Catherine's, with all their beauty annihilated.

"What's your business here?" he demanded grimly. "Who are you?"

"My name *was* Isabella Linton," I replied. "You've seen me before, sir. I'm lately married to Mr. Heathcliff; and he has brought me here—I suppose by your permission."

"Is he come back, then?" asked the hermit, glaring like a hungry wolf.

"Yes—we came just now," I said; "but he left me by the kitchen door; and when I would have gone in, your little boy played sentinel over the place, and frightened me off by the help of a bull-dog."

"It's well the hellish villain has kept his word!" growled my future host, searching the darkness beyond me in expectation of discovering Heathcliff; and then he indulged in a soliloquy of execrations, and threats of what he would have done had the "fiend" deceived him.

---

[4]"Mim" suggests prim, genteel speech. "Namby pamby! Did ever a Christian hear anything like it? Mincing and mouthing! How can I tell what you say?"

[5]"Not I!"

[6]"I've got something else to do."

[7]Sober.

I repented having tried this second entrance, and was almost inclined to slip away before he finished cursing, but ere I could execute that intention, he ordered me in, and shut and refastened the door.

There was a great fire, and that was all the light in the huge apartment, whose floor had grown a uniform grey; and the once brilliant pewter dishes which used to attract my gaze when I was a girl partook of a similar obscurity, created by tarnish and dust.

I inquired whether I might call the maid, and be conducted to a bed-room? Mr. Earnshaw vouchsafed no answer. He walked up and down, with his hands in his pockets, apparently quite forgetting my presence; and his abstraction was evidently so deep, and his whole aspect so misanthropical, that I shrank from disturbing him again.

You'll not be surprised, Ellen, at my feeling particularly cheerless, seated in worse than solitude on that inhospitable hearth, and remembering that four miles distant lay my delightful home, containing the only people I loved on earth; and there might as well be the Atlantic to part us, instead of those four miles, I could not overpass them!

I questioned with myself—where must I turn for comfort? and—mind you don't tell Edgar, or Catherine—above every sorrow beside, this rose pre-eminent—despair at finding nobody who could or would be my ally against Heathcliff!

I had sought shelter at Wuthering Heights, almost gladly, because I was secured by that arrangement from living alone with him; but he knew the people we were coming amongst, and he did not fear their intermeddling.

I sat and thought a doleful time; the clock struck eight, and nine, and still my companion paced to and fro, his head bent on his breast, and perfectly silent, unless a groan or a bitter ejaculation forced itself out at intervals.

I listened to detect a woman's voice in the house, and filled the interim with wild regrets and dismal anticipations, which, at last, spoke audibly in irrepressible sighing and weeping.

I was not aware how openly I grieved, till Earnshaw halted opposite, in his measured walk, and gave me a stare of newly awakened surprise. Taking advantage of his recovered attention, I exclaimed—

"I'm tired with my journey, and I want to go to bed! Where is the maid-servant? Direct me to her, as she won't come to me!"

"We have none," he answered; "you must wait on yourself!"

"Where must I sleep, then?" I sobbed—I was beyond regarding self-respect, weighed down by fatigue and wretchedness.

"Joseph will show you Heathcliff's chamber," said he; "open that door—he's in there."

I was going to obey, but he suddenly arrested me, and added in the strangest tone—

"Be so good as to turn your lock, and draw your bolt—don't omit it!"

"Well!" I said. "But why, Mr. Earnshaw?" I did not relish the notion of deliberately fastening myself in with Heathcliff.

"Look here!" he replied, pulling from his waistcoat a curiously constructed pistol, having a double-edged spring knife attached to the barrel. "That's a great tempter to a desperate man, is it not? I cannot resist going up with this, every night, and trying his door. If once I find it open, he's done for! I do it invariably, even though the minute before I have been recalling a hundred reasons that should make me refrain—it is some devil that urges me to thwart my own schemes by killing him—you fight against that devil, for love, as long as you may; when the time comes, not all the angels in heaven shall save him!"

I surveyed the weapon inquisitively; a hideous notion struck me. How powerful I should be possessing such an instrument! I took it from his hand, and touched the blade. He looked astonished at the expression my face assumed during a brief second. It was not horror, it was covetousness. He snatched the pistol back, jealously; shut the knife, and returned it to its concealment.

"I don't care if you tell him," said he. "Put him on his guard, and watch for him. You know the terms we are on, I see; his danger does not shock you."

"What has Heathcliff done to you?" I asked. "In what has he wronged you to warrant this appalling hatred? Wouldn't it be wiser to bid him quit the house?"

"No," thundered Earnshaw, "should he offer to leave me, he's a dead man, persuade him to attempt it, and you are a murderess! Am I to lose *all*, without a chance of retrieval? Is Hareton to be a beggar? Oh, damnation! I *will* have it back; and I'll have *his* gold too; and then his blood; and hell shall have his soul! It will be ten times blacker with that guest than ever it was before!"

You've acquainted me, Ellen, with your old master's habits. He is clearly on the verge of madness—he was so last night, at least. I shuddered to be near him, and thought on the servant's ill-bred moroseness as comparatively agreeable.

He now recommenced his moody walk, and I raised the latch, and escaped into the kitchen.

Joseph was bending over the fire, peering into a large pan that swung above it; and a wooden bowl of oatmeal stood on the settle close by. The contents of the pan began to boil, and he turned to plunge his hand into the bowl; I conjectured that this preparation was probably for our supper, and, being hungry, I resolved it should be eatable—so crying out sharply, "*I'll* make the porridge!" I removed the vessel out of his reach, and proceeded to take off my hat and riding habit. "Mr. Earnshaw," I continued, "directs me to wait on myself—I will—I'm not going to act the lady among you, for fear I should starve."

"Gooid Lord!" he muttered, sitting down, and stroking his ribbed stockings from the knee to the ankle. "If they's tuh be fresh ortherings—just when Aw getten used tuh two maisters, if Aw mun hev a *mistress* set o'er my heead, it's loike time tuh be flitting. Aw niver *did* think tuh say t' day ut Aw mud lave th' owld place—but Aw daht it's nigh at hend!"[8]

This lamentation drew no notice from me; I went briskly to work, sighing to remember a period when it would have been all merry fun; but compelled speedily to drive off the remembrance. It racked me to recall past happiness, and the greater peril there was of conjuring up its apparition, the quicker the thible[9] ran round, and the faster the handfuls of meal fell into the water.

Joseph beheld my style of cookery with growing indignation.

"Thear!" he ejaculated. "Hareton, thah willn't sup thy porridge tuh neeght; they'll be nowt bud lumps as big as maw nave. Thear, agean! Aw'd fling in bowl un' all, if Aw wer yah! Thear, pale t'

---

[8]"If there are to be new arrangements [or ways of doing things]—just when I've gotten used to two masters, if I must have a *mistress* over my head, it's about time to be going. I never did think to see the day that I must leave the old place—but I doubt [I'm afraid] it's near at hand!"

[9]Wooden stick for stirring porridge or other food in a pot.

guilp off, un' then yah'll hae done wi't. Bang, bang. It's a marcy t' bothom isn't deaved aht!"[10]

It *was* rather a rough mess, I own, when poured into the basins; four had been provided, and a gallon pitcher of new milk was brought from the dairy, which Hareton seized and commenced drinking and spilling from the expansive lip.

I expostulated, and desired that he should have his in a mug; affirming that I could not taste the liquid treated so dirtily. The old cynic chose to be vastly offended at this nicety; assuring me, repeatedly, that "the barn was every bit as gooid" as I, "and every bit as wollsome,"[11] and wondering how I could fashion to be[12] so conceited; meanwhile, the infant ruffian continued sucking, and glowered up at me defyingly, as he slavered[13] into the jug.

"I shall have my supper in another room," I said. "Have you no place you call a parlour?"

"*Parlour!*" he echoed, sneeringly, "*parlour!* Nay, we've noa *parlours*. If yah dunnut loike wer company, they's maister's; un' if yah dunnut loike maister, they's us."[14]

"Then I shall go upstairs," I answered; "shew me a chamber!"

I put my basin on a tray, and went myself to fetch some more milk.

With great grumblings, the fellow rose, and preceded me in my ascent. We mounted to the garrets; he opening a door, now and then, to look into the apartments we passed.

"Here's a rahm," he said, at last, flinging back a cranky board on hinges. "It's weel eneugh to ate a few porridge in. They's a pack uh corn i' t' corner, thear, meeterly clane; if yah're feared uh muckying yer grand silk cloes, spread yer hankerchir ut t' top on't."[15]

---

[10]"There! . . . thou will not eat thy porridge tonight; there will be nothing but lumps as big as my fist. There, again! I'd fling in the bowl and all, if I were you! There, peel the scum off [skim it], and then you'll have done with it. Bang, bang. It's a mercy the bottom isn't knocked out!"

[11]"The child was every bit as good . . . and every bit as wholesome."

[12]Contrive to be.

[13]Drooled.

[14]"No, we don't have parlors. If you don't like our company, there's the master's; and if you don't like master, there's us."

[15]"Here's a room," . . . flinging back a shaky board . . . "It's good enough to eat some porridge in. There's a pack of grain in the corner, there, tolerably clean; if you're afraid of dirtying your grand silk clothes, spread your handkerchief on the top of it."

The "rahm" was a kind of lumber-hole smelling strong of malt and grain; various sacks of which articles were piled around, leaving a wide, bare space in the middle.

"Why, man!" I exclaimed, facing him angrily, "this is not a place to sleep in. I wish to see my bed-room."

"*Bed-rume!*" he repeated, in a tone of mockery. "Yah's see all t' *bedrumes* thear is—yon's mine."

He pointed into the second garret, only differing from the first in being more naked about the walls, and having a large, low, curtainless bed with an indigo-coloured quilt, at one end.

"What do I want with yours?" I retorted. "I suppose Mr. Heathcliff does not lodge at the top of the house, does he?"

"Oh! it's Maister *Hathecliff's* yah're wenting?" cried he, as if making a new discovery. "Couldn't ye uh said soa, at onst? un' then, Aw mud uh telled ye, baht all this wark, ut that's just one ye cannut sea—he allas keeps it locked, un' nob'dy iver mells on't but hisseln."[16]

"You've a nice house, Joseph," I could not refrain from observing, "and pleasant inmates; and I think the concentrated essence of all the madness in the world took up its abode in my brain the day I linked my fate with theirs! However, that is not to the present purpose—there are other rooms. For heaven's sake, be quick, and let me settle somewhere!"

He made no reply to this adjuration; only plodding doggedly down the wooden steps, and halting before an apartment which, from that halt, and the superior quality of its furniture, I conjectured to be the best one.

There was a carpet, a good one, but the pattern was obliterated by dust; a fire-place hung with cut paper[17] dropping to pieces; a handsome oak-bedstead with ample crimson curtains of rather expensive material and modern make. But they had evidently experienced rough usage: the valances hung in festoons, wrenched from their rings, and the iron rod supporting them was bent in an arc, on

[16]"Couldn't you have said so, at once? And then, I might have told you, without all this work, that that's just the one you cannot see—he always keeps it locked, and nobody ever meddles in it but himself."

[17]The room has been decorated according to current feminine taste, probably by Hindley's wife Frances, but has deteriorated during Hindley's struggle with Heathcliff. Cutting colored paper in patterns to decorate fire screens or mantlepieces was a womanly hobby like needlework.

one side, causing the drapery to trail upon the floor. The chairs were also damaged, many of them severely; and deep indentations deformed the panels of the walls.

I was endeavouring to gather resolution for entering, and taking possession, when my fool of a guide announced—

"This here is t' maister's."

My supper by this time was cold, my appetite gone, and my patience exhausted. I insisted on being provided instantly with a place of refuge, and means of repose.

"Whear the divil?" began the religious elder. "The Lord bless us! The Lord forgie us! Whear the *hell* wold ye gang? ye marred, wearisome nowt! Yah seen all bud Hareton's bit uf a cham'er. They's nut another hoile tuh lig dahn in i' th' hahse!"[18]

I was so vexed, I flung my tray and its contents on the ground; and then seated myself at the stairs-head, hid my face in my hands, and cried.

"Ech! ech!" exclaimed Joseph. "Weel done, Miss Cathy! weel done, Miss Cathy! Hahsiver, t' maister sall just tum'le o'er them brocken pots; un' then we's hear summut; we's hear hah it's tuh be. Gooid-for-naught madling! yah desarve pining froo this tuh Churstmas, flinging t' precious gifts uh God under fooit i' yer flaysome rages! Bud, Aw'm mista'en if yah shew yer sperrit lang. Will Hathecliff bide sich bonny ways, think ye? Aw nobbut wish he may cotch ye i' that plisky. Aw nobbut wish he may."[19]

And so he went on scolding to his den beneath, taking the candle with him, and I remained in the dark.

The period of reflection succeeding this silly action compelled me to admit the necessity of smothering my pride, and choking my wrath, and bestirring myself to remove its effects.

[18]"Where the devil? . . . The Lord forgive us! Where the hell would you go? You spoiled, wearisome nothing! You've seen all but Hareton's bit of a chamber. There's not another hole to lie down in in the house!"

[19]"Well done, Miss Cathy! . . . However, the master shall just tumble over those broken pots, and then we shall hear something. . . . Good-for-nothing blockhead! you deserve to pine away from now till Christmas, flinging the precious gifts of God underfoot in your awful rages! But I'm mistaken if you'll show your spirit for long. Do you think Heathcliff will stand such cute tricks? I only wish he might catch you in that trantrum. I only wish he might." Joseph's sarcastic praise of Catherine suggests either that she's the one that created Isabella's misery or that Isabella is acting like Catherine.

An unexpected aid presently appeared in the shape of Throttler, whom I now recognised as a son of our old Skulker; it had spent its whelphood at the Grange, and was given by my father to Mr. Hindley. I fancy it knew me—it pushed its nose against mine by way of salute, and then hastened to devour the porridge, while I groped from step to step, collecting the shattered earthenware, and drying the spatters of milk from the banister with my pocket-handkerchief.

Our labours were scarcely over when I heard Earnshaw's tread in the passage; my assistant tucked in his tail, and pressed to the wall; I stole into the nearest doorway. The dog's endeavour to avoid him was unsuccessful; as I guessed by a scutter down stairs, and a prolonged, piteous yelping. I had better luck. He passed on, entered his chamber, and shut the door.

Directly after, Joseph came up with Hareton, to put him to bed. I had found shelter in Hareton's room, and the old man, on seeing me, said—

"They's rahm fur boath yah un' yer pride, nah, Aw sud think, i' the hahse. It's empty; yah muh hev it all tuh yerseln, un' Him as allas maks a third, i' sich ill company!"[20]

Gladly did I take advantage of this intimation; and the minute I flung myself into a chair, by the fire, I nodded, and slept.

My slumber was deep and sweet, though over far too soon. Mr. Heathcliff awoke me; he had just come in, and demanded, in his loving manner, what I was doing there?

I told him the cause of my staying up so late—that he had the key of our room in his pocket.

The adjective *our* gave mortal offence. He swore it was not, nor ever should be mine; and he'd—but I'll not repeat his language, nor describe his habitual conduct; he is ingenious and unresting in seeking to gain my abhorrence! I sometimes wonder at him with an intensity that deadens my fear; yet, I assure you, a tiger or a venomous serpent could not rouse terror in me equal to that which he wakens. He told me of Catherine's illness, and accused my brother of causing it; promising that I should be Edgar's proxy in suffering, till he could get hold of him.

[20]"There's room for both you and your pride, now, I should think, in the house. It's empty; you may have it all to yourself, and He who always makes a third [the Devil], in such bad company!"

I do hate him—I am wretched—I have been a fool! Beware of
uttering one breath of this to any one at the Grange. I shall expect
you every day—don't disappoint me!

ISABELLA.

## Chapter 14

As soon as I had perused this epistle, I went to the master, and informed him that his sister had arrived at the Heights, and sent me a
letter expressing her sorrow for Mrs. Linton's situation, and her ardent desire to see him; with a wish that he would transmit to her, as
early as possible, some token of forgiveness by me.

"Forgiveness?" said Linton. "I have nothing to forgive her,
Ellen—you may call at Wuthering Heights this afternoon, if you
like, and say that I am not *angry*, but I'm *sorry* to have lost her: especially as I can never think she'll be happy. It is out of the question
my going to see her, however; we are eternally divided; and should
she really wish to oblige me, let her persuade the villain she has
married to leave the country."

"And you won't write her a little note, sir?" I asked, imploringly.

"No," he answered. "It is needless. My communication with
Heathcliff's family shall be as sparing as his with mine. It shall
not exist!"

Mr. Edgar's coldness depressed me exceedingly; and all the way
from the Grange I puzzled my brains how to put more heart into
what he said, when I repeated it; and how to soften his refusal of
even a few lines to console Isabella.

I dare say she had been on the watch for me since morning: I saw
her looking through the lattice, as I came up the garden causeway,
and I nodded to her; but she drew back, as if afraid of being observed.

I entered without knocking. There never was such a dreary, dismal scene as the formerly cheerful house presented! I must confess
that, if I had been in the young lady's place, I would, at least, have
swept the hearth, and wiped the tables with a duster. But she already partook of the pervading spirit of neglect which encom-
passed her. Her pretty face was wan and listless; her hair
uncurled—some locks hanging lankly down, and some carelessly
twisted round her head. Probably she had not touched her dress
since yester evening.

Hindley was not there. Mr. Heathcliff sat at a table, turning over some papers in his pocket-book; but he rose when I appeared, asked me how I did, quite friendly, and offered me a chair.

He was the only thing there that seemed decent, and I thought he never looked better. So much had circumstances altered their positions, that he would certainly have struck a stranger as a born and bred gentleman, and his wife as a thorough little slattern!

She came forward eagerly to greet me; and held out one hand to take the expected letter.

I shook my head. She wouldn't understand the hint, but followed me to a sideboard, where I went to lay my bonnet, and importuned me in a whisper to give her directly what I had brought.

Heathcliff guessed the meaning of her manoeuvres, and said—

"If you have got anything for Isabella, as no doubt you have, Nelly, give it to her. You needn't make a secret of it; we have no secrets between us."

"Oh, I have nothing," I replied, thinking it best to speak the truth at once. "My master bade me tell his sister that she must not expect either a letter or a visit from him at present. He sends his love, ma'am, and his wishes for your happiness, and his pardon for the grief you have occasioned; but he thinks that after this time, his household and the household here should drop intercommunication, as nothing good could come of keeping it up."

Mrs. Heathcliff's lip quivered slightly, and she returned to her seat in the window. Her husband took his stand on the hearthstone, near me, and began to put questions concerning Catherine.

I told him as much as I thought proper of her illness, and he extorted from me, by cross-examination, most of the facts connected with its origin.

I blamed her, as she deserved, for bringing it all on herself; and ended by hoping that he would follow Mr. Linton's example, and avoid future interference with his family, for good or evil.

"Mrs. Linton is now just recovering," I said; "she'll never be like she was, but her life is spared, and if you really have a regard for her, you'll shun crossing her way again. Nay, you'll move out of this country entirely; and that you may not regret it, I'll inform you Catherine Linton is now as different now from your old friend Catherine Earnshaw, as that young lady is different from me! Her appearance is changed greatly, her character much more so; and the person who is compelled, of necessity, to be her companion, will only sustain his affection hereafter by the remembrance of what she once was, by common humanity, and a sense of duty!"

"That is quite possible," remarked Heathcliff, forcing himself to seem calm, "quite possible that your master should have nothing but common humanity and a sense of duty to fall back upon. But do you imagine that I shall leave Catherine to his *duty* and *humanity?* and can you compare my feelings respecting Catherine, to his? Before you leave this house, I must exact a promise from you, that you'll get me an interview with her—consent, or refuse, I *will* see her! What do you say?"

"I say, Mr. Heathcliff," I replied, "you must not—you never shall through my means. Another encounter between you and the master would kill her altogether!"

"With your aid that may be avoided," he continued; "and should there be danger of such an event—should he be the cause of adding a single trouble more to her existence—Why, I think I shall be justified in going to extremes! I wish you had sincerity enough to tell me whether Catherine would suffer greatly from his loss. The fear that she would restrains me. And there you see the distinction between our feelings—Had he been in my place, and I in his, though I hated him with a hatred that turned my life to gall, I never would have raised a hand against him. You may look incredulous, if you please! I never would have banished him from her society, as long as she desired his. The moment her regard ceased, I would have torn his heart out, and drank his blood! But, till then—if you don't believe me, you don't know me—till then, I would have died by inches before I touched a single hair of his head!"

"And yet," I interrupted, "you have no scruples in completely ruining all hopes of her perfect restoration, by thrusting yourself into her remembrance, now, when she has nearly forgotten you, and involving her in a new tumult of discord and distress."

"You suppose she has nearly forgotten me?" he said. "Oh Nelly! you know she has not! You know as well as I do, that for every thought she spends on Linton, she spends a thousand on me! At a most miserable period of my life, I had a notion of the kind. It haunted me on my return to the neighbourhood, last summer, but only her own assurance could make me admit the horrible idea again. And then, Linton would be nothing, nor Hindley, nor all the dreams that ever I dreamt. Two words would comprehend my future, *death* and *hell*—existence, after losing her, would be hell.

"Yet I was a fool to fancy for a moment that she valued Edgar Linton's attachment more than mine—If he loved with all the powers of his puny being, he couldn't love as much in eighty years, as I could in a day. And Catherine has a heart as deep as I have; the sea could be as readily contained in that horse-trough, as her whole affection be monopolized by him—Tush! He is scarcely a degree dearer to her than her dog, or her horse—It is not in him to be loved like me, how can she love in him what he has not?"

"Catherine and Edgar are as fond of each other as any two people can be!" cried Isabella with sudden vivacity. "No one has a right to talk in that manner, and I won't hear my brother depreciated in silence!"

"Your brother is wondrous fond of you too, isn't he?" observed Heathcliff scornfully. "He turns you adrift on the world with surprising alacrity."

"He is not aware of what I suffer," she replied. "I didn't tell him that."

"You have been telling him something, then—you have written, have you?"

"To say that I was married, I did write—you saw the note."

"And nothing since?"

"No."

"My young lady is looking sadly the worse for her change of condition," I remarked. "Somebody's love comes short in her case, obviously—whose I may guess; but, perhaps, I shouldn't say."

"I should guess it was her own," said Heathcliff. "She degenerates into a mere slut! She is tired of trying to please me, uncommonly early—You'd hardly credit it, but the very morrow of our wedding, she was weeping to go home. However, she'll suit this house so much the better for not being over nice, and I'll take care she does not disgrace me by rambling abroad."

"Well, sir," returned I, "I hope you'll consider that Mrs. Heathcliff is accustomed to be looked after, and waited on; and that she has been brought up like an only daughter whom every one was ready to serve—You must let her have a maid to keep things tidy about her, and you must treat her kindly—Whatever be your notion of Mr. Edgar, you cannot doubt that she has a capacity for strong attachments or she wouldn't have abandoned the elegancies, and comforts, and friends of her former home, to fix contentedly, in such a wilderness as this, with you."

"She abandoned them under a delusion," he answered, "picturing in me a hero of romance, and expecting unlimited indulgences from my chivalrous devotion. I can hardly regard her in the light of a rational creature, so obstinately has she persisted in forming a fabulous notion of my character, and acting on the false impressions she cherished. But, at last, I think she begins to know me—I don't perceive the silly smiles and grimaces that provoked me at first; and the senseless incapability of discerning that I was in earnest when I gave her my opinion of her infatuation, and herself—It was a marvellous effort of perspicacity to discover that I did not love her. I believed, at one time, no lessons could teach her that! and yet it is poorly learnt; for this morning she announced, as a piece of appalling intelligence, that I had actually succeeded in making her hate me! A positive labour of Hercules, I assure you! If it be achieved I have cause to return thanks—Can I trust your assertion, Isabella, are you sure you hate me? If I let you alone for half-a-day, won't you come sighing and wheedling to me again? I dare say she would rather I had seemed all tenderness before you; it wounds her vanity to have the truth exposed. But I don't care who knows that the passion was wholly on one side, and I never told her a lie about it. She cannot accuse me of showing one bit of deceitful softness. The first thing she saw me do, on coming out of the Grange, was to hang up her little dog, and when she pleaded for it the first words I uttered were a wish that I had the hanging of every being belonging to her, except one: possibly she took that exception for herself—But no brutality disgusted her—I suppose she has an innate admiration of it, if only her precious person were secure from injury! Now, was it not the depth of absurdity—of genuine idiocy, for that pitiful, slavish, mean-minded brach[1] to dream that I could love her? Tell your master, Nelly, that I never, in all my life, met with such an abject thing as she is—She even disgraces the name of Linton; and I've sometimes relented, from pure lack of invention, in my experiments on what she could endure, and still creep shamefully cringing back! But tell him, also, to set his frater-

[1] Bitch-hound.

nal and magisterial heart at ease, that I keep strictly within the limits of the law—I have avoided, up to this period, giving her the slightest right to claim a separation; and, what's more, she'd thank nobody for dividing us—if she desired to go she might—the nuisance of her presence outweighs the gratification to be derived from tormenting her!"

"Mr. Heathcliff," said I, "this is the talk of a madman, and your wife, most likely, is convinced you are mad; and, for that reason, she has borne with you hitherto; but now that you say she may go, she'll doubtless avail herself of the permission—You are not so bewitched ma'am, are you, as to remain with him of your own accord?"

"Take care, Ellen!" answered Isabella, her eyes sparkling irefully—there was no misdoubting by their expression, the full success of her partner's endeavours to make himself detested. "Don't put faith in a single word he speaks. He's a lying fiend, a monster, and not a human being! I've been told I might leave him before; and I've made the attempt, but I dare not repeat it! Only, Ellen, promise you'll not mention a syllable of his infamous conversation to my brother or Catherine—whatever he may pretend, he wishes to provoke Edgar to desperation—he says he has married me on purpose to obtain power over him; and he shan't obtain it—I'll die first! I just hope, I pray that he may forget his diabolical prudence, and kill me! The single pleasure I can imagine is to die, or to see him dead!"

"There—that will do for the present!" said Heathcliff. "If you are called upon in a court of law, you'll remember her language, Nelly! And take a good look at that countenance—she's near the point which would suit me. No, you're not fit to be your own guardian, Isabella, now; and I, being your legal protector, must retain you in my custody, however distasteful the obligation may be—Go upstairs; I have something to say to Ellen Dean, in private. That's not the way—upstairs, I tell you! Why, this is the road upstairs, child!"

He seized, and thrust her from the room; and returned muttering, "I have no pity! I have no pity! The more the worms writhe, the more I yearn to crush out their entrails! It is a moral teething, and I grind with greater energy, in proportion to the increase of pain."

"Do you understand what the word pity means?" I said, hastening to resume my bonnet. "Did you ever feel a touch of it in your life?"

"Put that down!" he interrupted, perceiving my intention to depart. "You are not going yet—Come here now, Nelly—I must either persuade or compel you to aid me in fulfilling my determination to see Catherine, and that without delay—I swear that I meditate no harm; I don't desire to cause any disturbance, or to exasperate or insult Mr. Linton; I only wish to hear from herself how she is, and why she has been ill; and to ask, if anything that I could do would be of use to her. Last night, I was in the Grange garden six hours, and I'll return there to-night; and every night I'll haunt the place, and every day, till I find an opportunity of entering. If Edgar Linton meets me I shall not hesitate to knock him down, and give him enough to assure his quiescence while I stay—If his servants oppose me, I shall threaten them off with these pistols—But wouldn't it be better to prevent my coming in contact with them, or their master? And you could do it so easily! I'd warn you when I came, and then you might let me in unobserved, as soon as she was alone, and watch till I departed, your conscience quite calm—you would be hindering mischief."

I protested against playing that treacherous part in my employer's house; and besides I urged the cruelty and selfishness of his destroying Mrs. Linton's tranquillity for his satisfaction.

"The commonest occurrence startles her painfully," I said. "She's all nerves, and she couldn't bear the surprise, I'm positive— Don't persist, sir! or else, I shall be obliged to inform my master of your designs, and he'll take measures to secure his house and its inmates from any such unwarrantable intrusions!"

"In that case, I'll take measures to secure you, woman!" exclaimed Heathcliff, "you shall not leave Wuthering Heights till tomorrow morning. It is a foolish story to assert that Catherine could not bear to see me; and as to surprising her, I don't desire it, you must prepare her—ask her if I may come. You say she never mentions my name, and that I am never mentioned to her. To whom should she mention me if I am a forbidden topic in the house? She thinks you are all spies for her husband—Oh, I've no doubt she's in hell among you! I guess, by her silence, as much as any thing, what she feels. You say she is often restless, and anxious looking—is that a proof of tranquillity? You talk of her mind being unsettled—How the devil could it be otherwise, in her frightful isolation. And that insipid, paltry creature attending her from *duty* and *humanity*! From *pity* and *charity*! He might as well plant an oak in a flower-pot, and expect it to thrive, as imagine he can restore her to vigour in the soil of his shallow cares! Let us settle it at once; will you stay here, and am I to fight my way to Catherine over Linton and his footmen? Or will you be my friend, as you have been hitherto, and do what I request? Decide! because there is no reason for my lingering another minute, if you persist in your stubborn ill-nature!"

Well, Mr. Lockwood, I argued, and complained, and flatly refused him fifty times; but in the long run he forced me to an agreement—I engaged to carry a letter from him to my mistress; and should she consent, I promised to let him have intelligence of Linton's next absence from home, when he might come, and get in as he was able—I wouldn't be there, and my fellow-servants should be equally out of the way.

Was it right, or wrong? I fear it was wrong, though expedient. I thought I prevented another explosion by my compliance; and I thought, too, it might create a favourable crisis in Catherine's mental illness. And then I remembered Mr. Edgar's stern rebuke of my carrying tales; and I tried to smooth away all disquietude on the subject by affirming, with frequent iteration, that that betrayal of trust, if it merited so harsh an appellation, should be the last.

Notwithstanding, my journey homeward was sadder than my journey thither; and many misgivings I had, ere I could prevail on myself to put the missive into Mrs. Linton's hand.

But here is Kenneth—I'll go down, and tell him how much better you are. My history is *dree*,[2] as we say, and will serve to while away another morning.


Dree, and dreary! I reflected, as the good woman descended to receive the doctor; and not exactly of the kind which I should have chosen to amuse me; but never mind! I'll extract wholesome medicines from Mrs. Dean's bitter herbs; and firstly, let me beware the fascination that lurks in Catherine Heathcliff's brilliant eyes. I should be in a curious taking[3] if I surrendered my heart to that young person, and the daughter turned out a second edition of the mother!

THE END OF VOLUME I.

[2]Sad, dreary.
[3]Strange situation; predicament.

# Volume 2

## Chapter 1/15

Another week over—and I am so many days nearer health, and spring! I have now heard all my neighbour's history, at different sittings, as the housekeeper could spare time from more important occupations. I'll continue it in her own words, only a little condensed. She is, on the whole, a very fair narrator and I don't think I could improve her style.

In the evening, she said, the evening of my visit to the Heights, I knew, as well as if I saw him, that Mr. Heathcliff was about the place; and I shunned going out, because I still carried his letter in my pocket, and didn't want to be threatened, or teased any more.

I had made up my mind not to give it till my master went somewhere, as I could not guess how its receipt would affect Catherine. The consequence was, that it did not reach her before the lapse of three days. The fourth was Sunday, and I brought it into her room, after the family were gone to church.

There was a man servant left to keep the house with me, and we generally made a practice of locking the doors during the hours of service; but on that occasion the weather was so warm and pleasant that I set them wide open, and, to fulfil my engagement, as I knew who would be coming, I told my companion that the mistress wished very much for some oranges, and he must run over to the village and get a few, to be paid for on the morrow. He departed, and I went upstairs.

Mrs. Linton sat in a loose, white dress, with a light shawl over her shoulders, in the recess of the open window, as usual. Her thick, long hair had been partly removed at the beginning of her illness, and now she wore it simply combed in its natural tresses over her temples and neck. Her appearance was altered, as I had told Heathcliff, but when she was calm, there seemed unearthly beauty in the change.

The flash of her eyes had been succeeded by a dreamy and melancholy softness: they no longer gave the impression of looking at the objects around her; they appeared always to gaze beyond, and far beyond—you would have said out of this world—Then, the paleness of her face, its haggard aspect having vanished as she recovered flesh, and the peculiar expression arising from her mental state, though painfully suggestive of their causes, added to the touching interest which she wakened, and invariably to me, I know, and to any person who saw her, I should think, refuted more tangible proofs of convalescence, and stamped her as one doomed to decay.

A book lay spread on the sill before her, and the scarcely perceptible wind fluttered its leaves at intervals. I believe Linton had laid it there, for she never endeavoured to divert herself with reading, or occupation of any kind; and he would spend many an hour in trying to entice her attention to some subject which had formerly been her amusement.

She was conscious of his aim, and in her better moods endured his efforts placidly, only showing their uselessness by now and then suppressing a wearied sigh, and checking him at last with the saddest of smiles and kisses. At other times, she would turn petulantly away, and hide her face in her hands, or even push him off angrily; and then he took care to let her alone, for he was certain of doing no good.

Gimmerton chapel bells were still ringing; and the full, mellow flow of the beck in the valley came soothingly on the ear. It was a sweet substitute for the yet absent murmur of the summer foliage, which drowned that music about the Grange when the trees were in leaf. At Wuthering Heights it always sounded on quiet days, following a great thaw, or a season of steady rain—and of Wuthering Heights Catherine was thinking as she listened; that is, if she thought, or listened, at all; but she had the vague, distant look I mentioned before, which expressed no recognition of material things either by ear or eye.

"There's a letter for you, Mrs. Linton," I said, gently inserting it in one hand that rested on her knee. "You must read it immediately, because it wants an answer. Shall I break the seal?"

"Yes," she answered, without altering the direction of her eyes.

I opened it—it was very short.

"Now," I continued, "read it."

She drew away her hand, and let it fall. I replaced it in her lap, and stood waiting till it should please her to glance down; but that movement was so long delayed that at last I resumed—

"Must I read it, ma'am? It is from Mr. Heathcliff."

There was a start and a troubled gleam of recollection, and a struggle to arrange her ideas. She lifted the letter, and seemed to peruse it; and when she came to the signature she sighed; yet still I found she had not gathered its import, for upon my desiring to hear her reply, she merely pointed to the name, and gazed at me with mournful and questioning eagerness.

"Well, he wishes to see you," said I, guessing her need of an interpreter. "He's in the garden by this time, and impatient to know what answer I shall bring."

As I spoke, I observed a large dog, lying on the sunny grass beneath, raise its ears as if about to bark, and then smoothing them back, announce by a wag of the tail that some one approached whom it did not consider a stranger.

Mrs. Linton bent forward, and listened breathlessly. The minute after a step traversed the hall; the open house was too tempting for Heathcliff to resist walking in: most likely he supposed that I was inclined to shirk my promise, and so resolved to trust to his own audacity.

With straining eagerness Catherine gazed towards the entrance of her chamber. He did not hit the right room directly; she motioned me to admit him; but he found it out, ere I could reach the door, and in a stride or two was at her side, and had her grasped in his arms.

He neither spoke, nor loosed his hold, for some five minutes, during which period he bestowed more kisses than ever he gave in his life before, I dare say; but then my mistress had kissed him first, and I plainly saw that he could hardly bear, for downright agony, to look into her face! The same conviction had stricken him as me, from the instant he beheld her, that there was no prospect of ultimate recovery there—she was fated, sure to die.

"Oh, Cathy! Oh, my life! how can I bear it?" was the first sentence he uttered, in a tone that did not seek to disguise his despair.

And now he stared at her so earnestly that I thought the very intensity of his gaze would bring tears into his eyes; but they burned with anguish, they did not melt.

"What now?" said Catherine, leaning back, and returning his look with a suddenly clouded brow—her humour was a mere vane for constantly varying caprices. "You and Edgar have broken my heart, Heathcliff! And you both come to bewail the deed to me, as if you were the people to be pitied! I shall not pity you, not I. You have killed me—and thriven on it, I think. How strong you are! How many years do you mean to live after I am gone?"

Heathcliff had knelt on one knee to embrace her; he attempted to rise, but she seized his hair, and kept him down.

"I wish I could hold you," she continued, bitterly, "till we were both dead! I shouldn't care what you suffered. I care nothing for your sufferings. Why shouldn't you suffer? I do! Will you forget me—will you be happy when I am in the earth? Will you say twenty years hence, 'That's the grave of Catherine Earnshaw. I loved her long ago, and was wretched to lose her; but it is past. I've loved many others since—my children are dearer to me than she was, and, at death, I shall not rejoice that I am going to her, I shall be sorry that I must leave them!' Will you say so, Heathcliff?"

"Don't torture me till I'm as mad as yourself," cried he, wrenching his head free, and grinding his teeth.

The two, to a cool spectator, made a strange and fearful picture. Well might Catherine deem that Heaven would be a land of exile to her, unless, with her mortal body, she cast away her mortal character also. Her present countenance had a wild vindictiveness in its white cheek, and a bloodless lip, and a scintillating eye; and she retained, in her closed fingers, a portion of the locks she had been grasping. As to her companion, while raising himself with one hand, he had taken her arm with the other; and so inadequate was his stock of gentleness to the requirements of her condition, that on his letting go, I saw four distinct impressions left blue in the colourless skin.

"Are you possessed with a devil," he pursued, savagely, "to talk in that manner to me, when you are dying? Do you reflect that all those words will be branded in my memory, and eating deeper eternally, after you have left me? You know you lie to say I have killed you; and, Catherine, you know that I could as soon forget you, as my existence! Is it not sufficient for your infernal selfishness that, while you are at peace, I shall writhe in the torments of hell?"

"I shall not be at peace," moaned Catherine, recalled to a sense of physical weakness by the violent, unequal throbbing of her heart, which beat visibly and audibly under this excess of agitation.

She said nothing further till the paroxysm was over; then she continued, more kindly—

"I'm not wishing you greater torment than I have, Heathcliff! I only wish us never to be parted—and should a word of mine distress you hereafter, think I feel the same distress underground, and for my own sake, forgive me! Come here and kneel down again! You never harmed me in your life. Nay, if you nurse anger, that will be worse to remember than my harsh words! Won't you come here again? Do!"

Heathcliff went to the back of her chair, and leant over, but not so far as to let her see his face, which was livid with emotion. She bent round to look at him; he would not permit it; turning abruptly, he walked to the fire-place, where he stood, silent, with his back towards us.

Mrs. Linton's glance followed him suspiciously: every movement woke a new sentiment in her. After a pause, and a prolonged gaze, she resumed, addressing me in accents of indignant disappointment.

"Oh, you see, Nelly! he would not relent a moment to keep me out of the grave! *That* is how I'm loved! Well, never mind! That is not *my* Heathcliff. I shall love mine yet; and take him with me— he's in my soul. And," added she, musingly, "the thing that irks me most is this shattered prison, after all. I'm tired, tired of being enclosed here. I'm wearying to escape into that glorious world, and to be always there; not seeing it dimly through tears, and yearning for it through the walls of an aching heart; but really with it, and in it. Nelly, you think you are better and more fortunate than I; in full health and strength—you are sorry for me—very soon that will be altered. I shall be sorry for *you*. I shall be incomparably beyond and above you all. I *wonder* he won't be near me!" she went on to herself. "I thought he wished it. Heathcliff, dear! you should not be sullen now. Do come to me, Heathcliff."

In her eagerness she rose, and supported herself on the arm of the chair. At that earnest appeal, he turned to her, looking absolutely desperate. His eyes, wide and wet at last, flashed fiercely on her; his breast heaved convulsively. An instant they held asunder; and then how they met I hardly saw, but Catherine made a spring, and he caught her, and they were locked in an embrace from which I thought my mistress would never be released alive. In fact, to my eyes, she seemed directly insensible. He flung himself into the nearest seat, and on my approaching hurriedly to ascertain if she had fainted, he gnashed at me, and foamed like a mad dog, and gathered her to him with greedy jealousy. I did not feel as if I were in the company of a creature of my own species; it appeared that he would not understand, though I spoke to him; so, I stood off, and held my tongue, in great perplexity.

A movement of Catherine's relieved me a little presently: she put up her hand to clasp his neck, and bring her cheek to his, as he held her: while he, in return, covering her with frantic caresses, said wildly—

"You teach me now how cruel you've been—cruel and false. *Why* did you despise me? *Why* did you betray your own heart, Cathy? I have not one word of comfort—you deserve this. You have killed yourself. Yes, you may kiss me, and cry; and wring out my kisses and tears. They'll blight you—they'll damn you. You loved me—then what *right* had you to leave me? What right—answer me—for the poor fancy you felt for Linton? Because misery, and degradation, and death, and nothing that God or Satan could inflict would have parted us, *you*, of your own will, did it. I have not broken your heart—*you* have broken it—and in breaking it you have broken mine. So much the worse for me, that I am strong. Do I want to live? What kind of living will it be when you—oh God! would *you* like to live with your soul in the grave?"

"Let me alone. Let me alone," sobbed Catherine. "If I've done wrong, I'm dying for it. It is enough! You left me too; but I won't upbraid you! I forgive you. Forgive me!"

"It is hard to forgive, and to look at those eyes, and feel those wasted hands," he answered. "Kiss me again; and don't let me see your eyes! I forgive what you have done to me. I love *my* murderer—but *yours*! How can I?"

They were silent—their faces hid against each other, and washed by each other's tears. At least, I suppose the weeping was on both sides; as it seemed Heathcliff *could* weep on a great occasion like this.

I grew very uncomfortable, meanwhile; for the afternoon wore fast away, the man whom I had sent off returned from his errand, and I could distinguish, by the shine of the westering sun up the valley, a concourse thickening outside Gimmerton chapel porch.

"Service is over," I announced. "My master will be here in half-an-hour."

Heathcliff groaned a curse, and strained Catherine closer—she never moved.

Ere long I perceived a group of the servants passing up the road towards the kitchen wing. Mr. Linton was not far behind; he opened the gate himself, and sauntered slowly up, probably enjoy-ing the lovely afternoon, that breathed as soft as summer.

"Now he is here," I exclaimed. "For Heaven's sake, hurry down! You'll not meet any one on the front stairs. Do be quick; and stay among the trees till he is fairly in."

"I must go, Cathy," said Heathcliff, seeking to extricate himself from his companion's arms. "But, if I live, I'll see you again before you are asleep. I won't stray five yards from your window."

"You must not go!" she answered, holding him as firmly as her strength allowed. "You shall not, I tell you."

"For one hour," he pleaded, earnestly.

"Not for one minute," she replied.

"I *must*—Linton will be up immediately," persisted the alarmed intruder.

He would have risen, and unfixed her fingers by the act—she clung fast, gasping; there was mad resolution in her face.

"No!" she shrieked. "Oh, don't, don't go. It is the last time! Edgar will not hurt us. Heathcliff, I shall die! I shall die!"

"Damn the fool. There he is!" cried Heathcliff, sinking back into his seat. "Hush, my darling! Hush, hush, Catherine! I'll stay. If he shot me so, I'd expire with a blessing on my lips."

And there they were fast again. I heard my master mounting the stairs—the cold sweat ran from my forehead; I was horrified.

"Are you going to listen to her ravings?" I said, passionately. "She does not know what she says. Will you ruin her, because she has not wit to help herself? Get up! You could be free instantly. That is the most diabolical deed that ever you did. We are all done for—master, mistress, and servant."

I wrung my hands, and cried out; and Mr. Linton hastened his step at the noise. In the midst of my agitation, I was sincerely glad to observe that Catherine's arms had fallen relaxed, and her head hung down.

"She's fainted or dead," I thought, "so much the better. Far bet-ter that she should be dead, than lingering a burden and a misery-maker to all about her."

Edgar sprang to his unbidden guest, blanched with astonish-ment and rage. What he meant to do, I cannot tell; however, the other stopped all demonstrations, at once, by placing the lifeless-looking form in his arms.

"Look there!" he said, "unless you be a fiend, help her first—then you shall speak to me!"

He walked into the parlour, and sat down. Mr. Linton summoned me, and with great difficulty, and after resorting to many means, we managed to restore her to sensation; but she was all bewildered; she sighed, and moaned, and knew nobody. Edgar, in his anxiety for her, forgot her hated friend. I did not. I went at the earliest opportunity, and besought him to depart, affirming that Catherine was better, and he should hear from me in the morning, how she passed the night.

"I shall not refuse to go out of doors," he answered; "but I shall stay in the garden; and, Nelly, mind you keep your word to-morrow. I shall be under those larch trees—mind! or I pay another visit, whether Linton be in or not."

He sent a rapid glance through the half-open door of the chamber, and ascertaining that what I stated was apparently true, delivered the house of his luckless presence.

## Chapter 2/16

About twelve o'clock, that night, was born the Catherine you saw at Wuthering Heights, a puny, seven months' child; and two hours after the mother died, having never recovered sufficient consciousness to miss Heathcliff, or know Edgar.

The latter's distraction at his bereavement is a subject too painful to be dwelt on; its after effects showed how deep the sorrow sunk.

A great addition, in my eyes, was his being left without an heir. I bemoaned that, as I gazed on the feeble orphan; and I mentally abused old Linton for—what was only natural partiality—the securing his estate to his own daughter, instead of his son's.

An unwelcomed infant it was, poor thing! It might have wailed out of life, and nobody cared a morsel, during those first hours of existence. We redeemed the neglect afterwards; but its beginning was as friendless as its end is likely to be.

Next morning—bright and cheerful out of doors—stole softened in through the blinds of the silent room, and suffused the couch and its occupant with a mellow, tender glow.

Edgar Linton had his head laid on the pillow, and his eyes shut. His young and fair features were almost as death-like as those of the form beside him, and almost as fixed; but *his* was the hush of exhausted anguish, and *hers* of perfect peace. Her brow smooth, her lids closed, her lips wearing the expression of a smile, no angel in heaven could be more beautiful than she appeared; and I partook of the infinite calm in which she lay. My mind was never in a holier frame than while I gazed on that untroubled image of Divine rest. I instinctively echoed the words she had uttered, a few hours before. "Incomparably beyond and above us all! Whether still on earth or now in Heaven, her spirit is at home with God!"

I don't know if it be a peculiarity in me, but I am seldom otherwise than happy while watching in the chamber of death, should no frenzied or despairing mourner share the duty with me. I see a repose that neither earth nor hell can break; and I feel an assurance of the endless and shadowless hereafter—the Eternity they have entered—where life is boundless in its duration, and love in its sympathy, and joy in its fulness. I noticed on that occasion how much selfishness there is even in a love like Mr. Linton's, when he so regretted Catherine's blessed release!

To be sure one might have doubted, after the wayward and impatient existence she had led, whether she merited a haven of peace at last. One might doubt in seasons of cold reflection, but not then, in the presence of her corpse. It asserted its own tranquillity, which seemed a pledge of equal quiet to its former inhabitant.

"Do you believe such people *are* happy in the other world, sir? I'd give a great deal to know."

I declined answering Mrs. Dean's question, which struck me as something heterodox. She proceeded:

"Retracing the course of Catherine Linton, I fear we have no right to think she is: but we'll leave her with her Maker."

The master looked asleep, and I ventured soon after sunrise to quit the room and steal out to the pure, refreshing air. The servants thought me gone to shake off the drowsiness of my protracted watch; in reality my chief motive was seeing Mr. Heathcliff. If he had remained among the larches all night he would have heard nothing of the stir at the Grange, unless, perhaps, he might catch the gallop of the messenger going to Gimmerton. If he had come nearer he would probably be aware, from the lights flitting to and fro, and the opening and shutting of the outer doors, that all was not right within.

I wished yet feared to find him. I felt the terrible news must be told, and I longed to get it over, but *how* to do it I did not know.

He was there—at least a few yards farther in the park; leant against an old ash tree, his hat off, and his hair soaked with the dew that had gathered on the budded branches, and fell pattering round him. He had been standing a long time in that position, for I saw a pair of ousels passing and repassing scarcely three feet from him, busy in building their nest, and regarding his proximity no more than that of a piece of timber. They flew off at my approach, and he raised his eyes and spoke:

"She's dead!" he said; "I've not waited for you to learn that. Put your handkerchief away—don't snivel before me. Damn you all! she wants none of *your* tears!"

I was weeping as much for him as her; we do sometimes pity creatures that have none of the feeling either for themselves or others; and when I first looked into his face I perceived that he had got intelligence of the catastrophe; and a foolish notion struck me that his heart was quelled, and he prayed, because his lips moved, and his gaze was bent on the ground.

"Yes, she's dead!" I answered, checking my sobs and drying my cheeks. "Gone to heaven, I hope, where we may, everyone, join her, if we take due warning, and leave our evil ways to follow good!"

"Did *she* take due warning, then?" asked Heathcliff, attempting a sneer. "Did she die like a saint? Come, give me a true history of the event. How did——"

He endeavoured to pronounce the name, but could not manage it; and compressing his mouth he held a silent combat with his inward agony, defying, meanwhile, my sympathy with an unflinching ferocious stare.

"How did she die?" he resumed at last—fain, notwithstanding his hardihood, to have a support behind him, for, after the struggle, he trembled, in spite of himself, to his very finger-ends.

"Poor wretch!" I thought; "you have a heart and nerves the same as your brother men! Why should you be anxious to conceal them? Your pride cannot blind God! You tempt Him to wring them, till He forces a cry of humiliation!"

"Quietly as a lamb!" I answered, aloud. "She drew a sigh, and stretched herself, like a child reviving, and sinking again to sleep; and five minutes after I felt one little pulse at her heart, and nothing more!"

"And—and did she ever mention me?" he asked, hesitating, as if he dreaded the answer to his question would introduce details that he could not bear to hear.

"Her senses never returned—she recognised nobody from the time you left her," I said. "She lies with a sweet smile on her face; and her latest ideas wandered back to pleasant early days. Her life closed in a gentle dream—may she wake as kindly in the other world!"

"May she wake in torment!" he cried, with frightful vehemence, stamping his foot, and groaning in a sudden paroxysm of ungovernable passion. "Why, she's a liar to the end! Where is she? Not *there*—not in heaven—not perished—where? Oh! you said you cared nothing for my sufferings! And I pray one prayer—I repeat it till my tongue stiffens—Catherine Earnshaw, may you not rest, as long as I am living! You said I killed you—haunt me, then! The murdered *do* haunt their murderers. I believe—I know that ghosts *have* wandered on earth. Be with me always—take any form—drive me mad! only *do* not leave me in this abyss, where I cannot find you! Oh, God! it is unutterable! I *cannot* live without my life! I *cannot* live without my soul!"

He dashed his head against the knotted trunk; and, lifting up his eyes, howled, not like a man, but like a savage beast being goaded to death with knives and spears.

I observed several splashes of blood about the bark of the tree, and his hand and forehead were both stained; probably the scene I witnessed was a repetition of others acted during the night. It hardly moved my compassion—it appalled me; still I felt reluctant to quit him so. But the moment he recollected himself enough to notice me watching, he thundered a command for me to go, and I obeyed. He was beyond my skill to quiet or console!

Mrs. Linton's funeral was appointed to take place on the Friday following her decease; and till then her coffin remained uncovered, and strewn with flowers and scented leaves, in the great drawing-room. Linton spent his days and nights there, a sleepless guardian; and—a circumstance concealed from all but me—Heathcliff spent his nights, at least, outside, equally a stranger to repose.

I held no communication with him; still I was conscious of his design to enter, if he could; and on the Tuesday, a little after dark, when my master, from sheer fatigue, had been compelled to retire a couple of hours, I went and opened one of the windows, moved by his perseverance to give him a chance of bestowing on the faded image of his idol one final adieu.

He did not omit to avail himself of the opportunity, cautiously and briefly; too cautiously to betray his presence by the slightest noise; indeed, I shouldn't have discovered that he had been there, except for the disarrangement of the drapery about the corpse's face, and for observing on the floor a curl of light hair, fastened with a silver thread, which, on examination, I ascertained to have been taken from a locket hung round Catherine's neck. Heathcliff had opened the trinket and cast out its contents, replacing them by a black lock of his own. I twisted the two, and enclosed them together.

Mr. Earnshaw was, of course, invited to attend the remains of his sister to the grave; and he sent no excuse, but he never came; so that, besides her husband, the mourners were wholly composed of tenants and servants. Isabella was not asked.

The place of Catherine's interment, to the surprise of the villagers, was neither in the chapel, under the carved monument of the Lintons, nor yet by the tombs of her own relations, outside. It was dug on a green slope, in a corner of the kirkyard, where the wall is so low that heath and bilberry plants have climbed over it from the moor; and peat mould almost buries it. Her husband lies in the same spot, now; and they have each a simple headstone above, and a plain gray block at their feet, to mark the graves.

## Chapter 3/17

That Friday made the last of our fine days, for a month. In the evening, the weather broke; the wind shifted from south to northeast, and brought rain first, and then sleet and snow.

On the morrow one could hardly imagine that there had been three weeks of summer: the primroses and crocuses were hidden under wintry drifts: the larks were silent, the young leaves of the early trees smitten and blackened—And dreary, and chill, and dismal that morrow did creep over! My master kept his room—I took possession of the lonely parlour, converting it into a nursery; and there I was sitting, with the moaning doll of a child laid on my knee, rocking it to and fro, and watching, meanwhile, the still driving flakes build up the uncurtained window, when the door opened, and some person entered, out of breath and laughing!

My anger was greater than my astonishment for a minute; I supposed it one of the maids, and I cried,

"Have done! How dare you show your giddiness here? What would Mr. Linton say if he heard you?"

"Excuse me!" answered a familiar voice, "but I know Edgar is in bed, and I cannot stop myself."

With that, the speaker came forward to the fire, panting and holding her hand to her side.

"I have run the whole way from Wuthering Heights!" she continued, after a pause. "Except where I've flown—I couldn't count the number of falls I've had—Oh, I'm aching all over! Don't be alarmed—There shall be an explanation as soon as I can give it— only just have the goodness to step out and order the carriage to take me on to Gimmerton, and tell a servant to seek up a few clothes in my wardrobe."

The intruder was Mrs. Heathcliff—she certainly seemed in no laughing predicament: her hair streamed on her shoulders, dripping with snow and water; she was dressed in the girlish dress she commonly wore, befitting her age more than her position; a low frock, with short sleeves, and nothing on either head or neck. The frock was of light silk, and clung to her with wet, and her feet were protected merely by thin slippers; add to this a deep cut under one ear, which only the cold prevented from bleeding profusely, a white face scratched and bruised, and a frame hardly able to support itself through fatigue, and you may fancy my first fright was not much allayed when I had had leisure to examine her.

"My dear young lady," I exclaimed, "I'll stir nowhere, and hear nothing, till you have removed every article of your clothes, and put on dry things; and certainly you shall not go to Gimmerton tonight; so it is needless to order the carriage."

"Certainly, I shall," she said; "walking or riding—yet I've no objection to dress myself decently; and—ah, see how it flows down my neck now! The fire does make it smart."

She insisted on my fulfilling her directions, before she would let me touch her; and not till after the coachman had been instructed to get ready, and a maid set to pack up some necessary attire, did I obtain her consent for binding the wound and helping to change her garments.

"Now, Ellen," she said, when my task was finished, and she was seated in an easy chair on the hearth, with a cup of tea before her, "You sit down opposite me, and put poor Catherine's baby away—I don't like to see it! You mustn't think I care little for Catherine, because I behaved so foolishly on entering—I've cried, too, bitterly—yes, more than any one else has reason to cry—we parted unreconciled, you remember, and I shan't forgive myself. But for all that, I was not going to sympathise with him—the brute beast! O, give me the poker! This is the last thing of his I have about me"; she slipped the gold ring from her third finger, and threw it on the floor. "I'll smash it!" she continued, striking it with childish spite, "and then I'll burn it!" and she took and dropped the misused article among the coals. "There! he shall buy another, if he gets me back again. He'd be capable of coming to seek me, to tease Edgar—I dare not stay, lest that notion should possess his wicked head! And besides, Edgar has not been kind, has he? And I won't come suing for his assistance; nor will I bring him into more trouble—Necessity compelled me to seek shelter here; though if I had not learnt he was out of the way, I'd have halted at the kitchen, washed my face, warmed myself, got you to bring what I wanted, and departed again to anywhere out of the reach of my accursed—of that incarnate goblin! Ah, he was in such a fury—if he had caught me! It's a pity Earnshaw is not his match in strength—I wouldn't have run till I'd seen him all but demolished, had Hindley been able to do it!"

"Well, don't talk so fast, Miss!" I interrupted, "you'll disorder the handkerchief I have tied round your face, and make the cut bleed again—Drink your tea, and take breath, and give over laughing— Laughter is sadly out of place under this roof, and in your condition!"

"An undeniable truth," she replied. "Listen to that child! It maintains a constant wail—send it out of my hearing, for an hour; I shan't stay any longer."

I rang the bell, and committed it to a servant's care; and then I inquired what had urged her to escape from Wuthering Heights in such an unlikely plight—and where she meant to go, as she refused remaining with us?

"I ought, and I wish to remain," answered she, "to cheer Edgar and take care of the baby, for two things, and because the Grange is my right home—but I tell you, he wouldn't let me! Do you think he could bear to see me grow fat and merry; and could bear to think that we were tranquil, and not resolve on poisoning our comfort?

Now, I have the satisfaction of being sure that he detests me to the point of its annoying him seriously to have me within ear-shot, or eye-sight—I notice, when I enter his presence, the muscles of his countenance are involuntarily distorted into an expression of hatred; partly arising from his knowledge of the good causes I have to feel that sentiment for him, and partly from original aversion—It is strong enough to make me feel pretty certain that he would not chase me over England, supposing I contrived a clear escape; and therefore I must get quite away. I've recovered from my first desire to be killed by him. I'd rather he'd kill himself! He has extinguished my love effectually, and so I'm at my ease. I can recollect yet how I loved him; and can dimly imagine that I could still be loving him, if—No, no! Even if he had doted on me, the devilish nature would have revealed its existence, somehow. Catherine had an awfully perverted taste to esteem him so dearly, knowing him so well—Monster! would that he could be blotted out of creation, and out of my memory!"

"Hush, hush! He's a human being," I said. "Be more charitable; there are worse men than he is yet!"

"He's not a human being," she retorted; "and he has no claim on my charity—I gave him my heart, and he took and pinched it to death; and flung it back to me—people feel with their hearts, Ellen, and since he has destroyed mine, I have not power to feel for him, and I would not, though he groaned from this to his dying day, and wept tears of blood for Catherine! No, indeed, indeed, I wouldn't!" And here Isabella began to cry; but, immediately dashing the water from her lashes, she recommenced.

"You asked, what has driven me to flight at last? I was compelled to attempt it, because I had succeeded in rousing his rage a pitch above his malignity. Pulling out the nerves with red hot pincers requires more coolness than knocking on the head. He was worked up to forget the fiendish prudence he boasted of, and proceeding to murderous violence: I experienced pleasure in being able to exasperate him: the sense of pleasure woke my instinct of self-preservation, so I fairly broke free; and if ever I come into his hands again he is welcome to a signal revenge.

"Yesterday, you know, Mr. Earnshaw should have been at the funeral. He kept himself sober for the purpose—tolerably sober; not going to bed mad at six o'clock and getting up drunk at twelve. Consequently, he rose, in suicidal low spirits, as fit for the church as for a dance; and instead, he sat down by the fire, and swallowed gin or brandy by tumblerfuls.

"Heathcliff—I shudder to name him!—has been a stranger in the house from last Sunday till to-day—Whether the angels have fed him, or his kin beneath, I cannot tell; but he has not eaten a meal with us for nearly a week—He has just come home at dawn, and gone upstairs to his chamber; locking himself in—as if anybody dreamt of coveting his company! There he has continued, praying like a Methodist; only the deity he implored is senseless dust and ashes; and God, when addressed, was curiously confounded with his own black father! After concluding these precious orisons—and they lasted generally till he grew hoarse and his voice was strangled in his throat—he would be off again; always straight down to the Grange! I wonder Edgar did not send for a constable, and give him into custody! For me, grieved as I was about Catherine, it was impossible to avoid regarding this season of deliverance from degrading oppression as a holiday.

"I recovered spirits sufficient to hear Joseph's eternal lectures without weeping; and to move up and down the house, less with the foot of a frightened thief than formerly. You wouldn't think that I should cry at anything Joseph could say, but he and Hareton are detestable companions. I'd rather sit with Hindley, and hear his awful talk, than with 't' little maister,' and his stanch supporter, that odious old man!

"When Heathcliff is in, I'm often obliged to seek the kitchen, and their society, or starve among the damp, uninhabited chambers; when he is not, as was the case this week, I establish a table and chair at one corner of the house fire, and never mind how Mr. Earnshaw may occupy himself; and he does not interfere with my arrangements: he is quieter, now, than he used to be, if no one provokes him; more sullen and depressed, and less furious. Joseph affirms he's sure he's an altered man; that the Lord has touched his heart, and he is saved 'so as by fire.'[1] I'm puzzled to detect signs of the favourable change, but it is not my business.

"Yester-evening, I sat in my nook reading some old books till late on towards twelve. It seemed so dismal to go upstairs, with the wild

[1]In I Corinthians 3.15, Paul says the spiritual person may be saved though the physical person has been tested and failed, as if burned in a fire.

snow blowing outside, and my thoughts continually reverting to the kirkyard and the new made grave! I dared hardly lift my eyes from the page before me, that melancholy scene so instantly usurped its place.

"Hindley sat opposite, his head leant on his hand, perhaps meditating on the same subject. He had ceased drinking at a point below irrationality, and had neither stirred nor spoken during two or three hours. There was no sound through the house but the moaning wind which shook the windows every now and then, the faint crackling of the coals, and the click of my snuffers as I removed at intervals the long wick of the candle. Hareton and Joseph were probably fast asleep in bed. It was very, very sad, and while I read, I sighed, for it seemed as if all joy had vanished from the world, never to be restored.

"The doleful silence was broken, at length, by the sound of the kitchen latch—Heathcliff had returned from his watch earlier than usual, owing, I suppose, to the sudden storm.

"That entrance was fastened, and we heard him coming round to get in by the other. I rose with an irrepressible expression of what I felt on my lips, which induced my companion, who had been staring towards the door, to turn and look at me.

"'I'll keep him out five minutes,' he exclaimed. 'You won't object?'

"'No, you may keep him out the whole night, for me,' I answered. 'Do! put the key in the lock, and draw the bolts.'

"Earnshaw accomplished this ere his guest reached the front; he then came and brought his chair to the other side of my table, leaning over it and searching in my eyes for a sympathy with the burning hate that gleamed from his: as he both looked and felt like an assassin, he couldn't exactly find that; but he discovered enough to encourage him to speak.

"'You and I,' he said, 'have each a great debt to settle with the man out yonder! If we were neither of us cowards, we might combine to discharge it. Are you as soft as your brother? Are you willing to endure to the last, and not once attempt a repayment?'

"'I'm weary of enduring now,' I replied, 'and I'd be glad of a retaliation that wouldn't recoil on myself; but treachery and violence are spears pointed at both ends—they wound those who resort to them, worse than their enemies.'

"'Treachery and violence are a just return for treachery and violence!' cried Hindley. 'Mrs. Heathcliff, I'll ask you to do nothing, but sit still, and be dumb—Tell me now, can you? I'm sure you would have as much pleasure as I, in witnessing the conclusion of the fiend's existence: he'll be *your* death unless you overreach him—and he'll be *my* ruin—Damn the hellish villain! He knocks at the door as if he were master here already! Promise to hold your tongue, and before that clock strikes—it wants three minutes of one—you're a free woman!'

"He took the implements which I described to you in my letter from his breast, and would have turned down the candle—I snatched it away, however, and seized his arm.

"'I'll not hold my tongue!' I said, 'You mustn't touch him . . . Let the door remain shut and be quiet!'

"'No! I've formed my resolution, and by God, I'll execute it!' cried the desperate being. 'I'll do you a kindness in spite of yourself, and Hareton justice! And you needn't trouble your head to screen me, Catherine is gone—Nobody alive would regret me, or be ashamed, though I cut my throat this minute—and it's time to make an end!'

"I might as well have struggled with a bear, or reasoned with a lunatic. The only resource left me was to run to a lattice, and warn his intended victim of the fate which awaited him.

"'You'd better seek shelter somewhere else to-night!' I exclaimed in rather a triumphant tone. 'Mr. Earnshaw has a mind to shoot you, if you resist in endeavouring to enter.'

"'You'd better open the door, you—' he answered, addressing me by some elegant term that I don't care to repeat.

"'I shall not meddle in the matter,' I retorted again. 'Come in and get shot, if you please! I've done my duty.'

"With that I shut the window, and returned to my place by the fire; having too small a stock of hypocrisy at my command to pretend any anxiety for the danger that menaced him.

"Earnshaw swore passionately at me; affirming that I loved the villain yet, and calling me all sorts of names for the base spirit I evinced. And I, in my secret heart (and conscience never reproached me) thought what a blessing it would be for *him*, should Heathcliff put him out of misery, and what a blessing for *me*, should he send Heathcliff to his right abode! As I sat nursing these reflections, the casement behind me was banged on to the floor by a blow from the latter individual, and his black countenance looked blightingly through. The stanchions stood too close to suffer his shoulders to follow, and I smiled, exulting in my fancied security. His hair and clothes were whitened with snow, and his sharp cannibal teeth, revealed by cold and wrath, gleamed through the dark.

"'Isabella, let me in, or I'll make you repent!' he 'girned',[2] as Joseph calls it.

"'I cannot commit murder,' I replied. 'Mr. Hindley stands sentinel with a knife and loaded pistol.'

"'Let me in by the kitchen door!' he said.

"'Hindley will be there before me,' I answered. 'And that's a poor love of yours, that cannot bear a shower of snow! We were left at peace in our beds, as long as the summer moon shone, but the moment a blast of winter returns, you must run for shelter! Heathcliff, if I were you, I'd go stretch myself over her grave, and die like a faithful dog . . . The world is surely not worth living in now, is it? You had distinctly impressed on me the idea that Catherine was the whole joy of your life—I can't imagine how you think of surviving her loss.'

"'He's there . . . is he?' exclaimed my companion, rushing to the gap. 'If I can get my arm out I can hit him!'

"I'm afraid, Ellen, you'll set me down as really wicked—but you don't know all, so don't judge! I wouldn't have aided or abetted an attempt on even *his* life, for anything—Wish that he were dead, I must; and therefore I was fearfully disappointed, and unnerved by terror for the consequences of my taunting speech, when he flung himself on Earnshaw's weapon and wrenched it from his grasp.

"The charge exploded, and the knife, in springing back, closed into its owner's wrist. Heathcliff pulled it away by main force, slitting up the flesh as it passed on, and thrust it dripping into his pocket. He then took a stone, struck down the division between two windows and sprung in. His adversary had fallen senseless with excessive pain, and the flow of blood that gushed from an artery, or a large vein.

"The ruffian kicked and trampled on him, and dashed his head repeatedly against the flags; holding me with one hand, meantime, to prevent me summoning Joseph.

"He exerted preter-human self-denial in abstaining from finishing him completely; but getting out of breath, he finally desisted, and dragged the apparently inanimate body on to the settle.

[2]Snarled.

"There he tore off the sleeve of Earnshaw's coat, and bound up the wound with brutal roughness, spitting and cursing during the operation, as energetically as he had kicked before.

"Being at liberty, I lost no time in seeking the old servant; who, having gathered by degrees the purport of my hasty tale, hurried below, gasping, as he descended the steps two at once.

"'Whet is thur tuh do, nah? whet is thur tuh do, nah?'

"'There's this to do,' thundered Heathcliff, 'that your master's mad; and should he last another month, I'll have him to an asylum. And how the devil did you come to fasten me out, you toothless hound? Don't stand muttering and mumbling there. Come, I'm not going to nurse him. Wash that stuff away; and mind the sparks of your candle—it is more than half brandy!'

"'Und soa, yah been murthering on him?' exclaimed Joseph, lifting his hands and eyes in horror. 'If iver Aw seed a seeght loike this! May the Lord—'

"Heathcliff gave him a push onto his knees, in the middle of the blood, and flung a towel to him; but instead of proceeding to dry it up, he joined his hands, and began a prayer which excited my laughter from its odd phraseology. I was in the condition of mind to be shocked at nothing; in fact, I was as reckless as some malefactors show themselves at the foot of the gallows.

"'Oh, I forgot you,' said the tyrant, 'you shall do that. Down with you. And you conspire with him against me, do you, viper? There, that is work fit for you!'

"He shook me till my teeth rattled, and pitched me beside Joseph, who steadily concluded his supplications, and then rose, vowing he would set off for the Grange directly. Mr. Linton was a magistrate, and though he had fifty wives dead, he should inquire into this.

"He was so obstinate in his resolution that Heathcliff deemed it expedient to compel, from my lips, a recapitulation of what had taken place; standing over me, heaving with malevolence, as I reluctantly delivered the account in answer to his questions.

"It required a great deal of labour to satisfy the old man that he was not the aggressor; especially with my hardly wrung replies. However, Mr. Earnshaw soon convinced him that he was alive still; he hastened to administer a dose of spirits, and by their succour his master presently regained motion and consciousness.

"Heathcliff, aware that he was ignorant of the treatment received while insensible, called him deliriously intoxicated; and said he should not notice his atrocious conduct further, but advised him to get to bed. To my joy, he left us after giving this judicious counsel, and Hindley stretched himself on the hearth-stone. I departed to my own room, marvelling that I had escaped so easily.

"This morning, when I came down, about half-an-hour before noon, Mr. Earnshaw was sitting by the fire, deadly sick; his evil genius, almost as gaunt and ghastly, leant against the chimney. Neither appeared inclined to dine; and having waited till all was cold on the table, I commenced alone.

"Nothing hindered me from eating heartily; and I experienced a certain sense of satisfaction and superiority, as, at intervals, I cast a look towards my silent companions, and felt the comfort of a quiet conscience within me.

"After I had done, I ventured on the unusual liberty of drawing near the fire, going round Earnshaw's seat, and kneeling in the corner beside him.

"Heathcliff did not glance my way, and I gazed up and contemplated his features almost as confidently as if they had been turned to stone. His forehead, that I once thought so manly, and that I now think so diabolical, was shaded with a heavy cloud; his basilisk eyes were nearly quenched by sleeplessness—and weeping, perhaps, for the lashes were wet then: his lips devoid of their ferocious sneer, and sealed in an expression of unspeakable sadness. Had it been another, I would have covered my face, in the presence of such grief. In *his* case, I was gratified; and, ignoble as it seems to insult a fallen enemy, I couldn't miss this chance of sticking in a dart; his weakness was the only time when I could taste the delight of paying wrong for wrong."

"Fie, fie, Miss!" I interrupted. "One might suppose you had never opened a Bible in your life. If God afflict your enemies, surely that ought to suffice you.[3] It is both mean and presumptuous to add your torture to his!"

"In general, I'll allow that it would be, Ellen," she continued. "But what misery laid on Heathcliff could content me, unless I have a hand in it? I'd rather he suffered *less*, if I might cause his suf-

---

[3]Psalms 55 urges reliance on God to punish one's enemies (18–23).

ferings, and he might *know* that I was the cause. Oh, I owe him so much. On only one condition can I hope to forgive him. It is, if I may take an eye for an eye, a tooth for a tooth,[4] for every wrench of agony return a wrench, reduce him to my level. As he was the first to injure, make him the first to implore pardon; and then— why, then, Ellen, I might show you some generosity. But it is utterly impossible I can ever be revenged, and therefore I cannot forgive him. Hindley wanted some water, and I handed him a glass, and asked him how he was.

"'Not as ill as I wish,' he replied. 'But leaving out my arm, every inch of me is as sore as if I had been fighting with a legion of imps!'

"'Yes, no wonder,' was my next remark. 'Catherine used to boast that she stood between you and bodily harm—she meant that certain persons would not hurt you, for fear of offending her. It's well people don't *really* rise from their grave, or, last night, she might have witnessed a repulsive scene! Are not you bruised, and cut over your chest and shoulders?'

"'I can't say,' he answered; 'but what do you mean? Did he dare to strike me when I was down?'

"'He trampled on, and kicked you, and dashed you on the ground,' I whispered. 'And his mouth watered to tear you with his teeth; because he's only half a man—not so much.'

"Mr. Earnshaw looked up, like me, to the countenance of our mutual foe; who, absorbed in his anguish, seemed insensible to anything around him; the longer he stood, the plainer his reflections revealed their blackness through his features.

"'Oh, if God would but give me strength to strangle him in my last agony, I'd go to hell with joy,' groaned the impatient man, writhing to rise, and sinking back in despair, convinced of his inadequacy for the struggle.

"'Nay, it's enough that he has murdered one of you,' I observed aloud. 'At the Grange, every one knows your sister would have been living now, had it not been for Mr. Heathcliff. After all, it is preferable to be hated than loved by him. When I recollect how happy we were—how happy Catherine was before he came—I'm fit to curse the day.'

[4]The law of retributive justice in the Old Testament or Hebrew Bible (Exodus 21.24).

"Most likely, Heathcliff noticed more the truth of what was said, than the spirit of the person who said it. His attention was roused, I saw, for his eyes rained down tears among the ashes, and he drew his breath in suffocating sighs.

"I stared full at him, and laughed scornfully. The clouded windows of hell flashed a moment towards me; the fiend which usually looked out, however, was so dimmed and drowned that I did not fear to hazard another sound of derision.

"'Get up, and begone out of my sight,' said the mourner.

"I guessed he uttered those words, at least, though his voice was hardly intelligible.

"'I beg your pardon,' I replied. 'But I loved Catherine too; and her brother requires attendance which, for her sake, I shall supply. Now that she's dead, I see her in Hindley; Hindley has exactly her eyes, if you had not tried to gouge them out, and made them black and red, and her—'

"'Get up, wretched idiot, before I stamp you to death!' he cried, making a movement that caused me to make one also.

"'But, then,' I continued, holding myself ready to flee; 'if poor Catherine had trusted you, and assumed the ridiculous, contemptible, degrading title of Mrs. Heathcliff, she would soon have presented a similar picture! *She* wouldn't have borne your abominable behaviour quietly; her detestation and disgust must have found voice.'

"The back of the settle and Earnshaw's person interposed between me and him; so instead of endeavouring to reach me, he snatched a dinner knife from the table and flung it at my head. It struck beneath my ear, and stopped the sentence I was uttering; but, pulling it out, I sprang to the door and delivered another which I hope went a little deeper than his missile.

"The last glimpse I caught of him was a furious rush on his part, checked by the embrace of his host; and both fell locked together on the hearth.

"In my flight through the kitchen I bade Joseph speed to his master; I knocked over Hareton, who was hanging a litter of puppies from a chair-back in the doorway; and, blest as a soul escaped from purgatory, I bounded, leaped, and flew down the steep road: then, quitting its windings, shot direct across the moor, rolling over banks, and wading through marshes; precipitating myself, in fact, towards the beacon light of the Grange. And far rather would I be condemned to a perpetual dwelling in the infernal regions, than even for one night abide beneath the roof of Wuthering Heights again."

Isabella ceased speaking, and took a drink of tea; then she rose, and bidding me put on her bonnet, and a great shawl I had brought, and turning a deaf ear to my entreaties for her to remain another hour, she stepped onto a chair, kissed Edgar's and Catherine's portraits, bestowed a similar salute on me, and descended to the carriage accompanied by Fanny, who yelped wild with joy at recovering her mistress. She was driven away, never to revisit this neighbourhood; but a regular correspondence was established between her and my master when things were more settled.

I believe her new abode was in the south, near London; there she had a son born, a few months subsequent to her escape. He was christened Linton, and, from the first, she reported him to be an ailing, peevish creature.

Mr. Heathcliff, meeting me one day in the village, inquired where she lived. I refused to tell. He remarked that it was not of any moment, only she must beware of coming to her brother; she should not be with him, if he had to keep her himself.

Though I would give no information, he discovered, through some of the other servants, both her place of residence and the existence of the child. Still he didn't molest her; for which forbearance she might thank his aversion, I suppose.

He often asked about the infant, when he saw me; and on hearing its name, smiled grimly, and observed:

"They wish me to hate it too, do they?"

"I don't think they wish you to know any thing about it," I answered.

"But I'll have it," he said, "when I want it. They may reckon on that!"

Fortunately, its mother died before the time arrived, some thirteen years after the decease of Catherine, when Linton was twelve, or a little more.

On the day succeeding Isabella's unexpected visit, I had no opportunity of speaking to my master: he shunned conversation, and was fit for discussing nothing. When I could get him to listen, I saw it pleased him that his sister had left her husband, whom he abhorred with an intensity which the mildness of his nature would scarcely seem to al-

low. So deep and sensitive was his aversion, that he refrained from
going anywhere where he was likely to see or hear of Heathcliff.
Grief, and that together, transformed him into a complete hermit: he
threw up his office of magistrate, ceased even to attend church,
avoided the village on all occasions, and spent a life of entire seclusion within the limits of his park and grounds: only varied by solitary
rambles on the moors, and visits to the grave of his wife, mostly at
evening, or early morning before other wanderers were abroad.

But he was too good to be thoroughly unhappy long. *He* didn't
pray for Catherine's soul to haunt him. Time brought resignation,
and a melancholy sweeter than common joy. He recalled her memory with ardent, tender love, and hopeful aspiring to the better
world, where, he doubted not, she was gone.

And he had earthly consolation and affections, also. For a few
days, I said, he seemed regardless of the puny successor to the departed; that coldness melted as fast as snow in April, and ere the
tiny thing could stammer a word or totter a step, it wielded a
despot's sceptre in his heart.

It was named Catherine, but he never called it the name in full,
as he had never called the first Catherine short, probably because
Heathcliff had a habit of doing so. The little one was always Cathy:
it formed to him a distinction from the mother, and yet a connection with her; and his attachment sprang from its relation to her,
far more than from its being his own.

I used to draw a comparison between him and Hindley Earnshaw, and perplex myself to explain satisfactorily why their conduct
was so opposite in similar circumstances. They had both been fond
husbands, and were both attached to their children; and I could not
see how they shouldn't both have taken the same road, for good or
evil. But, I thought in my mind, Hindley, with apparently the
stronger head, has shown himself sadly the worse and the weaker
man. When his ship struck,[5] the captain abandoned his post; and the
crew, instead of trying to save her, rushed into riot and confusion,
leaving no hope for their luckless vessel. Linton, on the contrary, displayed the true courage of a loyal and faithful soul: he trusted God;
and God comforted him. One hoped, and the other despaired: they
chose their own lots, and were righteously doomed to endure them.

[5]Ran aground.

But you'll not want to hear my moralizing, Mr. Lockwood: you'll judge as well as I can, all these things; at least, you'll think you will, and that's the same.

The end of Earnshaw was what might have been expected: it followed fast on his sister's, there were scarcely six months between them. We, at the Grange, never got a very succinct account of his state preceding it; all that I did learn, was on occasion of going to aid in the preparations for the funeral. Mr. Kenneth came to announce the event to my master.

"Well, Nelly," said he, riding into the yard one morning, too early not to alarm me with an instant presentiment of bad news. "It's yours and my turn to go into mourning at present. Who's given us the slip now, do you think?"

"Who?" I asked in a flurry.

"Why, guess!" he returned, dismounting, and slinging his bridle on a hook by the door. "And nip up the corner of your apron; I'm certain you'll need it."

"Not Mr. Heathcliff, surely?" I exclaimed.

"What! would you have tears for him?" said the doctor. "No, Heathcliff's a tough young fellow; he looks blooming to-day—I've just seen him. He's rapidly regaining flesh since he lost his better half."

"Who is it, then, Mr. Kenneth?" I repeated impatiently.

"Hindley Earnshaw! Your old friend Hindley—" he replied, "and my wicked gossip; though he's been too wild for me this long while. There! I said we should draw water—But cheer up! He died true to his character, drunk as a lord—Poor lad; I'm sorry, too. One can't help missing an old companion; though he had the worst tricks with him that ever man imagined, and has done me many a rascally turn—He's barely twenty-seven, it seems; that's your own age; who would have thought you were born in one year!"

I confess this blow was greater to me than the shock of Mrs. Linton's death: ancient associations lingered round my heart; I sat down in the porch and wept as for a blood relation, desiring Mr. Kenneth to get another servant to introduce him to the master.

I could not hinder myself from pondering on the question—"Had he had fair play?" Whatever I did, that idea would bother me. It was so tiresomely pertinacious that I resolved on requesting leave to go to Wuthering Heights, and assist in the last duties to the dead. Mr. Linton was extremely reluctant to consent, but I pleaded eloquently for the friendless condition in which he lay; and I said my old master and foster-brother had a claim on my services as strong as his own. Besides, I reminded him that the child, Hareton, was his wife's nephew, and, in the absence of nearer kin, he ought to act as its guardian; and he ought to and must inquire how the property was left, and look over the concerns of his brother-in-law.

He was unfit for attending to such matters then, but he bid me speak to his lawyer; and at length permitted me to go. His lawyer had been Earnshaw's also: I called at the village, and asked him to accompany me. He shook his head, and advised that Heathcliff should be let alone; affirming, if the truth were known, Hareton would be found little else than a beggar.

"His father died in debt," he said; "the whole property is mortgaged, and the sole chance for the natural heir is to allow him an opportunity of creating some interest in the creditor's heart, that he may be inclined to deal leniently towards him."

When I reached the Heights, I explained that I had come to see everything carried on decently, and Joseph, who appeared in sufficient distress, expressed satisfaction at my presence. Mr. Heathcliff said he did not perceive that I was wanted, but I might stay and order the arrangements for the funeral, if I chose.

"Correctly," he remarked, "that fool's body should be buried at the cross-roads,[6] without ceremony of any kind—I happened to leave him ten minutes, yesterday afternoon; and, in that interval, he fastened the two doors of the house against me, and he has spent the night in drinking himself to death deliberately! We broke in this morning, for we heard him snorting like a horse; and there he was, laid over the settle—flaying and scalping would not have wakened him—I sent for Kenneth, and he came; but not till the beast had changed into carrion—he was both dead and cold, and stark; and so you'll allow, it was useless making more stir about him!"

The old servant confirmed this statement, but muttered,

"Aw'd rayther he'd goan hisseln fur t' doctor! Aw sud uh taen tent uh' t' maister better nur him—un' he warn't deead when Aw left, nowt uh t' soart!"[7]

---

[6]Because suicide is a mortal sin, the corpse is denied Christian burial in a churchyard.

[7]"I'd rather he'd gone himself for the doctor! I should have taken care of the master better than him—and he wasn't dead when I left, nothing of the sort!"

I insisted on the funeral being respectable—Mr. Heathcliff said I might have my own way there too; only, he desired me to remember that the money for the whole affair came out of his pocket.

He maintained a hard, careless deportment, indicative of neither joy nor sorrow; if anything, it expressed a flinty gratification at a piece of difficult work successfully executed. I observed once, indeed, something like exultation in his aspect. It was just when the people were bearing the coffin from the house; he had the hypocrisy to represent a mourner; and previous to following with Hareton, he lifted the unfortunate child on to the table, and muttered, with peculiar gusto,

"Now, my bonny lad, you are *mine*! And we'll see if one tree won't grow as crooked as another, with the same wind to twist it!"

The unsuspecting thing was pleased at this speech; he played with Heathcliff's whiskers, and stroked his cheek; but I divined its meaning, and observed tartly,

"That boy must go back with me to Thrushcross Grange, sir— There is nothing in the world less yours than he is!"

"Does Linton say so?" he demanded.

"Of course—he has ordered me to take him," I replied.

"Well," said the scoundrel, "We'll not argue the subject now; but I have a fancy to try my hand at rearing a young one, so intimate to your master that I must supply the place of this with my own, if he attempt to remove it; I don't engage to let Hareton go, undisputed; but I'll be pretty sure to make the other come! Remember to tell him."

This hint was enough to bind our hands. I repeated its substance on my return, and Edgar Linton, little interested at the commencement, spoke no more of interfering. I'm not aware that he could have done it to any purpose, had he been ever so willing.

The guest was now the master of Wuthering Heights: he held firm possession, and proved to the attorney, who, in his turn, proved it to Mr. Linton, that Earnshaw had mortgaged every yard of land he owned for cash to supply his mania for gaming; and he, Heathcliff, was the mortgagee.

In that manner, Hareton, who should now be the first gentleman in the neighbourhood, was reduced to a state of complete dependence on his father's inveterate enemy; and lives in his own house as a servant deprived of the advantage of wages, and quite unable to right himself, because of his friendlessness and his ignorance that he has been wronged.

## Chapter 4/18

The twelve years, continued Mrs. Dean, following that dismal period, were the happiest of my life: my greatest troubles, in their passage, rose from our little lady's trifling illnesses, which she had to experience in common with all children, rich and poor.

For the rest, after the first six months, she grew like a larch; and could walk and talk too, in her own way, before the heath blossomed a second time over Mrs. Linton's dust.

She was the most winning thing that ever brought sunshine into a desolate house—a real beauty in face—with the Earnshaws' handsome dark eyes, but the Lintons' fair skin, and small features, and yellow curling hair. Her spirit was high, though not rough, and qualified by a heart sensitive and lively to excess in its affections. That capacity for intense attachments reminded me of her mother; still she did not resemble her; for she could be soft and mild as a dove, and she had a gentle voice, and pensive expression: her anger was never furious; her love never fierce; it was deep and tender.

However, it must be acknowledged, she had faults to foil her gifts. A propensity to be saucy was one; and a perverse will that indulged children invariably acquire, whether they be good tempered or cross. If a servant chanced to vex her, it was always: "I shall tell papa!" And if he reproved her, even by a look, you would have thought it a heart-breaking business: I don't believe he ever did speak a harsh word to her.

He took her education entirely on himself, and made it an amusement: fortunately, curiosity and a quick intellect urged her into an apt scholar; she learnt rapidly and eagerly, and did honour to his teaching.

Till she reached the age of thirteen, she had not once been beyond the range of the park by herself. Mr. Linton would take her with him a mile or so outside, on rare occasions; but he trusted her to no one else. Gimmerton was an unsubstantial name in her ears; the chapel, the only building she had approached or entered, except her own home; Wuthering Heights and Mr. Heathcliff did not exist for her; she was a perfect recluse; and, apparently, perfectly contented. Sometimes, indeed, while surveying the country from her nursery window, she would observe—

"Ellen, how long will it be before I can walk to the top of those hills? I wonder what lies on the other side—is it the sea?"

"No, Miss Cathy," I would answer; "it is hills again just like these."

"And what are those golden rocks like, when you stand under them?" she once asked.

The abrupt descent of Penistone Craggs particularly attracted her notice, especially when the setting sun shone on it and the topmost Heights, and the whole extent of landscape besides lay in shadow.

I explained that they were bare masses of stone, with hardly enough earth in their clefts to nourish a stunted tree.

"And why are they bright so long after it is evening here?" she pursued.

"Because they are a great deal higher up than we are," replied I; "you could not climb them, they are too high and steep. In winter the frost is always there before it comes to us; and, deep into summer, I have found snow under that black hollow on the north-east side!"

"Oh, you have been on them!" she cried, gleefully. "Then I can go, too, when I am a woman. Has papa been, Ellen?"

"Papa would tell you, Miss," I answered hastily, "that they are not worth the trouble of visiting. The moors, where you ramble with him, are much nicer; and Thrushcross park is the finest place in the world."

"But I know the park, and I don't know those," she murmured to herself. "And I should delight to look round me from the brow of that tallest point—my little pony, Minny, shall take me some time."

One of the maids mentioning the Fairy cave, quite turned her head with a desire to fulfil this project; she teased Mr. Linton about it; and he promised she should have the journey when she got older: but Miss Catherine measured her age by months, and—

"Now, am I old enough to go to Penistone Crags?" was the constant question in her mouth.

The road thither wound close by Wuthering Heights. Edgar had not the heart to pass it; so she received as constantly the answer.

"Not yet, love, not yet."

I said Mrs. Heathcliff lived above a dozen years after quitting her husband. Her family were of a delicate constitution: she and

Edgar both lacked the ruddy health that you will generally meet in these parts. What her last illness was, I am not certain; I conjecture they died of the same thing, a kind of fever, slow at its commencement, but incurable, and rapidly consuming life towards the close. She wrote to inform her brother of the probable conclusion of a four months' indisposition under which she had suffered; and entreated him to come to her, if possible, for she had much to settle, and she wished to bid him adieu, and deliver Linton safely into his hands. Her hope was, that Linton might be left with him, as he had been with her; his father, she would fain convince herself, had no desire to assume the burden of his maintenance or education.

My master hesitated not a moment in complying with her request; reluctant as he was to leave home at ordinary calls, he flew to answer this; commending Catherine to my peculiar vigilance, in his absence, with reiterated orders that she must not wander out of the park, even under my escort; he did not calculate on her going unaccompanied.

He was away three weeks: the first day or two, my charge sat in a corner of the library, too sad for either reading or playing: in that quiet state she caused me little trouble; but it was succeeded by an interval of impatient, fretful weariness; and being too busy, and too old then, to run up and down amusing her, I hit on a method by which she might entertain herself.

I used to send her on her travels round the grounds—now on foot, and now on a pony; indulging her with a patient audience of all her real and imaginary adventures, when she returned.

The summer shone in full prime; and she took such a taste for this solitary rambling that she often contrived to remain out from breakfast till tea; and then the evenings were spent in recounting her fanciful tales. I did not fear her breaking bounds, because the gates were generally locked, and I thought she would scarcely venture forth alone, if they had stood wide open.

Unluckily, my confidence proved misplaced. Catherine came to me, one morning at eight o'clock, and said she was that day an Arabian merchant, going to cross the Desert with his caravan; and I must give her plenty of provision for herself and beasts: a horse, and three camels, personated by a large hound and a couple of pointers.

I got together good store of dainties, and slung them in a basket on one side of the saddle; and she sprang up as gay as a fairy, sheltered by her wide-brimmed hat and gauze veil from the July sun, and trotted off with a merry laugh, mocking my cautious counsel to avoid galloping, and come back early.

The naughty thing never made her appearance at tea. One traveller, the hound, being an old dog and fond of its ease, returned; but neither Cathy, nor the pony, nor the two pointers were visible in any direction; I despatched emissaries down this path, and that path, and, at last, went wandering in search of her myself.

There was a labourer working at a fence round a plantation, on the borders of the grounds. I enquired of him if he had seen our young lady.

"I saw her at morn," he replied; "she would have me to cut her a hazel switch, and then she leapt her galloway[1] over the hedge yonder, where it is lowest, and galloped out of sight."

You may guess how I felt at hearing this news. It struck me directly she must have started for Penistone Craggs.

"What will become of her?" I ejaculated, pushing through a gap which the man was repairing, and making straight to the high road.

I walked as if for a wager, mile after mile, till a turn brought me in view of the Heights, but no Catherine could I detect, far or near.

The Craggs lie about a mile and a half beyond Mr. Heathcliff's place, and that is four from the Grange, so I began to fear night would fall ere I could reach them.

"And what if she should have slipped in clambering among them," I reflected, "and been killed, or broken some of her bones?"

My suspense was truly painful; and, at first, it gave me delightful relief to observe, in hurrying by the farm-house, Charlie, the fiercest of the pointers, lying under a window, with swelled head and bleeding ear.

I opened the wicket and ran to the door, knocking vehemently for admittance. A woman whom I knew, and who formerly lived at Gimmerton, answered—she had been servant there since the death of Mr. Earnshaw.

"Ah," said she, "you are come a seeking your little mistress! don't be frightened. She's here safe—but I'm glad it isn't the master."

"He is not at home then, is he?" I panted, quite breathless with quick walking and alarm.

---

[1]A breed of small, strong horse.

"No, no," she replied, "both he and Joseph are off, and I think they won't return this hour or more. Step in and rest you a bit."

I entered, and beheld my stray lamb seated on the hearth, rocking herself in a little chair that had been her mother's, when a child. Her hat was hung against the wall, and she seemed perfectly at home, laughing and chattering, in the best spirits imaginable, to Hareton, now a great, strong lad of eighteen, who stared at her with considerable curiosity and astonishment; comprehending precious little of the fluent succession of remarks and questions which her tongue never ceased pouring forth.

"Very well, Miss," I exclaimed, concealing my joy under an angry countenance. "This is your last ride, till papa comes back. I'll not trust you over the threshold again, you naughty, naughty girl."

"Aha, Ellen!" she cried, gaily, jumping up and running to my side. "I shall have a pretty story to tell to-night—and so you've found me out. Have you ever been here in your life before?"

"Put that hat on, and home at once," said I. "I'm dreadfully grieved at you, Miss Cathy, you've done extremely wrong! It's no use pouting and crying; that won't repay the trouble I've had, scouring the country after you. To think how Mr. Linton charged me to keep you in; and you stealing off so; it shows you are a cunning little fox, and nobody will put faith in you any more."

"What have I done?" sobbed she, instantly checked. "Papa charged me nothing—he'll not scold me, Ellen—he's never cross, like you!"

"Come, come!" I repeated. "I'll tie the riband. Now, let us have no petulance. Oh, for shame. You thirteen years old, and such a baby!"

This exclamation was caused by her pushing the hat from her head, and retreating to the chimney out of my reach.

"Nay," said the servant, "don't be hard on the bonny lass, Mrs. Dean. We made her stop—she'd fain have ridden forwards, afeard you should be uneasy. But Hareton offered to go with her, and I thought he should. It's a wild road over the hills."

Hareton, during the discussion, stood with his hands in his pockets, too awkward to speak, though he looked as if he did not relish my intrusion.

"How long am I to wait?" I continued, disregarding the woman's interference. "It will be dark in ten minutes. Where is the pony, Miss Cathy? And where is Phenix? I shall leave you, unless you be quick, so please yourself."

"The pony is in the yard," she replied, "and Phenix is shut in there. He's bitten—and so is Charlie. I was going to tell you all about it; but you are in a bad temper, and don't deserve to hear."

I picked up her hat, and approached to reinstate it; but perceiving that the people of the house took her part, she commenced capering round the room; and, on my giving chase, ran like a mouse, over and under and behind the furniture, rendering it ridiculous for me to pursue.

Hareton and the woman laughed; and she joined them, and waxed more impertinent still; till I cried, in great irritation.

"Well, Miss Cathy, if you were aware whose house this is, you'd be glad enough to get out."

"It's *your* father's, isn't it?" said she, turning to Hareton.

"Nay," he replied, looking down, and blushing bashfully.

He could not stand a steady gaze from her eyes, though they were just his own.

"Whose, then—your master's?" she asked.

He coloured deeper, with a different feeling, muttered an oath, and turned away.

"Who is his master?" continued the tiresome girl, appealing to me. "He talked about 'our house,' and 'our folk.' I thought he had been the owner's son. And he never said, Miss; he should have done, shouldn't he, if he's a servant?"

Hareton grew black as a thunder-cloud, at this childish speech. I silently shook my questioner, and, at last, succeeded in equipping her for departure.

"Now, get my horse," she said, addressing her unknown kinsman as she would one of the stable-boys at the Grange. "And you may come with me. I want to see where the goblin hunter rises in the marsh, and to hear about the *fairishes*,[2] as you call them—but, make haste! What's the matter? Get my horse, I say."

"I'll see thee damned, before I be *thy* servant!" growled the lad.

"You'll see me *what*?" asked Catherine in surprise.

"Damned—thou saucy witch!" he replied.

"There, Miss Cathy! you see you have got into pretty company," I interposed. "Nice words to be used to a young lady! Pray don't begin to dispute with him—Come, let us seek for Minny ourselves, and begone."

[2]Fairies.

"But, Ellen," cried she, staring, fixed in astonishment. "How dare he speak so to me? Mustn't he be made to do as I ask him? You wicked creature, I shall tell papa what you said—Now then!"

Hareton did not appear to feel this threat; so the tears sprung into her eyes with indignation. "You bring the pony," she exclaimed, turning to the woman, "and let my dog free this moment!"

"Softly, Miss," answered the addressed. "You'll lose nothing, by being civil. Though Mr. Hareton, there, be not the master's son, he's your cousin; and I was never hired to serve you."

"*He* my cousin!" cried Cathy, with a scornful laugh.

"Yes, indeed," responded her reprover.

"Oh, Ellen! don't let them say such things," she pursued in great trouble. "Papa is gone to fetch my cousin from London—my cousin is a gentleman's son—That my——" she stopped, and wept outright; upset at the bare notion of relationship with such a clown.

"Hush, hush!" I whispered, "people can have many cousins and of all sorts, Miss Cathy, without being any the worse for it; only they needn't keep their company, if they be disagreeable and bad."

"He's not, he's not my cousin, Ellen!" she went on, gathering fresh grief from reflection, and flinging herself into my arms for refuge from the idea.

I was much vexed at her and the servant for their mutual revelations; having no doubt of Linton's approaching arrival, communicated by the former, being reported to Mr. Heathcliff; and feeling as confident that Catherine's first thought on her father's return would be to seek an explanation of the latter's assertion concerning her rude-bred kindred.

Hareton, recovering from his disgust at being taken for a servant, seemed moved by her distress; and, having fetched the pony round to the door, he took, to propitiate her, a fine crooked-legged terrier whelp from the kennel, and putting it into her hand, bid her wisht,[3] for he meant naught.

Pausing in her lamentations, she surveyed him with a glance of awe and horror, then burst forth anew.

I could scarcely refrain from smiling at this antipathy to the poor fellow; who was a well-made, athletic youth, good looking in features, and stout and healthy, but attired in garments befitting his daily occupations of working on the farm, and lounging

---

[3]Hush.

176 • *Wuthering Heights*

among the moors after rabbits and game. Still, I thought I could detect in his physiognomy a mind owning better qualities than his father ever possessed. Good things lost amid a wilderness of weeds, to be sure, whose rankness far over-topped their neglected growth; yet, notwithstanding, evidence of a wealthy soil that might yield luxuriant crops under other and favourable circumstances. Mr. Heathcliff, I believe, had not treated him physically ill; thanks to his fearless nature, which offered no temptation to that course of oppression; it had none of the timid susceptibility that would have given zest to ill-treatment, in Heathcliff's judgment. He appeared to have bent his malevolence on making him a brute: he was never taught to read or write; never rebuked for any bad habit which did not annoy his keeper; never led a single step towards virtue, or guarded by a single precept against vice. And from what I heard, Joseph contributed much to his deterioration by a narrow-minded partiality which prompted him to flatter and pet him, as a boy, because he was the head of the old family. And as he had been in the habit of accusing Catherine Earnshaw and Heathcliff, when children, of putting the master past his patience, and compelling him to seek solace in drink, by what he termed their "offalld[4] ways," so at present he laid the whole burden of Hareton's faults on the shoulders of the usurper of his property.

If the lad swore, he wouldn't correct him; nor however culpably he behaved. It gave Joseph satisfaction, apparently, to watch him go the worst lengths. He allowed that the lad was ruined; that his soul was abandoned to perdition; but then, he reflected that Heathcliff must answer for it. Hareton's blood would be required at his hands; and there lay immense consolation in that thought.

Joseph had instilled into him a pride of name, and of his lineage; he would, had he dared, have fostered hate between him and the present owner of the Heights, but his dread of that owner amounted to superstition; and he confined his feelings regarding him to muttered innuendoes and private comminations.

I don't pretend to be intimately acquainted with the mode of living customary in those days at Wuthering Heights. I only speak from hearsay; for I saw little. The villagers affirmed Mr.

---

[4]Dreadful, wicked.

Heathcliff was *near*,[5] and a cruel hard landlord to his tenants; but the house, inside, had regained its ancient aspect of comfort under female management; and the scenes of riot common in Hindley's time were not now enacted within its walls. The master was too gloomy to seek companionship with any people, good or bad, and he is yet—

This, however, is not making progress with my story. Miss Cathy rejected the peace-offering of the terrier, and demanded her own dogs, Charlie and Phenix. They came limping, and hanging their heads; and we set out for home, sadly out of sorts, every one of us.

I could not wring from my little lady how she had spent the day; except that, as I supposed, the goal of her pilgrimage was Penistone Craggs; and she arrived without adventure to the gate of the farmhouse, when Hareton happened to issue forth, attended by some canine followers who attacked her train.

They had a smart battle, before their owners could separate them: that formed an introduction. Catherine told Hareton who she was, and where she was going; and asked him to show her the way; finally, beguiling him to accompany her.

He opened the mysteries of the Fairy cave, and twenty other queer places; but, being in disgrace, I was not favoured with a description of the interesting objects she saw.

I could gather, however, that her guide had been a favourite till she hurt his feelings by addressing him as a servant, and Heathcliff's housekeeper hurt hers by calling him her cousin.

Then the language he had held to her rankled in her heart; she who was always "love," and "darling," and "queen," and "angel," with everybody at the Grange, to be insulted so shockingly by a stranger! She did not comprehend it; and hard work I had, to obtain a promise that she would not lay the grievance before her father.

I explained how he objected to the whole household at the Heights, and how sorry he would be to find she had been there; but I insisted most on the fact, that if she revealed my negligence of his orders, he would perhaps be so angry that I should have to leave; and Cathy couldn't bear that prospect: she pledged her word, and kept it, for my sake—after all, she was a sweet little girl.

[5]Miserly.

## Chapter 5/19

A letter, edged with black, announced the day of my master's return. Isabella was dead; and he wrote to bid me get mourning for his daughter, and arrange a room, and other accommodations, for his youthful nephew.

Catherine ran wild with joy at the idea of welcoming her father back: and indulged most sanguine anticipations of the innumerable excellencies of her "real" cousin.

The evening of their expected arrival came. Since early morning, she had been busy, ordering her own small affairs; and now, attired in her new black frock—poor thing! her aunt's death impressed her with no definite sorrow—she obliged me, by constant worrying, to walk with her down through the grounds to meet them.

"Linton is just six months younger than I am," she chattered, as we strolled leisurely over the swells and hollows of mossy turf, under shadow of the trees. "How delightful it will be to have him for a playfellow! Aunt Isabella sent papa a beautiful lock of his hair; it was lighter than mine—more flaxen, and quite as fine. I have it carefully preserved in a little glass box; and I've often thought what pleasure it would be to see its owner—Oh! I am happy—and papa, dear, dear papa! Come, Ellen, let us run! come run!"

She ran, and returned and ran again, many times before my sober footsteps reached the gate, and then she seated herself on the grassy bank beside the path, and tried to wait patiently; but that was impossible; she couldn't be still a minute.

"How long they are!" she exclaimed. "Ah, I see some dust on the road—they are coming! No! When will they be here? May we not go a little way—half a mile, Ellen, only just half a mile? Do say yes, to that clump of birches at the turn!"

I refused staunchly: and, at length, her suspense was ended: the travelling carriage rolled in sight.

Miss Cathy shrieked, and stretched out her arms, as soon as she caught her father's face looking from the window. He descended, nearly as eager as herself; and a considerable interval elapsed ere they had a thought to spare for any but themselves.

While they exchanged caresses, I took a peep in to see after Linton. He was asleep in a corner, wrapped in a warm, fur-lined cloak, as if it had been winter. A pale, delicate, effeminate boy, who might have been taken for my master's younger brother, so strong was the resemblance, but there was a sickly peevishness in his aspect that Edgar Linton never had.

The latter saw me looking; and having shaken hands, advised me to close the door, and leave him undisturbed; for the journey had fatigued him.

Cathy would fain have taken one glance; but her father told her to come on, and they walked together up the park, while I hastened before to prepare the servants.

"Now, darling," said Mr. Linton, addressing his daughter, as they halted at the bottom of the front steps, "Your cousin is not so strong or so merry as you are, and he has lost his mother, remember, a very short time since; therefore, don't expect him to play and run about with you directly. And don't harass him much by talking—let him be quiet this evening, at least, will you?"

"Yes, yes, papa," answered Catherine; "but I do want to see him; and he hasn't once looked out."

The carriage stopped; and the sleeper, being roused, was lifted to the ground by his uncle.

"This is your cousin Cathy, Linton," he said, putting their little hands together. "She's fond of you already; and mind you don't grieve her by crying to-night. Try to be cheerful now; the travelling is at an end, and you have nothing to do but rest and amuse yourself as you please."

"Let me go to bed, then," answered the boy, shrinking from Catherine's salute; and he put up his fingers to remove incipient tears.

"Come, come, there's a good child," I whispered, leading him in. "You'll make her weep too—see how sorry she is for you!"

I do not know whether it was sorrow for him, but his cousin put on as sad a countenance as himself, and returned to her father. All three entered, and mounted to the library, where tea was laid ready.

I proceeded to remove Linton's cap and mantle, and placed him on a chair by the table; but he was no sooner seated than he began to cry afresh. My master inquired what was the matter.

"I can't sit on a chair," sobbed the boy.

"Go to the sofa, then, and Ellen shall bring you some tea," answered his uncle, patiently.

He had been greatly tried during the journey, I felt convinced, by his fretful, ailing charge.

Linton slowly trailed himself off, and lay down. Cathy carried a foot-stool and her cup to his side.

At first she sat silent; but that could not last; she had resolved to make a pet of her little cousin, as she would have him to be; and she commenced stroking his curls, and kissing his cheek, and offering him tea in her saucer, like a baby. This pleased him, for he was not much better; he dried his eyes, and lightened into a faint smile.

"Oh, he'll do very well," said the master to me, after watching them a minute. "Very well, if we can keep him, Ellen. The company of a child of his own age will instil new spirit into him soon: and by wishing for strength he'll gain it."

"Aye, if we can keep him!" I mused to myself; and sore misgivings came over me that there was slight hope of that. And then, I thought, however will that weakling live at Wuthering Heights, between his father and Hareton? What playmates and instructors they'll be.

Our doubts were presently decided; even earlier than I expected. I had just taken the children upstairs, after tea was finished, and seen Linton asleep—he would not suffer me to leave him till that was the case—I had come down, and was standing by the table in the hall, lighting a bed-room candle for Mr. Edgar, when a maid stepped out of the kitchen and informed me that Mr. Heathcliff's servant, Joseph, was at the door, and wished to speak with the master.

"I shall ask him what he wants first," I said, in considerable trepidation. "A very unlikely hour to be troubling people, and the instant they have returned from a long journey. I don't think the master can see him."

Joseph had advanced through the kitchen, as I uttered these words, and now presented himself in the hall. He was donned in his Sunday garments, with his most sanctimonious and sourest face; and holding his hat in one hand, and his stick in the other, he proceeded to clean his shoes on the mat.

"Good evening, Joseph," I said, coldly. "What business brings you here to-night?"

"It's Maister Linton Aw mun spake tull," he answered, waving me disdainfully aside.

"Mr. Linton is going to bed; unless you have something particular to say, I'm sure he won't hear it now," I continued. "You had better sit down in there, and entrust your message to me."

"Which is his rahm?" pursued the fellow, surveying the range of closed doors.

I perceived he was bent on refusing my mediation; so very reluctantly I went up to the library, and announced the unseasonable visiter, advising that he should be dismissed till next day.

Mr. Linton had no time to empower me to do so, for Joseph mounted close at my heels, and pushing into the apartment, planted himself at the far side of the table, with his two fists clapped on the head of his stick, and began in an elevated tone, as if anticipating opposition.

"Hathecliff has sent me for his lad, un' Aw munn't goa back baht him."[1]

Edgar Linton was silent a minute; an expression of exceeding sorrow overcast his features; he would have pitied the child on his own account; but, recalling Isabella's hopes and fears, and anxious wishes for her son, and her commendations of him to his care, he grieved bitterly at the prospect of yielding him up, and searched in his heart how it might be avoided. No plan offered itself: the very exhibition of any desire to keep him would have rendered the claimant more peremptory: there was nothing left but to resign him. However, he was not going to rouse him from his sleep.

"Tell Mr. Heathcliff," he answered, calmly, "that his son shall come to Wuthering Heights to-morrow. He is in bed, and too tired to go the distance now. You may also tell him that the mother of Linton desired him to remain under my guardianship; and, at present, his health is very precarious."

"Noa!" said Joseph, giving a thud with his prop on the floor, and assuming an authoritative air. "Noa! that manes nowt—Hathecliff maks noa 'cahnt uh t' mother, nur yah norther—bud he'll hev his lad; und Aw mun tak him—soa nah yah knaw!"[2]

"You shall not to-night!" answered Linton, decisively. "Walk down stairs at once, and repeat to your master what I have said. Ellen, show him down. Go—"

And, aiding the indignant elder with a lift by the arm, he rid the room of him, and closed the door.

---

[1] "Heathcliff has sent me for his son, and I must not go back without him."

[2] "That means nothing—Heathcliff takes no account of the mother, nor of you, either—but he'll have his son; and I must take him—so now you know!"

"Varrah weel!" shouted Joseph, as he slowly drew off. "Tuh morn, he's come hisseln, un' thrust *him* aht, if yah darr!"[3]

## Chapter 6/20

To obviate the danger of this threat being fulfilled, Mr. Linton commissioned me to take the boy home early, on Catherine's pony, and, said he—

"As we shall now have no influence over his destiny, good or bad, you must say nothing of where he is gone to my daughter; she cannot associate with him hereafter; and it is better for her to remain in ignorance of his proximity, lest she should be restless, and anxious to visit the Heights—merely tell her, his father sent for him suddenly, and he has been obliged to leave us."

Linton was very reluctant to be roused from his bed at five o'clock, and astonished to be informed that he must prepare for further travelling: but I softened off the matter by stating that he was going to spend some time with his father, Mr. Heathcliff, who wished to see him so much, he did not like to defer the pleasure till he should recover from his late journey.

"My father?" he cried, in strange perplexity. "Mamma never told me I had a father. Where does he live? I'd rather stay with uncle."

"He lives a little distance from the Grange," I replied, "just beyond those hills—not so far but you may walk over here, when you get hearty. And you should be glad to go home, and to see him. You must try to love him, as you did your mother, and then he will love you."

"But why have I not heard of him before?" asked Linton; "why didn't mamma and he live together, as other people do?"

"He had business to keep him in the north," I answered; "and your mother's health required her to reside in the south."

"And why didn't mamma speak to me about him?" persevered the child. "She often talked of uncle, and I learnt to love him long ago. How am I to love papa? I don't know him."

"Oh, all children love their parents," I said. "Your mother, perhaps, thought you would want to be with him, if she mentioned him often to you. Let us make haste. An early ride on such a beautiful morning is much preferable to an hour's more sleep."

[3]"Very well! . . . In the morning, he'll come himself, and throw *him* out if you dare!"

"Is *she* to go with us," he demanded. "The little girl I saw yesterday?"

"Not now," replied I.

"Is uncle?" he continued.

"No, I shall be your companion there," I said.

Linton sank back on his pillow, and fell into a brown study.

"I won't go without uncle," he cried at length; "I can't tell where you mean to take me."

I attempted to persuade him of the naughtiness of showing reluctance to meet his father: still he obstinately resisted any progress towards dressing; and I had to call for my master's assistance in coaxing him out of bed.

The poor thing was finally got off with several delusive assurances that his absence should be short; that Mr. Edgar and Cathy would visit him; and other promises, equally ill-founded, which I invented and reiterated, at intervals, throughout the way.

The pure heather-scented air, and the bright sunshine, and the gentle canter of Minny relieved his despondency, after a while. He began to put questions concerning his new home, and its inhabitants, with greater interest and liveliness.

"Is Wuthering Heights as pleasant a place as Thrushcross Grange?" he inquired, turning to take a last glance into the valley, whence a light mist mounted and formed a fleecy cloud on the skirts of the blue.

"It is not so buried in trees," I replied, "and it is not quite so large, but you can see the country beautifully, all round; and the air is healthier for you—fresher, and dryer. You will, perhaps, think the building old and dark, at first—though it is a respectable house, the next best in the neighbourhood. And you will have such nice rambles on the moors! Hareton Earnshaw—that is Miss Cathy's other cousin, and so yours in a manner—will show you all the sweetest spots; and you can bring a book in fine weather, and make a green hollow your study; and, now and then, your uncle may join you in a walk; he does, frequently, walk out on the hills."

"And what is my father like?" he asked. "Is he as young and handsome as uncle?"

"He's as young," said I, "but he has black hair and eyes, and looks sterner, and he is taller and bigger altogether. He'll not seem to you so gentle and kind at first, perhaps, because it is not his way—still, mind you be frank and cordial with him; and naturally he'll be fonder of you than any uncle, for you are his own."

"Black hair and eyes!" mused Linton. "I can't fancy him. Then I am not like him, am I?"

"Not much," I answered . . . Not a morsel, I thought: surveying with regret the white complexion and slim frame of my companion, and his large languid eyes . . . his mother's eyes save that, unless a morbid touchiness kindled them a moment, they had not a vestige of her sparkling spirit.

"How strange that he should never come to see mama and me," he murmured. "Has he ever seen me? If he have, I must have been a baby—I remember not a single thing about him!"

"Why, Master Linton," said I, "three hundred miles is a great distance; and ten years seem very different in length to a grown up person, compared with what they do to you. It is probable Mr. Heathcliff proposed going, from summer to summer, but never found a convenient opportunity; and now it is too late—Don't trouble him with questions on the subject, it will disturb him for no good."

The boy was fully occupied with his own cogitations for the remainder of the ride, till we halted before the farm-house garden gate. I watched to catch his impressions in his countenance. He surveyed the carved front and low-browed lattices, the straggling gooseberry bushes and crooked firs, with solemn intentness, and then shook his head: his private feelings entirely disapproved of the exterior of his new abode; but he had sense to postpone complaining—there might be compensation within.

Before he dismounted, I went and opened the door. It was half-past six; the family had just finished breakfast; the servant was clearing and wiping down the table. Joseph stood by his master's chair telling some tale concerning a lame horse; and Hareton was preparing for the hay-field.

"Hallo, Nelly!" cried Mr. Heathcliff, when he saw me. "I feared I should have to come down and fetch my property myself—You've brought it, have you? Let us see what we can make of it."

He got up and strode to the door. Hareton and Joseph followed in gaping curiosity. Poor Linton ran a frightened eye over the faces of the three.

"Sure-ly," said Joseph after a grave inspection, "he's swopped wi' ye, maister, an' yon's his lass!"

Heathcliff, having stared his son into an ague of confusion, uttered a scornful laugh.

"God! what a beauty! what a lovely, charming thing!" he exclaimed. "Haven't they reared it on snails and sour milk, Nelly? Oh, damn my soul! but that's worse than I expected—and the devil knows I was not sanguine!"

I bid the trembling and bewildered child get down, and enter. He did not thoroughly comprehend the meaning of his father's speech, or whether it were intended for him: indeed, he was not yet certain that the grim, sneering stranger was his father; but he clung to me with growing trepidation; and on Mr. Heathcliff's taking a seat, and bidding him "come hither," he hid his face on my shoulder, and wept.

"Tut, tut!" said Heathcliff, stretching out a hand and dragging him roughly between his knees, and then holding up his head by the chin. "None of that nonsense! We're not going to hurt thee, Linton—isn't that thy name? Thou art thy mother's child, entirely! Where is *my* share in thee, puling chicken?"

He took off the boy's cap and pushed back his thick flaxen curls, felt his slender arms, and his small fingers; during which examination Linton ceased crying, and lifted his great blue eyes to inspect the inspector.

"Do you know me?" asked Heathcliff, having satisfied himself that the limbs were all equally frail and feeble.

"No!" said Linton, with a gaze of vacant fear.

"You've heard of me, I dare say?"

"No," he replied again.

"No? What a shame of your mother, never to waken your filial regard for me! You are my son, then, I'll tell you; and your mother was a wicked slut to leave you in ignorance of the sort of father you possessed—Now, don't wince and colour up! Though it *is* something to see you have not white blood—Be a good lad; and I'll do for you—Nelly, if you be tired, you may sit down; if not, get home again—I guess you'll report what you hear, and see, to the cipher at the Grange; and this thing won't be settled while you linger about it."

"Well," replied I, "I hope you'll be kind to the boy, Mr. Heathcliff, or you'll not keep him long, and he's all you have akin in the wide world that you will ever know—remember."

"I'll be *very* kind to him, you needn't fear!" he said, laughing. "Only nobody else must be kind to him—I'm jealous of monopolizing his affection—And, to begin my kindness, Joseph! bring the lad some breakfast.—Hareton, you infernal calf, begone to your work. Yes, Nell," he added, when they had departed, "my son is prospective owner of your place, and I should not wish him to die till I was certain of being his successor. Besides, he's *mine*, and I want the triumph of seeing *my* descendant fairly lord of their estates; my child hiring their children, to till their fathers' lands for wages—That is the sole consideration which can make me endure the whelp—I despise him for himself, and hate him for the memories he revives! But, that consideration is sufficient; he's safe with me, and shall be tended as carefully as your master tends his own—I have a room up-stairs, furnished for him in handsome style—I've engaged a tutor, also, to come three times a week, from twenty miles distance, to teach him what he pleases to learn. I've ordered Hareton to obey him: and, in fact, I've arranged every thing with a view to preserve the superior and the gentleman in him, above his associates—I do regret, however, that he so little deserves the trouble—if I wished any blessing in the world, it was to find him a worthy object of pride, and I'm bitterly disappointed with the whey-faced whining wretch!"

While he was speaking, Joseph returned, bearing a basin of milk-porridge, and placed it before Linton. He stirred round the homely mess with a look of aversion, and affirmed he could not eat it.

I saw the old man servant shared largely in his master's scorn of the child, though he was compelled to retain the sentiment in his heart, because Heathcliff plainly meant his underlings to hold him in honour.

"Cannot ate it?" repeated he, peering in Linton's face, and subduing his voice to a whisper, for fear of being overheard. "But Maister Hareton nivir ate nowt else, when he wer a little un; und what wer gooid eneugh fur him's gooid eneugh fur yah, Aw's rayther think!"[1]

"I *shan't* eat it!" answered Linton, snappishly. "Take it away."

Joseph snatched up the food indignantly, and brought it to us.

[1] "Cannot eat it? . . . But Master Hareton never ate anything else, when he was a little one; and what was good enough for him is good enough for you, I rather think!" And following: "Is there anything wrong with the food?" "Well, that dainty boy says he can't eat it. But I guess that's right. His mother was just that way—we were almost too filthy to sow the wheat for making her bread."

"Is there owt ails th' victuals?" he asked, thrusting the tray under Heathcliff's nose.

"What should ail them?" he said.

"Wah!" answered Joseph, "yon dainty chap says he cannut ate 'em. Bud Aw guess it's raight! His mother were just soa—we wer a'most too mucky tuh sow t' corn for makking her breead."

"Don't mention his mother to me," said the master angrily. "Get him something that he can eat, that's all. What is his usual food, Nelly?"

I suggested boiled milk or tea; and the housekeeper received instructions to prepare some.

Come, I reflected, his father's selfishness may contribute to his comfort. He perceives his delicate constitution, and the necessity of treating him tolerably. I'll console Mr. Edgar by acquainting him with the turn Heathcliff's humour has taken.

Having no excuse for lingering longer, I slipped out, while Linton was engaged in timidly rebuffing the advances of a friendly sheep-dog. But he was too much on the alert to be cheated—as I closed the door, I heard a cry, and a frantic repetition of the words—

"Don't leave me! I'll not stay here! I'll not stay here!"

Then the latch was raised and fell—they did not suffer him to come forth. I mounted Minny, and urged her to a trot; and so my brief guardianship ended.

## Chapter 7/21

We had sad work with little Cathy that day: she rose in high glee, eager to join her cousin; and such passionate tears and lamentations followed the news of his departure, that Edgar himself was obliged to sooth her, by affirming he should come back soon; he added, however, "if I can get him;" and there were no hopes of that.

This promise poorly pacified her; but time was more potent; and though still, at intervals, she inquired of her father when Linton would return, before she did see him again, his features had waxed so dim in her memory that she did not recognise him.

When I chanced to encounter the housekeeper of Wuthering Heights, in paying business-visits to Gimmerton, I used to ask how the young master got on; for he lived almost as secluded as Catherine herself, and was never to be seen. I could gather from her that he continued in weak health, and was a tiresome inmate. She said Mr. Heathcliff seemed to dislike him ever longer and worse, though he took some trouble to conceal it. He had an antipathy to the sound of his voice, and could not do at all with his sitting in the same room with him many minutes together.

There seldom passed much talk between them; Linton learnt his lessons and spent his evenings in a small apartment they called the parlour; or else lay in bed all day; for he was constantly getting coughs, and colds, and aches, and pains of some sort.

"And I never knew such a faint-hearted creature," added the woman; "nor one so careful of hisseln. He *will* go on, if I leave the window open, a bit late in the evening. Oh! it's killing, a breath of night air! And he must have a fire in the middle of summer; and Joseph's 'bacca pipe is poison; and he must always have sweets and dainties, and always milk, milk for ever—heeding naught how the rest of us are pinched in winter—and there he'll sit, wrapped in his furred cloak in his chair by the fire, and some toast and water or other slop on the hob to sip at; and if Hareton, for pity, comes to amuse him—Hareton is not bad-natured, though he's rough—they're sure to part, one swearing and the other crying. I believe the master would relish Earnshaw's thrashing him to a mummy, if he were not his son: and, I'm certain, he would be fit to turn him out of doors, if he knew half the nursing he gives hisseln. But then, he won't go into danger of temptation; he never enters the parlour, and should Linton show those ways in the house[1] where he is, he sends him upstairs directly."

I divined, from this account, that utter lack of sympathy had rendered young Heathcliff selfish and disagreeable, if he were not so originally; and my interest in him, consequently, decayed; though still I was moved with a sense of grief at his lot, and a wish that he had been left with us.

Mr. Edgar encouraged me to gain information; he thought a great deal about him, I fancy, and would have run some risk to see him; and he told me once to ask the housekeeper whether he ever came into the village?

She said he had only been twice, on horseback, accompanying his father: and both times he pretended to be quite knocked up for three or four days afterwards.

[1]There are two sitting rooms at Wuthering Heights, the large communal one commonly called "the house," and another "small apartment they called the parlour," where Linton spends much of his time.

That housekeeper left, if I recollect rightly, two years after he came; and another, whom I did not know, was her successor: she lives there still.

Time wore on at the Grange in its former pleasant way, till Miss Cathy reached sixteen. On the anniversary of her birth we never manifested any signs of rejoicing, because it was also the anniversary of my late mistress's death. Her father invariably spent that day alone in the library; and walked, at dusk, as far as Gimmerton kirkyard, where he would frequently prolong his stay beyond midnight. Therefore Catherine was thrown on her own resources for amusement.

This twentieth of March was a beautiful spring day, and when her father had retired, my young lady came down dressed for going out, and said she asked to have a ramble on the edge of the moor with me; and Mr. Linton had given her leave, if we went only a short distance, and were back within the hour.

"So make haste, Ellen!" she cried. "I know where I wish to go; where a colony of moor game[2] are settled; I want to see whether they have made their nests yet."

"That must be a good distance up," I answered; "they don't breed on the edge of the moor."

"No, it's not," she said. "I've gone very near with papa."

I put on my bonnet and sallied out, thinking nothing more of the matter. She bounded before me, and returned to my side, and was off again like a young greyhound; and, at first, I found plenty of entertainment in listening to the larks singing far and near; and enjoying the sweet, warm sunshine; and watching her, my pet, and my delight, with her golden ringlets flying loose behind, and her bright cheek, as soft and pure in its bloom as a wild rose, and her eyes radiant with cloudless pleasure. She was a happy creature, and an angel, in those days. It's a pity she could not be content.

"Well," said I, "where are your moor-game, Miss Cathy? We should be at them—the Grange park-fence is a great way off now."

"Oh, a little further—only a little further, Ellen," was her answer, continually. "Climb to that hillock, pass that bank, and by the time you reach the other side, I shall have raised the birds."

[2]Grouse.

But there were so many hillocks and banks to climb and pass, that, at length, I began to be weary, and told her we must halt, and retrace our steps.

I shouted to her, as she had outstripped me, a long way; she either did not hear or did not regard, for she still sprang on, and I was compelled to follow. Finally, she dived into a hollow; and before I came in sight of her again, she was two miles nearer Wuthering Heights than her own home; and I beheld a couple of persons arrest her, one of whom I felt convinced was Mr. Heathcliff himself.

Cathy had been caught in the fact of plundering, or, at least, hunting out the nests of the grouse.

The Heights were Heathcliff's land, and he was reproving the poacher.

"I've neither taken any nor found any," she said, as I toiled to them, expanding her hands in corroboration of the statement.

"I didn't mean to take them; but papa told me there were quantities up here, and I wished to see the eggs."

Heathcliff glanced at me with an ill-meaning smile, expressing his acquaintance with the party, and, consequently, his malevolence towards it, and demanded who "papa" was?

"Mr. Linton of Thrushcross Grange," she replied. "I thought you did not know me, or you wouldn't have spoken in that way."

"You suppose papa is highly esteemed and respected then?" he said, sarcastically.

"And what are you?" inquired Catherine, gazing curiously on the speaker. "That man I've seen before. Is he your son?"

She pointed to Hareton, the other individual, who had gained nothing but increased bulk and strength by the addition of two years to his age: he seemed as awkward and rough as ever.

"Miss Cathy," I interrupted, "it will be three hours instead of one that we are out, presently. We really must go back."

"No, that man is not my son," answered Heathcliff, pushing me aside. "But I have one, and you have seen him before too; and, though your nurse is in a hurry, I think both you and she would be the better for a little rest. Will you just turn this nab[3] of heath, and walk into my house? You'll get home earlier for the ease; and you shall receive a kind welcome."

[3]A jutting edge of the range of moorland hills.

I whispered Catherine that she mustn't, on any account, accede to the proposal; it was entirely out of the question.

"Why?" she asked, aloud. "I'm tired of running, and the ground is dewy—I can't sit here. Let us go, Ellen! Besides, he says I have seen his son. He's mistaken, I think; but I guess where he lives—at the farm-house I visited in coming from Penistone Craggs. Don't you?"

"I do. Come, Nelly, hold your tongue—it will be a treat for her to look in on us. Hareton, get forwards with the lass. You shall walk with me, Nelly."

"No, she's not going to any such place," I cried, struggling to release my arm, which he had seized; but she was almost at the door-stones already, scampering round the brow at full speed. Her appointed companion did not pretend to escort her; he shyed off by the road side, and vanished.

"Mr. Heathcliff, it's very wrong," I continued, "you know you mean no good; and there she'll see Linton, and all will be told, as soon as ever we return; and I shall have the blame."

"I want her to see Linton," he answered. "He's looking better these few days; it's not often he's fit to be seen. And we'll soon persuade her to keep the visit secret—where is the harm of it?"

"The harm of it is, that her father would hate me, if he found I suffered her to enter your house; and I am convinced you have a bad design in encouraging her to do so," I replied.

"My design is as honest as possible. I'll inform you of its whole scope," he said. "That the two cousins may fall in love, and get married. I'm acting generously to your master; his young chit has no expectations, and should she second my wishes, she'll be provided for, at once, as joint successor with Linton."

"If Linton died," I answered, "and his life is quite uncertain, Catherine would be the heir."

"No, she would not," he said. "There is no clause in the will to secure it so; his property would go to me; but, to prevent disputes, I desire their union, and am resolved to bring it about."

"And I am resolved she shall never approach your house with me again," I returned, as we reached the gate, where Miss Cathy waited our coming.

Heathcliff bid me be quiet; and preceding us up the path, hastened to open the door. My young lady gave him several looks, as if she could not exactly make up her mind what to think of him; but now he smiled when he met her eye, and softened his voice in addressing her, and I was foolish enough to imagine the memory of her mother might disarm him from desiring her injury.

Linton stood on the hearth. He had been out, walking in the fields; for his cap was on, and he was calling to Joseph to bring him dry shoes.

He had grown tall of his age, still wanting some months of sixteen. His features were pretty yet, and his eye and complexion brighter than I remembered them, though with merely temporary lustre borrowed from the salubrious air and genial sun.

"Now, who is that?" asked Mr. Heathcliff, turning to Cathy. "Can you tell?"

"Your son?" she said, having doubtfully surveyed first one and then the other.

"Yes, yes," answered he; "but is this the only time you have beheld him? Think! Ah! you have a short memory. Linton, don't you recall your cousin, that you used to tease us so with wishing to see?"

"What, Linton!" cried Cathy, kindling into joyful surprise at the name. "Is that little Linton? He's taller than I am! Are you Linton?"

The youth stepped forward, and acknowledged himself. She kissed him fervently, and they gazed with wonder at the change time had wrought in the appearance of each.

Catherine had reached her full height; her figure was both plump and slender, elastic as steel, and her whole aspect sparkling with health and spirits. Linton's looks and movements were very languid, and his form extremely slight; but there was a grace in his manner that mitigated these defects, and rendered him not unpleasing.

After exchanging numerous marks of fondness with him, his cousin went to Mr. Heathcliff, who lingered by the door, dividing his attention between the objects inside and those that lay without, pretending, that is, to observe the latter, and really noting the former alone.

"And you are my uncle, then!" she cried, reaching up to salute him. "I thought I liked you, though you were cross, at first. Why don't you visit at the Grange with Linton? To live all these years such close neighbours, and never see us, is odd; what have you done so for?"

"I visited it once or twice too often before you were born," he answered. "There—damn it! If you have any kisses to spare, give them to Linton—they are thrown away on me."

"Naughty Ellen!" exclaimed Catherine, flying to attack me next with her lavish caresses. "Wicked Ellen! to try to hinder me from entering. But I'll take this walk every morning in future—may I, uncle—and sometimes bring papa? Won't you be glad to see us?"

"Of course!" replied the uncle, with a hardly suppressed grimace, resulting from his deep aversion to both the proposed visiters. "But stay," he continued, turning towards the young lady. "Now I think of it, I'd better tell you. Mr. Linton has a prejudice against me; we quarrelled at one time of our lives, with unchristian ferocity; and, if you mention coming here to him, he'll put a veto on your visits altogether. Therefore, you must not mention it, unless you be careless of seeing your cousin hereafter—you may come, if you will, but you must not mention it."

"Why did you quarrel?" asked Catherine, considerably crestfallen.

"He thought me too poor to wed his sister," answered Heathcliff, "and was grieved that I got her—his pride was hurt, and he'll never forgive it."

"That's wrong!" said the young lady: "some time, I'll tell him so; but Linton and I have no share in your quarrel. I'll not come here, then, he shall come to the Grange."

"It will be too far for me," murmured her cousin, "to walk four miles would kill me. No, come here, Miss Catherine, now and then, not every morning, but once or twice a week."

The father launched towards his son a glance of bitter contempt.

"I am afraid, Nelly, I shall lose my labour," he muttered to me. "Miss Catherine, as the ninny calls her, will discover his value, and send him to the devil. Now, if it had been Hareton—do you know that, twenty times a day, I covet Hareton, with all his degradation? I'd have loved the lad had he been some one else. But I think he's safe from *her* love. I'll pit him against that paltry creature, unless it bestir itself briskly. We calculate it will scarcely last till it is eighteen. Oh, confound the vapid thing. He's absorbed in drying his feet, and never looks at her—Linton!"

"Yes, father," answered the boy.

"Have you nothing to show your cousin, anywhere about; not even a rabbit, or a weasel's nest? Take her into the garden, before you change your shoes; and into the stable to see your horse."

"Wouldn't you rather sit here?" asked Linton, addressing Cathy in a tone which expressed reluctance to move again.

"I don't know," she replied, casting a longing look to the door, and evidently eager to be active.

He kept his seat, and shrank closer to the fire.

Heathcliff rose, and went into the kitchen, and from thence to the yard, calling out for Hareton.

Hareton responded, and presently the two re-entered. The young man had been washing himself, as was visible by the glow on his cheeks, and his wetted hair.

"Oh, I'll ask *you*, uncle," cried Miss Cathy, recollecting the housekeeper's assertion. "That's not my cousin, is he?"

"Yes," he replied, "your mother's nephew. Don't you like him?"

Catherine looked queer.

"Is he not a handsome lad?" he continued.

The uncivil little thing stood on tiptoe, and whispered a sentence in Heathcliff's ear.

He laughed; Hareton darkened; I perceived he was very sensitive to suspected slights, and had obviously a dim notion of his inferiority. But his master or guardian chased[4] the frown by exclaiming—

"You'll be the favourite among us, Hareton! She says you are a——What was it? Well, something very flattering. Here! you go with her round the farm. And behave like a gentleman, mind! Don't use any bad words; and don't stare, when the young lady is not looking at you, and be ready to hide your face when she is; and, when you speak, say your words slowly, and keep your hands out of your pockets. Be off, and entertain her as nicely as you can."

He watched the couple walking past the window. Earnshaw had his countenance completely averted from his companion. He seemed studying the familiar landscape with a stranger's and an artist's interest.

Catherine took a sly look at him, expressing small admiration. She then turned her attention to seeking out objects of amusement for herself, and tripped merrily on, lilting a tune to supply the lack of conversation.

"I've tied his tongue," observed Heathcliff. "He'll not venture a single syllable, all the time! Nelly, you recollect me at his age—nay, some years younger—Did I ever look so stupid, so 'gaumless,'[5] as Joseph calls it?"

[4]Chased away.
[5]Witless.

"Worse," I replied, "because more sullen with it."

"I've a pleasure in him!" he continued, reflecting aloud. "He has satisfied my expectations—If he were a born fool I should not enjoy it half so much—But he's no fool; and I can sympathise with all his feelings, having felt them myself—I know what he suffers now, for instance, exactly—it is merely a beginning of what he shall suffer, though. And he'll never be able to emerge from his bathos[6] of coarseness and ignorance. I've got him faster[7] than his scoundrel of a father secured me, and lower; for he takes a pride in his brutishness. I've taught him to scorn everything extra-animal as silly and weak—Don't you think Hindley would be proud of his son, if he could see him? almost as proud as I am of mine—But there's this difference; one is gold put to the use of paving stones, and the other is tin polished to ape a service of silver—*Mine* has nothing valuable about it; yet I shall have the merit of making it go as far as such poor stuff can go. *His* had first-rate qualities, and they are lost—rendered worse than unavailing—I have nothing to regret; he would have more than any, but I, are aware of—And the best of it is, Hareton is damnably fond of me! You'll own that I've out-matched Hindley there—If the dead villain could rise from his grave to abuse me for his offspring's wrongs, I should have the fun of seeing the said offspring fight him back again, indignant that he should dare to rail at the one friend he has in the world!"

Heathcliff chuckled a fiendish laugh at the idea; I made no reply, because I saw that he expected none.

Meantime, our young companion, who sat too removed from us to hear what was said, began to evince symptoms of uneasiness: probably repenting that he had denied himself the treat of Catherine's society, for fear of a little fatigue.

His father remarked the restless glances wandering to the window, and the hand irresolutely extended towards his cap.

"Get up, you idle boy!" he exclaimed with assumed heartiness. "Away after them . . . they are just at the corner, by the stand of hives."

Linton gathered his energies, and left the hearth. The lattice was open and, as he stepped out, I heard Cathy inquiring of her unsociable attendant, what was that inscription over the door?

[6]Depth.

[7]More securely.

Hareton stared up, and scratched his head like a true clown.
"It's some damnable writing," he answered. "I cannot read it."
"Can't read it?" cried Catherine, "I can read it . . . it's English . . .
but I want to know why it is there."

Linton giggled—the first appearance of mirth he had exhibited.
"He does not know his letters," he said to his cousin. "Could
you believe in the existence of such a colossal dunce?"

"Is he all as he should be?" asked Miss Cathy seriously, "or is
he simple . . . not right? I've questioned him twice now, and each
time he looked so stupid I think he does not understand me; I can
hardly understand *him*, I'm sure!"

Linton repeated his laugh, and glanced at Hareton tauntingly,
who certainly did not seem quite clear of comprehension at that
moment.

"There's nothing the matter, but laziness, is there, Earnshaw?" he
said. "My cousin fancies you are an idiot . . . There you experience
the consequence of scorning 'book-larning,' as you would say . . .
Have you noticed, Catherine, his frightful Yorkshire pronunciation?"

"Why, where the devil is the use on't?" growled Hareton, more
ready in answering his daily companion. He was about to enlarge
further, but the two youngsters broke into a noisy fit of merriment;
my giddy Miss being delighted to discover that she might turn his
strange talk to matter of amusement.

"Where is the use of the devil in that sentence?" tittered Linton.
"Papa told you not to say any bad words, and you can't open your
mouth without one . . . Do try to behave like a gentleman, now do!"

"If thou wern't more a lass than a lad, I'd fell thee this minute, I
would; pitiful lath of a crater!"[8] retorted the angry boor, retreating,
while his face burnt with mingled rage and mortification; for he was
conscious of being insulted, and embarrassed how to resent it.

Mr. Heathcliff, having overheard the conversation as well as I,
smiled when he saw him go, but immediately afterwards cast a
look of singular aversion on the flippant pair, who remained chattering in the door-way: the boy finding animation enough while
discussing Hareton's faults and deficiencies, and relating anecdotes
of his goings on; and the girl relishing his pert and spiteful sayings,
without considering the ill-nature they evinced. But I began to dis-

[8]Thin stick of a creature: a weakling.

like, more than to compassionate, Linton, and to excuse his father, in some measure, for holding him cheap.

We staid till afternoon: I could not tear Miss Cathy away, before: but happily my master had not quitted his apartment, and remained ignorant of our prolonged absence.

As we walked home, I would fain have enlightened my charge on the characters of the people we had quitted; but she got it into her head that I was prejudiced against them.

"Aha!" she cried, "you take papa's side, Ellen—you are partial . . . I know, or else you wouldn't have cheated me so many years into the notion that Linton lived a long way from here. I'm really extremely angry, only, I'm so pleased, I can't show it! But you must hold your tongue about my uncle . . . he's *my* uncle, remember, and I'll scold papa for quarrelling with him."

And so she ran on, till I dropped endeavouring to convince her of her mistake.

She did not mention the visit that night, because she did not see Mr. Linton. Next day it all came out, sadly to my chagrin; and still I was not altogether sorry: I thought the burden of directing and warning would be more efficiently borne by him than me, but he was too timid in giving satisfactory reasons for his wish that she would shun connection with the household of the Heights, and Catherine liked good reasons for every restraint that harassed her petted will.

"Papa!" she exclaimed, after the morning's salutations, "guess whom I saw yesterday, in my walk on the moors . . . Ah, papa, you started! you've not done right, have you, now? I saw—But listen, and you shall hear how I found you out, and Ellen, who is in league with you, and yet pretended to pity me so, when I kept hoping, and was always disappointed about Linton's coming back!"

She gave a faithful account of her excursion and its consequences; and my master, though he cast more than one reproachful look at me, said nothing till she had concluded. Then he drew her to him, and asked if she knew why he had concealed Linton's near neighbourhood from her? Could she think it was to deny her a pleasure that she might harmlessly enjoy?

"It was because you disliked Mr. Heathcliff," she answered.

"Then you believe I care more for my own feelings than yours, Cathy?" he said. "No, it was not because I disliked Mr. Heathcliff, but because Mr. Heathcliff dislikes me; and is a most diabolical man, delighting to wrong and ruin those he hates, if they give him the slightest opportunity. I knew that you could not keep up an acquaintance with your cousin, without being brought into contact with him; and I knew he would detest you, on my account; so, for your own good, and nothing else, I took precautions that you should not see Linton again—I meant to explain this some time as you grew older, and I'm sorry I delayed it!"

"But Mr. Heathcliff was quite cordial, papa," observed Catherine, not at all convinced; "and *he* didn't object to our seeing each other: he said I might come to his house when I pleased, only I must not tell you, because you had quarrelled with him, and would not forgive him for marrying aunt Isabella. And you won't—*you* are the one to be blamed—he is willing to let *us* be friends, at least; Linton and I—and you are not."

My master, perceiving that she would not take his word for her uncle-in-law's evil disposition, gave a hasty sketch of his conduct to Isabella, and the manner in which Wuthering Heights became his property. He could not bear to discourse long upon the topic, for though he spoke little of it, he still felt the same horror and detestation of his ancient enemy that had occupied his heart ever since Mrs. Linton's death. "She might have been living yet, if it had not been for him!" was his constant bitter reflection; and, in his eyes, Heathcliff seemed a murderer.

Miss Cathy, conversant with no bad deeds except her own slight acts of disobedience, injustice and passion, arising from hot temper and thoughtlessness, and repented of on the day they were committed, was amazed at the blackness of spirit that could brood on and cover[9] revenge for years, and deliberately prosecute its plans without a visitation of remorse. She appeared so deeply impressed and shocked at this new view of human nature—excluded from all her studies and all her ideas till now—that Mr. Edgar deemed it unnecessary to pursue the subject. He merely added,

"You will know hereafter, darling, why I wish you to avoid his house and family—now, return to your old employments and amusements, and think no more about them!"

Catherine kissed her father, and sat down quietly to her lessons for a couple of hours, according to custom; then she accompanied

[9]Conceal.

him into the grounds, and the whole day passed as usual. But in the evening, when she had retired to her room, and I went to help her to undress, I found her crying, on her knees by the bedside.

"Oh, fie, silly child!" I exclaimed. "If you had any real griefs, you'd be ashamed to waste a tear on this little contrariety. You never had one shadow of substantial sorrow, Miss Catherine. Suppose, for a minute, that master and I were dead, and you were by yourself in the world—how would you feel, then? Compare the present occasion with such an affliction as that, and be thankful for the friends you have, instead of coveting more."

"I'm not crying for myself, Ellen," she answered, "it's for him—He expected to see me again to-morrow, and there, he'll be so disappointed—and he'll wait for me, and I shan't come!"

"Nonsense!" said I, "do you imagine he has thought as much of you, as you have of him? Hasn't he Hareton for a companion? Not one in a hundred would weep at losing a relation they had just seen twice, for two afternoons—Linton will conjecture how it is, and trouble himself no further about you."

"But may I not write a note to tell him why I cannot come?" she asked, rising to her feet. "And just send those books I promised to lend him—his books are not as nice as mine, and he wanted to have them extremely, when I told him how interesting they were— May I not, Ellen?"

"No, indeed, no, indeed!" replied I with decision. "Then he would write to you, and there'd never be an end of it—No, Miss Catherine, the acquaintance must be dropped entirely—so papa expects, and I shall see that it is done!"

"But how can one little note—" she recommenced, putting on an imploring countenance.

"Silence!" I interrupted. "We'll not begin with your little notes—Get into bed!"

She threw at me a very naughty look, so naughty that I would not kiss her good-night at first. I covered her up, and shut her door, in great displeasure—but, repenting half-way, I returned softly, and lo! there was Miss, standing at the table with a bit of blank paper before her and a pencil in her hand, which she guiltily slipped out of sight, on my re-entrance.

"You'll get nobody to take that, Catherine," I said, "if you write it; and at present I shall put out your candle."

I set the extinguisher on the flame, receiving as I did so a slap on my hand, and a petulant "cross thing!" I then quitted her again, and she drew the bolt in one of her worst, most peevish humours.

The letter was finished and forwarded to its destination by a milk-fetcher who came from the village, but that I didn't learn till some time afterwards. Weeks passed on, and Cathy recovered her temper, though she grew wondrous fond of stealing off to corners by herself, and often, if I came near her suddenly while reading, she would start and bend over the book, evidently desirous to hide it; and I detected edges of loose paper sticking out beyond the leaves.

She also got a trick of coming down early in the morning, and lingering about the kitchen, as if she were expecting the arrival of something; and she had a small drawer in a cabinet in the library which she would trifle over for hours, and whose key she took special care to remove when she left it.

One day, as she inspected this drawer, I observed that the playthings and trinkets, which recently formed its contents, were transmuted into bits of folded paper.

My curiosity and suspicions were roused; I determined to take a peep at her mysterious treasures; so, at night, as soon as she and my master were safe upstairs, I searched and readily found among my house keys one that would fit the lock. Having opened, I emptied the whole contents into my apron, and took them with me to examine at leisure in my own chamber.

Though I could not but suspect, I was still surprised to discover that they were a mass of correspondence—daily almost, it must have been—from Linton Heathcliff, answers to documents forwarded by her. The earlier dated were embarrassed and short; gradually, however, they expanded into copious love letters, foolish as the age of the writer rendered natural, yet with touches, here and there, which I thought were borrowed from a more experienced source.

Some of them struck me as singularly odd compounds of ardour and flatness; commencing in strong feeling, and concluding in the affected, wordy way that a school-boy might use to a fancied, incorporeal sweetheart.

Whether they satisfied Cathy, I don't know, but they appeared very worthless trash to me.

After turning over as many as I thought proper, I tied them in a handkerchief, and set them aside, re-locking the vacant drawer.

Following her habit, my young lady descended early, and visited the kitchen: I watched her go to the door, on the arrival of a certain little boy; and, while the dairy maid filled his can, she tucked something into his jacket pocket, and plucked something out.

I went round by the garden, and laid wait for the messenger, who fought valorously to defend his trust, and we spilt the milk between us; but I succeeded in abstracting the epistle; and threatening serious consequences if he did not look sharp home, I remained under the wall, and perused Miss Cathy's affectionate composition. It was more simple and more eloquent than her cousin's, very pretty and very silly. I shook my head, and went meditating into the house.

The day being wet, she could not divert herself with rambling about the park; so, at the conclusion of her morning studies, she resorted to the solace of the drawer. Her father sat reading at the table; and I, on purpose, had sought a bit of work in some unripped fringes of the window curtain, keeping my eye steadily fixed on her proceedings.

Never did any bird flying back to a plundered nest which it had left brim-ful of chirping young ones, express more complete despair in its anguished cries and flutterings, than she by her single "Oh!" and the change that transfigured her late happy countenance. Mr. Linton looked up.

"What is the matter, love? Have you hurt yourself?" he said.

His tone and look assured her *he* had not been the discoverer of the hoard.

"No, papa—" she gasped. "Ellen! Ellen! come upstairs—I'm sick!"

I obeyed her summons, and accompanied her out.

"Oh, Ellen! you have got them," she commenced immediately, dropping on her knees, when we were enclosed alone. "O, give them to me, and I'll never never do so again! Don't tell papa—You have not told papa, Ellen, say you have not! I've been exceedingly naughty, but I won't do it any more!"

With a grave severity in my manner, I bid her stand up.

"So," I exclaimed, "Miss Catherine, you are tolerably far on, it seems—you may well be ashamed of them! A fine bundle of trash you study in your leisure hours, to be sure—Why, it's good enough to be printed! And what do you suppose the master will think, when I display it before him? I haven't shown it yet, but you needn't imagine I shall keep your ridiculous secrets—For shame! And you must have led the way in writing such absurdities; he would not have thought of beginning, I'm certain."

"I didn't! I didn't!" sobbed Cathy, fit to break her heart. "I didn't once think of loving him till—"

"*Loving!*" cried I, as scornfully as I could utter the word. "*Loving!* Did anybody ever hear the like! I might just as well talk of loving the miller who comes once a year to buy our corn. Pretty loving, indeed, and both times together you have seen Linton hardly four hours in your life! Now here is the babyish trash. I'm going with it to the library; and we'll see what your father says to such *loving*."

She sprang at her precious epistles, but I held them above my head; and then she poured out further frantic entreaties that I would burn them—do anything rather than show them. And being really fully as inclined to laugh as scold, for I esteemed it all girlish vanity, I at length relented in a measure, and asked,

"If I consent to burn them, will you promise faithfully, neither to send nor receive a letter again, nor a book—for I perceive you have sent him books—nor locks of hair, nor rings, nor playthings?"

"We don't send playthings!" cried Catherine, her pride overcoming her shame.

"Nor anything at all, then, my lady!" I said. "Unless you will, here I go."

"I promise, Ellen!" she cried, catching my dress."Oh, put them in the fire, do, do!"

But when I proceeded to open a place with the poker, the sacrifice was too painful to be borne—She earnestly supplicated that I would spare her one or two.

"One or two, Ellen, to keep for Linton's sake!"

I unknotted the handkerchief, and commenced dropping them in from an angle, and the flame curled up the chimney.

"I will have one, you cruel wretch!" she screamed, darting her hand into the fire, and drawing forth some half consumed fragments, at the expense of her fingers.

"Very well—and I will have some to exhibit to papa!" I answered, shaking back the rest into the bundle, and turning anew to the door.

She emptied her blackened pieces into the flames, and motioned me to finish the immolation. It was done; I stirred up the ashes, and interred them under a shovel full of coals; and she mutely, and with a sense of intense injury, retired to her private apartment. I descended to tell my master that the young lady's qualm of sickness was almost gone, but I judged it best for her to lie down a while. She wouldn't dine; but she re-appeared at tea, pale, and red about the eyes, and marvellously subdued in outward aspect.

Next morning I answered the letter by a slip of paper inscribed, "Master Heathcliff is requested to send no more notes to Miss Linton, as she will not receive them." And, thenceforth, the little boy came with vacant pockets.

## Chapter 8/22

Summer drew to an end, and early Autumn—it was past Michaelmas,[1] but the harvest was late that year, and a few of our fields were still uncleared.

Mr. Linton and his daughter would frequently walk out among the reapers: at the carrying of the last sheaves, they stayed till dusk, and the evening happening to be chill and damp, my master caught a bad cold that, settling obstinately on his lungs, confined him indoors throughout the whole of the winter, nearly without intermission.

Poor Cathy, frightened from her little romance, had been considerably sadder and duller since its abandonment, and her father insisted on her reading less, and taking more exercise. She had his companionship no longer; I esteemed it a duty to supply its lack, as much as possible, with mine; an inefficient substitute, for I could only spare two or three hours, from my numerous diurnal occupations, to follow her footsteps, and then, my society was obviously less desirable than his.

On an afternoon in October, or the beginning of November, a fresh watery afternoon, when the turf and paths were rustling with moist, withered leaves, and the cold, blue sky was half hidden by clouds—dark grey streamers, rapidly mounting from the west, and boding abundant rain—I requested my young lady to forego her

---

[1]September 29, the feast of St. Michael. England's Christian and agricultural calendar shaped the business calendar as well; contracts for farm labor and real estate, among others, came due at Michaelmas or the other three quarters of the year.

ramble because I was certain of showers. She refused; and I unwillingly donned a cloak, and took my umbrella to accompany her on a stroll to the bottom of the park; a formal walk which she generally affected if low-spirited—and that she invariably was when Mr. Edgar had been worse than ordinary; a thing never known from his confession, but guessed both by her and me from his increased silence, and the melancholy of his countenance.

She went sadly on; there was no running or bounding now, though the chill wind might well have tempted her to a race. And often, from the side of my eye, I could detect her raising a hand, and brushing something off her cheek.

I gazed round for a means of diverting her thoughts. On one side of the road rose a high, rough bank, where hazels and stunted oaks, with their roots half exposed, held uncertain tenure. The soil was too loose for the latter; and strong winds had blown some nearly horizontal. In summer, Miss Catherine delighted to climb along these trunks, and sit in the branches, swinging twenty feet above the ground; and I, pleased with her agility and her light, childish heart, still considered it proper to scold every time I caught her at such an elevation; but so that she knew there was no necessity for descending. From dinner to tea she would lie in her breeze-rocked cradle, doing nothing except singing old songs—my nursery lore—to herself, or watching the birds, joint tenants, feed and entice their young ones to fly, or nestling with closed lids, half thinking, half dreaming, happier than words can express.

"Look, Miss!" I exclaimed, pointing to a nook under the roots of one twisted tree. "Winter is not here yet. There's a little flower, up yonder, the last bud from the multitude of blue-bells that clouded those turf steps in July with a lilac mist. Will you clamber up, and pluck it to show to papa?"

Cathy stared a long time at the lonely blossom trembling in its earthy shelter, and replied, at length—

"No, I'll not touch it—but it looks melancholy, does it not, Ellen?"

"Yes," I observed, "about as starved and sackless[2] as you—your cheeks are bloodless; let us take hold of hands and run. You're so low, I dare say I shall keep up with you."

---

[2]Frozen and sluggish.

"No," she repeated, and continued sauntering on, pausing, at intervals, to muse over a bit of moss, or a tuft of blanched grass, or a fungus spreading its bright orange among the heaps of brown foliage; and, ever and anon, her hand was lifted to her averted face.

"Catherine, why are you crying, love?" I asked, approaching and putting my arm over her shoulder. "You mustn't cry because papa has a cold; be thankful it is nothing worse."

She now put no further restraint on her tears; her breath was stifled by sobs.

"Oh, it *will* be something worse," she said. "And what shall I do when papa and you leave me, and I am by myself? I can't forget your words, Ellen, they are always in my ear. How life will be changed, how dreary the world will be, when papa and you are dead!"

"None can tell, whether you won't die before us," I replied. "It's wrong to anticipate evil—we'll hope there are years and years to come before any of us go—master is young, and I am strong, and hardly forty-five. My mother lived till eighty, a canty[3] dame to the last. And suppose Mr. Linton were spared till he saw sixty, that would be more years than you have counted, Miss. And would it not be foolish to mourn a calamity above twenty years beforehand?"

"But Aunt Isabella was younger than papa," she remarked, gazing up with timid hope to seek further consolation.

"Aunt Isabella had not you and me to nurse her," I replied. "She wasn't as happy as master; she hadn't as much to live for. All you need do, is to wait well on your father, and cheer him by letting him see you cheerful; and avoid giving him anxiety on any subject—mind that, Cathy! I'll not disguise but you might kill him, if you were wild and reckless, and cherished a foolish, fanciful affection for the son of a person who would be glad to have him in his grave—and allowed him to discover that you fretted over the separation he has judged it expedient to make."

"I fret about nothing on earth except papa's illness," answered my companion. "I care for nothing in comparison with papa. And I'll never—never—oh, never, while I have my senses, do an act or say a word to vex him. I love him better than myself, Ellen; and I know it by this—I pray every night that I may live after him; because I would rather be miserable than that he should be—that proves I love him better than myself."

[3]Lively, spry (see Nelly as a "cant lass" in childhood, p. 50).

"Good words," I replied. "But deeds must prove it also; and after he is well, remember you don't forget resolutions formed in the hour of fear."

As we talked, we neared a door that opened on the road; and my young lady, lightening[4] into sunshine again, climbed up, and seated herself on the top of the wall, reaching over to gather some hips that bloomed scarlet on the summit branches of the wild rose trees, shadowing the highway side. The lower fruit had disappeared, but only birds could touch the upper, except from Cathy's present station.

In stretching to pull them, her hat fell off; and as the door was locked, she proposed scrambling down to recover it. I bid her be cautious lest she got a fall, and she nimbly disappeared.

But the return was no such easy matter; the stones were smooth and neatly cemented, and the rosebushes and blackberry stragglers could yield no assistance in re-ascending. I, like a fool, didn't recollect that till I heard her laughing, and exclaiming—

"Ellen! you'll have to fetch the key, or else I must run round to the porter's lodge. I can't scale the ramparts on this side!"

"Stay where you are," I answered, "I have my bundle of keys in my pocket; perhaps I may manage to open it; if not, I'll go."

Catherine amused herself with dancing to and fro before the door, while I tried all the large keys in succession. I had applied the last, and found that none would do; so, repeating my desire that she would remain there, I was about to hurry home as fast as I could, when an approaching sound arrested me. It was the trot of a horse; Cathy's dance stopped; and in a minute the horse stopped also.

"Who is that?" I whispered.

"Ellen, I wish you could open the door," whispered back my companion, anxiously.

"Ho, Miss Linton!" cried a deep voice (the rider's). "I'm glad to meet you. Don't be in haste to enter, for I have an explanation to ask and obtain."

"I shan't speak to you, Mr. Heathcliff!" answered Catherine. "Papa says you are a wicked man, and you hate both him and me; and Ellen says the same."

"That is nothing to the purpose," said Heathcliff. (He it was.) "I don't hate my son, I suppose, and it is concerning him that I demand your attention. Yes! you have cause to blush. Two or three

[4]Brightening up.

months since, were you not in the habit of writing to Linton? making love in play, eh? You deserved, both of you, flogging for that! You especially, the elder, and less sensitive, as it turns out. I've got your letters, and if you give me any pertness, I'll send them to your father. I presume you grew weary of the amusement, and dropped it, didn't you? Well, you dropped Linton with it, into a Slough of Despond.[5] He was in earnest—in love—really. As true as I live, he's dying for you—breaking his heart at your fickleness, not figuratively, but actually. Though Hareton has made him a standing jest for six weeks, and I have used more serious measures, and attempted to frighten him out of his idiocy, he gets worse daily, and he'll be under the sod before summer, unless you restore him!"

"How can you lie so glaringly to the poor child!" I called from the inside. "Pray ride on! How can you deliberately get up such paltry falsehoods? Miss Cathy, I'll knock the lock off with a stone. You won't believe that vile nonsense. You can feel in yourself, it is impossible that a person should die for love of a stranger."

"I was not aware there were eaves-droppers," muttered the detected villain. "Worthy Mrs. Dean, I like you, but I don't like your double dealing," he added, aloud. "How could *you* lie so glaringly, as to affirm I hated the 'poor child?' And invent bugbear stories to terrify her from my door-stones? Catherine Linton (the very name warms me), my bonny lass, I shall be from home all this week; go and see if I have not spoken truth; do, there's a darling! Just imagine your father in my place, and Linton in yours; then think how you would value your careless lover, if he refused to stir a step to comfort you, when your father, himself, entreated him; and don't, from pure stupidity, fall into the same error. I swear, on my salvation, he's going to his grave, and none but you can save him!"

The lock gave way, and I issued out.

"I swear Linton is dying," repeated Heathcliff, looking hard at me. "And grief and disappointment are hastening his death. Nelly, if you won't let her go, you can walk over yourself. But I shall not return till this time next week; and I think your master himself would scarcely object to her visiting her cousin!"

[5]In John Bunyan's *The Pilgrim's Progress* (1678), the marsh that is the allegory of despair.

"Come in," said I, taking Cathy by the arm and half forcing her to re-enter, for she lingered, viewing with troubled eyes the features of the speaker, too stern to express his inward deceit.

He pushed his horse close, and, bending down, observed—

"Miss Catherine, I'll own to you that I have little patience with Linton—and Hareton and Joseph have less. I'll own that he's with a harsh set. He pines for kindness, as well as love; and a kind word from you would be his best medicine. Don't mind Mrs. Dean's cruel cautions, but be generous, and contrive to see him. He dreams of you day and night, and cannot be persuaded that you don't hate him, since you neither write nor call."

I closed the door, and rolled a stone to assist the loosened lock in holding it; and spreading my umbrella, I drew my charge underneath, for the rain began to drive through the moaning branches of the trees, and warned us to avoid delay.

Our hurry prevented any comment on the encounter with Heathcliff, as we stretched[6] towards home; but I divined instinctively that Catherine's heart was clouded now in double darkness. Her features were so sad, they did not seem hers; she evidently regarded what she had heard as every syllable true.

The master had retired to rest before we came in. Cathy stole to his room to inquire how he was; he had fallen asleep. She returned, and asked me to sit with her in the library. We took our tea together; and afterwards she lay down on the rug, and told me not to talk for she was weary.

I got a book, and pretended to read. As soon as she supposed me absorbed in my occupation, she recommenced her silent weeping; it appeared, at present, her favourite diversion. I suffered her to enjoy it a while; then, I expostulated; deriding and ridiculing all Mr. Heathcliff's assertions about his son, as if I were certain she would coincide. Alas! I hadn't skill to counteract the effect his account had produced; it was just what he intended.

"You may be right, Ellen," she answered; "but I shall never feel at ease till I know—and I must tell Linton it is not my fault that I don't write; and convince him that I shall not change."

What use were anger and protestations against her silly credulity? We parted that night hostile—but next day beheld me on

[6]Rushed.

the road to Wuthering Heights, by the side of my wilful young mistress's pony. I couldn't bear to witness her sorrow, to see her pale, dejected countenance and heavy eyes; and I yielded in the faint hope that Linton himself might prove, by his reception of us, how little of the tale was founded on fact.

## Chapter 9/23

The rainy night had ushered in a misty morning—half frost, half drizzle—and temporary brooks crossed our path, gurgling from the uplands. My feet were thoroughly wetted; I was cross and low, exactly the humour suited for making the most of these disagreeable things.

We entered the farm-house by the kitchen way to ascertain whether Mr. Heathcliff were really absent; because I put slight faith in his own affirmation.

Joseph seemed sitting in a sort of elysium alone, beside a roaring fire; a quart of ale on the table near him, bristling with large pieces of toasted oat cake; and his black, short pipe in his mouth.

Catherine ran to the hearth to warm herself. I asked if the master were in?

My question remained so long unanswered, that I thought the old man had grown deaf, and repeated it louder.

"Na—ay!" he snarled, or rather screamed through his nose. "Na—ay! yah muh goa back whear yah coom frough."

"Joseph," cried a peevish voice, simultaneously with me, from the inner room. "How often am I to call you? There are only a few red ashes now. Joseph! come this moment."

Vigorous puffs, and a resolute stare into the grate, declared he had no ear for this appeal. The housekeeper and Hareton were invisible; one gone on an errand, and the other at his work, probably. We knew Linton's tones and entered.

"Oh, I hope you'll die in a garret! starved to death," said the boy, mistaking our approach for that of his negligent attendant.

He stopped, on observing his error; his cousin flew to him.

"Is that you, Miss Linton?" he said, raising his head from the arm of the great chair in which he reclined. "No—don't kiss me. It takes my breath—dear me! Papa said you would call," continued he, after recovering a little from Catherine's embrace; while she stood by looking very contrite. "Will you shut the door, if you please? you left it open—and those—those *detestable* creatures won't bring coals to the fire. It's so cold!"

I stirred up the cinders, and fetched a scuttle full myself. The invalid complained of being covered with ashes; but he had a tiresome cough, and looked feverish and ill, so I did not rebuke his temper.

"Well, Linton," murmured Catherine, when his corrugated brow relaxed, "are you glad to see me? Can I do you any good?"

"Why didn't you come before?" he asked. "You should have come, instead of writing. It tired me dreadfully, writing those long letters. I'd far rather have talked to you. Now, I can neither bear to talk, nor anything else. I wonder where Zillah is! Will you (looking at me) step into the kitchen and see?"

I had received no thanks for my other service; and being unwilling to run to and fro at his behest, I replied—

"Nobody is out there but Joseph."

"I want to drink," he exclaimed, fretfully, turning away. "Zillah is constantly gadding off to Gimmerton since papa went. It's miserable! And I'm obliged to come down here—they resolved never to hear me upstairs."

"Is your father attentive to you, Master Heathcliff?" I asked, perceiving Catherine to be checked in her friendly advances.

"Attentive? He makes *them* a little more attentive, at least," he cried. "The wretches! Do you know, Miss Linton, that brute Hareton laughs at me—I hate him—indeed, I hate them all—they are odious beings."

Cathy began searching for some water; she lighted on a pitcher in the dresser, filled a tumbler, and brought it. He bid her add a spoonful of wine from a bottle on the table; and having swallowed a small portion, appeared more tranquil, and said she was very kind.

"And are you glad to see me?" asked she, reiterating her former question, and pleased to detect the faint dawn of a smile.

"Yes, I am—It's something new to hear a voice like yours!" he replied, "but I *have* been vexed, because you wouldn't come—And papa swore it was owing to me; he called me a pitiful, shuffling, worthless thing; and said you despised me; and if he had been in my place, he would be more the master of the Grange than your father, by this time. But you don't despise me, do you, Miss——"

"I wish you would say Catherine, or Cathy!" interrupted my young lady. "Despise you? No! Next to papa, and Ellen, I love you better than anybody living. I don't love Mr. Heathcliff, though; and I dare not come when he returns; will he stay away many days?"

"Not many," answered Linton, "but he goes onto the moors frequently, since the shooting season commenced, and you might spend an hour or two with me, in his absence—Do! say you will! I think I should not be peevish with you; you'd not provoke me, and you'd always be ready to help me, wouldn't you?"

"Yes," said Catherine, stroking his long soft hair, "if I could only get papa's consent, I'd spend half my time with you—Pretty Linton! I wish you were my brother!"

"And then you would like me as well as your father?" observed he more cheerfully. "But papa says you would love me better than him, and all the world, if you were my wife—so I'd rather you were that!"

"No! I should never love anybody better than papa," she returned gravely. "And people hate their wives, sometimes, but not their sisters and brothers; and if you were the latter, you would live with us, and papa would be as fond of you as he is of me."

Linton denied that people ever hated their wives; but Cathy affirmed they did, and in her wisdom, instanced his own father's aversion to her aunt.

I endeavoured to stop her thoughtless tongue—I couldn't succeed till everything she knew was out. Master Heathcliff, much irritated, asserted her relation was false.

"Papa told me; and papa does not tell falsehoods!" she answered pertly.

"*My* papa scorns yours!" cried Linton. "He calls him a sneaking fool!"

"Yours is a wicked man," retorted Catherine, "and you are very naughty to dare to repeat what he says—He must be wicked, to have made aunt Isabella leave him as she did!"

"She didn't leave him," said the boy, "you shan't contradict me!"

"She did!" cried my young lady.

"Well, I'll tell *you* something!" said Linton. "Your mother hated your father, now then."

"Oh!" exclaimed Catherine, too enraged to continue.

"And she loved mine!" added he.

"You little liar! I hate you now," she panted, and her face grew red with passion.

"She did! she did!" sang Linton, sinking into the recess of his chair, and leaning back his head to enjoy the agitation of the other disputant, who stood behind.

"Hush, Master Heathcliff!" I said, "that's your father's tale too, I suppose."

"It isn't—you hold your tongue!" he answered; "she did, she did, Catherine, she did, she did!"

Cathy, beside herself, gave the chair a violent push, and caused him to fall against one arm. He was immediately seized by a suffocating cough that soon ended his triumph.

It lasted so long, that it frightened even me. As to his cousin, she wept with all her might, aghast at the mischief she had done, though she said nothing.

I held him, till the fit exhausted itself. Then he thrust me away; and leant his head down, silently—Catherine quelled her lamentations also, took a seat opposite, and looked solemnly into the fire.

"How do you feel now, Master Heathcliff?" I inquired, after waiting ten minutes.

"I wish *she* felt as I do," he replied, "spiteful, cruel thing! Hareton never touches me, he never struck me in his life—And I was better to-day—and there—" his voice died in a whimper.

"*I* didn't strike you!" muttered Cathy, chewing her lip to prevent another burst of emotion.

He sighed and moaned like one under great suffering; and kept it up for a quarter of an hour, on purpose to distress his cousin, apparently, for whenever he caught a stifled sob from her, he put renewed pain and pathos into the inflexions of his voice.

"I'm sorry I hurt you, Linton!" she said at length, racked beyond endurance. "But *I* couldn't have been hurt by that little push; and I had no idea that you could, either—you're not much, are you, Linton? Don't let me go home thinking I've done you harm! Answer, speak to me."

"I can't speak to you," he murmured, "you've hurt me so, that I shall lie awake all night, choking with this cough! If you had it you'd know what it was—but *you'll* be comfortably asleep, while I'm in agony—and nobody near me! I wonder how you would like to pass those fearful nights!" And he began to wail aloud for very pity of himself.

"Since you are in the habit of passing dreadful nights," I said, "it won't be miss who spoils your ease; you'd be the same, had she never come—However, she shall not disturb you again—and perhaps you'll get quieter when we leave you."

"Must I go?" asked Catherine dolefully, bending over him. "Do you want me to go, Linton?"

"You can't alter what you've done," he replied pettishly, shrinking from her, "unless you alter it for the worse, by teasing me into a fever!"

"Well, then I must go?" she repeated.

"Let me alone, at least," said he, "I can't bear your talking!"

She lingered, and resisted my persuasions to departure a tiresome while; but as he neither looked up nor spoke, she finally made a movement to the door and I followed.

We were recalled by a scream—Linton had slid from his seat on to the hearth-stone, and lay writhing in the mere perverseness of an indulged plague of a child, determined to be as grievous and harassing as it can.

I thoroughly gauged his disposition from his behaviour, and saw at once it would be folly to attempt humouring him. Not so my companion: she ran back in terror, knelt down, and cried, and soothed, and entreated, till he grew quiet from lack of breath, by no means from compunction at distressing her.

"I shall lift him on to the settle," I said, "and he may roll about as he pleases; we can't stop to watch him—I hope you are satisfied, Miss Cathy, that *you* are not the person to benefit him, and that his condition of health is not occasioned by attachment to you. Now then, there he is! Come away—as soon as he knows there is nobody by to care for his nonsense, he'll be glad to lie still!"

She placed a cushion under his head, and offered him some water; he rejected the latter, and tossed uneasily on the former, as if it were a stone, or a block of wood.

She tried to put it more comfortably.

"I can't do with that," he said, "it's not high enough!"

Catherine brought another to lay above it.

"That's *too* high!" murmured the provoking thing.

"How must I arrange it, then?" she asked despairingly.

He twined himself up to her, as she half knelt by the settle, and converted her shoulder into a support.

"No, that won't do!" I said. "You'll be content with the cushion, Master Heathcliff! Miss has wasted too much time on you, already; we cannot remain five minutes longer."

"Yes, yes, we can!" replied Cathy. "He's good and patient, now—He's beginning to think I shall have far greater misery than he will to-night, if I believe he is the worse for my visit; and then, I dare not come again—Tell the truth about it, Linton—for I mustn't come, if I have hurt you."

"You must come, to cure me," he answered. "You ought to come because you have hurt me—You know you have, extremely! I was not as ill when you entered, as I am at present—was I?"

"But you've made yourself ill by crying, and being in a passion. I didn't do it all," said his cousin. "However, we'll be friends now. And you want me—you would wish to see me sometimes, really?"

"I told you I did!" he replied impatiently. "Sit on the settle and let me lean on your knee—That's as mamma used to do, whole afternoons together—Sit quite still, and don't talk, but you may sing a song if you can sing, or you may say a nice, long interesting ballad—one of those you promised to teach me, or a story—I'd rather have a ballad, though: begin."

Catherine repeated the longest she could remember. The employment pleased both mightily. Linton would have another, and after that another, notwithstanding my strenuous objections; and so they went on until the clock struck twelve, and we heard Hareton in the court, returning for his dinner.

"And to-morrow, Catherine, will you be here to-morrow?" asked young Heathcliff, holding her frock, as she rose reluctantly.

"No!" I answered, "nor next day neither." She, however, gave a different response, evidently, for his forehead cleared as she stooped and whispered in his ear.

"You won't go to-morrow, recollect, Miss!" I commenced, when we were out of the house. "You are not dreaming of it, are you?"

She smiled.

"Oh, I'll take good care!" I continued, "I'll have that lock mended, and you can escape by no way else."

"I can get over the wall," she said, laughing. "The Grange is not a prison, Ellen, and you are not my jailer. And besides, I'm almost seventeen. I'm a woman—and I'm certain Linton would recover quickly if he had me to look after him—I'm older than he is, you know, and wiser, less childish, am I not? And he'll soon do as I direct him, with some slight coaxing—He's a pretty little darling when he's good. I'd make such a pet of him, if he were mine. We should never quarrel, should we, after we were used to each other? Don't you like him, Ellen?"

"Like him?" I exclaimed. "The worst-tempered bit of a sickly slip that ever struggled into its teens! Happily, as Mr. Heathcliff conjectured, he'll not win[1] twenty! I doubt whether he'll see spring, indeed—and small loss to his family, whenever he drops off; and lucky it is for us that his father took him—The kinder he was treated, the more tedious and selfish he'd be! I'm glad you have no chance of having him for a husband, Miss Catherine!"

My companion waxed serious at hearing this speech—To speak of his death so regardlessly wounded her feelings.

"He's younger than I," she answered, after a protracted pause of meditation, "and he ought to live the longest. He will— he must live as long as I do. He's as strong now as when he first came into the North, I'm positive of that! It's only a cold that ails him, the same as papa has—You say papa will get better, and why shouldn't he?"

"Well, well," I cried, "after all, we needn't trouble ourselves; for listen, Miss—and mind, I'll keep my word—if you attempt going to Wuthering Heights again, with or without me, I shall inform Mr. Linton, and unless he allow it, the intimacy with your cousin must not be revived."

"It has been revived!" muttered Cathy sulkily.

"Must not be continued, then!" I said.

"We'll see!" was her reply, and she set off at a gallop, leaving me to toil in the rear.

We both reached home before our dinner-time; my master supposed we had been wandering through the park, and therefore he demanded no explanation of our absence. As soon as I entered, I hastened to change my soaked shoes and stockings; but sitting such a while at the Heights had done the mischief. On the succeeding morning, I was laid up; and during three weeks I remained inca-

[1]Reach.

pacitated for attending to my duties—a calamity never experienced prior to that period, and never, I am thankful to say, since.

My little mistress behaved like an angel in coming to wait on me, and cheer my solitude. The confinement brought me exceedingly low—It is wearisome, to a stirring active body—but few have slighter reasons for complaint than I had. The moment Catherine left Mr. Linton's room, she appeared at my bed-side. Her day was divided between us; no amusement usurped a minute. She neglected her meals, her studies, and her play; and she was the fondest nurse that ever watched. She must have had a warm heart, when she loved her father so, to give so much to me!

I said her days were divided between us; but the master retired early, and I generally needed nothing after six o'clock, thus the evening was her own.

Poor thing, I never considered what she did with herself after tea. And though frequently, when she looked in to bid me good-night, I remarked a fresh colour in her cheeks, and a pinkness over her slender fingers; instead of fancying the hue borrowed from a cold ride across the moors, I laid it to the charge of a hot fire in the library.

## Chapter 10/24

At the close of three weeks, I was able to quit my chamber, and move about the house. And on the first occasion of my sitting up in the evening, I asked Catherine to read to me, because my eyes were weak. We were in the library, the master having gone to bed: she consented, rather unwillingly, I fancied; and imagining my sort of books did not suit her, I bid her please herself in the choice of what she perused.

She selected one of her own favourites, and got forward steadily about an hour; then came frequent questions.

"Ellen, are not you tired? Hadn't you better lie down now? You'll be sick, keeping up so long, Ellen."

"No, no, dear, I'm not tired," I returned, continually.

Perceiving me immovable, she essayed another method of showing her dis-relish for her occupation. It changed to yawning, and stretching, and—

"Ellen, I'm tired."

"Give over then and talk," I answered.

That was worse; she fretted and sighed, and looked at her watch till eight; and finally went to her room, completely over-done[1] with sleep, judging by her peevish, heavy look, and the constant rubbing she inflicted on her eyes.

The following night she seemed more impatient still; and on the third from recovering my company, she complained of a head-ache, and left me.

I thought her conduct odd; and having remained alone a long while, I resolved on going and inquiring whether she were better, and asking her to come and lie on the sofa, instead of upstairs, in the dark.

No Catherine could I discover upstairs, and none below. The servants affirmed they had not seen her. I listened at Mr. Edgar's door—all was silence. I returned to her apartment, extinguished my candle, and seated myself in the window.

The moon shone bright; a sprinkling of snow covered the ground, and I reflected that she might, possibly, have taken it into her head to walk about the garden, for refreshment. I did detect a figure creeping along the inner fence of the park; but it was not my young mistress; on its emerging into the light, I recognised one of the grooms.

He stood a considerable period, viewing the carriage-road through the grounds; then started off at a brisk pace, as if he had detected something, and reappeared presently, leading Miss's pony; and there she was, just dismounted, and walking by its side.

The man took his charge stealthily across the grass towards the stable. Cathy entered by the casement-window[2] of the drawing-room, and glided noiselessly up to where I awaited her.

She put the door gently to, slipped off her snowy shoes, untied her hat, and was proceeding, unconscious of my espionage, to lay aside her mantle, when I suddenly rose and revealed myself. The surprise petrified her an instant; she uttered an inarticulate exclamation, and stood fixed.

"My dear Miss Catherine," I began, too vividly impressed by her recent kindness to break into a scold, "where have you been riding out at this hour? And why should you try to deceive me, by telling a tale? Where have you been? Speak!"

---

[1]Overcome.

[2]Here, French window—one that pivots open rather than being raised vertically.

"To the bottom of the park," she stammered. "I didn't tell a tale."

"And no where else?" I demanded.

"No," was the muttered reply.

"Oh, Catherine," I cried, sorrowfully. "You know you have been doing wrong, or you wouldn't be driven to uttering an untruth to me. That does grieve me. I'd rather be three months ill, than hear you frame a deliberate lie."

She sprang forward, and bursting into tears, threw her arms round my neck.

"Well, Ellen, I'm so afraid of you being angry," she said. "Promise not to be angry, and you shall know the very truth. I hate to hide it."

We sat down in the window-seat; I assured her I would not scold, whatever her secret might be, and I guessed it, of course; so she commenced—

"I've been to Wuthering Heights, Ellen, and I've never missed going a day since you fell ill; except thrice before, and twice after you left your room. I gave Michael books and pictures to prepare Minny every evening, and to put her back in the stable; you mustn't scold *him* either, mind. I was at the Heights by half-past six, and generally stayed till half-past eight, and then galloped home. It was not to amuse myself that I went; I was often wretched all the time. Now and then, I was happy, once in a week perhaps. At first, I expected there would be sad work persuading you to let me keep my word to Linton, for I had engaged to call again next day when we quitted him; but, as you stayed upstairs on the morrow, I escaped that trouble; and while Michael was refastening the lock of the park door in the afternoon, I got possession of the key, and told him how my cousin wished me to visit him, because he was sick, and couldn't come to the Grange: and how papa would object to my going. And then I negotiated with him about the pony. He is fond of reading, and he thinks of leaving soon to get married, so he offered, if I would lend him books out of the library, to do what I wished; but I preferred giving him my own, and that satisfied him better.

"On my second visit, Linton seemed in lively spirits; and Zillah—that is their housekeeper—made us a clean room and a good fire, and told us that, as Joseph was out at a prayer-meeting, and Hareton Earnshaw was off with his dogs—robbing our woods of pheasants, as I heard afterwards—we might do what we liked.

"She brought me some warm wine and gingerbread, and appeared exceedingly good-natured; and Linton sat in the arm-chair, and I in the little rocking chair on the hearthstone, and we laughed and talked so merrily, and found so much to say; we planned where we would go, and what we would do in summer. I needn't repeat that, because you would call it silly.

"One time, however, we were near quarrelling. He said the pleasantest manner of spending a hot July day was lying from morning till evening on a bank of heath in the middle of the moors, with the bees humming dreamily about among the bloom, and the larks singing high up over head, and the blue sky and bright sun shining steadily and cloudlessly. That was his most perfect idea of heaven's happiness—mine was rocking in a rustling green tree, with a west wind blowing, and bright, white clouds flitting rapidly above; and not only larks, but throstles, and blackbirds, and linnets, and cuckoos pouring out music on every side, and the moors seen at a distance, broken into cool dusky dells, but close by, great swells of long grass undulating in waves to the breeze; and woods and sounding water, and the whole world awake and wild with joy. He wanted all to lie in an ecstasy of peace; I wanted all to sparkle, and dance in a glorious jubilee.

"I said his heaven would be only half alive, and he said mine would be drunk; I said I should fall asleep in his, and he said he could not breathe in mine, and began to grow very snappish. At last, we agreed to try both as soon as the right weather came; and then we kissed each other and were friends. After sitting still an hour, I looked at the great room with its smooth uncarpeted floor, and thought how nice it would be to play in, if we removed the table; and I asked Linton to call Zillah in to help us—and we'd have a game at blind-man's buff—she should try to catch us—you used to, you know, Ellen. He wouldn't; there was no pleasure in it, he said; but he consented to play at ball with me. We found two in a cupboard, among a heap of old toys; tops, and hoops, and battle-doors, and shuttlecocks. One was marked C., and the other H.; I wished to have the C., because that stood for Catherine, and the H. might be for Heathcliff, his name; but the bran came out of H., and Linton didn't like it.

"I beat him constantly; and he got cross again, and coughed, and returned to his chair. That night, though, he easily recovered

his good humour; he was charmed with two or three pretty songs—
*your* songs, Ellen; and when I was obliged to go, he begged and entreated me to come the following evening, and I promised.

"Minny and I went flying home as light as air: and I dreamt of
Wuthering Heights, and my sweet, darling cousin, till morning.

"On the morrow, I was sad; partly because you were poorly,
and partly that I wished my father knew, and approved of my ex-
cursions; but it was beautiful moonlight after tea; and, as I rode on,
the gloom cleared.

"I shall have another happy evening, I thought to myself, and
what delights me more, my pretty Linton will.

"I trotted up their garden, and was turning round to the back,
when that fellow Earnshaw met me, took my bridle, and bid me
go in by the front entrance. He patted Minny's neck, and said she
was a bonny beast, and appeared as if he wanted me to speak to
him. I only told him to leave my horse alone, or else it would
kick him.

"He answered in his vulgar accent.

"'It wouldn't do mitch hurt if it did,' and surveyed its legs with
a smile.

"I was half inclined to make it try; however, he moved off to
open the door, and, as he raised the latch, he looked up to the inscription above, and said, with a stupid mixture of awkwardness
and elation:

"'Miss Catherine! I can read yon, nah.'

"'Wonderful,' I exclaimed. 'Pray let us hear you—you *are*
grown clever!'

"He spelt, and drawled over by syllables, the name—

"'Hareton Earnshaw.'

"'And the figures?' I cried encouragingly, perceiving that he
came to a dead halt.

"'I cannot tell them yet,' he answered.

"'Oh, you dunce!' I said, laughing heartily at his failure.

"The fool stared, with a grin hovering about his lips, and a
scowl gathering over his eyes, as if uncertain whether he might not
join in my mirth; whether it were not pleasant familiarity, or what
it really was, contempt.

"I settled his doubts by suddenly retrieving my gravity, and desiring him to walk away, for I came to see Linton not him.

"He reddened—I saw that by the moonlight—dropped his hand from the latch, and skulked off, a picture of mortified vanity. He imagined himself to be as accomplished as Linton, I suppose, because he could spell his own name; and was marvellously discomfited that I didn't think the same."

"Stop, Miss Catherine, dear!" I interrupted. "I shall not scold, but I don't like your conduct there. If you had remembered that Hareton was your cousin, as much as Master Heathcliff, you would have felt how improper it was to behave in that way. At least, it was praiseworthy ambition for him to desire to be as accomplished as Linton: and probably he did not learn merely to show off; you had made him ashamed of his ignorance before, I have no doubt; and he wished to remedy it and please you. To sneer at his imperfect attempt was very bad breeding—had *you* been brought up in his circumstances, would you be less rude? He was as quick and as intelligent a child as ever you were, and I'm hurt that he should be despised now, because that base Heathcliff has treated him so unjustly."

"Well, Ellen, you won't cry about it, will you?" she exclaimed, surprised at my earnestness. "But wait, and you shall hear if he conned his A B C to please me; and if it were worth while being civil to the brute. I entered; Linton was lying on the settle and half got up to welcome me.

"'I'm ill to-night, Catherine, love,' he said, 'and you must have all the talk, and let me listen. Come, and sit by me—I was sure you wouldn't break your word, and I'll make you promise again, before you go.'

"I knew now that I mustn't tease him, as he was ill; and I spoke softly and put no questions, and avoided irritating him in any way. I had brought some of my nicest books for him; he asked me to read a little of one, and I was about to comply, when Earnshaw burst the door open, having gathered venom with reflection. He advanced direct to us, seized Linton by the arm, and swung him off the seat.

"'Get to thy own room!' he said in a voice almost inarticulate with passion, and his face looked swelled and furious. 'Take her there if she comes to see thee—thou shalln't keep me out of this. Begone, wi' ye both!'

"He swore at us, and left Linton no time to answer, nearly throwing him into the kitchen; and he clenched his fist, as I followed, seemingly longing to knock me down. I was afraid, for a moment, and I let one volume fall; he kicked it after me, and shut us out.

"I heard a malignant, crackly laugh by the fire, and turning beheld that odious Joseph, standing rubbing his bony hands, and quivering.

"'Aw wer sure he'd sarve ye aht! He's a grand lad! He's getten t' raight sperrit in him! *He* knaws—Aye, he knaws, as weel as Aw do, who sud be t' maister yonder—Ech, ech, ech! He mad ye skift properly![3] Ech, ech, ech!'

"'Where must we go?' I asked of my cousin, disregarding the old wretch's mockery.

"Linton was white and trembling. He was not pretty then, Ellen—Oh, no! he looked frightful! for his thin face and large eyes were wrought into an expression of frantic, powerless fury. He grasped the handle of the door, and shook it—it was fastened inside.

"'If you don't let me in I'll kill you! If you don't let me in I'll kill you!' he rather shrieked than said. 'Devil! devil! I'll kill you, I'll kill you!'

"Joseph uttered his croaking laugh again.

"'Thear, that's t' father!' he cried. 'That's father! We've allas summut uh orther side[4] in us—Niver heed, Hareton, lad—dunnut be 'feard—he cannot get at thee!'

"I took hold of Linton's hands, and tried to pull him away; but he shrieked so shockingly that I dared not proceed. At last, his cries were choked by a dreadful fit of coughing; blood gushed from his mouth, and he fell on the ground.

"I ran into the yard, sick with terror; and called for Zillah, as loud as I could. She soon heard me; she was milking the cows in a shed behind the barn, and hurrying from her work, she inquired what there was to do?[5]

"I hadn't breath to explain; dragging her in, I looked about for Linton. Earnshaw had come out to examine the mischief he had caused, and he was then conveying the poor thing upstairs. Zillah

[3]"I was sure he'd serve you out [get back at you]. . . . He's got the right spirit in him! *He* knows . . . as well as I do, who should be the master yonder. . . . He made you skip properly [sure made you scram]!"

[4]"We always have something of either side," that is, Linton is showing the "father" side of his personality, or Heathcliff's murderous spirit.

[5]What was the matter?

and I ascended after him; but he stopped me at the top of the steps, and said I shouldn't go in, I must go home.

"I exclaimed that he had killed Linton and I *would* enter.

"Joseph locked the door, and declared I should do 'no sich stuff,' and asked me whether I were 'bahn to be as mad as him.'[6]

"I stood crying, till the housekeeper re-appeared; she affirmed he would be better in a bit, but he couldn't do with that shrieking and din; and she took me, and nearly carried me into the house.

"Ellen, I was ready to tear my hair off my head! I sobbed and wept so that my eyes were almost blind; and the ruffian you have such sympathy with stood opposite, presuming every now and then to bid me 'wisht,' and denying that it was his fault; and finally, frightened by my assertions that I would tell papa, and that he should be put in prison and hanged, he commenced blubbering himself, and hurried out to hide his cowardly agitation.

"Still, I was not rid of him: when at length they compelled me to depart, and I had got some hundred yards off the premises, he suddenly issued from the shadow of the road-side, and checked Minny and took hold of me.

"'Miss Catherine, I'm ill grieved,' he began, 'but it's rayther too bad—'

"I gave him a cut with my whip, thinking perhaps he would murder me—He let go, thundering one of his horrid curses, and I galloped home more than half out of my senses.

"I didn't bid you good-night, that evening; and I didn't go to Wuthering Heights, the next—I wished to, exceedingly; but I was strangely excited, and dreaded to hear that Linton was dead, sometimes; and sometimes shuddered at the thought of encountering Hareton.

"On the third day I took courage; at least, I couldn't bear longer suspense and stole off, once more. I went at five o'clock, and walked, fancying I might manage to creep into the house, and up to Linton's room, unobserved. However, the dogs gave notice of my approach. Zillah received me, and saying 'the lad was mending nicely,' showed me into a small, tidy, carpeted apartment, where, to my inexpressible joy, I beheld Linton laid on a little sofa, reading one of my books. But he would neither speak to me nor look at me

---

[6]Going to be as crazy as he was. *Bahn* may be "born" or "bound" or "going."

through a whole hour, Ellen—He has such an unhappy temper—
and what quite confounded me, when he did open his mouth it was
to utter the falsehood that I had occasioned the uproar, and Hareton was not to blame!

"Unable to reply, except passionately, I got up and walked from
the room. He sent after me a faint 'Catherine!' He did not reckon
on being answered so—but I wouldn't turn back; and the morrow
was the second day on which I stayed at home, nearly determined
to visit him no more.

"But it was so miserable going to bed, and getting up, and
never hearing anything about him, that my resolution melted into
air, before it was properly formed. It *had* appeared wrong to take
the journey once; now it seemed wrong to refrain. Michael came to
ask if he must saddle Minny; I said 'Yes,' and considered myself doing a duty as she bore me over the hills.

"I was forced to pass the front windows to get to the court; it
was no use trying to conceal my presence.

"'Young master is in the house,' said Zillah, as she saw me
making for the parlour.

"I went in; Earnshaw was there also, but he quitted the room
directly. Linton sat in the great arm chair half asleep; walking up to
the fire, I began in a serious tone, partly meaning it to be true.

"'As you don't like me, Linton, and as you think I come on purpose to hurt you, and pretend that I do so every time, this is our last
meeting—let us say good-bye; and tell Mr. Heathcliff that you have
no wish to see me, and that he mustn't invent any more falsehoods
on the subject.'

"'Sit down and take your hat off, Catherine,' he answered.
'You are so much happier than I am, you ought to be better. Papa
talks enough of my defects, and shows enough scorn of me, to
make it natural I should doubt myself—I doubt whether I am not
altogether as worthless as he calls me, frequently; and then I feel so
cross and bitter, I hate everybody! I *am* worthless, and bad in temper, and bad in spirit, almost always—and if you choose, you *may*
say good-bye—you'll get rid of an annoyance—Only, Catherine, do
me this justice; believe that if I might be as sweet, and as kind, and
as good as you are, I would be, as willingly, and more so, than as
happy and as healthy. And believe that your kindness has made me
love you deeper than if I deserved your love, and though I couldn't,

and cannot help showing my nature to you, I regret it and repent it, and shall regret and repent it, till I die!'

"I felt he spoke the truth; and I felt I must forgive him; and, though he should quarrel the next moment, I must forgive him again. We were reconciled, but we cried, both of us, the whole time I stayed. Not entirely for sorrow, yet I *was* sorry Linton had that distorted nature. He'll never let his friends be at ease, and he'll never be at ease himself!

"I have always gone to his little parlour, since that night; because his father returned the day after. About three times, I think, we have been merry and hopeful, as we were the first evening; the rest of my visits were dreary and troubled—now with his selfishness and spite, and now with his sufferings; but I've learnt to endure the former with nearly as little resentment as the latter.

"Mr. Heathcliff purposely avoids me. I have hardly seen him at all. Last Sunday, indeed, coming earlier than usual, I heard him abusing poor Linton, cruelly, for his conduct of the night before. I can't tell how he knew of it, unless he listened. Linton had certainly behaved provokingly; however, it was the business of nobody but me; and I interrupted Mr. Heathcliff's lecture by entering and telling him so. He burst into a laugh, and went away, saying he was glad I took that view of the matter. Since then, I've told Linton he must whisper his bitter things.

"Now, Ellen, you have heard all; and I can't be prevented from going to Wuthering Heights, except by inflicting misery on two people—whereas, if you'll only not tell papa, my going need disturb the tranquillity of none. You'll not tell, will you? It will be very heartless if you do."

"I'll make up my mind on that point by to-morrow, Miss Catherine," I replied. "It requires some study; and so I'll leave you to your rest, and go think it over."

I thought it over aloud, in my master's presence; walking straight from her room to his, and relating the whole story, with the exception of her conversations with her cousin, and any mention of Hareton.

Mr. Linton was alarmed and distressed more than he would acknowledge to me. In the morning, Catherine learnt my betrayal of her confidence, and she learnt also that her secret visits were to end.

In vain she wept and writhed against the interdict, and implored her father to have pity on Linton. All she got to comfort her was a promise that he would write, and give him leave to come to the Grange when he pleased; but explaining that he must no longer expect to see Catherine at Wuthering Heights. Perhaps, had he been aware of his nephew's disposition and state of health, he would have seen fit to withhold even that slight consolation.

## Chapter 11/25

"These things happened last winter, sir," said Mrs. Dean; "hardly more than a year ago. Last winter, I did not think, at another twelve months' end, I should be amusing a stranger to the family with relating them! Yet, who knows how long you'll be a stranger? You're too young to rest always contented, living by yourself; and I some way fancy, no one could see Catherine Linton, and not love her. You smile; but why do you look so lively and interested, when I talk about her—and why have you asked me to hang her picture over your fireplace? and why—"

"Stop, my good friend!" I cried. "It may be very possible that *I* should love her; but would she love me? I doubt it too much to venture my tranquillity by running into temptation; and then my home is not here. I'm of the busy world, and to its arms I must return. Go on. Was Catherine obedient to her father's commands?"

"She was," continued the housekeeper. "Her affection for him was still the chief sentiment in her heart; and he spoke without anger; he spoke in the deep tenderness of one about to leave his treasure amid perils and foes, where his remembered words would be the only aid that he could bequeath to guide her.

He said to me, a few days afterwards,

"I wish my nephew would write, Ellen, or call. Tell me, sincerely, what you think of him—is he changed for the better, or is there a prospect of improvement, as he grows a man?"

"He's very delicate, sir," I replied; "and scarcely likely to reach manhood; but this I can say, he does not resemble his father; and if Miss Catherine had the misfortune to marry him, he would not be beyond her control, unless she were extremely and foolishly indulgent. However, master, you'll have plenty of time to get acquainted with him, and see whether he would suit her—it wants four years and more to his being of age."

Edgar sighed; and, walking to the window, looked out towards Gimmerton Kirk. It was a misty afternoon, but the February sun shone dimly, and we could just distinguish the two fir trees in the yard, and the sparely scattered gravestones.

"I've prayed often," he half soliloquized, "for the approach of what is coming; and now I begin to shrink, and fear it. I thought the memory of the hour I came down that glen a bridegroom would be less sweet than the anticipation that I was soon, in a few months, or possibly weeks, to be carried up, and laid in its lonely hollow! Ellen, I've been very happy with my little Cathy. Through winter nights and summer days she was a living hope at my side—but I've been as happy musing by myself among those stones, under that old church—lying, through the long June evenings, on the green mound of her mother's grave, and wishing, yearning for the time when I might lie beneath it. What can I do for Cathy? How must I quit her? I'd not care one moment for Linton being Heathcliff's son; nor for his taking her from me, if he could console her for my loss. I'd not care that Heathcliff gained his ends, and triumphed in robbing me of my last blessing! But should Linton be unworthy—only a feeble tool to his father—I cannot abandon her to him! And, hard though it be to crush her buoyant spirit, I must persevere in making her sad while I live, and leaving her solitary when I die. Darling! I'd rather resign her to God, and lay her in the earth before me."

"Resign her to God, as it is, sir," I answered, "and if we should lose you—which may He forbid—under His providence, I'll stand her friend and counsellor to the last. Miss Catherine is a good girl; I don't fear that she will go wilfully wrong; and people who do their duty are always finally rewarded."

Spring advanced; yet my master gathered no real strength, though he resumed his walks in the grounds with his daughter. To her inexperienced notions, this itself was a sign of convalescence; and then his cheek was often flushed, and his eyes were bright; she felt sure of his recovery.

On her seventeenth birthday, he did not visit the churchyard. It was raining, and I observed—

"You'll surely not go out to-night, sir?"

He answered—

"No, I'll defer it, this year, a little longer."

He wrote again to Linton, expressing his great desire to see him; and, had the invalid been presentable, I've no doubt his father would have permitted him to come. As it was, being instructed, he returned an answer, intimating that Mr. Heathcliff objected to his calling at the Grange; but his uncle's kind remembrance delighted him, and he hoped to meet him, sometimes, in his rambles, and personally to petition that his cousin and he might not remain long so utterly divided.

That part of his letter was simple, and probably his own. Heathcliff knew he could plead eloquently enough for Catherine's company, then—

"I do not ask," he said, "that she may visit here; but, am I never to see her, because my father forbids me to go to her home, and you forbid her to come to mine? Do, now and then, ride with her towards the Heights; and let us exchange a few words, in your presence! We have done nothing to deserve this separation; and you are not angry with me—you have no reason to dislike me—you allow—yourself. Dear uncle! send me a kind note to-morrow; and leave to join you anywhere you please, except at Thrushcross Grange. I believe an interview would convince you that my father's character is not mine; he affirms I am more your nephew than his son; and though I have faults which render me unworthy of Catherine, she has excused them, and, for her sake, you should also. You inquire after my health—it is better; but while I remain cut off from all hope, and doomed to solitude, or the society of those who never did and never will like me, how can I be cheerful and well?"

Edgar, though he felt for the boy, could not consent to grant his request; because he could not accompany Catherine.

He said, in summer, perhaps, they might meet. Meantime, he wished him to continue writing at intervals, and engaged to give him what advice and comfort he was able by letter; being well aware of his hard position in his family.

Linton complied; and had he been unrestrained, would probably have spoiled all by filling his epistles with complaints and lamentations; but his father kept a sharp watch over him; and, of course, insisted on every line that my master sent being shown; so, instead of penning his peculiar personal sufferings and distresses, the themes constantly uppermost in his thoughts, he harped on the cruel obligation of being held asunder from his friend and love; and gently intimated that Mr. Linton must allow an interview soon, or he should fear he was purposely deceiving him with empty promises.

Cathy was a powerful ally at home; and, between them, they at length persuaded my master to acquiesce in their having a ride or a walk together, about once a week, under my guardianship, and on the moors nearest the Grange; for June found him still declining; and, though he had set aside, yearly, a portion of his income for my young lady's fortune, he had a natural desire that she might retain—or, at least, return in a short time to—the house of her ancestors; and he considered her only prospect of doing that was by a union with his heir. He had no idea that the latter was failing almost as fast as himself, nor had any one, I believe; no doctor visited the Heights, and no one saw Master Heathcliff to make report of his condition, among us.

I, for my part, began to fancy my forebodings were false, and that he must be actually rallying, when he mentioned riding and walking on the moors, and seemed so earnest in pursuing his object.

I could not picture a father treating a dying child as tyrannically and wickedly as I afterwards learnt Heathcliff had treated him, to compel this apparent eagerness; his efforts redoubling the more imminently his avaricious and unfeeling plans were threatened with defeat by death.

## Chapter 12/26

Summer was already past its prime, when Edgar reluctantly yielded his assent to their entreaties, and Catherine and I set out on our first ride to join her cousin.

It was a close, sultry day; devoid of sunshine, but with a sky too dappled and hazy to threaten rain; and our place of meeting had been fixed at the guide-stone, by the crossroads. On arriving there, however, a little herd-boy, despatched as a messenger, told us that—

"Maister Linton wer just ut this side th' Heights: and he'd be mitch obleeged to us to gang on a bit further."

"Then Master Linton has forgot the first injunction of his uncle," I observed: "he bid us keep on the Grange land, and here we are, off at once."

"Well, we'll turn our horses' heads round, when we reach him," answered my companion, "our excursion shall lie towards home."

But when we reached him, and that was scarcely a quarter of a mile from his own door, we found he had no horse, and we were forced to dismount, and leave ours to graze.

He lay on the heath, awaiting our approach, and did not rise till we came within a few yards. Then, he walked so feebly, and looked so pale, that I immediately exclaimed—

"Why, Master Heathcliff, you are not fit for enjoying a ramble, this morning. How ill you do look!"

Catherine surveyed him with grief and astonishment; and changed the ejaculation of joy on her lips, to one of alarm; and the congratulation on their long postponed meeting to an anxious inquiry, whether he were worse than usual?

"No—better—better!" he panted, trembling, and retaining her hand as if he needed its support, while his large blue eyes wandered timidly over her; the hollowness round them transforming to haggard wildness the languid expression they once possessed.

"But you have been worse," persisted his cousin, "worse than when I saw you last—you are thinner, and—"

"I'm tired," he interrupted hurriedly. "It is too hot for walking, let us rest here. And, in the morning, I often feel sick—papa says I grow so fast."

Badly satisfied, Cathy sat down, and he reclined beside her.

"This is something like your paradise," said she, making an effort at cheerfulness. "You recollect the two days we agreed to spend in the place and way each thought pleasantest? This is nearly yours, only there are clouds; but then, they are so soft and mellow, it is nicer than sunshine. Next week, if you can, we'll ride down to the Grange Park, and try mine."

Linton did not appear to remember what she talked of; and he had evidently great difficulty in sustaining any kind of conversation. His lack of interest in the subjects she started, and his equal incapacity to contribute to her entertainment, were so obvious, that she could not conceal her disappointment. An indefinite alteration had come over his whole person and manner. The pettishness that might be caressed into fondness, had yielded to a listless apathy; there was less of the peevish temper of a child which frets and teases on purpose to be soothed, and more of the self-absorbed moroseness of a confirmed invalid, repelling consolation, and ready to regard the good-humoured mirth of others as an insult.

Catherine perceived, as well as I did, that he held it rather a punishment, than a gratification, to endure our company; and she made no scruple of proposing, presently, to depart.

That proposal, unexpectedly, roused Linton from his lethargy, and threw him into a strange state of agitation. He glanced fearfully towards the Heights, begging she would remain another half-hour, at least.

"But, I think," said Cathy, "you'd be more comfortable at home than sitting here; and I cannot amuse you to-day, I see, by my tales, and songs, and chatter; you have grown wiser than I, in these six months; you have little taste for my diversions now; or else, if I could amuse you, I'd willingly stay."

"Stay to rest yourself," he replied. "And, Catherine, don't think or say that I'm *very* unwell—it is the heavy weather and heat that make me dull; and I walked about, before you came, a great deal, for me. Tell uncle, I'm in tolerable health, will you?"

"I'll tell him that *you* say so, Linton. I couldn't affirm that you are," observed my young lady, wondering at his pertinacious assertion of what was evidently an untruth.

"And be here again next Thursday," continued he, shunning her puzzled gaze. "And give him my thanks for permitting you to come—my best thanks, Catherine. And—and, if you *did* meet my father, and he asked you about me, don't lead him to suppose that I've been extremely silent and stupid—don't look sad and downcast, as you *are* doing—he'll be angry."

"I care nothing for his anger," exclaimed Cathy, imagining she would be its object.

"But I do," said her cousin, shuddering. "*Don't* provoke him against me, Catherine, for he is very hard."

"Is he severe to you, Master Heathcliff?" I inquired. "Has he grown weary of indulgence, and passed from passive to active hatred?"

Linton looked at me, but did not answer; and, after keeping her seat by his side another ten minutes, during which his head fell drowsily on his breast, and he uttered nothing except suppressed moans of exhaustion or pain, Cathy began to seek solace in looking for bilberries, and sharing the produce of her researches with me. She did not offer them to him, for she saw further notice would only weary and annoy.

"Is it half an hour now, Ellen!" she whispered in my ear, at last. "I can't tell why we should stay. He's asleep, and papa will be wanting us back."

"Well, we must not leave him asleep," I answered; "wait till he wakes and be patient. You were mighty eager to set off, but your longing to see poor Linton has soon evaporated!"

"Why did *he* wish to see me?" returned Catherine. "In his crossest humours, formerly, I liked him better than I do in his present curious mood. It's just as if it were a task he was compelled to perform—this interview—for fear his father should scold him. But I'm hardly going to come to give Mr. Heathcliff pleasure; whatever reason he may have for ordering Linton to undergo this penance. And, though I'm glad he's better in health, I'm sorry he's so much less pleasant, and so much less affectionate to me."

"You think *he is* better in health, then?" I said.

"Yes," she answered; "because he always made such a great deal of his sufferings, you know. He is not tolerably well, as he told me to tell papa, but he's better, very likely."

"There you differ with me, Miss Cathy," I remarked; "I should conjecture him to be far worse."

Linton here started from his slumber in bewildered terror, and asked if any one had called his name.

"No," said Catherine; "unless in dreams. I cannot conceive how you manage to doze, out of doors, in the morning."

"I thought I heard my father," he gasped, glancing up to the frowning nab above us. "You are sure nobody spoke?"

"Quite sure," replied his cousin. "Only Ellen and I were disputing concerning your health. Are you truly stronger, Linton, than when we separated in winter? If you be, I'm certain one thing is not stronger—your regard for me—speak, are you?"

The tears gushed from Linton's eyes as he answered—

"Yes, yes, I am!"

And, still under the spell of the imaginary voice, his gaze wandered up and down to detect its owner.

Cathy rose.

"For to-day we must part," she said. "And I won't conceal that I have been sadly disappointed with our meeting, though I'll mention it to nobody but you—not that I stand in awe of Mr. Heathcliff!"

"Hush," murmured Linton; "for God's sake, hush! He's coming." And he clung to Catherine's arm, striving to detain her; but, at that announcement she hastily disengaged herself, and whistled to Minny, who obeyed her like a dog.

"I'll be here next Thursday," she cried, springing to the saddle. "Good-bye. Quick, Ellen!"

And so we left him, scarcely conscious of our departure, so absorbed was he in anticipating his father's approach.

Before we reached home, Catherine's displeasure softened into a perplexed sensation of pity and regret, largely blended with vague, uneasy doubts about Linton's actual circumstances, physical and social; in which I partook, though I counselled her not to say much, for a second journey would make us better judges.

My master requested an account of our ongoings. His nephew's offering of thanks was duly delivered, Miss Cathy gently touching on the rest. I, also, threw little light on his inquiries, for I hardly knew what to hide, and what to reveal.

## Chapter 13/27

Seven days glided away, every one marking its course by the henceforth rapid alteration of Edgar Linton's state. The havoc that months had previously wrought was now emulated by the inroads of hours.

Catherine, we would fain have deluded yet, but her own quick spirit refused to delude her. It divined, in secret, and brooded on the dreadful probability, gradually ripening into certainty.

She had not the heart to mention her ride, when Thursday came round; I mentioned it for her, and obtained permission to order her out of doors; for the library, where her father stopped a short time daily—the brief period he could bear to sit up—and his chamber, had become her whole world. She grudged each moment that did not find her bending over his pillow, or seated by his side. Her countenance grew wan with watching and sorrow, and my master gladly dismissed her to what he flattered himself would be a happy change of scene and society, drawing comfort from the hope that she would not now be left entirely alone after his death.

He had a fixed idea, I guessed by several observations he let fall, that as his nephew resembled him in person, he would resemble him in mind; for Linton's letters bore few or no indications of his defective character. And I through pardonable weakness refrained from correcting the error; asking myself what good there would be in disturbing his last moments with information that he had neither power nor opportunity to turn to account.

We deferred our excursion till the afternoon; a golden afternoon of August—every breath from the hills so full of life, that it seemed whoever respired it, though dying, might revive.

Catherine's face was just like the landscape—shadows and sunshine flitting over it, in rapid succession; but the shadows rested longer and the sunshine was more transient, and her poor little heart reproached itself for even that passing forgetfulness of its cares.

We discerned Linton watching at the same spot he had selected before. My young mistress alighted, and told me that as she was resolved to stay a very little while, I had better hold the pony and remain on horseback; but I dissented, I wouldn't risk losing sight of the charge committed to me a minute; so we climbed the slope of heath together.

Master Heathcliff received us with greater animation on this occasion; not the animation of high spirits though, nor yet of joy; it looked more like fear.

"It is late!" he said, speaking short, and with difficulty. "Is not your father very ill? I thought you wouldn't come."

"*Why* won't you be candid?" cried Catherine, swallowing her greeting. "Why cannot you say at once, you don't want me? It is strange, Linton, that for the second time you have brought me here on purpose, apparently, to distress us both, and for no reason besides!"

Linton shivered, and glanced at her, half supplicating, half ashamed, but his cousin's patience was not sufficient to endure this enigmatical behaviour.

"My father *is* very ill," she said, "and why am I called from his bedside—why didn't you send to absolve me from my promise, when you wished I wouldn't keep it? Come! I desire an explanation—playing and trifling are completely banished out of my mind: and I can't dance attendance on your affectations, now!"

"My affectations!" he murmured, "what are they? For Heaven's sake, Catherine, don't look so angry! Despise me as much as you please; I am a worthless, cowardly wretch—I can't be scorned enough! but I'm too mean for your anger—hate my father, and spare me for contempt!"

"Nonsense!" cried Catherine in a passion. "Foolish, silly boy! And there! he trembles, as if I were really going to touch him! You needn't bespeak[1] contempt, Linton; anybody will have it sponta-

---

[1] Beg for, order, or reserve (as in shop, hotel, or restaurant).

neously, at your service. Get off! I shall return home—it is folly dragging you from the hearth-stone, and pretending—what do we pretend? Let go my frock—if I pitied you for crying, and looking so very frightened, you should spurn such pity! Ellen, tell him how disgraceful this conduct is. Rise, and don't degrade yourself into an abject reptile—*don't*."

With streaming face and an expression of agony, Linton had thrown his nerveless frame along the ground; he seemed convulsed with exquisite terror.

"Oh!" he sobbed, "I cannot bear it! Catherine, Catherine, I'm a traitor too, and I dare not tell you! But leave me and I shall be killed! *Dear* Catherine, my life is in your hands; and you have said you loved me—and if you did, it wouldn't harm you. You'll not go then? kind, sweet, good Catherine! And perhaps you *will* consent—and he'll let me die with you!"

My young lady, on witnessing his intense anguish, stooped to raise him. The old feeling of indulgent tenderness overcame her vexation, and she grew thoroughly moved and alarmed.

"Consent to what?" she asked. "To stay? Tell me the meaning of this strange talk, and I will. You contradict your own words, and distract me! Be calm and frank, and confess at once all that weighs on your heart. You wouldn't injure me, Linton, would you? You wouldn't let any enemy hurt me, if you could prevent it? I'll believe you are a coward, for yourself, but not a cowardly betrayer of your best friend."

"But my father threatened me," gasped the boy, clasping his attenuated fingers, "and I dread him—I dread him! I *dare* not tell!"

"Oh well!" said Catherine, with scornful compassion, "keep your secret, *I'm* no coward—save yourself, I'm not afraid!"

Her magnanimity provoked his tears; he wept wildly, kissing her supporting hands, and yet could not summon courage to speak out.

I was cogitating what the mystery might be, and determined Catherine should never suffer to benefit him or any one else, by my goodwill; when hearing a rustle among the ling,[2] I looked up, and saw Mr. Heathcliff almost close upon us, descending the Heights. He didn't cast a glance towards my companions, though they were sufficiently near for Linton's sobs to be audible; but hailing me in

[2]Heather.

the almost hearty tone he assumed to none besides, and the sincerity of which I couldn't avoid doubting, he said,

"It is something to see you so near to my house, Nelly! How are you at the Grange? Let us hear! The rumour goes," he added in a lower tone, "that Edgar Linton is on his death-bed—perhaps they exaggerate his illness?"

"No; my master is dying," I replied, "it is true enough. A sad thing it will be for us all, but a blessing for him!"

"How long will he last, do you think?" he asked.

"I don't know," I said.

"Because," he continued, looking at the two young people, who were fixed under his eye—Linton appeared as if he could not venture to stir, or raise his head, and Catherine could not move, on his account—"Because that lad yonder seems determined to beat me—and I'd thank his uncle to be quick, and go before him—Hallo! Has the whelp been playing that game long? I *did* give him some lessons about snivelling. Is he pretty lively with Miss Linton generally?"

"Lively? no—he has shown the greatest distress," I answered. "To see him, I should say, that instead of rambling with his sweetheart on the hills, he ought to be in bed, under the hands of a doctor."

"He shall be, in a day or two," muttered Heathcliff. "But first—get up, Linton! Get up!" he shouted. "Don't grovel on the ground, there—up this moment!"

Linton had sunk prostrate again in another paroxysm of helpless fear, caused by his father's glance towards him, I suppose; there was nothing else to produce such humiliation. He made several efforts to obey, but his little strength was annihilated for the time, and he fell back again with a moan.

Mr. Heathcliff advanced, and lifted him to lean against a ridge of turf.

"Now," said he, with curbed ferocity, "I'm getting angry—and if you don't command that paltry spirit of yours—*Damn* you! Get up, directly!"

"I will, father!" he panted. "Only, let me alone, or I shall faint! I've done as you wished—I'm sure. Catherine will tell you that I—that I—have been cheerful—Ah! keep by me, Catherine; give me your hand."

"Take mine," said his father, "stand on your feet! There now—she'll lend you her arm . . . that's right, look at *her*. You would imagine I was the devil himself, Miss Linton, to excite such horror. Be so kind as to walk home with him, will you? He shudders, if I touch him."

"Linton, dear!" whispered Catherine, "I can't go to Wuthering Heights . . . papa has forbidden me . . . He'll not harm you, why are you so afraid?"

"I can never re-enter that house," he answered. "I am *not* to re-enter it without you!"

"Stop . . ." cried his father. "We'll respect Catherine's filial scruples. Nelly, take him in, and I'll follow your advice concerning the doctor, without delay."

"You'll do well," replied I, "but I must remain with my mistress. To mind your son is not my business."

"You are very stiff!" said Heathcliff, "I know that—but you'll force me to pinch the baby, and make it scream, before it moves your charity. Come then, my hero. Are you willing to return, escorted by me?"

He approached once more, and made as if he would seize the fragile being; but shrinking back, Linton clung to his cousin, and implored her to accompany him, with a frantic importunity that admitted no denial.

However I disapproved, I couldn't hinder her; indeed, how could she have refused him herself? What was filling him with dread, we had no means of discerning, but there he was, powerless under its gripe, and any addition seemed capable of shocking him into idiocy.

We reached the threshold; Catherine walked in; and I stood waiting till she had conducted the invalid to a chair, expecting her out immediately; when Mr. Heathcliff, pushing me forward, exclaimed—

"My house is not stricken with the plague, Nelly; and I have a mind to be hospitable to-day; sit down, and allow me to shut the door."

He shut and locked it also. I started.

"You shall have tea, before you go home," he added. "I am by myself. Hareton is gone with some cattle to the Lees[3]—and Zillah and Joseph are off on a journey of pleasure. And, though I'm used to being alone, I'd rather have some interesting company, if I can get it. Miss Linton, take your seat by *him*. I give you what I have;

---

[3]High grazing ground.

the present is hardly worth accepting; but, I have nothing else to offer. It is Linton, I mean. How she does stare! It's odd what a savage feeling I have to anything that seems afraid of me! Had I been born where laws are less strict, and tastes less dainty, I should treat myself to a slow vivisection of those two, as an evening's amusement."

He drew in his breath, struck the table, and swore to himself. "By hell! I hate them."

"I'm not afraid of you!" exclaimed Catherine, who could not hear the latter part of his speech.

She stepped close up; her black eyes flashing with passion and resolution.

"Give me that key—I will have it!" she said. "I wouldn't eat or drink here, if I were starving."

Heathcliff had the key in his hand that remained on the table. He looked up, seized with a sort of surprise at her boldness, or, possibly, reminded by her voice and glance, of the person from whom she had inherited it.

She snatched at the instrument, and half succeeded in getting it out of his loosened fingers; but her action recalled him to the present; he recovered it speedily.

"Now, Catherine Linton," he said, "stand off, or I shall knock you down; and that will make Mrs. Dean mad."

Regardless of this warning, she captured his closed hand and its contents again.

"We *will* go!" she repeated, exerting her utmost efforts to cause the iron muscles to relax; and finding that her nails made no impression, she applied her teeth pretty sharply.

Heathcliff glanced at me a glance that kept me from interfering a moment. Catherine was too intent on his fingers to notice his face. He opened them, suddenly, and resigned the object of dispute; but, ere she had well secured it, he seized her with the liberated hand, and pulling her on his knee, administered with the other a shower of terrific slaps on both sides of the head, each sufficient to have fulfilled his threat, had she been able to fall.

At this diabolical violence, I rushed on him furiously.

"You villain!" I began to cry, "you villain!"

A touch on the chest silenced me; I am stout, and soon put out of breath; and, what with that and the rage, I staggered dizzily back, and felt ready to suffocate, or to burst a blood-vessel.

The scene was over in two minutes; Catherine, released, put her two hands to her temples, and looked just as if she were not sure whether her ears were off or on. She trembled like a reed, poor thing, and leant against the table perfectly bewildered.

"I know how to chastise children, you see," said the scoundrel, grimly, as he stooped to repossess himself of the key, which had dropped to the floor. "Go to Linton now, as I told you; and cry at your ease! I shall be your father to-morrow—all the father you'll have in a few days—and you shall have plenty of that—you can bear plenty—you're no weakling—you shall have a daily taste, if I catch such a devil of a temper in your eyes again!"

Cathy ran to me instead of Linton, and knelt down, and put her burning cheek on my lap, weeping aloud. Her cousin had shrunk into a corner of the settle, as quiet as a mouse, congratulating himself, I dare say, that the correction had lighted on another than him.

Mr. Heathcliff, perceiving us all confounded, rose, and expeditiously made the tea himself. The cups and saucers were laid ready. He poured it out, and handed me a cup.

"Wash away your spleen," he said. "And help your own naughty pet and mine. It is not poisoned, though I prepared it. I'm going out to seek your horses."

Our first thought, on his departure, was to force an exit somewhere. We tried the kitchen door, but that was fastened outside; we looked at the windows—they were too narrow for even Cathy's little figure.

"Master Linton," I cried, seeing we were regularly imprisoned, "you know what your diabolical father is after, and you shall tell us, or I'll box your ears, as he has done your cousin's."

"Yes, Linton; you must tell," said Catherine. "It was for your sake I came; and it will be wickedly ungrateful if you refuse."

"Give me some tea, I'm thirsty, and then I'll tell you," he answered. "Mrs. Dean, go away. I don't like you standing over me. Now, Catherine, you are letting your tears fall into my cup! I won't drink that. Give me another."

Catherine pushed another to him, and wiped her face. I felt disgusted at the little wretch's composure, since he was no longer in terror for himself. The anguish he had exhibited on the moor subsided as soon as ever he entered Wuthering Heights; so I guessed he had been menaced with an awful visitation of wrath, if he failed in decoying us there; and, that accomplished, he had no further immediate fears.

"Papa wants us to be married," he continued, after sipping some of the liquid. "And he knows your papa wouldn't let us marry now; and he's afraid of my dying, if we wait; so we are to be married in the morning, and you are to stay here all night; and, if you do as he wishes, you shall return home next day, and take me with you."

"Take you with her, pitiful changeling?" I exclaimed. "*You* marry! Why, the man is mad, or he thinks us fools, every one. And, do you imagine that beautiful young lady, that healthy, hearty girl, will tie herself to a little perishing monkey like you? Are you cherishing the notion that *anybody*, let alone Miss Catherine Linton, would have you for a husband? You want whipping for bringing us in here at all, with your dastardly, puling tricks; and—don't look so silly now! I've a very good mind to shake you severely, for your contemptible treachery, and your imbecile conceit."

I did give him a slight shaking, but it brought on the cough, and he took to his ordinary resource of moaning and weeping, and Catherine rebuked me.

"Stay all night? No!" she said, looking slowly round. "Ellen, I'll burn that door down, but I'll get out."

And she would have commenced the execution of her threat directly, but Linton was up in alarm, for his dear self, again. He clasped her in his two feeble arms, sobbing—

"Won't you have me, and save me—not let me come to the Grange? Oh! darling Catherine! you mustn't go, and leave me, after all. You *must* obey my father, you *must*!"

"I must obey my own," she replied, "and relieve him from this cruel suspense. The whole night! What would he think? he'll be distressed already. I'll either break or burn a way out of the house. Be quiet! You're in no danger—but, if you hinder me—Linton, I love papa better than you!"

The mortal terror he felt of Mr. Heathcliff's anger, restored to the boy his coward's eloquence. Catherine was near distraught—still, she persisted that she must go home, and tried entreaty, in her turn, persuading him to subdue his selfish agony.

While they were thus occupied, our jailer re-entered.

"Your beasts have trotted off," he said, "and—Now, Linton! snivelling again? What has she been doing to you? Come, come—

have done, and get to bed. In a month or two, my lad, you'll be able to pay her back her present tyrannies, with a vigorous hand—you're pining for pure love, are you not? nothing else in the world—and she shall have you! There, to bed! Zillah won't be here to-night; you must undress yourself. Hush! hold your noise! Once in your own room, I'll not come near you, you needn't fear. By chance, you've managed tolerably. I'll look to the rest."

He spoke these words, holding the door open for his son to pass; and the latter achieved his exit exactly as a spaniel might which suspected the person who attended on it of designing a spiteful squeeze.

The lock was re-secured. Heathcliff approached the fire, where my mistress and I stood silent. Catherine looked up, and instinctively raised her hand to her cheek—his neighbourhood revived a painful sensation. Anybody else would have been incapable of regarding the childish act with sternness, but he scowled on her, and muttered—

"Oh, you are not afraid of me? Your courage is well disguised—you *seem* damnably afraid!"

"I *am* afraid now," she replied; "because if I stay, papa will be miserable; and how can I endure making him miserable—when he—when he—Mr. Heathcliff, *let* me go home! I promise to marry Linton—papa would like me to, and I love him—why should you wish to force me to do what I'll willingly do of myself?"

"Let him dare to force you!" I cried. "There's law in the land, thank God, there is! though we *be* in an out-of-the-way place. I'd inform, if he were my own son, and it's felony without benefit of clergy!"[4]

"Silence!" said the ruffian. "To the devil with your clamour! I don't want *you* to speak. Miss Linton, I shall enjoy myself remarkably in thinking your father will be miserable; I shall not sleep for satisfaction. You could have hit on no surer way of fixing your residence under my roof, for the next twenty-four hours, than informing me that such an event would follow. As to your promise to

---

[4]Strictly, the exemption of clergy from the jurisdiction of ordinary courts of law, but Nelly seems to mean it is a crime to marry outside the Church of England (which requires a public announcement of the wedding on three successive Sundays in the parish church [reading or publication of the banns], or less commonly at that time, a marriage license).

marry Linton, I'll take care you shall keep it; for you shall not quit this place till it is fulfilled."

"Send Ellen then, to let papa know I'm safe!" exclaimed Catherine, weeping bitterly. "Or marry me now. Poor papa! Ellen, he'll think we're lost. What shall we do?"

"Not he! He'll think you are tired of waiting on him, and run off, for a little amusement," answered Heathcliff. "You cannot deny that you entered my house of your own accord, in contempt of his injunctions to the contrary. And it is quite natural that you should desire amusement at your age; and that you would weary of nursing a sick man, and that man *only* your father. Catherine, his happiest days were over when your days began. He cursed you, I dare say, for coming into the world (I did, at least). And it would just do if he cursed you as *he* went out of it. I'd join him. I don't love you! How should I? Weep away. As far as I can see, it will be your chief diversion hereafter, unless Linton make amends for other losses; and your provident parent appears to fancy he may. His letters of advice and consolation entertained me vastly. In his last, he recommended my jewel to be careful of his; and kind to her when he got her. Careful and kind—that's paternal! But Linton requires his whole stock of care and kindness for himself. Linton can play the little tyrant well. He'll undertake to torture any number of cats if their teeth be drawn, and their claws pared. You'll be able to tell his uncle fine tales of his *kindness* when you get home again, I assure you."

"You're right there!" I said, "explain your son's character. Show his resemblance to yourself; and then, I hope, Miss Cathy will think twice, before she takes the cockatrice!"[5]

"I don't much mind speaking of his amiable qualities now," he answered, "because she must either accept him, or remain a prisoner, and you along with her, till your master dies. I can detain you both, quite concealed, here. If you doubt, encourage her to retract her word, and you'll have an opportunity of judging!"

"I'll not retract my word," said Catherine. "I'll marry him, within this hour, if I may go to Thrushcross Grange afterwards. Mr. Heathcliff, you're a cruel man, but you're not a fiend; and you won't, from *mere* malice, destroy, irrevocably, all my happiness. If papa thought I had left him on purpose, and if he died before I re-

---

[5]Little poisonous monster.

turned, could I bear to live? I've given over crying; but I'm going to kneel here, at your knee; and I'll not get up, and I'll not take my eyes from your face, till you look back at me! No, don't turn away! *do* look! You'll see nothing to provoke you. I don't hate you. I'm not angry that you struck me. Have you never loved *anybody*, in all your life, uncle? *never?* Ah! you must look once—I'm so wretched—you can't help being sorry and pitying me."

"Keep your eft's fingers[6] off; and move, or I'll kick you!" cried Heathcliff, brutally repulsing her. "I'd rather be hugged by a snake. How the devil can you dream of fawning on me? I *detest* you!"

He shrugged his shoulders—shook himself, indeed, as if his flesh crept with aversion, and thrust back his chair; while I got up and opened my mouth, to commence a downright torrent of abuse; but I was rendered dumb in the middle of the first sentence, by a threat that I should be shown into a room by myself, the very next syllable I uttered.

It was growing dark—we heard a sound of voices at the garden gate. Our host hurried out, instantly; *he* had his wits about him; *we* had not. There was a talk of two or three minutes, and he returned alone.

"I thought it had been your cousin Hareton," I observed to Catherine. "I wish he would arrive! Who knows but he might take our part?"

"It was three servants sent to seek you from the Grange," said Heathcliff, overhearing me. "You should have opened a lattice, and called out; but I could swear that chit is glad you didn't. She's glad to be obliged to stay, I'm certain."

At learning the chance we had missed, we both gave vent to our grief without control, and he allowed us to wail on till nine o'clock; then he bid us go upstairs, through the kitchen, to Zillah's chamber; and I whispered my companion to obey; perhaps we might contrive to get through the window there, or into a garret, and out by its skylight.

The window, however, was narrow, like those below, and the garret trap was safe from our attempts; for we were fastened in as before.

We neither of us lay down. Catherine took her station by the lattice, and watched anxiously for morning—a deep sigh being the only answer I could obtain to my frequent entreaties that she would try to rest.

[6]An eft is a lizard.

I seated myself in a chair, and rocked, to and fro, passing harsh judgment on my many derelictions of duty; from which, it struck me then, all the misfortunes of my employers sprang. It was not the case, in reality, I am aware; but it was, in my imagination, that dismal night, and I thought Heathcliff himself less guilty than I.

At seven o'clock he came, and inquired if Miss Linton had risen. She ran to the door immediately, and answered—

"Yes."

"Here then," he said, opening it, and pulling her out.

I rose to follow, but he turned the lock again. I demanded my release.

"Be patient," he replied; "I'll send up your breakfast in a while."

I thumped on the panels, and rattled the latch angrily; and Catherine asked why I was still shut up? He answered, I must try to endure it another hour, and they went away.

I endured it two or three hours; at length, I heard a footstep, not Heathcliff's.

"I've brought you something to eat," said a voice; "oppen t' door!"

Complying eagerly, I beheld Hareton, laden with food enough to last me all day.

"Tak it!" he added, thrusting the tray into my hand.

"Stay one minute," I began.

"Nay!" cried he, and retired, regardless of any prayers I could pour forth to detain him.

And there I remained enclosed, the whole day, and the whole of the next night; and another, and another. Five nights and four days I remained, altogether, seeing nobody but Hareton, once every morning, and he was a model of a jailer—surly, and dumb, and deaf to every attempt at moving his sense of justice or compassion.

## Chapter 14/28

In the fifth morning, or rather afternoon, a different step approached—lighter and shorter—and, this time, the person entered the room. It was Zillah; donned in her scarlet shawl, with a black silk bonnet on her head, and a willow basket swung to her arm.

"Eh, dear! Mrs. Dean," she exclaimed. "Well! there is a talk about you at Gimmerton. I never thought, but you were sunk in the Blackhorse marsh, and Missy with you, till master told me you'd been found, and he'd lodged you here! What, and you must have got on an island, sure? And how long were you in the hole? Did master save you, Mrs. Dean? But you're not so thin—you've not been so poorly, have you?"

"Your master is a true scoundrel!" I replied. "But he shall answer for it. He needn't have raised that tale—it shall all be laid bare!"

"What do you mean?" asked Zillah. "It's not his tale—they tell that in the village—about your being lost in the marsh; and I calls to Earnshaw, when I come in—"

"'Eh, they's queer things, Mr. Hareton, happened since I went off. It's a sad pity of that likely young lass, and cant Nelly Dean.'

"He stared. I thought he had not heard aught, so I told him the rumour.

"The master listened, and he just smiled to himself, and said—

"'If they have been in the marsh, they are out now, Zillah. Nelly Dean is lodged, at this minute, in your room. You can tell her to flit, when you go up; here is the key. The bog-water got into her head, and she would have run home, quite flighty, but I fixed her, till she came round to her senses. You can bid her go to the Grange, at once, if she be able, and carry a message from me, that her young lady will follow in time to attend the Squire's funeral.'"

"Mr. Edgar is not dead?" I gasped. "Oh! Zillah, Zillah!"

"No, no—sit you down, my good mistress," she replied, "you're right sickly yet. He's not dead: Doctor Kenneth thinks he may last another day—I met him on the road and asked."

Instead of sitting down, I snatched my outdoor things, and hastened below, for the way was free.

On entering the house, I looked about for some one to give information of Catherine.

The place was filled with sunshine, and the door stood wide open, but nobody seemed at hand.

As I hesitated whether to go off at once, or return and seek my mistress, a slight cough drew my attention to the hearth.

Linton lay on the settle, sole tenant, sucking a stick of sugar-candy, and pursuing my movements with apathetic eyes.

"Where is Miss Catherine?" I demanded, sternly, supposing I could frighten him into giving intelligence, by catching him thus, alone.

He sucked on like an innocent.

"Is she gone?" I said.

"No," he replied; "she's upstairs—she's not to go; we won't let her."

"You won't let her, little idiot!" I exclaimed. "Direct me to her room immediately, or I'll make you sing out sharply."

"Papa would make you sing out, if you attempted to get there," he answered. "He says I'm not to be soft with Catherine—she's my wife, and it's shameful that she should wish to leave me! He says, she hates me, and wants me to die, that she may have my money, but she shan't have it; and she shan't go home! she never shall! she may cry, and be sick as much as she pleases!"

He resumed his former occupation, closing his lids, as if he meant to drop asleep.

"Master Heathcliff," I resumed, "have you forgotten all Catherine's kindness to you, last winter, when you affirmed you loved her, and when she brought you books, and sung you songs, and came many a time through wind and snow to see you? She wept to miss one evening, because you would be disappointed; and you felt then, that she was a hundred times too good to you; and now you believe the lies your father tells, though you know he detests you both! And you join him against her. That's fine gratitude, is it not?"

The corner of Linton's mouth fell, and he took the sugar-candy from his lips.

"Did she come to Wuthering Heights, because she hated you?" I continued. "Think for yourself! As to your money, she does not even know that you will have any. And you say she's sick; and yet, you leave her alone, up there in a strange house! *You*, who have felt what it is to be so neglected! You could pity your own sufferings, and she pitied them, too, but you won't pity hers! I shed tears, Master Heathcliff, you see—an elderly woman, and a servant merely—and you, after pretending such affection, and having reason to worship her, almost, store every tear you have for yourself, and lie there quite at ease. Ah! you're a heartless, selfish boy!"

"I can't stay with her," he answered crossly. "I'll not stay, by myself. She cries so I can't bear it. And she won't give over, though I say I'll call my father—I did call him once; and he threatened to strangle her, if she was not quiet; but she began again, the instant he left the room, moaning and grieving all night long, though I screamed for vexation that I couldn't sleep."

"Is Mr. Heathcliff out?" I inquired, perceiving that the wretched creature had no power to sympathise with his cousin's mental tortures.

"He's in the court," he replied, "talking to Doctor Kenneth, who says uncle is dying, truly, at last—I'm glad, for I shall be master of the Grange after him—and Catherine always spoke of it as *her* house. It isn't hers! It's mine—papa says everything she has is mine. All her nice books are mine—she offered to give me them, and her pretty birds, and her pony Minny, if I would get the key of our room, and let her out: but I told her she had nothing to give, they were all, all mine. And then she cried, and took a little picture from her neck, and said I should have that—two pictures in a gold case: on one side her mother, and on the other, uncle, when they were young. That was yesterday—I said *they* were mine, too; and tried to get them from her. The spiteful thing wouldn't let me; she pushed me off, and hurt me. I shrieked out—that frightens her—she heard papa coming, and she broke the hinges, and divided the case and gave me her mother's portrait; the other she attempted to hide; but papa asked what was the matter and I explained it. He took the one I had away, and ordered her to resign hers to me; she refused, and he—he struck her down, and wrenched it off the chain, and crushed it with his foot."

"And were you pleased to see her struck?" I asked: having my designs in encouraging his talk.

"I winked," he answered. "I wink to see my father strike a dog, or a horse, he does it so hard—yet I was glad at first—she deserved punishing for pushing me: but when papa was gone, she made me come to the window and showed me her cheek cut on the inside, against her teeth, and her mouth filling with blood; and then she gathered up the bits of the picture, and went and sat down with her face to the wall, and she has never spoken to me since; and I sometimes think she can't speak for pain. I don't like to think so! but she's a naughty thing for crying continually; and she looks so pale and wild, I'm afraid of her!"

"And you can get the key if you choose?" I said.

"Yes, when I am upstairs," he answered; "but I can't walk upstairs now."

"In what apartment is it?" I asked.

"Oh," he cried, "I shan't tell *you* where it is! It is our secret. Nobody, neither Hareton, nor Zillah are to know. There! you've tired me—go away, go away!" And he turned his face on to his arm, and shut his eyes, again.

I considered it best to depart without seeing Mr. Heathcliff; and bring a rescue for my young lady, from the Grange.

On reaching it, the astonishment of my fellow servants to see me, and their joy also, was intense; and when they heard that their little mistress was safe, two or three were about to hurry up, and shout the news at Mr. Edgar's door: but I bespoke[1] the announcement of it, myself.

How changed I found him, even in those few days! He lay an image of sadness, and resignation, waiting his death. Very young he looked: though his actual age was thirty-nine, one would have called him ten years younger, at least. He thought of Catherine, for he murmured her name. I touched his hand, and spoke.

"Catherine is coming, dear master!" I whispered; "she is alive, and well; and will be here I hope to-night."

I trembled at the first effects of this intelligence: he half rose up, looked eagerly round the apartment, and then sank back in a swoon.

As soon as he recovered, I related our compulsory visit, and detention at the Heights. I said Heathcliff forced me to go in, which was not quite true; I uttered as little as possible against Linton; nor did I describe all his father's brutal conduct—my intentions being to add no bitterness, if I could help it, to his already overflowing cup.[2]

He divined that one of his enemy's purposes was to secure the personal property, as well as the estate, to his son, or rather himself; yet why he did not wait till his decease, was a puzzle to my master, because ignorant how nearly he and his nephew would quit the world together.

However, he felt that his will had better be altered—instead of leaving Catherine's fortune at her own disposal, he determined to put it in the hands of trustees, for her use during life; and for her children, if she had any, after her. By that means, it could not fall to Mr. Heathcliff should Linton die.

Having received his orders, I despatched a man to fetch the attorney, and four more, provided with serviceable weapons, to de-

---

[1]Claimed, reserved.

[2]See Psalm 23: "The Lord is my shepherd. . . . Thou preparest a table before me in the presence of mine enemies: thou anointest my head with oil; my cup runneth over" (23.1–5).

mand my young lady of her jailer. Both parties were delayed very late. The single servant returned first.

He said Mr. Green, the lawyer, was out when he arrived at his house, and he had to wait two hours for his re-entrance: and then Mr. Green told him he had a little business in the village, that must be done, but he would be at Thrushcross Grange before morning.

The four men came back unaccompanied, also. They brought word that Catherine was ill, too ill to quit her room, and Heathcliff would not suffer them to see her.

I scolded the stupid fellows well, for listening to that tale, which I would not carry to my master; resolving to take a whole bevy up to the Heights, at daylight, and storm it, literally, unless the prisoner were quietly surrendered to us.

Her father *shall* see her, I vowed, and vowed again, if that devil be killed on his own door-stones in trying to prevent it!

Happily, I was spared the journey, and the trouble.

I had gone down stairs at three o'clock to fetch a jug of water; and was passing through the hall with it in my hand, when a sharp knock at the front door made me jump.

"Oh! it is Green"—I said, recollecting myself—"only Green," and I went on, intending to send somebody else to open it; but the knock was repeated, not loud, and still importunately.

I put the jug on the banister, and hastened to admit him, myself.

The harvest moon shone clear outside. It was not the attorney. My own sweet little mistress sprang on my neck, sobbing,

"Ellen! Ellen! Is papa alive?"

"Yes!" I cried, "yes, my angel, he is! God be thanked, you are safe with us again!"

She wanted to run, breathless as she was, upstairs to Mr. Linton's room; but I compelled her to sit down on a chair, and made her drink, and washed her pale face, chafing it into a faint colour with my apron. Then I said I must go first, and tell of her arrival; imploring her to say, she should be happy with young Heathcliff. She stared, but soon comprehending why I counselled her to utter the falsehood, she assured me she would not complain.

I couldn't abide to be present at their meeting. I stood outside the chamber-door a quarter of an hour, and hardly ventured near the bed, then.

All was composed, however; Catherine's despair was as silent as her father's joy. She supported him calmly, in appearance; and he fixed on her features his raised eyes, that seemed dilating with ecstasy.

He died blissfully, Mr. Lockwood; he died so. Kissing her cheek, he murmured,

"I am going to her, and you, darling child, shall come to us;" and never stirred or spoke again, but continued that rapt, radiant gaze, till his pulse imperceptibly stopped, and his soul departed. None could have noticed the exact minute of his death, it was so entirely without a struggle.

Whether Catherine had spent her tears, or whether the grief were too weighty to let them flow, she sat there dry-eyed till the sun rose— she sat till noon, and would still have remained, brooding over that death-bed, but I insisted on her coming away, and taking some repose.

It was well I succeeded in removing her, for at dinner-time appeared the lawyer, having called at Wuthering Heights to get his instructions how to behave. He had sold himself to Mr. Heathcliff, and that was the cause of his delay in obeying my master's summons. Fortunately, no thought of worldly affairs crossed the latter's mind, to disturb him, after his daughter's arrival.

Mr. Green took upon himself to order everything and everybody about the place. He gave all the servants but me, notice to quit. He would have carried his delegated authority to the point of insisting that Edgar Linton should not be buried beside his wife, but in the chapel, with his family. There was the will, however, to hinder that, and my loud protestations against any infringement of its directions.

The funeral was hurried over; Catherine, Mrs. Linton Heathcliff now, was suffered to stay at the Grange, till her father's corpse had quitted it.

She told me that her anguish had at last spurred Linton to incur the risk of liberating her. She heard the men I sent, disputing at the door, and she gathered the sense of Heathcliff's answer. It drove her desperate—Linton, who had been conveyed up to the little parlour soon after I left, was terrified into fetching the key before his father re-ascended.

He had the cunning to unlock, and re-lock the door, without shutting it; and when he should have gone to bed, he begged to sleep with Hareton, and his petition was granted, for once.

Catherine stole out before break of day. She dare not try the doors, lest the dogs should raise an alarm; she visited the empty chambers, and examined their windows; and, luckily, lighting on her mother's, she got easily out of its lattice, and onto the ground, by means of the fir tree, close by. Her accomplice suffered for his share in the escape, notwithstanding his timid contrivances.

## Chapter 15/29

The evening after the funeral, my young lady and I were seated in the library; now musing mournfully, one of us despairingly, on our loss, now venturing conjectures as to the gloomy future.

We had just agreed the best destiny which could await Catherine, would be a permission to continue resident at the Grange, at least during Linton's life: he being allowed to join her there, and I to remain as housekeeper. That seemed rather too favourable an arrangement to be hoped for, and yet I did hope, and began to cheer up under the prospect of retaining my home, and my employment, and, above all, my beloved young mistress, when a servant—one of the discarded ones, not yet departed—rushed hastily in, and said, "that devil Heathcliff" was coming through the court: should he fasten the door in his face?

If we had been mad enough to order that proceeding, we had not time. He made no ceremony of knocking, or announcing his name; he was master, and availed himself of the master's privilege to walk straight in, without saying a word.

The sound of our informant's voice directed him to the library: he entered, and motioning him out, shut the door.

It was the same room into which he had been ushered, as a guest, eighteen years before: the same moon shone through the window; and the same autumn landscape lay outside. We had not yet lighted a candle, but all the apartment was visible, even to the portraits on the wall—the splendid head of Mrs. Linton, and the graceful one of her husband.

Heathcliff advanced to the hearth. Time had little altered his person either. There was the same man; his dark face rather sallower, and more composed, his frame a stone or two heavier, perhaps, and no other difference.

Catherine had risen with an impulse to dash out, when she saw him.

"Stop!" he said, arresting her by the arm. "No more runnings away! Where would you go? I'm come to fetch you home; and I hope you'll be a dutiful daughter, and not encourage my son to further disobedience. I was embarrassed how to punish him, when I discovered his part in the business—he's such a cobweb, a pinch would annihilate him—but you'll see by his look that he has received his due! I brought him down one evening, the day before yesterday, and just set him in a chair, and never touched him afterwards. I sent Hareton out, and we had the room to ourselves. In two hours, I called Joseph to carry him up again; and since then, my presence is as potent on his nerves as a ghost; and I fancy he sees me often, though I am not near. Hareton says he wakes and shrieks in the night by the hour together; and calls you to protect him from me; and whether you like your precious mate or not, you must come—he's your concern now; I yield all my interest in him to you."

"Why not let Catherine continue here?" I pleaded, "and send Master Linton to her. As you hate them both, you'd not miss them—they *can* only be a daily plague to your unnatural heart."

"I'm seeking a tenant for the Grange," he answered; "and I want my children about me, to be sure—besides, that lass owes me her services for her bread; I'm not going to nurture her in luxury and idleness after Linton is gone. Make haste and get ready now. And don't oblige me to compel you."

"I shall," said Catherine. "Linton is all I have to love in the world, and, though you have done what you could to make him hateful to me, and me to him, you *cannot* make us hate each other! and I defy you to hurt him when I am by, and I defy you to frighten me."

"You are a boastful champion!" replied Heathcliff; "but I don't like you well enough to hurt him—you shall get the full benefit of the torment, as long as it lasts. It is not I who will make him hateful to you—it is his own sweet spirit. He's as bitter as gall at your desertion, and its consequences—don't expect thanks for this noble devotion. I heard him draw a pleasant picture to Zillah of what he would do, if he were as strong as I—the inclination is there, and his very weakness will sharpen his wits to find a substitute for strength."

"I know he has a bad nature," said Catherine; "he's your son. But I'm glad I've a better, to forgive it; and I know he loves me and for that reason I love him. Mr. Heathcliff, *you* have *nobody* to love you; and, however miserable you make us, we shall still have the revenge of thinking that your cruelty arises from your greater misery! You *are* miserable, are you not? Lonely, like the devil, and envious like him? *Nobody* loves you—*nobody* will cry for you, when you die! I wouldn't be you!"

Catherine spoke with a kind of dreary triumph. She seemed to have made up her mind to enter into the spirit of her future family, and draw pleasure from the griefs of her enemies.

"You shall be sorry to be yourself presently," said her father-in-law, "if you stand there another minute. Begone, witch, and get your things."

She scornfully withdrew.

In her absence, I began to beg for Zillah's place at the Heights, offering to resign her mine; but he would suffer it on no account. He bid me be silent, and then, for the first time, allowed himself a glance round the room, and a look at the pictures. Having studied Mrs. Linton's, he said—

"I shall have that at home. Not because I need it, but—"

He turned abruptly to the fire, and continued, with what, for lack of a better word, I must call a smile—

"I'll tell you what I did yesterday! I got the sexton, who was digging Linton's grave, to remove the earth off her coffin lid, and I opened it. I thought, once, I would have stayed there, when I saw her face again—it is hers yet—he had hard work to stir me; but he said it would change, if the air blew on it, and so I struck one side of the coffin loose—and covered it up—not Linton's side, damn him! I wish he'd been soldered in lead—and I bribed the sexton to pull it away, when I'm laid there, and slide mine out too—I'll have it made so, and then, by the time Linton gets to us, he'll not know which is which!"

"You are very wicked, Mr. Heathcliff!" I exclaimed; "were you not ashamed to disturb the dead?"

"I disturbed nobody, Nelly," he replied; "and I gave some ease to myself. I shall be a great deal more comfortable now; and you'll have a better chance of keeping me underground, when I get there. Disturbed her? No! she has disturbed me, night and day, through eighteen years—incessantly—remorselessly—till yesternight—and yesternight, I was tranquil. I dreamt I was sleeping the last sleep, by that sleeper, with my heart stopped, and my cheek frozen against hers."

"And if she had been dissolved into earth, or worse, what would you have dreamt of then?" I said.

"Of dissolving with her, and being more happy still!" he answered. "Do you suppose I dread any change of that sort? I expected such a transformation on raising the lid, but I'm better pleased that it should not commence till I share it. Besides, unless I had received a distinct impression of her passionless features, that strange feeling would hardly have been removed. It began oddly. You know, I was wild after she died, and eternally, from dawn to dawn, praying her to return to me—her spirit—I have a strong faith in ghosts; I have a conviction that they can, and do exist, among us!

"The day she was buried there came a fall of snow. In the evening I went to the churchyard. It blew bleak as winter—all round was solitary: I didn't fear that her fool of a husband would wander up the den[1] so late—and no one else had business to bring them there.

"Being alone, and conscious two yards of loose earth was the sole barrier between us, I said to myself—

"'I'll have her in my arms again! If she be cold, I'll think it is this north wind that chills *me*; and if she be motionless, it is sleep.'

"I got a spade from the toolhouse, and began to delve with all my might—it scraped the coffin; I fell to work with my hands; the wood commenced cracking about the screws, I was on the point of attaining my object, when it seemed that I heard a sigh from some one above, close at the edge of the grave, and bending down.—'If I can only get this off,' I muttered, 'I wish they may shovel in the earth over us both!' and I wrenched at it more desperately still. There was another sigh, close at my ear. I appeared to feel the warm breath of it displacing the sleet-laden wind. I knew no living thing in flesh and blood was by—but as certainly as you perceive the approach to some substantial body in the dark, though it cannot be discerned, so certainly I felt that Cathy was there, not under me, but on the earth.

"A sudden sense of relief flowed from my heart through every limb. I relinquished my labour of agony, and turned consoled at once, unspeakably consoled. Her presence was with me; it remained while I re-filled the grave, and led me home. You may laugh, if you will, but I was sure I should see her there. I was sure she was with me, and I could not help talking to her.

[1]The hollow.

"Having reached the Heights, I rushed eagerly to the door. It was fastened; and, I remember, that accursed Earnshaw and my wife opposed my entrance. I remember stopping to kick the breath out of him, and then hurrying upstairs, to my room, and hers—I looked round impatiently—I felt her by me—I could *almost* see her, and yet I *could not*! I ought to have sweat blood then, from the anguish of my yearning, from the fervour of my supplications to have but one glimpse! I had not one. She showed herself, as she often was in life, a devil to me! And, since then, sometimes more, and sometimes less, I've been the sport of that intolerable torture! Infernal—keeping my nerves at such a stretch, that, if they had not resembled catgut, they would, long ago, have relaxed to the feebleness of Linton's.

"When I sat in the house with Hareton, it seemed that on going out, I should meet her; when I walked on the moors I should meet her coming in. When I went from home, I hastened to return: she *must* be somewhere at the Heights, I was certain! And when I slept in her chamber—I was beaten out of that—I couldn't lie there; for the moment I closed my eyes, she was either outside the window, or sliding back the panels, or entering the room, or even resting her darling head on the same pillow as she did when a child. And I must open my lids to see. And so I opened and closed them a hundred times a night—to be always disappointed! It racked me! I've often groaned aloud, till that old rascal Joseph no doubt believed that my conscience was playing the fiend inside of me.

"Now, since I've seen her, I'm pacified—a little. It was a strange way of killing, not by inches, but by fractions of hairbreadths, to beguile me with the spectre of a hope, through eighteen years!"

Mr. Heathcliff paused and wiped his forehead—his hair clung to it, wet with perspiration; his eyes were fixed on the red embers of the fire; the brows not contracted, but raised next the temples, diminishing the grim aspect of his countenance, but imparting a peculiar look of trouble, and a painful appearance of mental tension towards one absorbing subject. He only half addressed me, and I maintained silence—I didn't like to hear him talk!

After a short period, he resumed his meditation on the picture, took it down, and leant it against the sofa to contemplate it at better advantage; and while so occupied Catherine entered, announcing that she was ready, when her pony should be saddled.

"Send that over to-morrow," said Heathcliff to me, then turn-ing to her, he added, "You may do without your pony—it is a fine evening, and you'll need no ponies at Wuthering Heights, for what journeys you take, your own feet will serve you—Come along."

"Good-bye, Ellen!" whispered my dear little mistress. As she kissed me, her lips felt like ice. "Come and see me, Ellen, don't forget."

"Take care you do no such thing, Mrs. Dean!" said her new fa-ther. "When I wish to speak to you I'll come here. I want none of your prying at my house!"

He signed her to precede him; and casting back a look that cut my heart, she obeyed.

I watched them from the window, walk down the garden. Heathcliff fixed Catherine's arm under his, though she disputed the act at first, evidently, and with rapid strides, he hurried her into the alley, whose trees concealed them.

## Chapter 16/30

I have paid a visit to the Heights, but I have not seen her since she left; Joseph held the door in his hand, when I called to ask after her, and wouldn't let me pass. He said Mrs. Linton was "thrang,"[1] and the master was not in. Zillah has told me something of the way they go on, otherwise I should hardly know who was dead, and who living.

She thinks Catherine haughty, and does not like her, I can guess by her talk. My young lady asked some aid of her, when she first came, but Mr. Heathcliff told her to follow her own business, and let his daughter-in-law look after herself, and Zillah willingly ac-quiesced, being a narrow-minded selfish woman. Catherine evinced a child's annoyance at this neglect; repaid it with contempt, and thus enlisted my informant among her enemies, as securely as if she had done her some great wrong.

I had a long talk with Zillah, about six weeks ago, a little be-fore you came, one day, when we foregathered on the moor; and this is what she told me.

"The first thing Mrs. Linton did," she said, "on her arrival at the Heights, was to run upstairs without even wishing good-

---

[1] Busy.

evening to me and Joseph; she shut herself into Linton's room, and remained till morning—then, while the master and Earnshaw were at breakfast, she entered the house and asked all in a quiver if the doctor might be sent for? her cousin was very ill."

"'We know that!' answered Heathcliff, 'but his life is not worth a farthing, and I won't spend a farthing on him.'

"'But I cannot tell how to do,' she said, 'and if nobody will help me, he'll die!'

"'Walk out of the room!' cried the master, 'and let me never hear a word more about him! None here care what becomes of him; if you do, act the nurse; if you do not, lock him up and leave him.'

"Then she began to bother me, and I said I'd had enough plague with the tiresome thing; we each had our tasks, and hers was to wait on Linton, Mr. Heathcliff bid me leave that labour to her.

"How they managed together, I can't tell. I fancy he fretted a great deal, and moaned hisseln,[2] night and day; and she had precious little rest, one could guess by her white face, and heavy eyes—she sometimes came into the kitchen all wildered like,[3] and looked as if she would fain beg assistance. But I was not going to disobey the master—I never dare disobey him, Mrs. Dean, and though I thought it wrong that Kenneth should not be sent for, it was no concern of mine, either to advise or complain; and I always refused to meddle.

"Once or twice, after we had gone to bed, I've happened to open my door again and seen her sitting crying, on the stairs' top; and then I've shut myself in, quick, for fear of being moved to interfere. I did pity her then, I'm sure; still I didn't wish to lose my place, you know!

"At last, one night she came boldly into my chamber, and frightened me out of my wits, by saying—

"'Tell Mr. Heathcliff that his son is dying—I'm sure he is, this time.—Get up, instantly, and tell him!'

"Having uttered this speech, she vanished again. I lay a quarter of an hour listening and trembling—Nothing stirred—the house was quiet.

"She's mistaken, I said to myself. 'He's got over it. I needn't disturb them.' And I began to doze. But my sleep was marred a second

[2]To himself.
[3]Bewildered.

time, by a sharp ringing of the bell—the only bell we have, put up on purpose for Linton; and the master called to me, to see what was the matter, and inform them that he wouldn't have that noise repeated.

"I delivered Catherine's message. He cursed to himself, and in a few minutes, came out with a lighted candle, and proceeded to their room. I followed—Mrs. Heathcliff was seated by the bedside, with her hands folded on her knees. Her father-in-law went up, held the light to Linton's face, looked at him, and touched him; afterwards he turned to her.

"'Now—Catherine,' he said, 'how do you feel?'

"She was dumb.

"'How do you feel, Catherine?' he repeated.

"'He's safe, and I'm free,' she answered. 'I should feel well—but,' she continued, with a bitterness she couldn't conceal, 'You have left me so long to struggle against death, alone, that I feel and see only death! I feel like death!'

"And she looked like it, too! I gave her a little wine. Hareton and Joseph, who had been wakened by the ringing and the sound of feet, and heard our talk from outside, now entered. Joseph was fain,[4] I believe, of the lad's removal; Hareton seemed a thought bothered, though he was more taken up with staring at Catherine than thinking of Linton. But the master bid him get off to bed again—we didn't want his help. He afterwards made Joseph remove the body to his chamber, and told me to return to mine, and Mrs. Heathcliff remained by herself.

"In the morning, he sent me to tell her she must come down to breakfast—she had undressed, and appeared going to sleep, and said she was ill; at which I hardly wondered. I informed Mr. Heathcliff, and he replied,

"'Well, let her be till after the funeral; and go up now and then to get her what is needful; and as soon as she seems better, tell me.'"

Cathy stayed upstairs a fortnight, according to Zillah, who visited her twice a day, and would have been rather more friendly, but her attempts at increasing kindness were proudly and promptly repelled.

Heathcliff went up once, to show her Linton's will. He had bequeathed the whole of his, and what had been her movable property to his father. The poor creature was threatened, or coaxed,

---

[4]Glad of; preferring.

into that act during her week's absence, when his uncle died. The
lands, being a minor, he could not meddle with. However, Mr.
Heathcliff has claimed and kept them in his wife's right, and his
also—I suppose legally: at any rate Catherine destitute of cash and
friends, cannot disturb his possession.

"Nobody," said Zillah, "ever approached her door, except that
once, but I . . . and nobody asked anything about her. The first occasion of her coming down into the house, was on a Sunday afternoon.

"She had cried out, when I carried up her dinner, that she
couldn't bear any longer being in the cold; and I told her the master
was going to Thrushcross Grange, and Earnshaw and I needn't hinder her from descending; so, as soon as she heard Heathcliff's horse
trot off, she made her appearance, donned in black, and her yellow
curls combed back behind her ears, as plain as a Quaker. She could-
n't comb them out.

"Joseph and I generally go to chapel on Sundays," (the Kirk,
you know, has no minister now, explained Mrs. Dean, and they call
the Methodists' or Baptists' place, I can't say which it is, at Gimmerton a chapel[5]). "Joseph has gone," she continued, "but I
thought proper to bide at home. Young folks are always the better
for an elder's over-looking,[6] and Hareton, with all his bashfulness,
isn't a model of nice behaviour. I let him know that his cousin
would very likely sit with us, and she had been always used to see
the Sabbath respected, so he had as good leave his guns and bits of
in-door work alone, while she stayed.

"He coloured up at the news, and cast his eyes over his hands
and clothes. The train-oil[7] and gunpowder were shoved out of sight
in a minute. I saw he meant to give her his company; and I guessed,
by his way, he wanted to be presentable; so, laughing, as I durst not
laugh when the master is by, I offered to help him, if he would, and
joked at his confusion. He grew sullen, and began to swear.

---

[5]Zillah and Joseph, like rural servants at the Brontës' Haworth, attend a Dissenting
chapel, not the "Kirk" or Church of England. As one of the gentry, Catherine would
attend the Church of England rather than a meeting of the Society of Friends (Quak-
ers) or the chapel; but the Church cannot appoint a minister in a parish of scant attendance (a problem faced by Patrick Brontë and others in Yorkshire). Catherine
does expect Hareton to observe the Sabbath (not work on Sunday). Nelly, as a
higher-class servant, identifies with the religion of the Lintons.
[6]Superintendence (not ignoring).
[7]Oil from whales or seals for his gun or other equipment.

"Now, Mrs. Dean," she went on, seeing me not pleased by her manner, "you happen[8] think your young lady too fine for Mr. Hareton, and happen you're right—but, I own, I should love well to bring her pride a peg lower. And what will all her learning and her daintiness do for her, now? She's as poor as you or I—poorer, I'll be bound—you're saving, and I'm doing my little, all that road."[9]

Hareton allowed Zillah to give him her aid; and she flattered him into a good humour; so, when Catherine came, half forgetting her former insults, he tried to make himself agreeable, by the house-keeper's account.

"Missis walked in," she said, "as chill as an icicle, and as high as a princess. I got up and offered her my seat in the arm-chair. No, she turned up her nose at my civility. Earnshaw rose too, and bade her come to the settle, and sit close by the fire; he was sure she was starved.[10]

"'I've been starved a month and more,' she answered, resting on the word as scornful as she could.

"And she got a chair for herself, and placed it at a distance from both of us.

"Having sat till she was warm, she began to look round, and discovered a number of books in the dresser; she was instantly upon her feet again, stretching to reach them; but they were too high up.

"Her cousin, after watching her endeavours a while, at last summoned courage to help her; she held her frock, and he filled it with the first that came to hand.

"That was a great advance for the lad—she didn't thank him; still, he felt gratified that she had accepted his assistance, and ventured to stand behind as she examined them, and even to stoop and point out what struck his fancy in certain old pictures which they contained—nor was he daunted by the saucy style in which she jerked the page from his finger; he contented himself with going a bit farther back, and looking at her, instead of the book.

"She continued reading, or seeking for something to read. His attention became, by degrees, quite centred in the study of her thick, silky curls—her face he couldn't see, and she couldn't see him. And,

[8]Perhaps (*hap* is an old word for *chance* or *fortune*).
[9]"My bit [of saving] in that way."
[10]Frozen.

perhaps not quite awake to what he did, but attracted like a child to a candle, at last he proceeded from staring to touching; he put out his hand and stroked one curl, as gently as if it were a bird. He might have stuck a knife into her neck, she started round in such a taking.[11]

"'Get away this moment! How dare you touch me? Why are you stopping[12] there?' she cried, in a tone of disgust. 'I can't endure you! I'll go upstairs again, if you come near me.'

"Mr. Hareton recoiled, looking as foolish as he could do; he sat down in the settle, very quiet, and she continued turning over her volumes, another half hour—finally, Earnshaw crossed over, and whispered to me.

"'Will you ask her to read to us, Zillah? I'm stalled of[13] doing naught—and I do like—I could like to hear her! Dunnot say I wanted it, but ask of yourseln.'

"'Mr. Hareton wishes you would read to us, ma'am,' I said, immediately. 'He'd take it very kind—he'd be much obliged.'

"She frowned; and, looking up, answered,

"'Mr. Hareton, and the whole set of you, will be good enough to understand that I reject any pretence at kindness you have the hypocrisy to offer! I despise you, and will have nothing to say to any of you! When I would have given my life for one kind word, even to see one of your faces, you all kept off. But I won't complain to you! I'm driven down here by the cold, not either to amuse you, or enjoy your society.'

"'What could I ha' done?' began Earnshaw. 'How was I to blame?'

"'Oh! you are an exception,' answered Mrs. Heathcliff. 'I never missed such a concern[14] as you.'

"'But, I offered more than once, and asked,' he said, kindling up at her pertness, 'I asked Mr. Heathcliff to let me wake for you[15]—'

"'Be silent! I'll go out of doors, or anywhere, rather than have your disagreeable voice in my ear!' said my lady.

"Hareton muttered, she might go to hell, for him! and unslinging his gun, restrained himself from his Sunday occupations no longer.

[11]Such a state (of anger).

[12]Staying (he should stop hanging around her).

[13]Weary of.

[14]Such a person, creature.

[15]Stay up or watch over the sick room so she could rest.

"He talked now, freely enough; and she presently saw fit to retreat to her solitude; but the frost had set in, and, in spite of her pride, she was forced to condescend to our company, more and more. However, I took care there should be no further scorning at my good nature—ever since, I've been as stiff as herself—and she has no lover or liker among us—and she does not deserve one—for, let them say the least word to her, and she'll curl back[16] without respect of any one! She'll snap at the master himself, and as good as dares him to thrash her; and the more hurt she gets, the more venomous she grows."

At first, on hearing this account from Zillah, I determined to leave my situation, take a cottage, and get Catherine to come and live with me; but Mr. Heathcliff would as soon permit that, as he would set up Hareton in an independent house; and I can see no remedy, at present, unless she could marry again; and that scheme, it does not come within my province to arrange.

Thus ended Mrs. Dean's story. Notwithstanding the doctor's prophecy, I am rapidly recovering strength, and, though it be only the second week in January, I propose getting out on horseback, in a day or two, and riding over to Wuthering Heights, to inform my landlord that I shall spend the next six months in London; and, if he likes, he may look out for another tenant to take the place, after October—I would not pass another winter here, for much.

## Chapter 17/31

Yesterday was bright, calm, and frosty. I went to the Heights as I proposed; my housekeeper entreated me to bear a little note from her to her young lady, and I did not refuse, for the worthy woman was not conscious of anything odd in her request.

The front door stood open, but the jealous gate was fastened, as at my last visit; I knocked and invoked Earnshaw from among the garden beds; he unchained it, and I entered. The fellow is as handsome a rustic as need be seen. I took particular notice of him this time; but then, he does his best, apparently, to make the least of his advantages.

[16]Recoil.

I asked if Mr. Heathcliff were at home? He answered, no; but he would be in at dinner-time. It was eleven o'clock, and I announced my intention of going in, and waiting for him, at which he immediately flung down his tools and accompanied me, in the office of watchdog, not as a substitute for the host.

We entered together; Catherine was there, making herself useful in preparing some vegetables for the approaching meal; she looked more sulky and less spirited than when I had seen her first. She hardly raised her eyes to notice me, and continued her employment with the same disregard to common forms of politeness, as before; never returning my bow and good morning by the slightest acknowledgment.

"She does not seem so amiable," I thought, "as Mrs. Dean would persuade me to believe. She's a beauty, it is true; but not an angel."

Earnshaw surlily bid her remove her things to the kitchen.

"Remove them yourself," she said, pushing them from her, as soon as she had done, and retiring to a stool by the window, where she began to carve figures of birds and beasts, out of the turnip parings in her lap.

I approached her, pretending to desire a view of the garden; and, as I fancied, adroitly dropped Mrs. Dean's note on to her knee, unnoticed by Hareton—but she asked aloud—

"What is that?" And chucked it off.

"A letter from your old acquaintance, the housekeeper at the Grange," I answered, annoyed at her exposing my kind deed, and fearful lest it should be imagined a missive of my own.

She would gladly have gathered it up, at this information, but Hareton beat her; he seized and put it in his waistcoat, saying Mr. Heathcliff should look at it first.

Thereat, Catherine silently turned her face from us, and very stealthily drew out her pocket-handkerchief and applied it to her eyes; and her cousin, after struggling a while to keep down his softer feelings, pulled out the letter and flung it on the floor beside her as ungraciously as he could.

Catherine caught and perused it eagerly; then she put a few questions to me concerning the inmates, rational and irrational, of her former home; and gazing towards the hills, murmured in soliloquy.

"I should like to be riding Minny down there! I should like to be climbing up there—Oh, I'm tired—I'm *stalled*,[1] Hareton!"

And she leant her pretty head back against the sill, with half a yawn and half a sigh, and lapsed into an aspect of abstracted sadness, neither caring nor knowing whether we remarked her.

"Mrs. Heathcliff," I said, after sitting some time mute, "you are not aware that I am an acquaintance of yours? so intimate, that I think it strange you won't come and speak to me. My housekeeper never wearies of talking about and praising you; and she'll be greatly disappointed if I return with no news of, or from you, except that you received her letter and said nothing!"

She appeared to wonder at this speech, and asked,

"Does Ellen like you?"

"Yes, very well," I replied hesitatingly.

"You must tell her," she continued, "that I would answer her letter, but I have no materials for writing, not even a book from which I might tear a leaf."

"No books!" I exclaimed. "How do you contrive to live here without them? If I may take the liberty to inquire—Though provided with a large library, I'm frequently very dull at the Grange—take my books away, and I should be desperate!"

"I was always reading, when I had them," said Catherine, "and Mr. Heathcliff never reads; so he took it into his head to destroy my books. I have not had a glimpse of one, for weeks. Only once, I searched through Joseph's store of theology, to his great irritation. And once, Hareton, I came upon a secret stock in your room . . . some Latin and Greek, and some tales and poetry; all old friends— I brought the last here—and you gathered them, as a magpie gathers silver spoons, for the mere love of stealing! They are of no use to you—or else you concealed them in the bad spirit, that as you cannot enjoy them, nobody else shall. Perhaps *your* envy counselled Mr. Heathcliff to rob me of my treasures? But I've most of them written on my brain and printed in my heart, and you cannot deprive me of those!"

Earnshaw blushed crimson, when his cousin made this revelation of his private literary accumulations, and stammered an indignant denial of her accusations.

[1]Weary.

"Mr. Hareton is desirous of increasing his amount of knowledge," I said, coming to his rescue. "He is not *envious* but *emulous* of your attainments—He'll be a clever scholar in a few years!"

"And he wants *me* to sink into a dunce, meantime," answered Catherine. "Yes, I hear him trying to spell and read to himself, and pretty blunders he makes! I wish you would repeat Chevy Chase, as you did yesterday—It was extremely funny! I heard you . . . and I heard you turning over the dictionary, to seek out the hard words, and then cursing, because you couldn't read their explanations!"

The young man evidently thought it too bad that he should be laughed at for his ignorance, and then laughed at for trying to remove it. I had a similar notion, and, remembering Mrs. Dean's anecdote of his first attempt at enlightening the darkness in which he had been reared, I observed,

"But, Mrs. Heathcliff, we have each had a commencement, and each stumbled and tottered on the threshold, and had our teachers scorned, instead of aiding us, we should stumble and totter yet."

"Oh!" she replied, "I don't wish to limit his acquirements . . . still, he has no right to appropriate what is mine, and make it ridiculous to me with his vile mistakes and mis-pronunciations! Those books, both prose and verse, are consecrated to me by other associations, and I hate to have them debased and profaned in his mouth! Besides, of all, he has selected my favourite pieces that I love the most to repeat, as if out of deliberate malice!"

Hareton's chest heaved in silence a minute; he laboured under a severe sense of mortification and wrath, which it was no easy task to suppress.

I rose, and from a gentlemanly idea of relieving his embarrassment, took up my station in the door-way, surveying the external prospect as I stood.

He followed my example, and left the room, but presently reappeared, bearing half-a-dozen volumes in his hands, which he threw into Catherine's lap, exclaiming,

"Take them! I never want to hear, or read, or think of them again!"

"I won't have them, now!" she answered. "I shall connect them with you, and hate them!"

She opened one that had obviously been often turned over, and read a portion in the drawling tone of a beginner; then laughed, and threw it from her.

"And listen!" she continued provokingly, commencing a verse of an old ballad in the same fashion.

But his self-love would endure no further torment—I heard, and not altogether disapprovingly, a manual check given to her saucy tongue—The little wretch had done her utmost to hurt her cousin's sensitive though uncultivated feelings, and a physical argument was the only mode he had of balancing the account and repaying its effects on the inflicter.

He afterwards gathered the books and hurled them on the fire. I read in his countenance what anguish it was to offer that sacrifice to spleen—I fancied that as they consumed, he recalled the pleasure they had already imparted, and the triumph and ever-increasing pleasure he had anticipated from them—and I fancied I guessed the incitement to his secret studies, also. He had been content with daily labour and rough animal enjoyments, till Catherine crossed his path—Shame at her scorn, and hope of her approval were his first prompters to higher pursuits; and instead of guarding him from one, and winning him the other, his endeavours to raise himself had produced just the contrary result.

"Yes, that's all the good that such a brute as you can get from them!" cried Catherine, sucking her damaged lip, and watching the conflagration with indignant eyes.

"You'd *better* hold your tongue, now!" he answered fiercely.

And his agitation precluding further speech, he advanced hastily to the entrance, where I made way for him to pass. But, ere he had crossed the door-stones, Mr. Heathcliff, coming up the causeway, encountered him and laying hold of his shoulder, asked,

"What's to do now, my lad?"

"Naught, naught!" he said, and broke away, to enjoy his grief and anger in solitude.

Heathcliff gazed after him, and sighed.

"It will be odd, if I thwart myself!" he muttered, unconscious that I was behind him. "But, when I look for his father in his face, I find *her* every day more! How the devil is he so like? I can hardly bear to see him."

He bent his eyes to the ground, and walked moodily in. There was a restless, anxious expression in his countenance I had never remarked there before, and he looked sparer in person.

His daughter-in-law, on perceiving him through the window, immediately escaped to the kitchen, so that I remained alone.

"I'm glad to see you out of doors again, Mr. Lockwood," he said, in reply to my greeting, "from selfish motives partly: I don't think I could readily supply your loss in this desolation. I've wondered, more than once, what brought you here."

"An idle whim, I fear, sir," was my answer, "or else an idle whim is going to spirit me away—I shall set out for London next week, and I must give you warning, that I feel no disposition to retain Thrushcross Grange beyond the twelvemonths I agreed to rent it. I believe I shall not live there any more."

"Oh, indeed! you're tired of being banished from the world, are you?" he said. "But, if you be coming to plead off paying for a place you won't occupy, your journey is useless—I never relent in exacting my due, from any one."

"I'm coming to plead off nothing about it!" I exclaimed, considerably irritated. "Should you wish it, I'll settle with you now," and I drew my notebook from my pocket.

"No, no," he replied coolly, "you'll leave sufficient behind, to cover your debts, if you fail to return . . . I'm not in such a hurry— sit down and take your dinner with us—a guest that is safe from repeating his visit, can generally be made welcome—Catherine! bring the things in—where are you?"

Catherine re-appeared, bearing a tray of knives and forks.

"You may get your dinner with Joseph," muttered Heathcliff aside, "and remain in the kitchen till he is gone."

She obeyed his directions very punctually—perhaps she had no temptation to transgress. Living among clowns and misanthropists, she probably cannot appreciate a better class of people, when she meets them.

With Mr. Heathcliff, grim and saturnine, on one hand, and Hareton, absolutely dumb, on the other, I made a somewhat cheerless meal, and bade adieu early—I would have departed by the back way to get a last glimpse of Catherine, and annoy old Joseph; but Hareton received orders to lead up my horse, and my host himself escorted me to the door, so I could not fulfil my wish.

"How dreary life gets over in that house!" I reflected, while riding down the road. "What a realization of something more romantic than a fairy tale it would have been for Mrs. Linton Heathcliff, had she and I struck up an attachment, as her good nurse desired, and migrated together into the stirring atmosphere of the town!"

## Chapter 18/32

1802.—This September, I was invited to devastate the moors of a friend,[1] in the North; and, on my journey to his abode, I unexpectedly came within fifteen miles of Gimmerton. The hostler, at a roadside public-house, was holding a pail of water to refresh my horses, when a cart of very green oats, newly reaped, passed by, and he remarked—

"Yon's frough Gimmerton, nah! They're allas three wick after other folk wi' ther harvest."[2]

"Gimmerton?" I repeated—my residence in that locality had already grown dim and dreamy. "Ah! I know! How far is it from this?"

"Happen fourteen mile o'er th' hills, and a rough road," he answered.

A sudden impulse seized me to visit Thrushcross Grange. It was scarcely noon, and I conceived that I might as well pass the night under my own roof, as in an inn. Besides, I could spare a day easily, to arrange matters with my landlord, and thus save myself the trouble of invading the neighbourhood again.

Having rested a while, I directed my servant to inquire the way to the village; and, with great fatigue to our beasts, we managed the distance in some three hours.

I left him there, and proceeded down the valley alone. The grey church looked greyer, and the lonely churchyard lonelier. I distinguished a moor sheep cropping the short turf on the graves. It was sweet, warm weather—too warm for travelling; but the heat did not hinder me from enjoying the delightful scenery above and below; had I seen it nearer August, I'm sure it would have tempted me to waste a month among its solitudes. In winter, nothing more dreary, in summer, nothing more divine, than those glens shut in by hills, and those bluff, bold swells of heath.

---

[1]Gentlemen customarily spent the hunting season at each others' estates, and Lockwood jokes about slaughtering his host's game.

[2]"That's from Gimmerton, now! They're always three weeks behind other folks with their harvest."

I reached the Grange before sunset, and knocked for admittance; but the family had retreated into the back premises, I judged by one thin, blue wreath curling from the kitchen chimney, and they did not hear.

I rode into the court. Under the porch, a girl of nine or ten sat knitting, and an old woman reclined on the horse-steps, smoking a meditative pipe.

"Is Mrs. Dean within?" I demanded of the dame.

"Mistress Dean? Nay!" she answered, "shoo doesn't bide[3] here; shoo's up at th' Heights."

"Are you the housekeeper, then?" I continued.

"Eea, Aw keep th' hahse," she replied.

"Well, I'm Mr. Lockwood, the master—Are there any rooms to lodge me in, I wonder? I wish to stay all night."

"T' maister!" she cried in astonishment, "Whet, whoiver knew yah wur coming? Yah sud ha' send word. They's nowt norther dry nor mensful abaht t' place[4]—nowt there isn't!"

She threw down her pipe and bustled in, the girl followed, and I entered too; soon perceiving that her report was true, and, moreover, that I had almost upset her wits by my unwelcome apparition.

I bid her be composed—I would go out for a walk; and, meantime, she must try to prepare a corner of a sitting-room for me to sup in, and a bedroom to sleep in—No sweeping and dusting, only good fires and dry sheets were necessary.

She seemed willing to do her best; though she thrust the hearthbrush into the grates in mistake for the poker, and malappropriated several other articles of her craft; but I retired, confiding in her energy for a resting-place against[5] my return.

Wuthering Heights was the goal of my proposed excursion. An after-thought brought me back, when I had quitted the court.

"All well at the Heights?" I enquired of the woman.

"Eea, f'r owt Ee knaw!"[6] she answered, skurrying away with a pan of hot cinders.

---

[3]Live.

[4]"What, whoever knew you were coming? You should have sent word. There's nothing either dry or decent about the place."

[5]In preparation for.

[6]"Yes, for all I know."

I would have asked why Mrs. Dean had deserted the Grange; but it was impossible to delay her at such a crisis, so I turned away and made my exit, rambling leisurely along with the glow of a sinking sun behind, and the mild glory of a rising moon in front; one fading, and the other brightening, as I quitted the park, and climbed the stony by-road branching off to Mr. Heathcliff's dwelling.

Before I arrived in sight of it, all that remained of day was a beamless, amber light along the west; but I could see every pebble on the path, and every blade of grass, by that splendid moon.

I had neither to climb the gate, nor to knock—it yielded to my hand.

That is an improvement! I thought. And I noticed another, by the aid of my nostrils; a fragrance of stocks and wall flowers, wafted on the air, from amongst the homely fruit trees.

Both doors and lattices were open; and yet, as is usually the case in a coal district, a fine, red fire illuminated the chimney; the comfort which the eye derives from it, renders the extra heat endurable. But the house of Wuthering Heights is so large, that the inmates have plenty of space for withdrawing out of its influence; and, accordingly, what inmates there were had stationed themselves not far from one of the windows. I could both see them and hear them talk before I entered, and looked and listened in consequence, being moved thereto by a mingled sense of curiosity and envy that grew as I lingered.

"Con-*trary!*" said a voice, as sweet as a silver bell—"That for the third time, you dunce! I'm not going to tell you, again! Recollect, or I'll pull your hair!"

"Contrary, then," answered another, in deep but softened tones. "And now, kiss me for minding so well."

"No, read it over first correctly, without a single mistake."

The male speaker began to read—he was a young man, respectably dressed, and seated at a table, having a book before him. His handsome features glowed with pleasure, and his eyes kept impatiently wandering from the page to a small white hand over his shoulder, which recalled him by a smart slap on the cheek, whenever its owner detected such signs of inattention.

Its owner stood behind; her light shining ringlets blending, at intervals, with his brown locks, as she bent to superintend his studies; and her face—it was lucky he could not see her face, or he would never have been so steady—I could, and I bit my lip, in spite, at having thrown away the chance I might have had, of doing something besides staring at its smiting beauty.

The task was done, not free from further blunders, but the pupil claimed a reward, and received at least five kisses, which, however, he generously returned. Then, they came to the door, and from their conversation, I judged they were about to issue out and have a walk on the moors. I supposed I should be condemned in Hareton Earnshaw's heart, if not by his mouth, to the lowest pit in the infernal regions if I showed my unfortunate person in his neighbourhood then, and feeling very mean and malignant, I skulked round to seek refuge in the kitchen.

There was unobstructed admittance on that side also; and, at the door, sat my old friend, Nelly Dean, sewing and singing a song, which was often interrupted from within, by harsh words of scorn and intolerance, uttered in far from musical accents.

"Aw'd rayther, by th' haulf, hev 'em swearing i' my lugs frough morn to neeght, nur hearken yah, hahsiver!"[7] said the tenant of the kitchen, in answer to an unheard speech of Nelly's. "It's a blazing shaime, ut Aw cannut oppen t' Blessed Book, bud yah set up them glories tuh Sattan, un' all t' flaysome wickednesses that iver were born intuh th' warld! Oh! yah're a raight nowt; un' shoo's another; un' that poor lad 'ull be lost atween ye. Poor lad!" he added, with a groan; "he's witched, I'm sartin on't! O, Lord, judge 'em, for there's norther law nor justice amang wer rullers!"[8]

"No! or we should be sitting in flaming fagots,[9] I suppose," retorted the singer. "But wisht, old man, and read your Bible like a Christian, and never mind me. This is 'Fairy Annie's Wedding'—a bonny tune—it goes to a dance."

Mrs. Dean was about to recommence, when I advanced, and recognising me directly, she jumped to her feet, crying—

---

[7]I'd rather, by half [a whole lot], have them swearing in my ears from morn till night, than listen to you, anyway!"

[8]"It's a blazing shame, that I can't open the Blessed Book, but you start singing to the glory of Satan, and all the terrible wickednesses that ever were born into the world! Oh! You're a real nothing, and she's another, and that poor boy will be lost between you. . . . He's bewitched, I'm certain of it! . . . there's neither law nor justice among our rulers!"

[9]Burning logs (making fun of Joseph's damning people to burn in hell).

"Why, bless you, Mr. Lockwood! How could you think of returning in this way? All's shut up at Thrushcross Grange. You should have given us notice!"

"I've arranged to be accommodated there, for as long as I shall stay," I answered. "I depart again to-morrow. And how are you transplanted here, Mrs. Dean? tell me that."

"Zillah left, and Mr. Heathcliff wished me to come, soon after you went to London, and stay till you returned. But, step in, pray! Have you walked from Gimmerton this evening?"

"From the Grange," I replied; "and, while they make me lodging room there, I want to finish my business with your master, because I don't think of having another opportunity in a hurry."

"What business, sir?" said Nelly, conducting me into the house. "He's gone out, at present, and won't return soon."

"About the rent," I answered.

"Oh! then it is with Mrs. Heathcliff you must settle," she observed, "or rather with me. She has not learnt to manage her affairs yet, and I act for her; there's nobody else."

I looked surprised.

"Ah! you have not heard of Heathcliff's death, I see!" she continued.

"Heathcliff dead?" I exclaimed, astonished. "How long ago?"

"Three months since—but, sit down, and let me take your hat, and I'll tell you all about it. Stop, you have had nothing to eat, have you?"

"I want nothing. I have ordered supper at home. You sit down too. I never dreamt of his dying! Let me hear how it came to pass. You say you don't expect them back for some time—the young people?"

"No—I have to scold them every evening, for their late rambles—but they don't care for me. At least, have a drink of our old ale—it will do you good—you seem weary."

She hastened to fetch it, before I could refuse, and I heard Joseph asking whether "it warn't a crying scandal that she should have fellies[10] at her time of life? And then, to get them jocks[11] out o' t' Maister's cellar! He fair shaamed to bide still and see it."

[10]Fellows, admirers.
[11]Food, provisions.

She did not stay to retaliate, but re-entered, in a minute, bearing a reaming,[12] silver pint, whose contents I lauded with becoming earnestness. And afterwards she furnished me with the sequel of Heathcliff's history. He had a "queer" end, as she expressed it.

I was summoned to Wuthering Heights, within a fortnight of your leaving us, she said; and I obeyed joyfully, for Catherine's sake.

My first interview with her grieved and shocked me! she had altered so much since our separation. Mr. Heathcliff did not explain his reasons for taking a new mind about my coming here; he only told me he wanted me, and he was tired of seeing Catherine: I must make the little parlour my sitting room, and keep her with me. It was enough if he were obliged to see her once or twice a day.

She seemed pleased at this arrangement; and, by degrees, I smuggled over a great number of books, and other articles, that had formed her amusement at the Grange; and flattered myself we should get on in tolerable comfort.

The delusion did not last long. Catherine, contented at first, in a brief space grew irritable and restless. For one thing, she was forbidden to move out of the garden, and it fretted her sadly to be confined to its narrow bounds, as Spring drew on—for another, in following[13] the house, I was forced to quit her frequently, and she complained of loneliness; she preferred quarrelling with Joseph in the kitchen, to sitting at peace in her solitude.

I did not mind their skirmishes; but Hareton was often obliged to seek the kitchen also, when the master wanted to have the house to himself; and though, in the beginning, she either left it at his approach, or quietly joined in my occupations, and shunned remarking or addressing him—and though he was always as sullen and silent as possible—after a while, she changed her behaviour, and became incapable of letting him alone: talking at him; commenting on his stupidity and idleness; expressing her wonder how he could endure the life he lived—how he could sit a whole evening staring into the fire, and dozing.

"He's just like a dog, is he not, Ellen?" she once observed, "or a cart-horse? He does his work, eats his food, and sleeps, eternally!

[12]Foaming.
[13]Taking care of.

What a blank, dreary mind he must have! Do you ever dream, Hareton? And, if you do, what is it about? But, you can't speak to me!"

Then she looked at him; but he would neither open his mouth, nor look again.

"He's perhaps dreaming now," she continued. "He twitched his shoulder as Juno twitches hers. Ask him, Ellen."

"Mr. Hareton will ask the master to send you upstairs, if you don't behave!" I said. He had not only twitched his shoulder but clenched his fist, as if tempted to use it.

"I know why Hareton never speaks, when I am in the kitchen," she exclaimed, on another occasion. "He is afraid I shall laugh at him. Ellen, what do you think? He began to teach himself to read once; and, because I laughed, he burned his books, and dropped it—was he not a fool?"

"Were not you naughty?" I said; "answer me that."

"Perhaps I was," she went on, "but I did not expect him to be so silly. Hareton, if I gave you a book, would you take it now? I'll try!"

She placed one she had been perusing on his hand; he flung it off, and muttered, if she did not give over, he would break her neck.

"Well, I shall put it here," she said, "in the table drawer, and I'm going to bed."

Then she whispered me to watch whether he touched it, and departed. But he would not come near it, and so I informed her in the morning, to her great disappointment. I saw she was sorry for his persevering sulkiness and indolence—her conscience reproved her for frightening him off improving himself—she had done it effectually.

But her ingenuity was at work to remedy the injury; while I ironed, or pursued other such stationary employments as I could not well do in the parlour—she would bring some pleasant volume, and read it aloud to me. When Hareton was there, she generally paused in an interesting part, and left the book lying about—that she did repeatedly; but he was as obstinate as a mule, and, instead of snatching at her bait, in wet weather he took to smoking with Joseph, and they sat like automatons, one on each side of the fire, the elder happily too deaf to understand her wicked nonsense, as he would have called it, the younger doing his best to seem to disregard it. On fine evenings the latter followed his shooting expeditions, and Catherine yawned and sighed, and teased me to talk to her, and ran off into the court or garden, the moment I began; and, as a last resource, cried and said she was tired of living, her life was useless.

Mr. Heathcliff, who grew more and more disinclined to society, had almost banished Earnshaw from his apartment. Owing to an accident at the commencement of March, he became for some days a fixture in the kitchen. His gun burst while out on the hills by himself; a splinter cut his arm, and he lost a good deal of blood before he could reach home. The consequence was that, perforce, he was condemned to the fire-side and tranquility, till he made it up again.

It suited Catherine to have him there. At any rate, it made her hate her room upstairs more than ever; and she would compel me to find out business below, that she might accompany me.

On Easter Monday, Joseph went to Gimmerton fair with some cattle; and, in the afternoon, I was busy getting up linen in the kitchen—Earnshaw sat, morose as usual, at the chimney corner, and my little mistress was beguiling an idle hour with drawing pictures on the window panes, varying her amusement by smothered bursts of songs, and whispered ejaculations, and quick glances of annoyance and impatience in the direction of her cousin, who steadfastly smoked, and looked into the grate.

At a notice that I could do with her no longer, intercepting my light, she removed to the hearthstone. I bestowed little attention on her proceedings, but, presently, I heard her begin—

"I've found out, Hareton, that I want—that I'm glad—that I should like you to be my cousin, now, if you had not grown so cross to me, and so rough."

Hareton returned no answer.

"Hareton, Hareton, Hareton! do you hear?" she continued.

"Get off wi' ye!" he growled, with uncompromising gruffness.

"Let me take that pipe," she said, cautiously advancing her hand, and abstracting it from his mouth.

Before he could attempt to recover it, it was broken, and behind the fire. He swore at her and seized another.

"Stop," she cried; "you must listen to me, first; and I can't speak while those clouds are floating in my face."

"Will you go to the devil!" he exclaimed, ferociously, "and let me be!"

"No," she persisted, "I won't—I can't tell what to do to make you talk to me, and you are determined not to understand. When I call you stupid, I don't mean anything—I don't mean that I despise you. Come, you shall take notice of me, Hareton—you are my cousin, and you shall own me."

"I shall have naught to do wi' you, and your mucky[14] pride, and your damned, mocking tricks!" he answered. "I'll go to hell, body and soul, before I look sideways after you again! Side out o' t' gait,[15] now; this minute!"

Catherine frowned, and retreated to the window-seat, chewing her lip, and endeavouring, by humming an eccentric tune, to conceal a growing tendency to sob.

"You should be friends with your cousin, Mr. Hareton," I interrupted, "since she repents of her sauciness! It would do you a great deal of good—it would make you another man, to have her for a companion."

"A companion?" he cried; "when she hates me, and does not think me fit to wipe her shoon! Nay, if it made me a king, I'd not be scorned for seeking her good will any more."

"It is not I who hate you, it is you who hate me!" wept Cathy, no longer disguising her trouble. "You hate me as much as Mr. Heathcliff does, and more."

"You're a damned liar," began Earnshaw; "why have I made him angry, by taking your part then, a hundred times? and that, when you sneered at, and despised me, and—Go on plaguing me, and I'll step in yonder, and say you worried me out of the kitchen!"

"I didn't know you took my part," she answered, drying her eyes; "and I was miserable and bitter at every body; but, now I thank you, and beg you to forgive me, what can I do besides?"

She returned to the hearth, and frankly extended her hand.

He blackened, and scowled like a thunder cloud, and kept his fists resolutely clenched, and his gaze fixed on the ground.

Catherine, by instinct, must have divined it was obdurate perversity, and not dislike, that prompted this dogged conduct; for, after remaining an instant undecided, she stooped, and impressed on his cheek a gentle kiss.

The little rogue thought I had not seen her, and, drawing back, she took her former station by the window, quite demurely.

[14]Filthy.
[15]Get out of the way.

I shook my head reprovingly; and then she blushed, and whispered—

"Well! what should I have done, Ellen? He wouldn't shake hands, and he wouldn't look—I must show him some way that I like him, that I want to be friends."

Whether the kiss convinced Hareton, I cannot tell; he was very careful, for some minutes, that his face should not be seen; and when he did raise it, he was sadly puzzled where to turn his eyes.

Catherine employed herself in wrapping a handsome book neatly in white paper; and having tied it with a bit of ribband, and addressed it to "Mr. Hareton Earnshaw," she desired me to be her ambassadress, and convey the present to its destined recipient.

"And tell him, if he'll take it, I'll come and teach him to read it right," she said, "and, if he refuse it, I'll go upstairs, and never tease him again."

I carried it, and repeated the message, anxiously watched by my employer. Hareton would not open his fingers, so I laid it on his knee. He did not strike it off either. I returned to my work. Catherine leaned her head and arms on the table, till she heard the slight rustle of the covering being removed; then she stole away, and quietly seated herself beside her cousin. He trembled, and his face glowed—all his rudeness and all his surly harshness had deserted him—he could not summon courage, at first, to utter a syllable, in reply to her questioning look, and her murmured petition.

"Say you forgive me, Hareton, do! You can make me so happy, by speaking that little word."

He muttered something inaudible.

"And you'll be my friend?" added Catherine, interrogatively.

"Nay! you'll be ashamed of me every day of your life," he answered. "And the more, the more you know me, and I cannot bide it."

"So, you won't be my friend?" she said, smiling as sweet as honey, and creeping close up.

I overheard no further distinguishable talk; but, on looking round again, I perceived two such radiant countenances bent over the page of the accepted book, that I did not doubt the treaty had been ratified on both sides, and the enemies were, thenceforth, sworn allies.

The work they studied was full of costly pictures; and those, and their position, had charm enough to keep them unmoved, till

Joseph came home. He, poor man, was perfectly aghast at the spectacle of Catherine seated on the same bench with Hareton Earnshaw, leaning her hand on his shoulder; and confounded at his favourite's endurance of her proximity. It affected him too deeply to allow an observation on the subject that night. His emotion was only revealed by the immense sighs he drew, as he solemnly spread his large Bible on the table, and overlaid it with dirty bank-notes from his pocket-book, the produce of the day's transactions. At length, he summoned Hareton from his seat.

"Tak these in tuh t' maister, lad," he said, "un' bide theare; Aw's gang up tuh my awn rahm. This hoile's norther mensful nor seemly fur us—we mun side aht, and seearch another." [16]

• "Come, Catherine," I said, "we must 'side out' too—I've done my ironing, are you ready to go?"

"It is not eight o'clock!" she answered, rising unwillingly, "Hareton, I'll leave this book upon the chimney-piece, and I'll bring some more to-morrow."

"Ony books ut yah leave, Aw sall tak' intuh th' hahse," said Joseph, "un' it 'ull be mitch if yah find 'em agean; soa, yah muh plase yourseln!" [17]

Cathy threatened that his library should pay for hers; and, smiling as she passed Hareton, went singing upstairs, lighter of heart, I venture to say, than ever she had been under that roof before; except, perhaps, during her earliest visits to Linton.

The intimacy, thus commenced, grew rapidly; though it encountered temporary interruptions. Earnshaw was not to be civilized with a wish; and my young lady was no philosopher, and no paragon of patience; but both their minds tending to the same point—one loving and desiring to esteem, and the other loving and desiring to be esteemed—they contrived in the end to reach it.

You see, Mr. Lockwood, it was easy enough to win Mrs. Heathcliff's heart; but now, I'm glad you did not try—the crown of all my wishes will be the union of those two; I shall envy no one on their wedding-day—there won't be a happier woman than myself in England!

---

[16]"Take these in to the master, . . . and stay there; I'm going up to my own room. This room is neither decent nor seemly for us—we must get away, and find another."

[17]Any books that you leave, I shall take into the house . . . and it will be much [you'll be lucky] if you find them again; so, you may please yourself!"

## Chapter 19/33

On the morrow of that Monday, Earnshaw being still unable to follow his ordinary employments, and, therefore, remaining about the house, I speedily found it would be impracticable to retain my charge beside me, as heretofore.

She got down stairs before me, and out into the garden, where she had seen her cousin performing some easy work; and when I went to bid them come to breakfast, I saw she had persuaded him to clear a large space of ground from currant and gooseberry bushes, and they were busy planning together an importation of plants from the Grange.

I was terrified at the devastation which had been accomplished in a brief half hour; the black currant trees were the apple of Joseph's eye, and she had just fixed her choice of a flower bed in the midst of them!

"There! That will be all shewn to the master," I exclaimed, "the minute it is discovered. And what excuse have you to offer for taking such liberties with the garden? We shall have a fine explosion on the head of it:[1] see if we don't! Mr. Hareton, I wonder you should have no more wit, than to go and make that mess at her bidding!"

"I'd forgotten they were Joseph's," answered Earnshaw, rather puzzled, "but I'll tell him I did it."

We always ate our meals with Mr. Heathcliff. I held the mistress's post in making tea and carving; so I was indispensable at table. Catherine usually sat by me; but to-day she stole nearer to Hareton, and I presently saw she would have no more discretion in her friendship, than she had in her hostility.

"Now, mind you don't talk with and notice your cousin too much," were my whispered instructions as we entered the room. "It will certainly annoy Mr. Heathcliff, and he'll be mad at you both."

"I'm not going to," she answered.

The minute after, she had sidled to him, and was sticking primroses in his plate of porridge.

He dared not speak to her, there; he dared hardly look; and yet she went on teasing, till he was twice on the point of being provoked to laugh; and I frowned, and then she glanced toward the master, whose mind was occupied on other subjects than his com-

[1]On that head (or count); as soon as it's discovered.

pany, as his countenance evinced, and she grew serious for an instant, scrutinizing him with deep gravity. Afterwards she turned, and re-commenced her nonsense; at last, Hareton uttered a smothered laugh.

Mr. Heathcliff started; his eye rapidly surveyed our faces. Catherine met it with her accustomed look of nervousness, and yet defiance, which he abhorred.

"It is well you are out of my reach," he exclaimed. "What fiend possesses you to stare back at me, continually, with those infernal eyes? Down with them! and don't remind me of your existence again. I thought I had cured you of laughing!"

"It was me," muttered Hareton.

"What do you say?" demanded the master.

Hareton looked at his plate, and did not repeat the confession.

Mr. Heathcliff looked at him a bit, and then silently resumed his breakfast, and his interrupted musing.

We had nearly finished, and the two young people prudently shifted wider asunder, so I anticipated no further disturbance during that sitting; when Joseph appeared at the door, revealing by his quivering lip and furious eyes, that the outrage committed on his precious shrubs was detected.

He must have seen Cathy and her cousin about the spot before he examined it, for while his jaws worked like those of a cow chewing its cud, and rendered his speech difficult to understand, he began:

"Aw mun hev my wage, and Aw mun goa! Aw *hed* aimed tuh dee, wheare Aw'd sarved fur sixty year; un' Aw thowt Aw'd lug my books up intuh t' garret, un' all my bits uh stuff, un' they sud hev t' kitchen to theirseln; fur t' sake uh quietness. It wur hard tuh gie up my awn hearthstun, bud Aw thowt Aw *could* do that! Bud, nah, shoo's taan my garden frough me, un' by th' heart! Maister, Aw cannot stand it! Yah muh bend tuh th' yoak, an ye will—Aw'm noan used to't, and an ow'd man doesn't sooin get used tuh new barthens— Aw'd rayther arn my bite, an' my sup, wi' a hammer in th' road!"[2]

---

[2]"I must have my wages, and I must go! I *had* planned to die where I'd served for sixty years; and I thought I'd lug my books up into the garret, and all my bits of stuff, and they should have the kitchen to themselves; for the sake of quiet. It was hard to give up my own hearthstone, but I thought I *could* do that! But, no, she's taken my garden from me, and by the heart! Master, I cannot stand it! You may bend to the yoke, if you will—I'm not used to it, and an old man doesn't soon get used to a new paddock [a warm place for cattle]—I'd rather earn my food, and my drink, with a hammer in the road [doing road-building work]!"

"Now, now, idiot!" interrupted Heathcliff, "cut it short! What's your grievance? I'll interfere in no quarrels between you and Nelly—She may thrust you into the coal-hole for anything I care."

"It's noan Nelly!" answered Joseph. "Aw sudn't shift fur Nelly—nasty, ill nowt as shoo is. Thank God! *shoo* cannot stale t' sowl o' nob'dy! Shoo wer niver soa handsome, bud whet a body mud look at her baht winking. It's yon flaysome, graceless quean, ut's witched ahr lad, wi' her bold een, un' her forrard ways—till—Nay! It fair brusts my heart! He's forgotten all E done for him, un' made on him, un' goan un' riven up a whole row ut t' grandest currant trees, i' t' garden!"[3] and here he lamented outright, unmanned by a sense of his bitter injuries, and Earnshaw's ingratitude and dangerous condition.

"Is the fool drunk?" asked Mr. Heathcliff. "Hareton, is it you he's finding fault with?"

"I've pulled up two or three bushes," replied the young man, "but I'm going to set 'em again."

"And why have you pulled them up?" said the master.

Catherine wisely put in her tongue.

"We wanted to plant some flowers there," she cried. "I'm the only person to blame, for I wished him to do it."

"And who the devil gave *you* leave to touch a stick about the place?" demanded her father-in-law, much surprised. "And who ordered *you* to obey her?" he added, turning to Hareton.

The latter was speechless; his cousin replied—

"You shouldn't grudge a few yards of earth for me to ornament, when you have taken all my land!"

"Your land, insolent slut? You never had any!" said Heathcliff.

"And my money," she continued, returning his angry glare, and, meantime, biting a piece of crust, the remnant of her breakfast.

"Silence!" he exclaimed. "Get done, and begone!"

"And Hareton's land, and his money," pursued the reckless thing. "Hareton and I are friends now; and I shall tell him all about you!"

The master seemed confounded a moment: he grew pale, and rose up, eyeing her all the while, with an expression of mortal hate.

---

[3] "I shouldn't budge for Nelly—nasty, bad nothing as she is. Thank God! She can't steal anyone's soul away! She was never so handsome, but what a person might look at her without winking. It's that terrible, godforsaken slut, that's bewitched our lad, with her bold eyes, her forward ways—till—No! It about breaks my heart! He's forgotten all I've done for him, and made of him, and gone and torn up a whole row of the grandest currant trees, in the garden!"

"If you strike me, Hareton will strike you!" she said, "so you may as well sit down."

"If Hareton does not turn you out of the room, I'll strike him to Hell," thundered Heathcliff. "Damnable witch! dare you pretend to rouse him against me? Off with her! Do you hear? Fling her into the kitchen! I'll kill her, Ellen Dean, if you let her come into my sight again!"

Hareton tried, under his breath, to persuade her to go.

"Drag her away!" he cried savagely. "Are you staying to talk?" And he approached to execute his own command.

"He'll not obey you, wicked man, any more!" said Catherine, "and he'll soon detest you, as much as I do!"

"Wisht! wisht!" muttered the young man reproachfully. "I will not hear you speak so to him—Have done!"

"But you won't let him strike me?" she cried.

"Come then!" he whispered earnestly.

It was too late—Heathcliff had caught hold of her.

"Now *you* go!" he said to Earnshaw. "Accursed witch! this time she has provoked me, when I could not bear it; and I'll make her repent it for ever!"

He had his hand in her hair; Hareton attempted to release the locks, entreating him not to hurt her that once. Heathcliff's black eyes flashed, he seemed ready to tear Catherine in pieces, and I was just worked up to risk coming to the rescue, when of a sudden his fingers relaxed, he shifted his grasp from her head to her arm, and gazed intently in her face—Then, he drew his hand over his eyes, stood a moment to collect himself apparently, and turning anew to Catherine, said with assumed calmness,

"You must learn to avoid putting me in a passion, or I shall really murder you, some time! Go with Mrs. Dean, and keep with her, and confine your insolence to her ears. As to Hareton Earnshaw, if I see him listen to you, I'll send him seeking his bread where he can get it! Your love will make him an outcast, and a beggar—Nelly, take her, and leave me, all of you! Leave me!"

I led my young lady out; she was too glad of her escape, to resist; the other followed, and Mr. Heathcliff had the room to himself, till dinner.

I had counselled Catherine to get hers upstairs; but, as soon as he perceived her vacant seat, he sent me to call her. He spoke to none of us, ate very little, and went out directly afterwards, intimating that he should not return before evening.

The two new friends established themselves in the house, during his absence, where I heard Hareton sternly check his cousin, on her offering a revelation of her father-in-law's conduct to his father.

He said he wouldn't suffer a word to be uttered to him, in his disparagement; if he were the devil, it didn't signify; he would stand by him; and he'd rather she would abuse himself, as she used to, than begin on Mr. Heathcliff.

Catherine was waxing cross at this; but he found means to make her hold her tongue, by asking, how she would like *him* to speak ill of her father? and then she comprehended that Earnshaw took the master's reputation home to himself, and was attached by ties stronger than reason could break—chains, forged by habit, which it would be cruel to attempt to loosen.

She showed a good heart, thenceforth, in avoiding both complaints and expressions of antipathy concerning Heathcliff; and confessed to me her sorrow that she had endeavoured to raise a bad spirit between him and Hareton—indeed, I don't believe she has ever breathed a syllable, in the latter's hearing, against her oppressor, since.

When this slight disagreement was over, they were thick again, and as busy as possible, in their several occupations of pupil and teacher. I came in to sit with them, after I had done my work, and I felt so soothed and comforted to watch them, that I did not notice how time got on. You know, they both appeared, in a measure, my children: I had long been proud of one, and now, I was sure, the other would be a source of equal satisfaction. His honest, warm, and intelligent nature shook off rapidly the clouds of ignorance and degradation in which it had been bred; and Catherine's sincere commendations acted as a spur to his industry. His brightening mind brightened his features, and added spirit and nobility to their aspect—I could hardly fancy it the same individual I had beheld on the day I discovered my little lady at Wuthering Heights, after her expedition to the Crags.

While I admired, and they laboured, dusk drew on, and with it returned the master. He came upon us quite unexpectedly, entering by the front way, and had a full view of the whole three, ere we could raise our heads to glance at him.

Well, I reflected, there was never a pleasanter, or more harmless sight; and it will be a burning shame to scold them. The red firelight glowed on their two bonny heads, and revealed their faces, animated with the eager interest of children; for, though he was twenty-three, and she eighteen, each had so much of novelty to feel and learn, that neither experienced nor evinced the sentiments of sober disenchanted maturity.

They lifted their eyes together, to encounter Mr. Heathcliff—perhaps you have never remarked that their eyes are precisely similar, and they are those of Catherine Earnshaw. The present Catherine has no other likeness to her, except a breadth of forehead, and a certain arch of the nostril that makes her appear rather haughty, whether she will or not. With Hareton the resemblance is carried farther: it is singular, at all times—then, it was particularly striking: because his senses were alert, and his mental faculties wakened to unwonted activity.

I suppose this resemblance disarmed Mr. Heathcliff: he walked to the hearth in evident agitation, but it quickly subsided, as he looked at the young man; or, I should say, altered its character, for it was there yet.

He took the book from his hand, and glanced at the open page, then returned it without any observation; merely signing Catherine away—her companion lingered very little behind her, and I was about to depart also, but he bid me sit still.

"It is a poor conclusion, is it not," he observed, having brooded a while on the scene he had just witnessed. "An absurd termination to my violent exertions? I get levers and mattocks to demolish the two houses, and train myself to be capable of working like Hercules, and when everything is ready, and in my power, I find the will to lift a slate off either roof has vanished! My old enemies have not beaten me—now would be the precise time to revenge myself on their representatives—I could do it; and none could hinder me—But where is the use? I don't care for striking, I can't take the trouble to raise my hand! That sounds as if I had been labouring the whole time, only to exhibit a fine trait of magnanimity. It is far from being the case—I have lost the faculty of enjoying their destruction, and I am too idle to destroy for nothing.

"Nelly, there is a strange change approaching—I'm in its shadow at present—I take so little interest in my daily life, that I hardly remember to eat and drink—Those two, who have left the room, are the only objects which retain a distinct material appearance to me; and that appearance causes me pain, amounting to agony. About *her* I won't speak; and I don't desire to think; but I earnestly wish she were invisible—her presence invokes only maddening sensations. *He* moves me differently; and yet if I could do it without seeming insane, I'd never see him again! You'll perhaps think me rather inclined to become so," he added, making an effort to smile, "if I try to describe the thousand forms of past associations and ideas he awakens or embodies—But you'll not talk of what I tell you, and my mind is so eternally secluded in itself, it is tempting, at last, to turn it out to another.

"Five minutes ago, Hareton seemed a personification of my youth, not a human being—I felt to him in such a variety of ways, that it would have been impossible to have accosted him rationally.

"In the first place, his startling likeness to Catherine connected him fearfully with her—That, however, which you may suppose the most potent to arrest my imagination, is actually the least—for what is not connected with her to me? and what does not recall her? I cannot look down to this floor, but her features are shaped on the flags! In every cloud, in every tree—filling the air at night, and caught by glimpses in every object by day, I am surrounded with her image! The most ordinary faces of men and women—my own features—mock me with a resemblance. The entire world is a dreadful collection of memoranda that she did exist, and that I have lost her!

"Well, Hareton's aspect was the ghost of my immortal love, of my wild endeavours to hold my right, my degradation, my pride, my happiness, and my anguish—

"But it is frenzy to repeat these thoughts to you; only it will let you know why, with a reluctance to be always alone, his society is no benefit, rather an aggravation of the constant torment I suffer—and it partly contributes to render me regardless how he and his cousin go on together. I can give them no attention, any more."

"But what do you mean by a *change*, Mr. Heathcliff?" I said, alarmed at his manner, though he was neither in danger of losing his senses, nor dying; according to my judgment he was quite strong and healthy; and, as to his reason, from childhood he had a delight in dwelling on dark things, and entertaining odd fancies—

he might have had a monomania on the subject of his departed idol; but on every other point his wits were as sound as mine.

"I shall not know that, till it comes," he said, "I'm only half conscious of it now."

"You have no feeling of illness, have you?" I asked.

"No, Nelly, I have not," he answered.

"Then, you are not afraid of death?" I pursued.

"Afraid! No!" he replied. "I have neither a fear, nor a presentiment, nor a hope of death—Why should I? With my hard constitution, and temperate mode of living, and unperilous occupations, I ought to and probably *shall* remain above ground, till there is scarcely a black hair on my head—And yet I cannot continue in this condition!—I have to remind myself to breathe—almost to remind my heart to beat! And it is like bending back a stiff spring . . . it is by compulsion that I do the slightest act not prompted by one thought, and by compulsion, that I notice anything alive or dead, which is not associated with one universal idea . . . I have a single wish, and my whole being and faculties are yearning to attain it. They have yearned towards it so long, and so unwaveringly, that I'm convinced it *will* be reached—and *soon*—because it has devoured my existence—I am swallowed in the anticipation of its fulfilment.

"My confessions have not relieved me—but, they may account for some otherwise unaccountable phases of humour which I show. O, God! It is a long fight, I wish it were over!"

He began to pace the room, muttering terrible things to himself; till I was inclined to believe, as he said Joseph did, that conscience had turned his heart to an earthly hell—I wondered greatly how it would end.

Though he seldom before had revealed his state of mind, even by looks, it was his habitual mood, I had no doubt. He asserted it himself—but not a soul, from his general bearing, would have conjectured the fact. You did not, when you saw him, Mr. Lockwood—and at the period of which I speak, he was just the same as then, only fonder of continued solitude, and perhaps still more laconic in company.

## Chapter 20/34

For some days after that evening, Mr. Heathcliff shunned meeting us at meals; yet he would not consent, formally, to exclude Hareton and Cathy. He had an aversion to yielding so completely to his feelings, choosing rather to absent himself—And eating once in twenty-four hours seemed sufficient sustenance for him.

One night, after the family were in bed, I heard him go down stairs, and out at the front door: I did not hear him re-enter and, in the morning, I found he was still away.

We were in April then: the weather was sweet and warm, the grass as green as showers and sun could make it, and the two dwarf apple trees, near the southern wall, in full bloom.

After breakfast, Catherine insisted on my bringing a chair, and sitting, with my work, under the fir trees at the end of the house; and she beguiled Hareton, who had perfectly recovered from his accident, to dig and arrange her little garden, which was shifted to that corner by the influence of Joseph's complaints.

I was comfortably revelling in the spring fragrance around, and the beautiful soft blue overhead, when my young lady, who had run down near the gate to procure some primrose roots for a border, returned only half laden, and informed us that Mr. Heathcliff was coming in.

"And he spoke to me," she added, with a perplexed countenance.

"What did he say?" asked Hareton.

"He told me to begone as fast as I could," she answered. "But he looked so different from his usual look that I stopped a moment to stare at him."

"How?" he enquired.

"Why, almost bright and cheerful—No, almost nothing—*very much* excited, and wild and glad!" she replied.

"Night-walking amuses him, then," I remarked, affecting a careless manner: in reality, as surprised as she was; and, anxious to ascertain the truth of her statement, for to see the master looking glad would not be an every day spectacle, I framed an excuse to go in.

Heathcliff stood at the open door; he was pale, and he trembled; yet, certainly, he had a strange joyful glitter in his eyes, that altered the aspect of his whole face.

"Will you have some breakfast?" I said. "You must be hungry, rambling about all night!"

I wanted to discover where he had been; but I did not like to ask directly.

"No, I'm not hungry," he answered, averting his head, and speaking rather contemptuously, as if he guessed I was trying to divine the occasion of his good humour.

I felt perplexed—I didn't know whether it were not a proper opportunity to offer a bit of admonition.

"I don't think it right to wander out of doors," I observed, "instead of being in bed: it is not wise, at any rate, this moist season. I dare say you'll catch a bad cold, or a fever—you have something the matter with you now!"

"Nothing but what I can bear," he replied, "and with the greatest pleasure, provided you'll leave me alone—get in, and don't annoy me."

I obeyed; and, in passing, I noticed he breathed as fast as a cat.

"Yes!" I reflected to myself, "we shall have a fit of illness. I cannot conceive what he has been doing!"

That noon, he sat down to dinner with us, and received a heaped-up plate from my hands, as if he intended to make amends for previous fasting.

"I've neither cold nor fever, Nelly," he remarked, in allusion to my morning's speech. "And I'm ready to do justice to the food you give me."

He took his knife and fork, and was going to commence eating, when the inclination appeared to become suddenly extinct. He laid them on the table, looked eagerly towards the window, then rose and went out.

We saw him walking, to and fro, in the garden while we concluded our meal; and Earnshaw said he'd go and ask why he would not dine; he thought we had grieved him some way.

"Well, is he coming?" cried Catherine, when her cousin returned.

"Nay," he answered; "but he's not angry; he seemed rare and pleased indeed; only, I made him impatient by speaking to him twice; and then he bid me be off to you; he wondered how I could want the company of any body else."

I set his plate, to keep warm, on the fender: and after an hour or two he re-entered, when the room was clear, in no degree calmer—the same unnatural—it was unnatural—appearance of joy under his black brows; the same bloodless hue, and his teeth visible, now and then, in a kind of smile; his frame shivering, not as one shivers with chill or weakness, but as a tight-stretched cord vibrates—a strong thrilling, rather than trembling.

I will ask what is the matter, I thought, or who should? And I exclaimed—

"Have you heard any good news, Mr. Heathcliff? You look uncommonly animated."

"Where should good news come from, to me?" he said. "I'm animated with hunger; and, seemingly, I must not eat."

"Your dinner is here," I returned; "why won't you get it?"

"I don't want it now," he muttered, hastily. "I'll wait till supper. And, Nelly, once for all, let me beg you to warn Hareton and the other away from me. I wish to be troubled by nobody—I wish to have this place to myself."

"Is there some new reason for this banishment?" I inquired. "Tell me why you are so queer, Mr. Heathcliff? Where were you last night? I'm not putting the question through idle curiosity, but—"

"You are putting the question through very idle curiosity," he interrupted, with a laugh. "Yet, I'll answer it. Last night, I was on the threshold of hell. To-day, I am within sight of my heaven—I have my eyes on it—hardly three feet to sever me! And now you'd better go—You'll neither see nor hear anything to frighten you, if you refrain from prying."

Having swept the hearth and wiped the table, I departed more perplexed than ever.

He did not quit the house again that afternoon, and no one intruded on his solitude, till, at eight o'clock, I deemed it proper, though unsummoned, to carry a candle and his supper to him.

He was leaning against the ledge of an open lattice, but not looking out; his face was turned to the interior gloom. The fire had smouldered to ashes; the room was filled with the damp, mild air of the cloudy evening, and so still, that not only the murmur of the beck down Gimmerton was distinguishable, but its ripples and its gurgling over the pebbles, or through the large stones which it could not cover.

I uttered an ejaculation of discontent at seeing the dismal grate, and commenced shutting the casements, one after another, till I came to his.

"Must I close this?" I asked, in order to rouse him, for he would not stir.

The light flashed on his features, as I spoke. Oh, Mr. Lockwood, I cannot express what a terrible start I got, by the momentary view! Those deep black eyes! That smile, and ghastly paleness! It appeared to me, not Mr. Heathcliff, but a goblin; and, in my terror, I let the candle bend towards the wall, and it left me in darkness.

"Yes, close it," he replied, in his familiar voice. "There, that is pure awkwardness! Why did you hold the candle horizontally? Be quick, and bring another."

I hurried out in a foolish state of dread, and said to Joseph—

"The master wishes you to take him a light; and rekindle the fire." For I dare not go in myself again just then.

Joseph rattled some fire into the shovel, and went; but he brought it back, immediately, with the supper tray in his other hand, explaining that Mr. Heathcliff was going to bed, and he wanted nothing to eat till morning.

We heard him mount the stairs directly; he did not proceed to his ordinary chamber, but turned into that with the panelled bed— its window, as I mentioned before, is wide enough for anybody to get through, and it struck me that he plotted another midnight excursion, which he had rather we had no suspicion of.

"Is he a ghoul, or a vampire?" I mused. I had read of such hideous, incarnate demons. And then I set myself to reflect how I had tended him in infancy; and watched him grow to youth; and followed him almost through his whole course; and what absurd nonsense it was to yield to that sense of horror.

"But where did he come from, the little dark thing, harboured by a good man to his bane?" muttered superstition, as I dozed into unconsciousness. And I began, half dreaming, to weary myself with imagining some fit parentage for him; and repeating my waking meditations, I tracked his existence over again, with grim variations; at last, picturing his death and funeral; of which all I can remember is being exceedingly vexed at having the task of dictating an inscription for his monument, and consulting the sexton about it; and, as he had no surname, and we could not tell his age, we were obliged to content ourselves with the single word, "Heathcliff." That came true; we were. If you enter the kirkyard, you'll read on his headstone only that, and the date of his death.

Dawn restored me to common sense. I rose, and went into the garden as soon as I could see, to ascertain if there were any footmarks under his window. There were none.

"He has stayed at home," I thought, "and he'll be all right, to-day!"

I prepared breakfast for the household, as was my usual custom, but told Hareton and Catherine to get theirs ere the master came down, for he lay late. They preferred taking it out of doors, under the trees, and I set a little table to accommodate them. On my re-entrance, I found Mr. Heathcliff below. He and Joseph were conversing about some farming business; he gave clear, minute directions concerning the matter discussed, but he spoke rapidly, and turned his head continually aside, and had the same excited expression, even more exaggerated.

When Joseph quitted the room, he took his seat in the place he generally chose, and I put a basin of coffee before him. He drew it nearer, and then rested his arms on the table, and looked at the opposite wall, as I supposed, surveying one particular portion, up and down, with glittering, restless eyes, and with such eager interest that he stopped breathing during half a minute together.

"Come now," I exclaimed, pushing some bread against his hand. "Eat and drink that, while it is hot. It has been waiting near an hour."

He didn't notice me, and yet he smiled. I'd rather have seen him gnash his teeth than smile so.

"Mr. Heathcliff! master!" I cried. "Don't, for God's sake, stare as if you saw an unearthly vision."

"Don't, for God's sake, shout so loud," he replied. "Turn round, and tell me, are we by ourselves?"

"Of course," was my answer, "of course we are!"

Still, I involuntarily obeyed him, as if I was not quite sure.

With a sweep of his hand, he cleared a vacant space in front among the breakfast things, and leant forward to gaze more at his ease.

Now, I perceived he was not looking at the wall, for when I regarded him alone, it seemed, exactly, that he gazed at something within two yards distance. And whatever it was, it communicated, apparently, both pleasure and pain, in exquisite extremes: at least, the anguished, yet raptured expression of his countenance suggested that idea.

The fancied object was not fixed, either; his eyes pursued it with unwearied vigilance, and, even in speaking to me, were never weaned away.

I vainly reminded him of his protracted abstinence from food; if he stirred to touch anything in compliance with my entreaties, if he stretched his hand out to get a piece of bread, his fingers clenched, before they reached it, and remained on the table, forgetful of their aim.

I sat, a model of patience, trying to attract his absorbed attention from its engrossing speculation; till he grew irritable, and got up, asking why I would not allow him to have his own time in taking his meals? and saying that, on the next occasion, I needn't wait, I might set the things down, and go.

Having uttered these words, he left the house, slowly sauntered down the garden path, and disappeared through the gate.

The hours crept anxiously by: another evening came. I did not retire to rest till late, and when I did, I could not sleep. He returned after midnight, and, instead of going to bed, shut himself into the room beneath. I listened, and tossed about; and, finally, dressed, and descended. It was too irksome to lie there, harassing my brain with a hundred idle misgivings.

I distinguished Mr. Heathcliff's step, restlessly measuring the floor; and he frequently broke the silence by a deep inspiration, resembling a groan. He muttered detached words, also; the only one I could catch was the name of Catherine, coupled with some wild term of endearment, or suffering; and spoken as one would speak to a person present—low and earnest, and wrung from the depth of his soul.

I had not courage to walk straight into the apartment; but I desired to divert him from his reverie, and therefore fell foul of the kitchen fire; stirred it, and began to scrape the cinders. It drew him forth sooner than I expected. He opened the door immediately, and said—

"Nelly, come here—is it morning? Come in with your light."

"It is striking four," I answered; "you want a candle to take upstairs—you might have lit one at this fire."

"No, I don't wish to go upstairs," he said. "Come in, and kindle *me* a fire, and do anything there is to do about the room."

"I must blow the coals red first, before I can carry any," I replied, getting a chair and the bellows.

He roamed to and fro, meantime, in a state approaching distraction: his heavy sighs succeeding each other so thick as to leave no space for common breathing between.

"When day breaks, I'll send for Green," he said; "I wish to make some legal inquiries of him while I can bestow a thought on those matters, and while I can act calmly. I have not written my will yet, and how to leave my property, I cannot determine! I wish I could annihilate it from the face of the earth."

"I would not talk so, Mr. Heathcliff," I interposed. "Let your will be, a while—you'll be spared to repent of your many injustices, yet! I never expected that your nerves would be disordered—they are, at present, marvellously so, however; and, almost entirely, through your own fault. The way you've passed these three last days might knock up a Titan. Do take some food, and some repose. You need only look at yourself in a glass to see how you require both. Your cheeks are hollow, and your eyes blood-shot, like a person starving with hunger, and going blind with loss of sleep."

"It is not my fault, that I cannot eat or rest," he replied. "I assure you it is through no settled designs. I'll do both, as soon as I possibly can. But you might as well bid a man struggling in the water, rest within arm's length of the shore! I must reach it first, and then I'll rest. Well, never mind Mr. Green; as to repenting of my injustices, I've done no injustice, and I repent of nothing—I'm too happy, and yet I'm not happy enough. My soul's bliss kills my body, but does not satisfy itself."

"Happy, master?" I cried. "Strange happiness! If you would hear me without being angry, I might offer some advice that would make you happier."

"What is that?" he asked. "Give it."

"You are aware, Mr. Heathcliff," I said, "that from the time you were thirteen years old, you have lived a selfish, unchristian life; and probably hardly had a Bible in your hands, during all that period. You must have forgotten the contents of the book, and you may not have space to search it now. Could it be hurtful to send for some one—some minister of any denomination, it does not matter which, to explain it, and show you how very far you have erred from its precepts, and how unfit you will be for its heaven, unless a change takes place before you die?"

"I'm rather obliged than angry, Nelly," he said, "for you remind me of the manner in which I desire to be buried in—It is to be carried to the churchyard, in the evening. You and Hareton may, if you please, accompany me—and mind, particularly, to notice that the sexton obeys my directions concerning the two coffins! No minister need come; nor need anything be said over me—I tell you, I have nearly attained *my* heaven; and that of others is altogether un-valued and uncoveted by me!"

"And supposing you persevered in your obstinate fast, and died by that means, and they refused to bury you in the precincts of the Kirk?" I said, shocked at his godless indifference. "How would you like it?"

"They won't do that," he replied: "if they did, you must have me removed secretly; and if you neglect it, you shall prove, practi-cally, that the dead are not annihilated!"

As soon as he heard the other members of the family stirring he retired to his den, and I breathed freer—But in the afternoon, while Joseph and Hareton were at their work, he came into the kitchen again, and with a wild look, bid me come, and sit in the house—he wanted somebody with him.

I declined, telling him plainly that his strange talk and manner frightened me, and I had neither the nerve nor the will to be his companion, alone.

"I believe you think me a fiend!" he said, with his dismal laugh, "something too horrible to live under a decent roof!"

Then turning to Catherine, who was there, and who drew be-hind me at his approach, he added, half sneeringly.

"Will *you* come, chuck? I'll not hurt you. No! to you, I've made myself worse than the devil. Well, there is *one* who won't shrink from my company! By God! she's relentless. Oh, damn it! It's unut-terably too much for flesh and blood to bear, even mine."

He solicited the society of no one more. At dusk, he went into his chamber—through the whole night, and far into the morning, we heard him groaning, and murmuring to himself. Hareton was anxious to enter, but I bid him fetch Mr. Kenneth, and he should go in and see him.

When he came, and I requested admittance and tried to open the door, I found it locked; and Heathcliff bade us be damned. He was better, and would be left alone; so the doctor went away.

The following evening was very wet, indeed it poured down, till day-dawn; and, as I took my morning walk round the house, I ob-served the master's window swinging open, and the rain driving straight in.

He cannot be in bed, I thought, those showers would drench him through! He must either be up, or out. But I'll make no more ado, I'll go boldly, and look!

Having succeeded in obtaining entrance with another key, I ran to unclose the panels, for the chamber was vacant—quickly pushing them aside, I peeped in. Mr. Heathcliff was there—laid on his back. His eyes met mine so keen and fierce, I started; and then, he seemed to smile.

I could not think him dead—but his face and throat were washed with rain; the bed-clothes dripped, and he was perfectly still. The lattice, flapping to and fro, had grazed one hand that rested on the sill—no blood trickled from the broken skin, and when I put my fingers to it, I could doubt no more—he was dead and stark!

I hasped the window; I combed his black long hair from his forehead; I tried to close his eyes—to extinguish, if possible, that frightful, life-like gaze of exultation, before any one else beheld it. They would not shut—they seemed to sneer at my attempts, and his parted lips and sharp, white teeth sneered too! Taken with another fit of cowardice, I cried out for Joseph. Joseph shuffled up, and made a noise, but resolutely refused to meddle with him.

"Th' divil's harried off his soul," he cried, "and he muh hev his carcass intuh t' bargin, for owt Aw care! Ech! what a wicked un he looks girnning at death!"[1] and the old sinner grinned in mockery.

I thought he intended to cut a caper round the bed; but suddenly composing himself, he fell on his knees, and raised his hands, and returned thanks that the lawful master and the ancient stock were restored to their rights.

I felt stunned by the awful event; and my memory unavoidably recurred to former times with a sort of oppressive sadness. But poor Hareton, the most wronged, was the only one who really suffered much. He sat by the corpse all night, weeping in bitter earnest. He pressed its hand, and kissed the sarcastic, savage face that every one else shrank from contemplating; and bemoaned him with that strong grief which springs naturally from a generous heart, though it be tough as tempered steel.

Kenneth was perplexed to pronounce of what disorder the master died. I concealed the fact of his having swallowed nothing for

---

[1] "The devil's carried off his soul . . . and he may have his carcass into the bargain . . . grinning at death!"

four days, fearing it might lead to trouble, and then, I am persuaded he did not abstain on purpose; it was the consequence of his strange illness, not the cause.

We buried him, to the scandal of the whole neighbourhood, as he wished. Earnshaw and I, the sexton, and six men to carry the coffin, comprehended the whole attendance.

The six men departed when they had let it down into the grave. We stayed to see it covered. Hareton, with a streaming face, dug green sods, and laid them over the brown mould himself: at present it is as smooth and verdant as its companion mounds—and I hope its tenant sleeps as soundly. But the country folks, if you ask them, would swear on the Bible that he *walks*. There are those who speak to having met him near the church, and on the moor, and even within this house—Idle tales, you'll say, and so say I. Yet that old man by the kitchen fire affirms he has seen two on 'em, looking out of his chamber window, on every rainy night since his death—and an odd thing happened to me about a month ago.

I was going to the Grange one evening—a dark evening threatening thunder—and, just at the turn of the Heights, I encountered a little boy with a sheep and two lambs before him; he was crying terribly, and I supposed the lambs were skittish, and would not be guided.

"What is the matter, my little man?" I asked.

"They's Heathcliff and a woman, yonder, under t' Nab," he blubbered, "un' Aw darnut pass 'em."

I saw nothing; but neither the sheep nor he would go on, so I bid him take the road lower down.

He probably raised the phantoms from thinking, as he traversed the moors alone, on the nonsense he had heard his parents and companions repeat—yet still, I don't like being out in the dark, now—and I don't like being left by myself in this grim house—I cannot help it, I shall be glad when they leave it, and shift to the Grange!

"They are going to the Grange, then?" I said.

"Yes," answered Mrs. Dean, "as soon as they are married; and that will be on New Year's day."

"And who will live here then?"

"Why, Joseph will take care of the house, and, perhaps a lad to keep him company. They will live in the kitchen, and the rest will be shut up."

"For the use of such ghosts as choose to inhabit it," I observed.

"No, Mr. Lockwood," said Nelly, shaking her head. "I believe the dead are at peace, but it is not right to speak of them with levity." At that moment the garden gate swung to; the ramblers were returning.

"*They* are afraid of nothing," I grumbled, watching their approach through the window. "Together they would brave Satan and all his legions."

As they stepped on to the door-stones, and halted to take a last look at the moon, or, more correctly, at each other, by her light, I felt irresistibly impelled to escape them again; and pressing a remembrance[2] into the hand of Mrs. Dean, and disregarding her expostulations at my rudeness, I vanished through the kitchen, as they opened the house-door, and so should have confirmed Joseph in his opinion of his fellow-servant's gay indiscretions, had he not, fortunately, recognised me for a respectable character by the sweet ring of a sovereign at his feet.

My walk home was lengthened by a diversion in the direction of the kirk. When beneath its walls, I perceived decay had made progress, even in seven months—many a window showed black gaps deprived of glass; and slates jutted off, here and there, beyond the right line of the roof, to be gradually worked off in coming autumn storms.

I sought, and soon discovered, the three head-stones on the slope next the moor—the middle one grey, and half buried in heath—Edgar Linton's only harmonized by the turf, and moss creeping up its foot—Heathcliff's still bare.

I lingered round them, under that benign sky; watched the moths fluttering among the heath, and hare-bells; listened to the soft wind breathing through the grass; and wondered how any one could ever imagine unquiet slumbers for the sleepers in that quiet earth.

THE END

---

[2]A keepsake, literally, a tip.

# CONTEXTS

*Emily Brontë*
from a painting of a family group by Branwell Brontë.

Published by Harper & Brothers, New York.

Portrait of Emily Brontë by Branwell Brontë. An engraving of the fragment of the "Gun Group Portrait," from the Haworth Edition (1900).

Elizabeth Gaskell's drawing, "Haworth Church and Parsonage," from *The Life of Charlotte Brontë* (1857).

# Biographical

## Biographical Sketch

Emily Jane Brontë's life may seem a simple story: daughter of a clergyman; born, lived, and died (unmarried) in remote Yorkshire (apart from some months studying in Brussels); a private person who cooked and sewed, walked, and wrote every day, with interludes of reading, music, and drawing. She was fascinated by the moors no less than by the operatic conflicts in the tiny manuscripts of the four Brontë children. Her strongest bond as an adult was with her sister Anne—and her animals. She left behind almost no correspondence and no autobiography other than a few "diary papers." Although full-length biographies have been published, for the most part her life has been folded into the biography of the family, especially of the longest surviving, Charlotte. The biographical accounts of Emily by Charlotte and by Elizabeth Gaskell convey a striking but somewhat repellant personality; they express doubts about the value of Emily's writing, though they concede her genius. Since the middle of the nineteenth century, researchers have revised and amplified the early portrait of the author of *Wuthering Heights*. This seemingly narrow, uneventful life has proven far from simple to decipher.[1]

Emily Brontë was born on July 30, 1818, in Thornton, near Bradford, Yorkshire, the fifth child and fourth daughter of Maria Branwell and Patrick Brontë. Her mother had been raised in middle-class comfort in Cornwall; her father had escaped agricultural poverty in Ireland to enter Cambridge University and become a clergyman in the Church of England. Both earnestly religious par-

---

[1]What follows synthesizes many sources (see Further Reading), cited here on some of the more debated points.

ents had some writing talent; Patrick published volumes of poetry and a novel, *The Maid of Killarney* (1818). In 1820, Rev. Brontë moved his family of six young children five miles to Haworth, Yorkshire, to a better-paid appointment in the church. Maria Branwell Brontë, after a painful struggle with cancer, died in 1821, when Emily was just three.

A motherless family of young children was a serious challenge on a small income; Patrick proposed marriage to three eligible acquaintances—and was rejected.[2] In 1824, the girls were sent to the Clergy Daughters' School, Cowan Bridge, later condemned as "Lowood" in *Jane Eyre*. Emily enrolled there on November 25 (aged six years and four months), and the school record notes that she "reads very prettily, and works [sews] a little. Left June 1, 1825"; "Subsequent career—Governess." The former headmistress ("Miss Temple") recalled that Emily "was quite the pet nursling of the school" (LCB 61). The two eldest sisters, Maria and Elizabeth, fell ill and came home to die, and the two younger sisters were hastily withdrawn.

This ensured that their aunt Elizabeth Branwell, who had come to care for her dying sister, would remain in Haworth to help raise the remaining children. Sometimes caricatured—a zealous Methodist, a strict monitor of chores, a spinster who wore large, old-fashioned caps and went "clicking about in pattens" (wooden overshoes) on the cold stone floors of the parsonage (Nussey 26)—Aunt Branwell appears to have brought some broad views and interests with her from Cornwall and became a valued intellectual companion for Patrick Brontë and the children.

Patrick was a confirmed eccentric—eating simple foods alone in his study, wrapping his chin and throat in a thick white cravat, or forbidding curtains and linen or cotton clothing because of his dread of fire. According to Charlotte Brontë's school friend Ellen Nussey, "His manner and mode of speech always had the tone of high-bred courtesy" (26). Rather than a harsh father, he seems to have been unusually engaged for his day and encouraged the children's unlimited reading. He taught Emily Latin, a rare subject for

---

[2]Elizabeth Branwell, Mrs. Brontë's sister, who came to live with the family, was not one of them; it was illegal to marry one's deceased wife's sister. Without a fortune and with six little children, even a handsome, clever gentleman with a lifetime appointment was no attractive match.

girls in that period. Patrick's early ambitions as an author and his interest in politics influenced his children's writing.[3] He entertained the children with local "stories which made one shiver," as Ellen Nussey recalled, believing that Emily reproduced this material in *Wuthering Heights* (29).

Gaskell records Patrick Brontë's account of his attempt to "ascertain the hidden characters of his children," as she puts it.

> When my children were very young . . . thinking that they knew more than I had yet discovered, in order to make them speak with less timidity, . . . happening to have a mask in the house, I told them all to stand and speak boldly from under cover of the mask.
>
> I began with the youngest (Anne, afterwards Acton Bell), and asked what a child like her most wanted; she answered, "Age and experience." I asked the next (Emily, afterwards Ellis Bell), what I had best do with her brother Branwell, who was sometimes a naughty boy; she answered, "Reason with him, and when he won't listen to reason, whip him." I asked Branwell what was the best way of knowing the difference between the intellects of man and woman; he answered, "By considering the difference between them as to their bodies." I then asked Charlotte what was the best book in the world; she answered, "The Bible." And what was the next best; she answered, "The Book of Nature." (LCB 47–48)

This revealing if staged episode, which concludes with pious exchanges with the two eldest sisters, has focused much attention. The family seems to inhabit a workshop of philosophy and religious doctrine. The boy is both more privileged and more harshly disciplined than the girls. The scene supports other impressions of the author of *Wuthering Heights*: Patrick consults Emily as a peer, and Emily is closely attached to Branwell, less submissive than her sisters, and more attracted to cruelty. The Brontë juvenilia show that the children were keenly interested in geography, history, and politics as well as romances and adventure. By 1826, a set of Branwell's

---

[3]Rev. Brontë published in the newspapers, cooperated with rival religious groups (Dissenters), and cared for his parishioners and their education (the sisters taught in the parish school).

toy soldiers became the pretext for a series of tales, dramas, and poems. Emily collaborated with Charlotte on "bed plays" when they shared a bed, but in 1831 Emily and Anne separated their Kingdom of Gondal from Charlotte and Branwell's Kingdom of Angria.[4]

In 1835, Emily enrolled at Charlotte's former school, Roe Head, but she endured it little more than three months. Her health and spirits bounced back when she was allowed to return to the parsonage, where she studied French, German, and music and continued her artwork and writing (often in collaboration with Branwell). For six months in 1838–39, Emily taught at a school, Law Hill, near Halifax. Charlotte described the position as "hard labour from six in the morning to eleven at night, with only one half-hour of exercise between. This is slavery" (LCB 116), though the Brontës typically exaggerated their grievances. One student recalled that Emily once told her class of young girls that "the house-dog . . . was dearer to her than they were" (Chitham, *A Life*, 114). The Brontës evinced a dislike of children and they chafed at their teaching duties (see Duckett; Thormählen, *The Brontës and Education*).

Even so, at Law Hill Emily produced poetry of increasing strength, and it is likely that she gathered material for her novel. Law Hill was built by a "cuckoo" or usurper named Jack Sharp, who was adopted by an uncle and took over the family's business and property. Near Halifax, as well, were houses that are claimed as prototypes of Wuthering Heights (High Sunderland Hall) and Thrushcross Grange (Shibden Hall). Yet Emily became so homesick that she returned home in March 1839. A pleasant period ensued in 1840 when Rev. Brontë's curate, William Weightman, provided charming company for the sisters. (Charlotte, not Anne or Ellen Nussey, had a crush on him [Barker, *Brontës*, 326], but he died of cholera in 1842.) Charlotte nicknamed Emily "the Major," a mock protector of the other women from Weightman or other perils.[5]

Emily has long attracted fascination as a chronicler of the moors and houses in her own vicinity (were Top Withens and Ponden Hall replicated in the novel?). Ellen Nussey remembered her at

---

[4]Though other gifted families of Victorian children also produced domestic newspapers, magazines, plays, or series of tales, the Brontës sustained the projects with unusual intensity. As addictive as any fantasy series or virtual world today, Gondal and Angria were difficult to leave even when the creators were adults.

[5]Patrick Brontë taught Emily to fire the pistol he kept for defense in the parsonage.

a favorite stream: "half reclining on a slab of stone, [she] played like a young child with the tadpoles in the water, making them swim about, and then fell to moralizing on the strong and the weak, the brave and the cowardly, as she chased them with her hand" (27). She "had . . . a lithesome, graceful figure," Nussey recalled. "She was the tallest person in the house, except her father. Her hair, which was naturally as beautiful as Charlotte's, was in the same unbecoming tight curl and frizz, and there was the same want of complexion. She had very beautiful eyes—kind, kindling, liquid eyes; but she did not often look at you" (26–27).

With the plan of opening a school for girls, Emily and Charlotte enrolled at the Pensionnat Heger in Brussels in 1842 to strengthen their qualifications. In less than a year they returned to Haworth because of Aunt Branwell's death. Emily never returned to Brussels; someone had to serve in the role of housekeeper. Emily was an excellent baker and kept household accounts. It was she who invested (somewhat unwisely) in railway shares the small inheritances the sisters received from Aunt Branwell (Barker, *Brontës*, 449).

The year 1845 was pivotal in bringing *Wuthering Heights* into the world. Branwell was dismissed from his post as tutor because of his affair with the mother, Mrs. Robinson, and began a spectacular, alcohol-soaked self-destruction. Charlotte, also suffering from love for an older married person, languished more quietly. Emily, absorbed in her writing—probably the early chapters of her novel— "desir[ed] that every body could be as comfortable as myself," as her diary paper says. At this point Charlotte discovered her sister's poems; outraged, Emily finally agreed to a published collection, *Poems*, by Currer, Ellis, and Acton Bell (1846). Only two copies sold. No pupils had answered the advertisement for the Misses Brontë's Establishment for Young Ladies in 1844. The remaining way for educated women to gain decent independence was to write novels. By the summer of 1846, Emily had a one-volume novel ready to submit to publishers along with those by her two sisters; in 1847, Thomas Newby agreed to publish a two-volume work by Ellis Bell, *Wuthering Heights*.[6] Just as she had fiercely protected the invented world of Gondal, Ellis Bell refused to abandon her pseudonym. Although there is evidence that Emily had begun another novel, all

[6]Newby at last published 250 copies of the novels by Ellis and Acton Bell but never paid the £100 due to the authors (Chitham, *A Life*, 223).

hope was overwhelmed by Branwell's decline; he died on September 24. Emily, becoming ill after the funeral, refused any care, aggravating the symptoms of tuberculosis. She died scarcely three months later, on December 19, 1848.

A biographical summary only begins to portray this extraordinary writer. We gain glimpses through her contemporaries. In the diary papers, she is playful, slightly rebellious but fond of her housemates and curious about the effects of time. Her poems convey the visionary, her French "devoirs" reveal a logician and satirist.[7] Virginia Woolf in 1929 suggested that Emily Brontë was great precisely because she overcame personality (*Room of One's Own*, 75–76). Yet we still want to know as much as we can about Emily Brontë behind the mask of Ellis Bell.

# Emily Brontë in Elizabeth Gaskell's *The Life of Charlotte Brontë*

### Elizabeth Gaskell (1810–1865)

In the 1850s, Elizabeth Gaskell became fascinated by the famous novelist, Charlotte Brontë, and the two exchanged friendly visits and correspondence until Charlotte's death in 1855. They had much in common as renowned novelists living in the industrial North. Both had lost their mothers early. Gaskell was raised by an aunt in a country town, Knutsford, near Manchester. She married William Gaskell, a Unitarian minister, in 1832 and helped him with his social work in Manchester as she raised their four surviving daughters. In 1848, her novel, *Mary Barton*, on the conflict between industrial workers and masters, launched a successful if controversial career. Patrick Brontë and Charlotte's widower Arthur Nicholls asked her to write the official biography. One of the most critically esteemed of Gaskell's works, it has been considered one of the best Victorian biographies. Gaskell's zeal to represent Charlotte as a self-sacrificing woman encouraged her to exaggerate anecdotes of the Brontës' characters

[7]Regarding the French essays, Juliet Barker insists that Emily Brontë's "misanthropy—and her lack of conventional religious faith—have been vastly overstated" (*Brontës*, 388).

and behavior, including Emily's austerity and selfishness. Gaskell's version of Emily, whom she never met, has had a lasting impact. Glimpses of Emily emerge in Gaskell's depiction of the Brontës' daily life, well-disciplined by Aunt Branwell.

> People in Haworth have assured me that, according to the hour of day—nay, the very minute—could they have told what the inhabitants of the parsonage were about. At certain times the girls would be sewing in their aunt's bed-room . . . ; at certain (early) hours they had their meals; from six to eight, Miss Branwell read aloud to Mr Brontë; at punctual eight, the household assembled to evening prayers in his study; and by nine he, the aunt, and Tabby, were all in bed,—the girls free to pace up and down (like restless wild animals) in the parlour, talking over plans and projects, and thoughts of what was to be their future life. (LCB 147–48)

Gaskell produced a negative image of Emily as if to gain credit for the self-sacrificing Charlotte and submissive Anne.

> Emily and Anne were . . . like twins. The former from reserve, the latter from timidity, avoided all friendships and intimacies beyond their family. Emily was impervious . . . her own decision of what was right and fitting was a law for her conduct and appearance, with which she allowed no one to interfere. (LCB 128)

Gaskell suggests that Emily's homesickness was willful like Catherine's illness. Yet she does recognize that Emily was a handy housekeeper and clever student. "Any one passing by the kitchen-door, might have seen [Emily] studying German out of an open book, propped up before her, as she kneaded the dough; but no study, however interesting, interfered with the goodness of the bread, which was always light and excellent" (LCB 110).

The Brontë sisters made a strange impression at the Pensionnat:

> Emily had taken a fancy to the fashion, ugly and preposterous even during its reign, of gigot sleeves, and persisted in wearing them long after they were "gone out." Her petti-

coats, too, had not a curve or a wave in them, but hung down straight and long, clinging to her lank figure. The sisters spoke to no one but from necessity. (LCB 177)

M. Heger recognized their rare qualities.

He seems to have rated Emily's genius as something even higher than Charlotte's. . . . Emily had a head for logic, and a capability of argument, unusual in a man, and rare indeed in a woman, according to M. Héger. . . . "She should have been a man—a great navigator," said M. Héger. . . . "Her . . . strong imperious will would never have been daunted by opposition or difficulty; never have given way but with life." . . . She appeared egotistical and exacting compared to Charlotte, . . . and in the anxiety of the elder to make her younger sister contented, she allowed her to exercise a kind of unconscious tyranny over her. (LCB 177)

Gaskell describes the two sisters frequently walking together in the school garden in a strange anti-social bond, "Emily, though so much the taller, leaning on her sister. Charlotte would always answer when spoken to . . . ; Emily rarely spoke to any one" (LCB 189).

M. Heger decided on a program of reading aloud classics of French literature for them to interpret, evaluate, and imitate.

After explaining his plan to them, he awaited their reply. Emily spoke first; and said that she saw no good to be derived from it; and that, by adopting it, they should lose all originality of thought and expression. She would have entered into an argument on the subject, but for this, M. Héger had no time. Charlotte then spoke; she also doubted the success of the plan; but she would . . . obey him while she was his pupil. (LCB 178)

Charlotte wrote in a letter, "Emily and [M. Heger] don't draw well together at all. Emily works like a horse,[1] and she has had great difficulties," knowing little French beforehand (LCB 179). Charlotte later

[1]Horses that are not well matched in size, strength, or temperament do not "draw well together."

noted that "Monsieur and Madame Héger begin to recognise the valuable parts of her character, under her singularities" (LCB 186).

Gaskell founded the legend of a wild spirit attuned to animals, based on Charlotte's version of Emily in the heroine of *Shirley*, representing

> her way of sitting on the rug reading, with her arm round her rough bull-dog's neck; her calling to a strange dog, running past, with hanging head and lolling tongue, to give it a merciful draught of water, its maddened snap at her, her nobly stern presence of mind, going right into the kitchen, and taking up one of Tabby's red-hot Italian irons to sear the bitten place, and telling no one, till the danger[2] was well-nigh over. . . . [Keeper] loved to steal up-stairs, and stretch his square, tawny limbs, on the comfortable beds. . . . But the cleanliness of the parsonage arrangements was perfect. . . . In the gathering dusk of an autumn evening, Tabby came . . . to tell Emily that Keeper was lying on the best bed. . . . [Emily] went up-stairs, and Tabby and Charlotte stood in the gloomy passage below. . . . Down-stairs came Emily, dragging after her the unwilling Keeper, his hind legs set in a heavy attitude of resistance, held by the "scuft of his neck," but growling low and savagely all the time. The watchers would fain have spoken, but durst not, for fear of . . . causing her to avert her head for a moment from the enraged brute. She let him go, planted in a dark corner at the bottom of the stairs; . . . her bare clenched fist struck against his red fierce eyes, before he had time to make his spring . . . till his eyes were swelled up, and the half-blind, stupified [*sic*] beast was led to his accustomed lair, to have his swelled head fomented and cared for by the very Emily herself. The generous dog owed her no grudge; he loved her dearly ever after; he walked first among the mourners to her funeral; he slept moaning for nights at the door of her empty room. . . . (LCB 213–15)

After Branwell's death, Charlotte writes:

> Nov. 23rd, 1848. I told you Emily was ill. . . . I believe, if you were to see her, your impression would be that there is

---

[2]Of rabies. Charlotte published *Shirley* after Emily's death; the eponymous heroine cauterizes her own wound when she is bitten by a rabid dog.

no hope. A more hollow, wasted, pallid aspect I have not beheld. The deep tight cough continues; the breathing after the least exertion is a rapid pant; . . . She resolutely refuses to see a doctor; she will . . . scarcely allow her feelings to be alluded to. Our position is, and has been for some weeks, exquisitely painful. . . . I think Emily seems the nearest thing to my heart in the world. (LCB 291)

On December 10, 1848, Charlotte notes that she has consulted a London physician in writing, although Emily "declares 'no poisoning doctor' shall come near her." Gaskell describes Emily's last day:

One Tuesday morning, in December, she arose and dressed herself as usual, making many a pause, . . . and even endeavouring to take up her employment of sewing: the servants looked on, and knew what the catching, rattling breath, and the glazing of the eye too surely foretold. . . . On that morning Charlotte wrote thus,—probably in the very presence of her dying sister:—

"Tuesday.

"I should have written to you before, if I had had one word of hope. . . . She grows daily weaker. The physician . . . sent some medicine, which she would not take. Moments so dark as these I have never known. . . ."

The morning drew on to noon. Emily was worse: she could only whisper in gasps. Now, when it was too late, she said to Charlotte, "If you will send for a doctor, I will see him now." About two o'clock she died. (LCB 291–93)

Charlotte writes:

Yesterday we put her poor, wasted, mortal frame quietly under the church pavement. We are very calm at present. Why should we be otherwise? . . . No need now to tremble for the hard frost and the keen wind. Emily does not feel them. She died in a time of promise. We saw her taken from life in its prime. But it is God's will, and the place where she is gone is better than that she has left. (LCB 293)

# Writings by Emily Brontë

*Very little that Emily Brontë wrote remains to us. This section samples the few pieces of prose other than her novel: the text of her diary fragments and one of her French essays. In the following section, we exhibit a small anthology of Emily Brontë's poetry.*

*The "diary papers," written in collaboration with Anne Brontë, were designed to take stock of family circumstances and daily life on certain anniversary occasions, to be reread at intervals of years. These pages (in cursive and a minute "Brontë script" resembling the typeface of printed books) are characteristically scrawled, with erratic spelling and punctuation and curious sketches of the scene of writing. Topics shift abruptly from activities in the parsonage to British politics to ventures in the imaginary world of Gondal. Our transcription, although it loses the complex layout and illustrations of the original manuscripts, follows the text closely. A few missing letters or other details are inserted in brackets; a few surnames are capitalized for consistency.*

*Also in this section, we present a translation of one of Emily Brontë's writing assignments in Brussels, a French "devoir" on the character of cats. Its satire of human motives and its attraction to animal cruelty seem in keeping with the personality that might have created* Wuthering Heights. *Yet the essay, like the poems and the novel, should not be read as a direct expression of the author's views or feelings.*

## from "Diary Papers" (1834–1845)

### Diary Paper, November 24, 1834

November the 24 1834 Monday
Emily Jane Brontë
Anne Brontë

I fed Rainbow, Diamond Snowflake Jasper pheasent (alias) this morning Branwell went down to Mr. Drivers and brought news that Sir Robert Peel was going to be invited to stand for Leeds[1]   Anne

[1]The Brontës were interested in Sir Robert Peel (1788–1850), Prime Minister in 1834–35 and 1841–46, for several reasons: his schoolboy association with Byron; his service as chief secretary in Ireland enforcing Protestant rule (1812–18); and his role in Catholic Emancipation as Home Secretary under the Duke of Wellington (1828–30), a hero of the Brontës. He did not stand for election in Leeds (near Haworth) in 1834.

and I have been peeling apples for Charlotte to make us an apple
pudding and for Aunts nuts and apples   Charlotte said she made
puddings perfectly and she was of a quick but lim[i]ted intellect.[2]
Tabby said just now Come Anne pilloputate (i.e. pill a potato) Aunt
has come into the kitchen just now and said where are your feet
Anne   Anne answered On the floor Aunt   papa opened the parlour
door and gave Branwell a letter saying here Branwell read this and
show it to your Aunt and Charlotte—the Gondals are discovering
the interior of Gaaldine   Sally Mosley is washing in the back-Kitchin
    It is past Twelve o'clock   Anne and I have not tid[i]ed our-
selv[e]s, done our bed work or done our lessons and we want to go
out to play   we are going to have for Dinner Boiled Beef Turnips,
potatoes and applepudding. The Kitchin is in a very untidy state
Anne and I have not done our music exercise which consists of b
major   Taby said on my putting a pen in her face Ya pitter pottering
there instead of pilling a potate   I answered O Dear, O Dear, O dear
I will derectly with that I get up, take a knife and begin pilling (finished pilling the potatoes[)]   papa going to walk   Mr. Sunderland
expected.
    Anne and I say I wonder what we shall be like and what we shall
be and where we shall be if all goes on well in the year 1874—in
which year I shall be in my 57th year Anne will be going in her 55th
year   Branwell will be going in his 58th year   And Charlotte in her
59th year   hoping we shall all be well at that time we close our paper[3]

### Diary Paper, June 26, 1837

Monday evening June 26 1837

A bit past 4 o'clock Charlotte working in Aunts room   Branwell
reading *Eugene Aram*[4] to her   Anne and I writing in the drawing
room—Anne a poem beginning Fair was the evening and brightly
the Sun—I Augustus-Almeda's life 1st Vol—4th page from the

[2]A jest about conventional views of female capacities.

[3]Charlotte was born in 1816, Branwell in 1817, Emily in 1818, and Anne in 1820—
i.e. 1874 would be their 58th, 57th, 56th, and 54th years. Debate renumbers in ms.

[4]Self-taught linguist and Yorkshire tutor Eugene Aram (1704–59), despite his
protests of innocence, was convicted and hanged for the murder of his friend; his
story inspired a ballad by Thomas Hood (1829) and a three-decker novel by Bulwer
Lytton (1832).

last—fine rather coolish thin grey cloudy but sunny day    Aunt working in the little Room    papa—gone out.    Tabby in the Kitchin—the Emperors and Empresses of Gondal and Gaaldine preparing to depart from Gaaldine to Gondal to prepare for the coranation which will be on the 12th of July    Queen Vittiora ascended the throne this month    Northangerland in Moncey's Isle—Zamorna at Eversham. all tight and right in which condition it is hoped we shall all be on this day 4 years at which time Charlotte will be 25 and 2 months—Branwell just 24 it being his birthday— myself 22 and 10 months and a peice Anne 21 and nearly a half    I wonder where we shall be and how we shall be and what kind of a day it will be then let us hope for the best

Emily Jane Brontë—Anne Brontë[5]

I guess that this day 4 years we shall all be in this drawing room comfortable    I hope it may be so    Anne guesses we shall all be gone somewhere together comfortable    We hope it may be either

Aunt. Come Emily  its past 4 o'clock.

Emily. Yes Aunt

Anne. well do you intend to write in the evening

Emily. well what think you

(we agreed to go out 1st to make sure if we got into a humo[u]r   we may Stay [out?])

**Diary Paper, July 30, 1841**

A Paper to be opened
when Anne is
25 years old
or my next birthday after—
if
—all be well—
Emily Jane Brontë.  July the 30[th] 1841

It is Friday evening—near 9 o'clock—wild rainy weather    I am seated in the dining room alone—having just concluded tidying our desk-boxes—writing this document—Papa is in the parlour. Aunt

[5]Almost half of the page of this diary displays an ink sketch of Anne and Emily writing at a table; Emily sits with her back to the viewer with a labeled box for storing their papers at her right hand. The rest of the words are inserted in the margins, bottom and right vertical, of the sketch.

up stairs in her room—she has been reading Blackwood's Magazine to papa—Victoria and Adelaide are ensconced in the peat-house—Keeper is in the Kitchen—Nero in his cage[6]—We are all stout and hearty as I hope is the case with Charlotte, Branwell, and Anne, of whom the first is at Mr White Esqre Upperwood House, Rawden The second is at Luddenden foot and the third is I beleive at Scarborough—enditing perhaps a paper corresponding to this—

A scheme is at present in agitation for setting us up in a school of our own as yet nothing is determined but I hope and trust it may go on and prosper and answer our highest expectations— this day 4— years I wonder whether we shall still be dragging on in our present condition or established to our hearts' content Time will show—

I guess that at the time appointed for the opening of this paper—we (ie) Charlotte, Anne and I—shall be all merrily seated in our own sitting-room in some pleasant and flourishing seminary having just gathered in for the midsummer holydays our debts will be paid off and we shall have cash in hand to a considerable amount. papa Aunt and Branwell will either have been or be coming to visit us—it will be a fine warm summery evening very different from this bleak look-out Anne and I will perchance slip out into the garden [a] few minutes to peruse our papers. I hope either this [o]r some thing better will be the case—

The Gondalians are at present in a threatening state but there is no open rupture as yet—all the princes and princesses of the [Royal?] royalty are at the Palace of Instruction—I have a good many books on hand—but I am sorry to say that as usual I make small progress with any—however I have just made a new regularity paper! and I mean—verb sap[7]—to do great things—and now I close sending from far an ex[hortation] of courage courage to exiled and harassed Anne wishing she was here.

[6]Victoria and Adelaide are pet geese named after the Queen of England and her predecessor, Queen Consort of William IV; Keeper a dog; and Nero a hawk (often mistranscribed as "Hero"), named for the Roman emperor.

[7]Common abbreviation for Latin phrase, *verbum sat sapienti est*: a word to the wise is enough.

## Diary Paper, Thursday, July 30, 1845

Haworth—Thursday—July 30th 1845

My birthday—showery—breezy—cool—I am twenty seven years old today—this morning Anne and I opened the papers we wrote 4 years since on my twenty third birthday—this paper we intend, if all be well, to open on my 30th three years hence in 1848—since the 1841 paper, the following events have taken place

Our school-scheme has been abandoned and instead Charlotte and I went to Brussels on the 8th of Febr[u]ary 1842

Branwell left his place at Luddenden Foot

C and I returned from Brussels November 8th 1842 in consequence of Aunt's death—

Branwell went to Thorp Green as a tutor where Anne still continued—January 1843

Charlotte returned to Brussels the same month and after staying a year came back again on new years day 1844

Anne left her situation at Thorp Green of her own accord—June 1845

Branwell left—July 1845

Anne and I went our first long Journey by ourselves together—leaving Home on the 30th of June—Monday—sleeping at York—returning to Keighley Tuesday evening sleeping there and walking home on Wedensday morning—though the weather was broken, we enjoyed ourselves very much except during a few hours at Bradford and during our excursion we were Ronald Macelgin, Henry Angora, Juliet Augusteena, Rosabella Esmalden, Ella and Julian Egremont Catherine Navarre and Cordelia Fitzaphnold[8] escaping from the palaces of Instruction to join the Royalists who are hard driven at present by the victorious Republicans—The Gondals still flo[u]rish bright as ever     I am at present writing a work on the First Wars—Anne has been writing some articles on this and a book by Henry Sophona—We intend sticking firm by the rascals as long as they delight us which I am glad to say they do at present—I should have mentioned that last summer the school scheme was revived in full vigo[u]r—we had prospectuses

---

[8]Though Emily Brontë's spelling is erratic and her handwriting difficult to decipher, these are commonly accepted spellings of characters' names in the Gondal cycle (Ratchford, *Gondal's Queen*, 192).

printed despatched letters to all aquaintances imparting our plans and did our little all—but it was found no go—now I dont desire a school at all and none of us have any great longing for it—we have cash enough for our present wants with a prospect of accumolation—we are all in decent health—only that papa has a complaint in his eyes and with the exception of B who I hope will be better and do better, hereafter. I am quite contented for myself—not as idle as formerly, altogether as hearty and having learnt to make the most of the present and hope for the future with less fidget[i]ness that I cannot do all I wish—seldom or ever troubled with nothing to do, and merely desiring that every body could be as comfortable as myself and as undesponding and then we should have a very tolerable world of it—

By mistake I find we have opened the paper on the 31st instead of the 30th  Yesterday was much such a day as this but the morning was devine—

Tabby who was gone in our last paper is come back and has lived with us—two years and a half and is in good health—Martha who also departed is here too—We have got Flossey, got and lost Tiger—lost the Hawk Nero which with the geese was given away and is doubtless dead for when I came back from Brussels I enquired on all hands and could hear nothing of him—Tiger died early last year—Keeper and Flossey are well also the canary acquired 4 years since—

We are now all at home and likely to be there some time—Branwell went to Liverpool on Tuesday to stay a week—Tabby has just been teasing me to turn as formerly to "pilloputate"—Anne and I should have picked the black currants if it had been fine and sunshiny—I must hurry off now to my turning[9] and ironing    I have plenty of work on hands and writing and am altogether full of business    with best wishes for the whole House till 1848—July 30th and as much longer as may be I conclude

E J Brontë[10]

---

[9]*Turning* refurbishes clothing by resewing it with the inner surface of the fabric outward. *Work* in the following sentence refers to sewing.

[10]The bottom of this page of the diary is filled with Emily Brontë's sketch of herself seated, facing the interior of a bedroom, a cat asleep on the bed; in the foreground a dog, probably Keeper, fills almost as much space as the woman with her portable writing desk on her lap.

## "The Cat" (May 15, 1842)[1]                    Emily J. Brontë

I can say sincerely that I like cats; also I can give very good reasons why those who despise them are wrong.

A cat is an animal who has more human feelings than almost any other being. We cannot sustain a comparison with the dog, it is infinitely too good; but the cat, although it differs in some physical points, is extremely like us in disposition.

There may be people, in truth, who would say that this resemblance only comes close to the most wicked men; that it is limited to their excessive hypocrisy, cruelty, and ingratitude; detestable vices in our race and equally odious in that of cats.

Without disputing the limits that those individuals set on our affinity, I answer that if hypocrisy, cruelty, and ingratitude are exclusively the domain of the wicked, that class comprises everyone. Our education develops one of these qualities in great perfection, the others flourish without any care, and far from condemning them, we regard all three with great complacency. A cat, out of self-interest, sometimes hides its misanthropy under the guise of amiable gentleness; instead of tearing what it desires from its master's hand, it approaches with a caressing air, rubs its pretty little head against him, and advances a paw whose touch is soft as down. When it has gained its end, it resumes its character of Timon.[2] Such artfulness in it is called hypocrisy; in ourselves, we give it another name, it's politeness, and he who would not use it to disguise his real feelings would soon be hunted out of society.

"But," says some delicate lady, who has murdered a half-dozen lapdogs through pure affection, "the cat is such a cruel beast, he is not content to kill his prey, he torments it before its death; you cannot make that accusation against us." Just about so, Madame. Your husband, for example, likes hunting very much, but foxes being rare on his land, he would not have the means to pursue this amusement often, if he did not manage his supplies thus: once he has run an animal to its last breath, he snatches it from the jaws of the hounds and saves it to suffer the same torture two or three more times, ending finally in death. You yourself avoid a bloody spectacle because it

---

[1]Devoir composed at Pensionnat Heger, Brussels. See Lonoff (57–59). Translation and punctuation adapted.

[2]Lord Timon is a misanthrope in Shakespeare's play *The Life of Timon of Athens*.

wounds your weak nerves. But I have seen you embrace your child ecstatically, when he came to show you a beautiful butterfly crushed between his cruel little fingers; and at that moment, I really wanted to have a cat, with the tail of a half-devoured rat hanging from its mouth, to present as the image, the true copy, of your angel. You could not refuse to kiss him, and if he scratched us both in revenge, so much the better. Little boys are rather liable to acknowledge their friends' caresses in that way, and the resemblance would be more perfect. The ingratitude of cats is another name for discernment. They know how to value our favors at their true price, because they guess the motives that prompt us to grant them, and if those motives might sometimes be good, undoubtedly they always remember that they owe all their miseries and all their evil qualities to the great ancestor of humankind. For assuredly, the cat was not wicked in Paradise.

## Charlotte Brontë's Selection of Poems by Ellis Bell (1850)

Poems *by Currer, Ellis, and Acton Bell appeared at the authors' expense in 1846 and dropped like a stone. But the fame of* Jane Eyre *encouraged Charlotte's publisher, Smith, Elder, to republish the poetry collection in 1848. In the 1850 edition of* Wuthering Heights, *Charlotte reproduced a selection of Emily's poems, with heavy revisions including stanzas or poems of her own. Charlotte shapes a biographical sketch of a (belated) Romantic poet unable to live outside the unyielding landscape, overlooking Emily's religious searching and her use of dramatic personae: most of the poems are voiced by characters in the Gondal cycle of stories. Charlotte and later readers have recognized the rare qualities of the poems, direct, intense, unadorned. Their very existence—along with the diary papers and French essays—was largely against Emily Brontë's "scruples and wishes." Serving as a kind of posthumous agent, Charlotte sought to polish the image as well as protect her relatives' privacy, probably suppressing many other pages. In a sense, Charlotte stifled Emily's poetry; little of it can be dated after 1845, when Charlotte began her campaign for publication, and Emily must have become occupied with* Wuthering Heights *(Chitham, Birth, 173–81).*

*Edward Charles Morgan declared in 1932, "whoever wrote the poems wrote* Wuthering Heights, *the same unreality of this world, the same greater reality of another, being in them both" (Morgan, quoted in Hatfield 11). Some of Emily Brontë's poems were never published before the twentieth century, some attributed to other Brontës, and most of them more or less marked by editorial errors. C. W.* Hatfield *reconstructed the twenty-one poems in the 1846 collection, the seventeen additional poems published in 1850, and those later brought to light in his* The Complete Poems of Emily Jane Brontë *in 1941, more recently answered by Derek Roper and Edward Chitham in* The Poems of Emily Brontë (1995). *We approximate Emily Brontë's versions of the poems, with some standardization of spelling, spacing, and punctuation. Our selection, differing from Charlotte's, appears in chronological order of composition (as these scholars have recently determined it).*[1]

### from Prefatory Note, "Selections from Poems by Ellis Bell" (1850)

It would not have been difficult to compile a volume out of the papers left by my sisters, had I . . . dismissed . . . the scruples and the wishes of those whose written thoughts these papers held. . . .

It has been already said that my sisters wrote much in childhood and girlhood. Usually, it seems a sort of injustice to expose in print the crude thoughts of the unripe mind, the rude efforts of the unpractised hand; yet I venture to give three little poems of my sister Emily's, written in her sixteenth year, because they illustrate a point in her character.[2]

At that period she was sent to school.[3] Her previous life, with the exception of a single half-year,[4] had been passed in the absolute retirement of a village parsonage, amongst the hills bordering Yorkshire and Lancashire. The scenery of these hills is not grand—it is not romantic; it is scarcely striking. Long low moors, dark with heath, shut in little valleys, where a stream waters, here and there, a fringe of stunted copse. Mills and scattered cottages chase romance from these

[1]On Charlotte's prefatory note, see Dunn (318–20) and Marsden and Jack (445–46).

[2]This edition presents only one of the poems that Charlotte refers to as a teenage production, "A little while, a little while"; Emily was 20 when she wrote it. See Dunn (318–20). The 18 "Selections" in 1850 included one of unknown authorship.

[3]Emily joined Charlotte at Miss Wooler's Roe Head school in 1835. The first poem presented here instead responds in part to the lack of private time Emily endured as a teacher at Law Hill in 1837.

[4]Like Charlotte and their older sisters Maria and Elizabeth, Emily had attended the Clergy Daughters' School at Cowan Bridge.

valleys; it is only higher up, deep in amongst the ridges of the moors, that Imagination can find rest for the sole of her foot: and even if she finds it there, she must be a solitude-loving raven—no gentle dove. If she demand beauty to inspire her, she must bring it inborn. . . . The eye of the gazer must *itself* brim with a "purple light,"[5] intense enough to perpetuate the brief flower-flush of August on the heather. . . . Unless that light and freshness are innate and self-sustained, the drear prospect of a Yorkshire moor will be found as barren of poetic as of agricultural interest: where the love of wild nature is strong, the locality will perhaps be clung to with the more passionate constancy, because from the hill-lover's self comes half its charm.

My sister Emily loved the moors. Flowers brighter than the rose bloomed in the blackest of the heath for her; out of a sullen hollow in a livid hill-side her mind could make an Eden. . . .

Liberty was the breath of Emily's nostrils; without it, she perished. The change from her own home to a school, and from her own very noiseless, very secluded, but unrestricted and inartificial mode of life, to one of disciplined routine (though under the kindliest auspices), was what she failed in enduring. Her nature proved here too strong for her fortitude. Every morning when she woke, the vision of home and the moors rushed on her, and darkened and saddened the day. . . . Nobody knew what ailed her but me—I knew only too well. In this struggle her health was quickly broken. . . . I felt in my heart she would die if she did not go home. . . . After the age of twenty, having meantime studied alone with diligence and perseverance, she went with me to an establishment on the Continent: the same suffering and conflict ensued, heightened by the strong recoil of her . . . English spirit from the . . . foreign and Romish system.[6] Once more she seemed sinking, but this time she rallied through the mere force of resolution: with inward remorse and shame she looked back on her former failure, and resolved to conquer in this second ordeal. She did conquer: but the victory cost her dear. She was never happy till she carried her hard-won knowledge back to the remote English village, the old parsonage-house, and desolate Yorkshire hills. A very few years more, and she looked her last on those hills, and breathed her last in that house, and under the aisle of that obscure village church found her last lowly

[5]Samuel Taylor Coleridge, "Song of the Pixies," l. 12.
[6]That is, revulsion against the Catholicism in Brussels.

resting-place. Merciful was the decree that spared her when she was a stranger in a strange land.[7] . . .

The following pieces were composed at twilight, in the school-room, when the leisure of the evening play-hour brought back in full tide the thoughts of home.

### December 4th 1838[8]

A little while, a little while
The noisy crowd are barred away;
And I can sing and I can smile—
A little while I've holyday!

Where wilt thou go, my harassed heart?       5
Full many a land invites thee now;
And places near, and far apart
Have rest for thee, my weary brow—

There is a spot mid barren hills
Where winter howls and driving rain       10
But if the dreary tempest chills
There is a light that warms again

The house is old, the trees are bare
And moonless bends the misty dome
But what on earth is half so dear—       15
So longed for as the hearth of home?

The mute bird sitting on the stone,
The dank moss dripping from the wall,
The garden-walk with weeds o'er-grown
I love them—how I love them all!       20

Shall I go there? or shall I seek
Another clime, another sky—
Where tongues familiar music speak
In accents dear to memory?

[7]Moses speaks of himself as a stranger in a strange land during the exile in Egypt (Exodus 2.22); Patrick Brontë writes of suffering without companions through his wife's long last illness, "at Haworth, a stranger in a strange land" (November 27, 1821, in Barker, *Letters*, 1). The Brontës may be seen as Irish exiles in Yorkshire.
[8]Entitled "Stanzas" in the 1850 edition; poem number 40 in Roper (69–70).

Yes, as I mused, the naked room,                                    25
The flickering firelight died away
And from the midst of cheerless gloom
I passed to bright, unclouded day—

A little and a lone green lane
That opened on a common wide                                        30
A distant, dreamy, dim blue chain
Of mountains circling every side—

A heaven so clear, an earth so calm,
So sweet, so soft, so hushed in air
And, deepening still the dreamlike charm,                           35
Wild moor-sheep feeding every where—

That was the scene—I knew it well
I knew the pathways far and near
That winding o'er each billowy swell
Marked out the tracks of wandering deer                            40

Could I have lingered but an hour
It well had paid a week of toil
But truth has banished fancy's power;
I hear my dungeon bars recoil—

Even as I stood with raptured eye                                   45
Absorbed in bliss so deep and dear
My hour of rest had fleeted by
And given me back to weary care—

### September 11th 1840

Here again is the same mind in converse with a like abstraction.[9]
"The Night-Wind," breathing through an open window, has visited
an ear which discerned language in its whispers.[10]

---

[9]Charlotte Brontë links this poem with "Shall Earth no more inspire thee" and "Aye
there it is! It wakes to night" (see pp. 326–28), which preceded and followed it in the
1850 edition of *Wuthering Heights* (Hatfield 146–47, 163–66).

[10]Note by Charlotte Brontë.

## The Night-Wind[11]

In summer's mellow midnight
  A cloudless moon shone through
Our open parlour window
And rosetrees wet with dew—

I sat in silent musing—     5
  The soft wind waved my hair
It told me Heaven was glorious
And sleeping Earth was fair—

I needed not its breathing
To bring such thoughts to me     10
But still it whispered lowly
"How dark the woods will be!—

"The thick leaves in my murmur
Are rustling like a dream,
And all their myriad voices     15
Instinct with spirit seem"

I said, "Go, gentle singer,
Thy wooing voice is kind,
But do not think its music
Has power to reach my mind—     20

"Play with the scented flower,
The young tree's supple bough—
And leave my human feelings
In their own course to flow"

The Wanderer would not leave me     25
Its kiss grew warmer still—
"O come," it sighed so sweetly
"I'll win thee 'gainst thy will—

[11]The title provided in Charlotte's 1850 edition. Number 79 in Roper (107–8).

"Have we not been from childhood friends?
Have I not loved thee long?                               30
As long as thou hast loved the night
Whose silence wakes my song?

"And when thy heart is resting
Beneath the church-yard stone
I shall have time for mourning                            35
And thou for being alone"—

### May 16th 1841

The following little piece has no title but in it the Genius of a solitary region seems to address his wandering and wayward votary,
and to recall within his influence the proud mind which rebelled at
times against what it most loved.[12]

Shall Earth no more inspire thee,
Thou lonely dreamer now?
Since passion may not fire thee
Shall Nature cease to bow?

Thy mind is ever moving                                    5
In regions dark to thee;
Recall its useless roving—
Come back and dwell with me—

I know my mountain breezes
Enchant and soothe thee still—                            10
I know my sunshine pleases
Despite thy wayward will—

When day with evening blending
Sinks from the summer sky,
I've seen thy spirit bending                               15
In fond idolatry—

I've watched thee every hour—
I know my mighty sway—

[12]Note by Charlotte Brontë. Number 84 in Roper (121–22).

I know my magic power
To drive thy griefs away—                                        20

Few hearts to mortals given
On earth so wildly pine
Yet none would ask a Heaven
More like the Earth than thine—

Then let my winds caress thee—                                   25
Thy comrade let me be—
Since nought beside can bless thee—
Return and dwell with me—

## July 6th 1841

In these stanzas a louder gale has roused the sleeper on her pillow:
the wakened soul struggles to blend with the storm by which it is
swayed.[13]

Aye there it is! It wakes to night
Sweet thoughts that will not die
And feeling's fires flash all as bright
As in the years gone by!—

And I can tell by thine altered cheek                            5
And by thy kindled gaze
And by the words thou scarce dost speak,
How wildly fancy plays—

Yes I could swear that glorious wind
Has swept the world aside                                        10
Has dashed its memory from thy mind
Like foam-bells from the tide—

And thou art now a spirit pouring
Thy presence into all—

---

[13]Note by Charlotte Brontë, comparing this poem to "The Night-Wind." Number
85 in Roper (122).

The essence of the Tempest's roaring          15
And of the Tempest's fall—

A universal influence
From Thine own influence free—
A principle of life intense
Lost to mortality—          20

Thus truely when that breast is cold
Thy prisoned soul shall rise,
The Dungeon mingle with the mould—
        The captive with the skies—[14]

Jan 2d 1846

The following are the last lines my sister Emily ever wrote.[15]

No coward soul is mine
No trembler in the world's storm-troubled sphere
I see Heaven's glories shine
And Faith shines equal arming me from Fear

O God within my breast          5
Almighty ever-present Deity
Life, that in me hast rest
As I,—Undying Life, have power in Thee

Vain are the thousand creeds
That move men's hearts, unutterably vain,          10
Worthless as withered weeds
Or idlest froth amid the boundless main

---

[14]Charlotte made numerous changes and added these final lines:
  "Nature's deep being, thine shall hold, / Her spirit all thy spirit fold, / Her
  breath absorb thy sighs. / Mortal! Though soon life's tale is told; / Who once
  lives, never dies!" See Hatfield (165–66).

[15]Note by Charlotte Brontë. Emily did write a narrative poem of 264 lines (unfin-
ished), dated September 14, 1846 (Hatfield 244–52), and a short poem, "Why ask to
know what date what clime," dated May 13, 1848 (Roper's numbers 126 and 127
[184–93]). Roper identifies over 70 undated poems and fragments.

To waken doubt in one
Holding so fast by thy infinity
So surely anchored on                                    15
The steadfast rock of Immortality

With wide-embracing love
Thy Spirit animates eternal years
Pervades and broods above,
Changes, sustains, dissolves, creates, and rears        20

Though Earth and moon were gone
And suns and universes ceased to be
And Thou wert left alone
Every Existence would exist in thee

There is not room for Death                              25
Nor atom that his might could render void
Since thou art Being and Breath
And what thou art may never be destroyed

# Charlotte Brontë on Ellis Bell

*Charlotte Brontë, writing on September 13, 1850, to W. S. Williams,
"reader" or editor at Smith, Elder, recalled of the first publisher of*
Wuthering Heights *and* Agnes Grey:

> Mr. Newby undertook first to print 350 copies of "Wuthering
> Heights", but he afterwards declared he had only printed 250. I
> doubt whether he could be induced to return the £50[1] without a
> good deal of trouble. . . . The conclusion I drew from the whole of
> Mr. Newby's conduct to my Sisters—was that he is a man with
> whom it is desirable to have little to do. (Barker, *Letters*, 296)

*The reissue of her sisters' novels by Smith, Elder provided an opportu-
nity for Charlotte to shape their reputations. The surviving sibling sub-
merges the death of Branwell in this memorial, as an unspeakable*

[1]In an arrangement common at the time, the Brontës had agreed to co-publish their
novels, investing their own money to be recouped from sales—but Thomas Newby
refused to provide any repayment.

*catastrophe. At the same time, she attributes any unappealing aspects of either Emily's or Anne's works either to Branwell's ruin or to the Yorkshire environment, the torments of genius, and masochistic religious zeal. Charlotte's elegiac rhetoric and allusions enhance the impression that Emily had tapped into a reservoir of uncanny powers.*

## Charlotte Brontë, from "Biographical Notice of Ellis and Acton Bell" (1850)

It has been thought that all the works published under the names of Currer, Ellis, and Acton Bell, were, in reality, the production of one person. This mistake I endeavoured to rectify by a few words of disclaimer prefixed to the third edition of *Jane Eyre*. These, too, it appears, failed to gain general credence, and now, on the occasion of a reprint of *Wuthering Heights* and *Agnes Grey* I am advised distinctly to state how the case really stands.

Indeed, I feel myself that it is time the obscurity attending those two names—Ellis and Acton—was done away. The little mystery, which formerly yielded some harmless pleasure, has lost its interest; circumstances are changed. It becomes, then, my duty to explain briefly the origin and authorship of the books written by Currer, Ellis, and Acton Bell.

About five years ago, my two sisters and myself, after a somewhat prolonged period of separation, found ourselves reunited, and at home. Resident in a remote district where education had made little progress, and where, consequently, there was no inducement to seek social intercourse beyond our own domestic circle, we were wholly dependent on ourselves and each other, on books and study, for the enjoyments and occupations of life. The highest stimulus, as well as the liveliest pleasure we had known from childhood upwards, lay in attempts at literary composition; formerly we used to show each other what we wrote, but of late years this habit of communication and consultation had been discontinued; hence it ensued, that we were mutually ignorant of the progress we might respectively have made.

One day, in the autumn of 1845, I accidentally lighted on a MS. volume of verse in my sister Emily's handwriting. Of course, I was not surprised, knowing that she could and did write verse: I looked it over, and something more than surprise seized me,—a deep conviction that these were not common effusions, nor at all like the poetry women generally write. I thought them condensed and terse, vigorous and genuine. To my ear, they had also a peculiar music—wild, melancholy, and elevating.

My sister Emily was not a person of demonstrative character, nor one, on the recesses of whose mind and feelings, even those nearest and dearest to her could, with impunity, intrude unlicensed; it took hours to reconcile her to the discovery I had made, and days to persuade her that such poems merited publication. I knew, however, that a mind like hers could not be without some latent spark of honourable ambition. . . .

Meantime, my younger sister quietly produced some of her own compositions, intimating that, since Emily's had given me pleasure, I might like to look at hers. I could not but be a partial judge, yet I thought that these verses, too, had a sweet sincere pathos of their own.

We had very early cherished the dream of one day becoming authors. This dream, never relinquished even when distance divided and absorbing tasks occupied us, now suddenly acquired strength and consistency: it took the character of a resolve. We agreed to arrange a small selection of our poems and, if possible, get them printed. Averse to personal publicity, we veiled our own names under those of Currer, Ellis, and Acton Bell; the ambiguous choice being dictated by a sort of conscientious scruple at assuming Christian names positively masculine, while we did not like to declare ourselves women, because—without at that time suspecting that our mode of writing and thinking was not what is called "feminine"—we had a vague impression that authoresses are liable to be looked on with prejudice; we had noticed how critics sometimes use for their chastisement the weapon of personality, and for their reward, a flattery, which is not true praise.

The bringing out of our little book was hard work. As was to be expected, neither we nor our poems were at all wanted; but for this we had been prepared at the outset; though inexperienced ourselves, we had read the experience of others. The great puzzle lay in the difficulty of getting answers of any kind from the publishers to whom we applied. Being greatly harassed by this obstacle, I ventured to apply to the Messrs Chambers, of Edinburgh, for a word of advice; *they* may have forgotten the circumstance, but *I* have not, for from them I received a brief and business-like, but civil and sensible reply, on which we acted, and at last made a way.

The book was printed: it is scarcely known, and all of it that merits to be known are the poems of Ellis Bell. . . . Ill-success failed to crush us: the mere effort to succeed had given a wonderful zest to existence; it must be pursued. We each set to work on a prose tale: Ellis Bell produced *Wuthering Heights*, Acton Bell *Agnes Grey*, and Currer Bell also wrote a narrative in one volume.[2] These MSS. were perseveringly obtruded upon various publishers for the space of a year and a half; usually, their fate was an ignominious and abrupt dismissal.

At last *Wuthering Heights* and *Agnes Grey* were accepted on terms somewhat impoverishing to the two authors; Currer Bell's book found acceptance nowhere, nor any acknowledgment of merit. . . . As a forlorn hope, he tried one publishing house more—Messrs. Smith and Elder. Ere long . . . there came a letter, which he opened in the dreary expectation of finding two hard hopeless lines . . . and, instead, he took out of the envelope a letter of two pages. He read it trembling. It declined, indeed, to publish that tale, for business reasons, but it discussed its merits and demerits so courteously, so considerately, that this very refusal cheered the author. . . . It was added, that a work in three volumes would meet with careful attention.

I was then just completing *Jane Eyre*, at which I had been working while the one-volume tale was plodding its weary round in London: in three weeks I sent it off; friendly and skilful hands took it in. This was in the commencement of September 1847; it came out before the close of October following, while *Wuthering Heights* and *Agnes Grey*, my sisters' works, which had already been in the press for months, still lingered under a different management.

They appeared at last. Critics failed to do them justice. The immature but very real powers revealed in *Wuthering Heights* were scarcely recognised; its import and nature were misunderstood; the identity of its author was misrepresented; it was said that this was an earlier and ruder attempt of the same pen which had produced *Jane Eyre*. Unjust and grievous error! We laughed at it at first, but I deeply lament it now. Hence, I fear, arose a prejudice against the book. That writer who could attempt to palm off an inferior and immature production under cover of one successful effort, must indeed be unduly eager after the secondary and sordid result of authorship. . . .

[2]*The Professor*, first published, posthumously, in 1857. Charlotte's chronology must be in error, as she was already seeking a publisher for the Bells' three separate tales a month before the volume of poems was published in May 1846 (Marsden and Jack xiii–xiv).

It is my duty, as well as my pleasure, to acknowledge one exception to the general rule of criticism. One writer,[3] endowed with the keen vision and fine sympathies of genius, has discerned the real nature of *Wuthering Heights*, and has, with equal accuracy, noted its beauties and touched on its faults. Too often do reviewers remind us of the mob of Astrologers, Chaldeans, and Soothsayers gathered before the "writing on the wall," and unable to read the characters or make known the interpretation.[4] We have a right to rejoice when a true seer comes at last, some man . . . to whom ha[s] been given light . . . who can accurately read the "Mene, Mene, Tekel, Upharsin" of an original mind (however unripe, however inefficiently cultured and partially expanded that mind may be). . . .

Yet even the writer to whom I allude shares the mistake about the authorship. . . .

[A paragraph follows on Acton Bell and *The Tenant of Wildfell Hall*, suggesting that Anne had written this novel about alcoholism and vice out of religious duty to warn against "talents misused and faculties abused," the conduct she had witnessed "near at hand" in Branwell.]

Neither Ellis nor Acton allowed herself for one moment to sink under want of encouragement; energy nerved the one, and endurance upheld the other. They were both prepared to try again; I would fain think that hope and the sense of power was yet strong within them. But a great change approached. . . . In the very heat and burden of the day,[5] the labourers failed over their work.

My sister Emily first declined.[6] The details of her illness are deep-branded in my memory, but to dwell on them . . . is not in my power. Never in all her life had she lingered over any task that lay before her, and she did not linger now. . . . She made haste to leave us. Yet,

---

[3]See the *Palladium* for September 1850. [CB's note, referring to writer Sydney Dobell.]

[4]Daniel 5.7. King Belshazzar, at a blasphemous feast, sees a ghostly hand write on the wall the words "Mene, Mene, Tekel, Upharsin" (sometimes translated as [your days are] "Numbered, numbered, weighed, and divided"). The king's advisers fail, but Daniel warns Belshazzar that he will be brought down.

[5]Matthew 20.12. In the parable of the vineyard, laborers who came earliest complain of latecomers being paid equally "to those who have borne the burden and heat of the day." The allegorical theme, that it is never too late for salvation, appeals to Charlotte, who was consoled in the belief that Branwell accepted faith in his last days (see letter to W. S. Williams, October 6, 1848, Barker, *Letters*, 210).

[6]Branwell was apparently drinking himself to death when Anne produced *Tenant* (it went into a second edition in July 1848); he died September 24, 1848, and Emily died December 19, 1848, so she was not "first" to decline, though before Anne.

while physically she perished, mentally she grew stronger. . . . I have seen nothing like it; but, indeed, I have never seen her parallel in anything. Stronger than a man, simpler than a child, her nature stood alone. . . . Full of ruth for others, on herself she had no pity; the spirit was inexorable to the flesh; from the trembling hand, the unnerved limbs, the faded eyes, the same service was exacted as they had rendered in health. To stand by and witness this, and not dare to remonstrate, was a pain no words can render.

Two cruel months of hope and fear passed painfully by, and the day came at last when the terrors and pains of death were to be undergone by this treasure, which had grown dearer and dearer. . . . Towards the decline of that day, we had nothing of Emily but her mortal remains. . . . She died December 19, 1848.

We thought this enough; but we were utterly and presumptuously wrong. She was not buried ere Anne fell ill. . . . Accordingly, she followed in the same path with slower step, and with a patience that equalled the other's fortitude. I have said that she was religious, and . . . those Christian doctrines. . . . brought her through. She died May 28, 1849.

What more shall I say about them? . . . In externals, they were two unobtrusive women; a perfectly secluded life gave them retiring manners and habits. In Emily's nature the extremes of vigour and simplicity seemed to meet. Under an unsophisticated culture, inartificial tastes, and an unpretending outside, lay a secret power and fire that might have informed the brain and kindled the veins of a hero; but . . . her powers were unadapted to the practical business of life; she would fail to . . . consult her most legitimate advantage. An interpreter ought always to have stood between her and the world. Her will was not very flexible, and it generally opposed her interest. Her temper was magnanimous, but warm and sudden; her spirit altogether unbending.

Anne's character was milder and more subdued; she wanted the power, the fire, the originality of her sister, but was well-endowed with quiet virtues of her own. . . . Neither Emily nor Anne was learned; they had no thought of filling their pitchers at the wellspring of other minds; they always wrote from the impulse of nature, the dictates of intuition, and from such stores of observation as their limited experience had enabled them to amass. I may sum up all by saying, that for strangers they were nothing, for superficial observers less than nothing; but for those who had known them all their lives in the intimacy of close relationship, they were genuinely good and truly great.

This notice has been written, because I felt it a sacred duty to wipe the dust off their gravestones, and leave their dear names free from soil.

Currer Bell.

*September 19, 1850.*


### Charlotte Brontë, from "Editor's Preface" to the New Edition of *Wuthering Heights* (1850)

I HAVE just read over "Wuthering Heights," and, for the first time, have obtained a clear glimpse of what are termed (and, perhaps, really are) its faults; have gained a definite notion of how it appears . . . to strangers who knew nothing of the author; who are unacquainted with the locality where the scenes of the story are laid. . . .

To all such "Wuthering Heights" must appear a rude and strange production. The wild moors of the north of England can for them have no interest; the language, the manners, the very dwellings and household customs of the scattered inhabitants of those districts, must be to such readers in a great measure unintelligible, and—where intelligible—repulsive. Men and women who, perhaps, naturally very calm, and with feelings moderate in degree, and little marked in kind, have been trained from their cradle to observe the utmost evenness of manner and guardedness of language, will hardly know what to make of the rough, strong utterance, the harshly manifested passions, the unbridled aversions, and headlong partialities of unlettered moorland hinds and rugged moorland squires, who have grown up untaught and unchecked, except by mentors as harsh as themselves. A large class of readers, likewise, will suffer greatly from the introduction into the pages of this work of words printed with all their letters, which it has become the custom to represent by the initial and final letter only—a blank line filling the interval. I may as well say at once that, for this circumstance, it is out of my power to apologize. . . . The practice of hinting by single letters those expletives . . . strikes me as a proceeding which, however well meant, is weak and futile. . . .

With regard to the rusticity of "Wuthering Heights," I admit the charge, for I feel the quality. It is rustic all through. It is moorish, and wild, and knotty as a root of heath. Nor was it natural that it should be otherwise; the author being herself a native and nursling of the moors. Doubtless, had her lot been cast in a town, her writings, if she had written at all, would have possessed another character. . . . Had Ellis Bell been a lady or a gentleman accustomed to what is called "the world," her view of a remote and unreclaimed region, as well as of the dwellers therein, would have differed greatly from that actually taken by the homebred country girl. Doubtless it would have been wider—more comprehensive: whether it would have been more original or more truthful is not so certain. As far as the scenery and locality are concerned, it could scarcely have been so sympathetic: . . . her native hills were far more to her than a spectacle; they were what she lived in, and by, as much as the wild birds . . . or as the heather. . . . Her descriptions, then, of natural scenery, are what they should be, and all they should be.

Where delineation of human character is concerned, the case is different. I am bound to avow that she had scarcely more practical knowledge of the peasantry amongst whom she lived, than a nun has of the country people who sometimes pass her convent gates. My sister's disposition was not naturally gregarious; circumstances favoured and fostered her tendency to seclusion; except to go to church or take a walk on the hills, she rarely crossed the threshold of home. Though her feeling for the people round was benevolent, intercourse with them she never sought. . . . And yet she knew them: knew their ways, their language, their family histories; she could hear of them with interest, and talk of them with detail, minute, graphic, and accurate. . . . Hence it ensued that what her mind had gathered of the real concerning them, was too exclusively confined to those tragic and terrible traits of which, in listening to the secret annals of every rude vicinage, the memory is sometimes compelled to receive the impress. Her imagination . . . found in such traits material whence it wrought creations like Heathcliff, like Earnshaw, like Catherine. Having formed these beings, she did not know what she had done. If the auditor of her work, when read in manuscript, shuddered under the grinding influence of natures so relentless and implacable, of spirits so lost and fallen; if it was complained that the mere hearing of certain vivid and fearful scenes banished sleep by night, and disturbed mental peace by day, Ellis Bell would wonder what was meant, and suspect the complainant of affectation. Had she but lived, her mind would of itself have grown like a strong tree . . . and its matured fruits would have attained a mellower ripeness . . . ; but on that mind time and experience alone could work: to the influence of other intellects, it was not amenable.

Having avowed that over much of "Wuthering Heights" there broods "a horror of great darkness";[1] that, in its storm-heated and electrical atmosphere, we seem at times to breathe lightning, let me point to those spots where clouded daylight and the eclipsed sun still attest their existence. For a specimen of true benevolence and homely fidelity, look at the character of Nelly Dean; for an example of constancy and tenderness, remark that of Edgar Linton. (Some people will think these qualities do not shine so well incarnate in a man as they would do in a woman, but Ellis Bell could never be brought to comprehend this notion: nothing moved her more than any insinuation that the faithfulness and clemency, the long-suffering and loving-kindness which are esteemed virtues in the daughters of Eve, become foibles in the sons of Adam. She held that . . . what clothes the Godhead in glory, can disgrace no form of feeble humanity.) There is a dry saturnine humour in the delineation of old Joseph, and some glimpses of grace and gaiety animate the younger Catherine. Nor is even the first heroine of the name destitute of a certain strange beauty in her fierceness, or of honesty in the midst of perverted passion and passionate perversity.

Heathcliff, indeed, stands unredeemed; never once swerving in his arrow-straight course to perdition, from the time when "the little black-haired swarthy thing, as dark as if it came from the Devil," was first unrolled out of the bundle and set on its feet in the farmhouse kitchen, to the hour when Nelly Dean found the grim, stalwart corpse laid on its back in the panel-enclosed bed. . . .

Heathcliff betrays one solitary human feeling, and that is *not* his love for Catherine; which is a sentiment fierce and inhuman: a passion such as might boil and glow in the bad essence of some evil genius; a fire that might form the tormented centre—the ever-suffering soul of a magnate of the infernal world: and by its quenchless and ceaseless ravage . . . doom[ ] him to carry Hell with him wherever he wanders.[2] No; the single link that connects Heathcliff with humanity is his rudely confessed regard for Hareton Earnshaw— the young man whom he has ruined; and then his half-implied esteem for Nelly Dean. These solitary traits omitted, we should say

---

[1]Genesis 15.12, referring to the foreboding dream before Abram's covenant with God.

[2]Milton's Satan in *Paradise Lost* laments, "Which way I fly is hell" (4.75).

he was child neither of Lascar nor gipsy, but a man's shape animated by demon life—a Ghoul—an Afreet.[3]

Whether it is right or advisable to create beings like Heathcliff, I do not know: I scarcely think it is. But this I know; the writer who possesses the creative gift owns something of which he is not always master. . . . He may lay down rules and devise principles, . . . and then, haply without any warning of revolt, there comes a time when it will no longer consent "to harrow the vallies, or be bound with a band in the furrow"[4]—when it "laughs at the multitude of the city, and regards not the crying of the driver"—when, refusing absolutely to make ropes out of sea-sand any longer, it sets to work on statue-hewing, and you have a Pluto or a Jove, a Tisiphone or a Psyche, a Mermaid or a Madonna, as Fate or Inspiration direct.[5] Be the work grim or glorious, dread or divine, you have little choice left but . . . to work passively under dictates you neither delivered nor could question. . . . If the result be attractive, the World will praise you, who little deserve praise; if it be repulsive, the same World will blame you, who almost as little deserve blame.

"Wuthering Heights" was hewn in a wild workshop, with simple tools, out of homely materials. The statuary found a granite block on a solitary moor: gazing thereon, he saw how from the crag might be elicited a head, savage, swart, sinister; a form moulded with at least one element of grandeur—power. He wrought with a rude chisel, and from no model but the vision of his meditations. With time and labour, the crag took human shape; and there it stands colossal, dark, and frowning, half statue, half rock: in the former sense, terrible and goblin-like; in the latter, almost beautiful, for its colouring is of mellow grey, and moorland moss clothes it; and heath, with its blooming bells and balmy fragrance, grows faithfully close to the giant's foot.[6]

CURRER BELL.

---

[3]Arabic names (in folklore or the Qur'an) for demons that may take monstrous or human form; *ghoul* became a term for grave robber.

[4]Job 39.10. One in a series of rhetorical questions about untameable creatures: Who would harness a unicorn for farm work? Similarly, the wild ass "laughs" thus (Job 39.7).

[5]Pluto: ruler of the underworld; Jove: Roman supreme deity; Tisiphone: one of the Erinyes or Furies (the name means she avenges murder); Psyche: supremely beautiful maiden beloved by Eros (Cupid) in Apuleius's *The Golden Ass* (200 CE). Each pair represents low and lofty alternatives.

[6]Brontë here echoes the name Bell as well as the final words of *Wuthering Heights*: the (head)stones, moor, creeping moss, "heath, and hare-bells."

# *Historical, Social, and Legal*

## Heathcliff and the Unsettled Classes

*Wuthering Heights* seems to inhabit a backwater of historical time. Despite actual locations and dates (its first word is "1801"), its closed social circle of two families seems untouched by change. Yet contemporary upheavals register in the novel. Heathcliff's revenge is that of the laborer who becomes a self-made man. But he might also represent other kinds of outsiders who appeared to threaten Victorian order. Most unsettling, no one really knows Heathcliff's origin. Some critics have assigned him a literary genealogy: the Byronic hero, Milton's Satan, Shakespeare's Othello. But his racial ancestry remains an unsolvable mystery. Is he English? Irish? mixed race with some African blood? He arrives dirty and ragged and speaking "gibberish" (Gaelic?). He is called many things: a thief, a gypsy ("the son of the fortune-teller"), "a little Lascar, or an American or Spanish castaway" (pp. 46–47). Nelly tries to comfort him with self-help advice: Even "if you were a regular black" you should display "a good heart," she counsels as she cleans him up. "You're fit for a prince in disguise. Who knows, but your father was Emperor of China, and your mother an Indian queen, each of them able to buy up, with one week's income, Wuthering Heights and Thrushcross Grange together? And you were kidnapped by wicked sailors, and brought to England" (p. 53).

Heathcliff was found as a starving orphan on the streets of Liverpool,[1] one of the hubs of the slave trade until 1807 (owning slaves *in* England was illegal but was not abolished in English colonies until 1833). Noting the presence of African-descended people in the inland regions of England during the era of the novel, Christopher Heywood links Heathcliff to Africa. Terry Eagleton instead focuses on the Brontës' Irish background, Branwell's trip to Liverpool in 1845, and Ireland's Great Famine, which in 1845–49 produced a million deaths and two million refugees.

Before 1800, the British Midlands were already in an industrial revolution. Yorkshire faced economic instability and labor unrest. In 1811–12, Patrick Brontë witnessed attacks on machinery by Luddites (described in the excerpt from Samuel Smiles). Across the 1820s, workers went on strike in Bradford and Halifax, southeast of Haworth, and in Leeds, further to the east. Workers from as far away as Ireland converged where there was higher-wage work for wool combers and hand- or power-loom weavers; many continued to work on farms in season. A paper in Bradford in the 1820s described the district as "a Babel of different dialects" and observed the wool combers to be gifted speakers and performers (they "could recite with wonderful power") as well as active political and labor organizers (quoted in Thompson 283).

The Victorians began to form "scientific" approaches to the mobile populations. Dr. James Kay-Shuttleworth was one such authority; in retirement, he became a patron of writers, including Charlotte Brontë. (The Kay-Shuttleworths took Charlotte to the Lake District, where she met Elizabeth Gaskell.) Kay-Shuttleworth's *Report on the State of the Irish Poor in Great Britain* (1836) contrasted the skilled, self-respecting English laborers with the desperate Irish: "The Irish emigration into Britain is an example of a less civilized population spreading themselves, as a kind of substratum, beneath a more civilized community" (Thompson 432–35). It was all too easy to characterize displaced and suffering masses as inferior or as a threat of riot and disorder. Heathcliff appears to be an alien wanderer, but perhaps the worst nightmare is that he uses sober thrift and hard work as well as cunning to topple his masters.

[1]In cities such as Bristol, Liverpool, and New York, destitute children known as "street Arabs" might be institutionalized. From 1854 to 1929, orphans or children of "unfit" parents (often Irish) were sent on "orphan trains" from New York and other cities to work on farms in the Midwest. Native American and Australian Aboriginal children were removed from their families to be reeducated.

## *Nomads of City and Country*

As Eagleton suggests, Ireland figures as "Nature to England's Culture" (9). Racist concepts at this time located primitive humanity outside Anglo-Saxon civilization, especially in imperial possessions in India, Africa, and Asia (Meyer 112–15). There were domestic versions, too, of attempts to justify domination; attributes of poverty were interpreted as signs of biological inferiority and defective character. Experts such as Henry Mayhew sought to explain "the dangerous classes" in the midst of civilized society, with something of the physician's diagnosing and curing disease.

### Henry Mayhew (1812–1887)

*Henry Mayhew's venturesome life as a playwright, editor, and journalist carried over into his investigative reporting in London. His father, a solicitor, apprenticed each of his seven sons to the law (there were seventeen children), but Henry ran away to sea. In Paris as well as London, he was close friends with William Makepeace Thackeray (Charlotte Brontë's hero) and Douglas Jerrold (whose weekly reviewed* Wuthering Heights *in 1848); he married Jerrold's daughter in 1844. In 1841, Mayhew had co-founded the long-running humor magazine,* Punch, *a venue for Thackeray and others. Mayhew's successful articles in the* Morning Chronicle *(October 1849–December 1850) were developed into a two-volume study in 1851, with additional volumes in 1861. It is a pioneering work of ethnography.*

*Mayhew anticipates later studies of so-called deviant types that measure facial structure or other characteristics. He was fascinated as well as repelled by the wanderers, perhaps sensing a resource for renewed vitality, much as Heathcliff seems more alive than the Lintons. Some of the traits of the "nomad" or "nomade" could be attributed to Mayhew, with his erratic career.*

### from *London Labour and the London Poor,* Volume 1 (1861)

#### Of Wandering Tribes in General.

Of the thousand millions of human beings that are said to constitute the population of the entire globe, there are—socially, morally, and perhaps even physically considered—but two distinct and broadly

marked races, viz., the wanderers and the settlers—the vagabond and
the citizen—the nomadic and the civilized tribes. Between these two
extremes, however, ethnologists recognize a mediate variety, partaking
of the attributes of both. There is not only the race of hunters and manufacturers—those who live by shooting and fishing, and those who live
by producing—but, say they, there are also the herdsmen, or those
who live by tending and feeding, what they consume. Each of these
classes has its peculiar and distinctive physical as well as moral characteristics. . . . A greater relative development of the jaws and cheek
bones . . . indicates a more ample extension of the organs subservient
to sensation and the animal faculties. Such a configuration is adapted
to the wandering tribes; whereas, the greater relative development of
the bones of the skull—indicating as it does a greater expansion of the
brain, and consequently of the intellectual faculties—is especially
adapted to the civilized races or settlers, who depend mainly on their
knowledge . . . for the necessaries and comforts of life. Moreover it
would appear, that not only are all races divisible into wanderers and
settlers, but that each civilized or settled tribe has generally some wandering horde intermingled with, and in a measure preying upon, it. . . .

(1) There are two distinct races of men, viz.:—the wandering
and the civilized tribes; (2) to each of these tribes a different form of
head is peculiar. . . . (3) to each civilized tribe there is generally a
wandering horde attached; (4) such wandering hordes have frequently a different language from the more civilized portion of the
community, and that adopted with the intent of concealing their
designs and exploits from them. It is curious that no one has as yet
applied the above facts to the explanation of certain anomalies in
the present state of society among ourselves. . . .

The resemblance once discovered, however, becomes of great
service in enabling us to use the moral characteristics of the nomade
races of other countries, as a means of comprehending the more
readily those of the vagabonds and outcasts of our own. . . .

The nomad then is distinguished from the civilized man by his
repugnance to regular and continuous labour—by his want of providence in laying up a store for the future—by his inability to perceive consequences . . . —by his passion for stupefying herbs and
roots, and, when possible, for intoxicating fermented liquors—by
his extraordinary powers of enduring privation—by his comparative insensibility to pain—by an immoderate love of gaming, fre-

quently risking his own personal liberty upon a single cast—by his love of libidinous dances—by the pleasure he experiences in witnessing the suffering of sentient creatures—by his delight in warfare and all perilous sports—by his desire for vengeance—by the looseness of his notions as to property—by the absence of chastity among his women, and his disregard of female honour—and lastly, by his vague sense of religion—his rude idea of a Creator, and utter absence of all appreciation of the mercy of the Divine Spirit.

Strange to say, despite its privations, its dangers, and its hardships, those who have once adopted the savage and wandering mode of life, rarely abandon it. There are countless examples of white men adopting all the usages of the Indian hunter, but there is scarcely one example of the Indian hunter or trapper adopting the steady and regular habits of civilized life; indeed, the various missionaries who have visited nomade races have found their labours utterly unavailing, so long as a wandering life continued.

## *Self-Made Men and Luddites*

Mayhew's assertion that nomads never acquire the characteristics of the settled classes is belied in *Wuthering Heights*. Although Heathcliff's brutality is barely tamed, he shows that it is compatible with established laws. Patrick Brontë was a different sort of self-made man: Born in poverty, he became a clergyman with the rank if hardly the means of a gentleman. Smiles's *Self-Help* (1859) is full of similar stories of overcoming humble origins. Unlike Mayhew, Smiles believes self-determination outweighs birth. Smiles took an optimist's view of the mutual benefit of economic competition and individual success.

### Samuel Smiles (1812–1904)

*A Scotsman raised in strict Calvinism and trained as a medical practitioner, Smiles took on the rationalist outlook of the Unitarians and became editor of the Radical* Leeds Times *in 1838, and thus was within the orbit of the Brontës. In 1843–44, he published* A History of Ireland *that would have had immediate interest for readers in the Haworth parsonage. Smiles is best known today for his international best-seller,* Self-Help, *which began as a lecture to a working-men's association. In spite of similarities in name and circumstance, Heathcliff and the historical John Heathcoat would be almost opposite models to follow. Smiles portrays Heathcoat as an open-hearted, fatherly provider who ensures that the younger generation does not repeat a history of ignorance, deprivation, and unrest.*

## from *Self-Help* (1859)

### from Chapter I: Self-Help—National and Individual

"Heaven helps those who help themselves" is a well-tried maxim, embodying in a small compass the results of vast human experience. The spirit of self-help is the root of all genuine growth in the individual; and, exhibited in the lives of many, it constitutes the true source of national vigour and strength. . . . Whatever is done *for* men or classes, to a certain extent takes away the stimulus and necessity of doing for themselves. . . .

The spirit of self-help, as exhibited in the energetic action of individuals, has in all times been a marked feature in the English character, and furnishes the true measure of our power as a nation. Rising above the heads of the mass there were always to be found a series of individuals distinguished beyond others. . . . But our progress has also been owing to multitudes of smaller and less known men. Though only the generals' names may be remembered in the history of any great campaign, it has been in a great measure through the . . . heroism of the privates that victories have been won. . . . Even the humblest person, who sets before his fellows an example of industry, sobriety, and upright honesty . . . has a present as well as a future influence upon the well-being of his country; for his life and character pass unconsciously into the lives of others, and propagate good example. . . .

Daily experience shows that it is energetic individualism which produces the most powerful effects upon the life and action of others, and really constitutes the best practical education. Schools, academies, and colleges, give but the merest beginnings of culture in comparison with it. Far more influential is the life-education daily given in our homes, in the streets, behind counters, . . . at the loom and the plough, in counting-houses and manufactories. . . . For all experience serves to illustrate and enforce the lesson . . . that it is life rather than literature, action rather than study, and character rather than biography, which tend perpetually to renovate mankind.

Biographies of great, but especially of good men, are nevertheless most instructive and useful, as helps, guides, and incentives to others. Some of the best are almost equivalent to gospels—teaching high living, high thinking, and energetic action for their own and the world's good. The valuable examples which they furnish of the power of self-help, of patient purpose, resolute working, and steadfast integrity, . . . exhibit, in language not to be misunderstood, what it is in the power of each to accomplish for himself. . . .

Great men of science, literature, and art—apostles of great thoughts and lords of the great heart—have belonged to no exclusive class nor rank in life. They have come alike from colleges, workshops, and farmhouses,—from the huts of poor men and the mansions of the rich. . . . The poorest have sometimes taken the highest places; nor have difficulties apparently the most insuperable proved obstacles in their way. Those very difficulties, in many instances, would ever seem to have been their best helpers, by evoking their powers of labour and endurance, and stimulating into life faculties which might otherwise have lain dormant. . . .

No one knows to a certainty what Shakespeare was; but it is unquestionable that he sprang from a humble rank. His father was a butcher and grazier; and Shakespeare himself is supposed to have been in early life a woolcomber; whilst others aver that he was an usher in a school and afterwards a scrivener's clerk. He truly seems to have been "not one, but all mankind's epitome." For such is the accuracy of his sea phrases that a naval writer alleges that he must have been a sailor; whilst a clergyman infers, from internal evidence in his writings, that he was probably a parson's clerk. . . . The common class of day labourers has given us Brindley the engineer, Cook the navigator, and Burns the poet. Masons and bricklayers can boast of Ben Jonson, . . . Edwards and Telford the engineers, Hugh Miller the geologist, and Allan Cunningham the writer and sculptor; whilst among distinguished carpenters we find the names of Inigo Jones the architect, Harrison the chronometer-maker, John Hunter the physiologist, Romney and Opie the painters. . . .

### from Chapter II: Leaders of Industry—Inventors and Producers

John Heathcoat was the youngest son of a respectable small farmer at Duffield, Derbyshire, where he was born in 1783. When at school he made steady and rapid progress, but was early removed from it to be apprenticed to a frame-smith near Loughborough. The boy soon learnt to handle tools with dexterity, and he acquired a minute knowledge of the parts of which the stocking-frame was composed, as well as of the more intricate warp-machine. At his leisure he studied how to introduce improvements in them, and . . . as early as the age of sixteen, he conceived the idea of inventing a machine by which lace might be made similar to Buckingham or French lace, then all made by hand. . . . Many ingenious Nottingham mechanics had, during a long succession of years, been labouring at the problem of inventing a machine by which the mesh of threads should be *twisted* round each other on the formation of the net. Some of these men died in poverty, some were driven insane, and all alike failed in the object of their search. The old warp-machine held its ground.

When a little over twenty-one years of age, Heathcoat went to Nottingham, where he readily found employment . . . as a setter-up of hosiery and warp-frames, and was much respected for his talent for invention, general intelligence, and . . . conduct. He also continued to pursue the subject on which his mind had before been occupied. . . . He first studied the art of making the Buckingham or pillow-lace by hand, with the object of effecting the same motions by mechanical means. It was a long and laborious task, requiring the exercise of great perseverance and ingenuity. . . .

He eventually succeeded in working out his principle with extraordinary skill and success; and, at the age of twenty-four, he was enabled to secure his invention by a patent.

During this time his wife was kept in almost as great anxiety as himself. . . . The conversation which took place one eventful evening was vividly remembered. "Well," said the anxious wife, "will it work?" "No," was the sad answer; "I have had to take it all to pieces again." . . . [H]is poor wife could restrain her feelings no longer, but sat down and cried bitterly. She had, however, only a few more weeks to wait, for success, long laboured for and richly deserved, came at last, and a proud and happy man was John Heathcoat when he brought home the first narrow strip of bobbin-net made by his machine, and placed it in the hands of his wife.

As in the case of nearly all inventions which have proved productive, Heathcoat's rights as a patentee were disputed, and his claims as an inventor called in question. On the supposed invalidity of the patent, the lace-makers boldly adopted the bobbin-net machine, and set the inventor at defiance. But other patents were taken out for alleged improvements and adaptations; and it was only when these new patentees fell out and went to law with each other that Heathcoat's rights became established. . . .

To return to the personal history of Mr. Heathcoat. In 1809 we find him established as a lace-manufacturer at Loughborough, in Leicestershire. There he carried on a prosperous business for several years, giving employment to a large number of operatives, at wages varying from 5*l.* to 10*l.* a week. Notwithstanding the great increase in the number of hands employed in lace-making through the introduction of the new machines, it began to be whispered about among the workpeople that they were superseding labour, and an extensive conspiracy was formed for the purpose of destroying them wherever found. As early as the year 1811 disputes arose between the masters and men engaged in the stocking and lace trades. . . . As the machines were of so delicate a construction that a single blow of a hammer rendered them useless, and as the manufacture was carried on for the most part in detached buildings, . . . remote from towns, the opportunities of destroying them were unusually easy. In the neighbourhood of Nottingham, . . . the machine-breakers . . . held nocturnal meetings. . . . Probably with the view of inspiring confidence, they gave out that they were under the command of a leader named Ned Ludd, or General Ludd, and hence their designation of Luddites. Under this organization machine-breaking was carried on . . . during the winter of 1811, occasioning great distress, and throwing large numbers of workpeople out of employment. . . .

The Luddites . . . rapidly extended over the northern and midland manufacturing districts. The organization became more secret. . . . All machines were doomed by them to destruction, whether employed in the manufacture of cloths, calico, or lace; and a reign of terror began which lasted for years. In Yorkshire and Lancashire mills were boldly attacked by armed rioters, . . . so that it became necessary to guard them by soldiers and yeomanry. The masters themselves . . . were assaulted, and some were murdered. At length the law was vigorously set in motion; numbers of the misguided Luddites were apprehended; some were executed; and after several years' violent commotion . . . the machine-breaking riots were at length quelled. . . .

One bright sunny day, in the summer of 1816, a body of rioters entered [Heathcoat's] factory . . . and set fire to it, destroying thirty-seven lace-machines, above 10,000*l.* worth of property. Ten of the men were apprehended for the felony, and eight of them were executed. Mr. Heathcoat made a claim upon the county for compensation . . . of 10,000*l.* The magistrates sought to couple with the payment . . . the condition that Mr. Heathcoat should expend the money in the county of Leicester; but to this he would not assent. . . . At Tiverton, in Devonshire . . . Mr. Heathcoat bought the old mill, renovated and enlarged it, and there recommenced the manufacture of lace upon a larger scale than before; . . . employing a large number of artisans at good wages. . . .

Mr. Heathcoat was a man of great natural gifts. He possessed a sound understanding, quick perception, and a genius for business . . . uprightness, honesty, and integrity. . . . Himself a diligent self-educator, he gave ready encouragement to deserving youths in his employment. . . . During his own busy life, he contrived to save time to master French and Italian. . . . There were few subjects on which he had not formed for himself shrewd and accurate views. The two thousand workpeople in his employment regarded him almost as a father, and he carefully provided for their comfort and improvement. Prosperity did not spoil him . . . nor close his heart against the claims of the poor. . . . To provide for the education of the children of his workpeople, he built schools for them at a cost of about 6000*l.* He was also a man of singularly cheerful and buoyant disposition, a favourite with men of all classes, and most admired and beloved by those who knew him best.

# Women's Rights and Roles

## *Ellis Bell and Sarah Stickney Ellis*

Charlotte Brontë suggested that the pseudonyms Currer, Ellis, and Acton Bell were chosen to avoid falsely claiming to be men, and to gain due respect for their work: "authoresses are liable to be looked on with prejudice" (see p. 331). Bell may refer to the middle name of Arthur Bell Nicholls, their father's curate and Charlotte's future husband, or perhaps to the first and last letters of Branwell. In "The

Brontë Pseudonyms," Marianne Thormählen proposes that all the first names derive from the surnames of contemporary women who represented and advocated women's achievements in education, literature, and household management: the prominent book-collector Frances Mary Richardson Currer, who was a patron of the sisters' school at Cowan Bridge; the poet Eliza Acton, whose classic *Modern Cookery for Private Families* appeared in 1845; and Sarah Stickney Ellis, best known for her series of advice manuals, beginning with *The Women of England* (1839).

The Ellis connection may seem a stretch. If the Brontës might be associated with women's progress, Sarah Ellis has been viewed as out of step with it. For Ellis, England's women had "the high and holy duty of cherishing and protecting the minor morals of life, from whence springs all that is elevated in purpose, and glorious in action." Women should exert domestic influence that ultimately shapes the conduct of the empire. How could one possibly reconcile Ellis Bell—a sort of pagan force of nature—or the novel's hostile family environments with Sarah Ellis's model of self-effacing domesticity? Yet *Wuthering Heights* does provide a rich commentary on women's rights, education, and domestic roles, and it even seems to apply "Mrs. Ellis's" advice by negative example.

Sarah Ellis portrays a relatively new set of types, the alienated man of business or industry and his suburban wife no longer occupied in producing household goods. Ellis's confidence that men's passion for money and power will succumb to women's appeals to their better natures is belied in the marriages narrated in the novel. Hindley's wife Frances is impotent in influence, and Heathcliff treats his wife, daughter-in-law, and son with brutality; only Edgar behaves like the new type of *gentle*man. Compare Sarah Ellis's description of the failed hostess to the rude welcome Lockwood receives; or compare her examples to the first and second Catherines.

### Sarah Stickney Ellis (1799–1872)

*Sarah Stickney Ellis, the Yorkshire-born daughter of a Quaker farmer, shared many experiences and qualities with Emily Brontë, including the early loss of her mother and love of learning, outdoor activity, and housekeeping. Financial necessity led Ellis to work as an artist and in 1844 to found Rawdon House School for girls; Thackeray and others satirized Ellis for teaching women to manipulate men. In 1837, she married William Ellis, a Congregational minister.* The Women of England *and her other advice books (including* Daughters *[1842],* Wives *[1843], and* Mothers *[1843]) were very successful, and she published extensively in other genres.* The stories in Family Secrets *(1842) were groundbreaking exposes of middle-class alcoholism and may have influenced Anne Brontë's* The Tenant of Wildfell Hall *(Twycross-Martin).*

## from *The Women of England, Their Social Duties and Domestic Habits* (1839)

### from Chapter II: Influence of the Women of England

In our imperfect state of being, we seldom attain any great or national good without its accompaniment of evil. . . . Thus the great facilities of communication, not only throughout our own country, but with distant parts of the world, are rousing men of every description to tenfold exertion in the field of competition in which they are engaged; so that their whole being is becoming swallowed up in efforts and calculations relating to their pecuniary success. . . .

May it not be said to be the especial duty of women to look around them, and see in what way they can counteract this evil, by calling back the attention of man to those sunnier spots in his existence, by which the growth of his moral feelings have been encouraged, and his heart improved?

We cannot believe of the fathers who watched over our childhood, of the husbands who shared our intellectual pursuits, of the brothers who went hand in hand with us in our love of poetry and nature, that they are all gone over to the side of mammon,[1] that there does not lurk in some corner of their hearts a secret longing to return; yet every morning brings the same hurried and indifferent parting, every evening the same jaded, speechless, welcomeless return—until we almost fail to recognize the man, in the machine.

English homes have been much boasted of by English people, both at home and abroad. What would a foreigner think of those neat, and sometimes elegant residences, which form a circle of comparative gentility around our cities and our trading towns? What

[1]Committed themselves to materialism or making money for its own sake.

would he think, when told that the fathers of those families have not time to see their children, except on the Sabbath-day? . . .

What woman can look on without asking—"Is there nothing I can do, to call them back?" Surely there is. . . . Will an increase of intellectual attainments, or a higher style of accomplishments, effect this purpose? Will the common-place frivolities of morning calls, or an interminable range of superficial reading, enable them to assist their brothers, their husbands, or their sons in becoming happier and better men?

No: . . . man is a social being, and beneath the hard surface he puts on, to fit him for the wear and tear of every day, he has a heart as true to the kindly affections of our nature, as that of woman. . . . He has therefore need of all her sisterly services . . . to foster in his nature, and establish in his character, that higher tone of feeling, without which he can enjoy nothing beyond a kind of animal existence. . . .

The British throne being now graced by a female sovereign, . . . it is surely not a time for the female part of the community to fall away from the high standard of moral excellence. . . .

### from Chapter III: Modern Education

One of the most striking features in the character of the young ladies of the present day, is the absence of contentment. They are lively when excited, but no sooner does the excitement cease, than they fall back into their habitual listlessness, under which they so often complain . . . that one would suppose them to be victims of adversity. . . . For the sake of the poetry of the matter, one would scarcely deny to every young lady her little canker-worm to nurse in her bosom, since all must have their pets. But when they add selfishness to melancholy, and trouble their friends with their idle and fruitless complaints, the case becomes too serious for a jest.

### from Chapter VII:
### Domestic Habits,—Consideration and Kindness

We will imagine a woman . . . receiving her guest. . . . The visiter is permitted to see that her hostess has reluctantly laid down her book . . . ; or, after her guest has remained twenty minutes in a vacant, and by no means inviting parlour, she comes toiling up from the kitchen, with a countenance that makes it dreadful to be adding to her daily fatigues. . . .

One domestic then is ordered, in the hearing of the guest, to take all the luggage up stairs, to bring hot water, towels, soap—to turn the carpets—run for the best looking-glass—and see that tea is ready by the time the friend comes down. The party then ascend, accompanied by the panting servant, into a room, upon which no kind care has been bestowed. . . . The mistress of the house is angry at this neglect, and rings the bell. The servant ascends from the kitchen to the highest room, to learn that she must go down again. . . . The fire has dwindled to the lowest bar. The mistress looks for coals, but the usual receptacle is empty. She feels as if there were a conspiracy against her. There is—there *can* be no one to blame but the servant. With these complaints, and often-repeated apologies, the time is occupied until the appearance of the long-expected meal. . . .

. . . [T]he individual here described fails to exhibit the character of the *true English woman*, whose peculiar charm is that of diffusing happiness, . . . [like] a ministering angel, applying the magical key of sympathy.

## Harriet Martineau (1802–1876)

*Harriet Martineau was raised in Norwich in a prominent Unitarian family. When her father's textile firm failed in 1829, she turned to writing as a profession, having published pieces in the* Monthly Repository *since 1822. This Unitarian journal, founded in 1806, continued to publish Martineau's writings after W. J. Fox steered it toward national prominence beginning in 1828. She became famous as a writer on economics and social studies, and published widely. Deaf since late childhood, she had many rocky friendships in intellectual circles, including for a time with Charlotte Brontë. It was common for magazine articles to appear anonymously or under a pseudonym; this early essay by Martineau assumes a man's point of view, although she herself sought to emulate the learned women writers she lists at the end.*

## from "On Female Education" (1823)[1]

It is not so much my object to inquire whether the natural powers of women be equal to those of men, as to shew the expediency of

---

[1]Published as Discipulus, "On Female Education. Norwich, November, 1822." *Monthly Repository* 18 (1823): 77–81.

giving proper scope and employment to the powers which they do possess. It may be as well, notwithstanding, to inquire whether the difference be as great as is generally supposed between the mental structure of men and of women.

Doubtless the formation of the mind must depend in a great degree on the structure of the body. From this cause the strength of mind observable in men is supposed to arise; and the delicacy of the female mind is thought to be in agreement with the bodily frame. But it is impossible to ascertain how much may depend on early education. . . . We find that as long as the studies of children of both sexes continue the same, the progress they make is equal. . . . In the cultivated ranks of society, . . . the boy goes on continually increasing his stock of information . . . while the girl is probably confined to low pursuits, . . . she is taught to believe that solid information is unbecoming her sex, almost her whole time is expended on light accomplishments . . . ; and when the natural consequences of this mode of treatment arise, all mankind agree that the abilities of women are far inferior to those of men. . . .

The first great objection which is made to enlightening the female mind is, that if engaged in the pursuit of knowledge, women neglect their appropriate duties and peculiar employments.

2nd. That the greatest advances that the female mind can make in knowledge, must still fall far short of the attainments of the other sex.

3rd. That the vanity so universally ascribed to the sex is apt to be inflated by any degree of proficiency in knowledge, and that women therefore become forgetful of the subordinate station assigned them by law, natural and divine.

To the first objection I answer, that such a pursuit of knowledge as shall lead women to neglect their peculiar duties, is not that cultivation of mind for the utility of which I am contending. But these duties may be well performed without engaging the whole time and attention. If "great thoughts constitute great minds," what can be expected from a woman whose whole intellect is employed on the trifling cares and comparatively mean occupations, to which the advocates for female ignorance would condemn her? These cares . . . should never be pursued as the end itself. The knowledge of these necessary arts is so easily acquired, and they are so easily performed, that an active mind will feel a dismal vacuity, . . . and if nothing nobler and better is presented to it, it will waste its energies in the pursuit of folly, if not of vice. . . .

If we consider woman as the guardian and instructress of infancy, her claims to cultivation of mind become doubly urgent. It is evident that if the soul of the teacher is narrow and contracted, that of the pupil cannot be enlarged. . . .

With respect to the second objection, . . . I allow that the acquirements of women can seldom equal those of men, and it is not desirable that they should. I do not wish to excite a spirit of rivalry between the sexes; I do not desire that many females should seek for fame as authors. . . . I wish them to be companions to men, instead of playthings or servants, one of which an ignorant woman must commonly be. . . .

No Englishwoman, above the lower ranks of life, ought to be ignorant of the Evidences and Principles of her religious belief, of Sacred History, of the outline at least of General History, of the Elements of the Philosophy of Nature, and of the Human Mind; and to these should be added the knowledge of such living languages, and the acquirement of such accomplishments, as situation and circumstances may direct.

With respect to the third objection, . . . the most important part of education, the implanting of religious principles must be in part neglected, if the share of knowledge which women may appropriate, should be suffered to inflate their vanity, or excite feelings of pride. Christian humility should be one of the first requisites in female education. . . .

Let woman then be taught that . . . she is to be a rational companion to those of the other sex among whom her lot in life is cast, that her proper sphere is *home*. . . . She will engraft the vigorous qualities of the mind of man on her own blooming virtues, and insinuate into his mind those softer graces and milder beauties, which will smooth the ruggedness of his character. . . .

See what has already been done. In the present age, and in our own country, we can reckon among those who have rendered important services to society at large, . . . the names of More, Barbauld, Hamilton, Edgeworth, Carter. . . .[2]

---

[2]Martineau lists 11 surnames of eminent women writers. Hannah More (1745–1833), Anna Laetitia Aikin Barbauld (1743–1825), Elizabeth Hamilton (1756–1816), Maria Edgeworth (1767–1849), Elizabeth Carter (1717–1806)—all were renowned precedents for the Brontës.

I . . . conclude . . . with the hope, that these examples of what may be done may excite a noble emulation in their own sex, and in ours such a conviction of the value of the female mind. . . .

DISCIPULUS.

## *Wills, Women, and Property*

The Brontë sisters were likely to become spinsters,[1] given that they had no dowries and the eligible men in their vicinity tended to be poor curates. There were compensations in remaining independent, and there were precedents for unmarried women writers. Harriet Martineau, whom Charlotte Brontë befriended in London in 1849, remained single and established her own house in the Lake District. If Martineau or any woman like her had married without a settlement (a prenuptial trust), all her property and earnings would become her husband's, and her legal identity would become subsumed in his (the law of coverture). If the marriage produced children, the husband automatically had custody (divorce was difficult, extremely expensive, scandalous, and rare). These legal inequities for married women were being confronted in the 1830s–40s, in part by reforms instigated by the writer Lady Caroline Norton, whose abusive husband withheld her children and her income. The Infant Custody Act in 1839 (maternal custody of children under the age of seven) and the Matrimonial Causes Act in 1857 (property rights for married women) were some of the first measures of change. Norton's pamphlet, *English Laws for Women in the Nineteenth Century*, was published in the same year, 1854, as Barbara Bodichon's authoritative summary.

### Barbara Leigh Smith Bodichon (1827–1891)

*Barbara Leigh Smith Bodichon was the daughter and granddaughter of radical and abolitionist Members of Parliament and cousin of the founder of the nursing profession, Florence Nightingale; her friends*

---

[1] A "spinster" originally was someone employed in spinning yarn; from the 17th century, it designated a woman of any age who had never been married. For centuries it has also meant a woman beyond the usual age for marriage. In the 1840s, a woman's chances of marrying declined rapidly by the age of 25 (Barker, *Brontës*, 448), and the 1851 census revealed that as many as 750,000 women in England might never marry because of a lack of men.

*included the novelist George Eliot. Her parents never married. Illegiti-macy, combined with an excellent education and an independent income, provided Barbara Leigh Smith with extraordinary freedom to design her own career as a painter and an organizer of campaigns for education, employment, and legal rights for women. In 1857 she mar-ried Eugene Bodichon, a French physician; childless, they lived half the year in Algiers and half in England.*

## from *A Brief Summary, in Plain Language, of the Most Important Laws Concerning Women* (1854)

*Legal Condition of Unmarried Women or Spinsters.* A single woman has the same rights to property, to protection from the law, and has to pay the same taxes to the State, as a man. . . .

If [a woman's] father or mother die *intestate* (*i.e.*, without a will) she takes an equal share with her brothers and sisters of the personal property (*i.e.*, goods, chattels, moveables), but her eldest brother, if she have one, and his children, even daughters, will take the *real* property (*i.e.*, not personal property, but all other, as land, &c.), as the heir-at-law; males and their issue being preferred to females. . . . If she be an only child, she is entitled to all the intestate real and personal property.

The church and nearly all offices under government are closed to women. . . . The professions of law and medicine, whether or not closed by law, are [in England] closed in fact. [Women] may engage in trade, and may occupy inferior situations, such as matron of a charity. . . .

*Laws Concerning Married Women.* . . .

A man and wife are one person in law; a wife loses all her rights as a single woman, and her existence is entirely absorbed in that of her husband. He is civilly responsible for her acts; she lives under his protection or cover, and her condition is called coverture.

A woman's body belongs to her husband; she is in his custody, and he can enforce his right by a writ of *habeus corpus*.

What was her personal property before marriage, such as money in hand, money at the bank, jewels, household goods, clothes, &c., becomes absolutely her husband's, . . . whether he and his wife live together or not. . . .

The legal custody of children belongs to the father. During the life-time of a sane father, the mother has no rights over her children, except a limited power over infants, and the father may take them from her and dispose of them as he thinks fit. . . .

As the wife acts under the command and control of her husband, she is excused from punishment for certain offences, such as theft, burglary, housebreaking, &c., if committed in his presence. . . . A wife cannot be found guilty of concealing her felon husband. . . . She cannot be found guilty of stealing from her husband or of setting his house on fire, as they are one person in law. A husband and wife cannot be found guilty of conspiracy, as that offence cannot be committed unless there are two persons.

*Usual Precautions against the Laws Concerning the Property of Married Women.*

. . . It is usual, before marriage, in order to secure a wife and her children against the power of the husband, to make with his consent a settlement of some property on the wife. . . .

Although the Common Law does not allow a married woman to possess any property, yet in respect of property settled for her separate use, Equity endeavours to treat her as a single woman. . . .

There are great difficulties and complexities in making settlements, and they should always be made by a competent lawyer.


# A Tale of Two Houses: Interiors and Servants

Wuthering Heights is named, in the Earnshaw's dialect, for its weather-exposed location. Can the reader adapt to such a hostile environment? The stunted trees suggest we should look elsewhere for comfort and entertainment—perhaps lower down, in the cozy-sounding vale of Thrushcross Grange, where trees bloom along the protective garden wall.

At Wuthering Heights, the pewter plate, silver tankards, rough furniture, exposed beams, and open hearth that feels like the mouth of hell suggest the "Gothic." John Ruskin's aesthetic criticism, "The Nature of Gothic" (1851–53), played a large part in a Victorian Gothic revival, a reaction against the industrialization that made mass-produced carpets, china, and upholstered furniture widely available. Charles Eastlake (1833–1906) followed Ruskin in applying Gothic aesthetics to interior design, stressing that old-fashioned quality was compatible with comfort and taste. Eastlake's *Hints on Household Taste* (1868) was widely accepted as a model of domestic design; it sought to reconcile "the poetry" of medieval art and design with "practical advantages" (39–40), as if to unite Wuthering Heights with Thrushcross Grange.

## *Interiors*

The scarcity of specific description in *Wuthering Heights* has encouraged some critics to regard it as timeless. The challenge more recently has been to resituate the novel in its own time and place. What are the historical markings on those two seemingly mythic residences? Reading the shape of rooms, furnishings, and amenities—as well as the question of hospitality—reveals a conflicted cultural history and a ranking of characters according to the comforts and service they expect.

Witold Rybczynski in his history of the idea of "home" emphasizes that comfort and privacy are largely modern concepts. In early housing, a "family" (which included employees) shared a central hearth and space (24–32). Not until the eighteenth century did rooms gain specialized functions, with comfortable chairs (81). The two dates that anchor the novel near the beginning, 1500 and 1801, seem to relate to the two houses, which could be models of Rybczynski's early and modern ideas of home. But to take just one point of contrast between these interiors, compare the sparse furniture at the Heights, "high-backed, primitive structures" painted green or black, to the crimson carpet and "crimson-covered chairs and tables" at the Grange. The high-backed settle common in English houses for centuries at the Grange has been replaced by a sofa. Comfort is a measure of character in the novel; the weak or peevish characters resort to sofas or crave the fire.[1] Many readers may imagine that they would be happiest wandering free on the moors. But there is something to be said for reading a novel in good lighting on a comfortable chair.

---

[1]Coal mining fueled industrial development in Yorkshire and provided the cheapest heating: "as is usually the case in a coal district, a fine, red fire illuminated the chimney," Lockwood observes (p. 270).

# John Ruskin (1819–1900)

> Modern Painters *(1843–60), by influential critic John Ruskin, was a revelation to Charlotte Brontë when she read it. Her first conversation with novelist Elizabeth Gaskell touched on their shared admiration (LCB 353), and she praised* The Stones of Venice *as "nobly laid and chiseled" (375). Despite his Oxford education, later appointment as Slade Professor of Fine Art, and avid travels in Europe, Ruskin seems almost a character from one of the Brontës' novels: the sheltered, only child of Evangelical parents (his father was a prosperous wine merchant), suffering from emotional torment throughout his life, his marriage annulled after six years, and gradually losing his sanity in old age. But Ruskin inspired many with his vision of the moral meaning of art and his resistance to modern alienation. For both Brontë and Ruskin, the Gothic celebrates imperfect freedom over enlightened control, and the potential development of the manual laborer as true gentleman.*

## from "The Nature of Gothic," *The Stones of Venice* (1851–1853)

### from Volume 2, Chapter 6

I believe, then, that the characteristics or moral elements of Gothic are the following, placed in the order of their importance:

1. Savageness.
2. Changefulness.
3. Naturalism.
4. Grotesqueness.
5. Rigidity.
6. Redundance. . . .

(1.) SAVAGENESS. I am not sure when the word "Gothic" was first generically applied to the architecture of the North; but I presume that, whatever the date of its original usage, it was intended to imply reproach, and express the barbaric character of the nations among whom that architecture arose. It never implied . . . that their architecture had been originally invented by the Goths themselves; but it did imply that they and their buildings together exhibited a degree of sternness and rudeness. . . . Perhaps some among us, in our admiration of the magnificent science . . . and sacredness of

[Gothic architecture] . . . might desire that the term of ancient reproach should be withdrawn. . . .

The Greek gave the lower workman no subject which he could not perfectly execute. The Assyrian gave him subjects which he could only execute imperfectly, but fixed a legal standard for his imperfection. The workman was, in both systems, a slave. But in the Medieval, or especially Christian, system of ornament, this slavery is done away with altogether; Christianity having recognized, in small things as well as great, the individual value of every soul. . . .

If you will make a man of the working creature, you cannot make a tool. Let him but begin to imagine, to think, to try to do anything worth doing; and the engine-turned precision is lost at once. Out come all his roughness, all his dulness, all his incapability. . . .

And now, reader, look round this English room of yours, about which you have been proud so often, because the work of it was so good and strong, and the ornaments of it so finished. Examine again all those accurate mouldings, and perfect polishings, and unerring adjustments of the seasoned wood and tempered steel. . . . These perfectnesses are signs of a slavery in our England a thousand times more bitter and more degrading than that of the scourged African, or helot[1] Greek. . . .

And, on the other hand, go forth again to gaze upon the old cathedral front, where you have smiled so often at the fantastic ignorance of the old sculptors: examine once more those ugly goblins, . . . and stern statues, . . . but do not mock at them, for they are signs of life and liberty of every workman who struck the stone; . . .

Choose whether you will pay for the lovely form or the perfect finish, and choose at the same moment whether you will make the worker a man or a grindstone. . . . Accurately speaking, no good work whatever can be perfect, and *the demand for perfection is always a sign of a misunderstanding of the ends of art.* . . .

Great art whether expressing itself in words, colours, or stones, does *not* say the same thing over and over again; . . . that to repeat itself is no more a characteristic of genius in marble than it is of genius in print; and that we may, without offending any laws of good taste, require of an architect, as we do of a novelist, that he should be not only correct, but entertaining.

---

[1]Serf or slave.

## *Domestic Servants*

Patrick Brontë's annual income of about £180 placed the family at the poor end of the middle class, able to maintain only one or two women as live-in servants. In 1825, a family with ten times this income could just about afford three women and two men as servants (Burnett 155). The Brontë sisters shared a twinned aversion to becoming servants—that is, governesses—in other people's houses and to bringing a stranger into their household service. When Tabitha Aykroyd[1] fell ill, their resistance to having a replacement went so far as a hunger strike. Gaskell reproduces a letter from Charlotte:

> December 21st, 1839.
>
> [D]uring the last month, . . . we have been without a servant. . . . I manage the ironing, and keep the rooms clean; Emily does the baking, and attends to the kitchen. We are such odd animals, that we prefer this mode of contrivance to having a new face amongst us. . . . I am much happier black-leading the stoves, making the beds, and sweeping the floors at home, than I should be living like a fine lady anywhere else. . . . I *hate* and *abhor* the very thoughts of governess-ship. . . . (LCB 143–44)

Like the Brontës, the Earnshaws regarded old servants as members of the family, quite at odds with the professional distance maintained by the modern wife in Isabella Beeton's rules of management.

In the historical span of *Wuthering Heights* (1760–1840), the vast majority of households (even on limited incomes) depended on some hours of female labor for heat, light, clothing, and other essentials.[2] The Lintons employ several maids, male servants, and farm laborers. The less manicured Wuthering Heights has a sparser staff: one woman, one man, and one or more boys.[3] As

[1]Biographical interest in the Brontës extended to their servants; Nancy and Sarah Garrs and Martha and Tabitha Brown were sources.

[2]In 1831, 670,491 female domestic servants were listed (Thompson 234). In the census of 1851, according to John Burnett, 751,641 women in Great Britain were counted as domestic servants, about 25 percent of all the women who held paid jobs (136–38).

[3]In 1830–70, farms in the West Riding (Yorkshire) mostly raised sheep, and farm laborers were scarce because of better-paid industrial work (Stephens 86).

Lockwood mutters when Joseph functions as both groom and but-ler: "Here we have the whole establishment of domestics, I sup-pose." There is evidently no gardener, as "the grass grows up between the flags" (pp. 3–4).

*Wuthering Heights*, largely narrated by a servant,[4] is surpris-ingly preoccupied with the treatment and status of servants, from Lockwood's and Isabella's dismay at the lack of service at the Heights to the difficulty of how to receive the gentlemanly Heathcliff at the Grange: Edgar is dismayed that Catherine enter-tains a "runaway servant," but she satirically orders Nelly to "set two tables . . . one for your master and Miss Isabella, being gentry; the other for Heathcliff and myself, being of the lower orders" (p. 87). The orders and disorders in both households come into sharper focus in the perspective of Isabella Beeton's *Book of Household Management*.

### Isabella Beeton (1836–1865)

*The Martha Stewart of her day, Isabella Beeton married the wealthy publisher Samuel Orchart Beeton in 1856 and was soon contribut-ing regularly to his* Englishwoman's Domestic Magazine. *A series of her articles from this journal were adapted as a single volume with the telling title,* The Book of Household Management; Comprising Information for the Mistress, Housekeeper, Cook, [etc., and] All Things Connected with Home Life and Comfort. *She died at the age of 28 after giving birth to her fourth child. This prototype of mod-ern cookbooks sold nearly two million copies by 1868 and was still in use in the twentieth century. Beeton's citations of classic literature and her wide-ranging advice appealed to the aspirations of newly prosperous readers. Her charts of the staffing needs and rates of pay provide useful guides to money and standards of living in the Victorian era.*

[4]Edward Chitham suggests that Brontë added later housekeepers in revising *Wuther-ing Heights* from one volume to two during 1846–47; these servants are necessary either not to tell the story too soon to Lockwood or to fill in events at the Heights during Nelly's stay at the Grange (*Birth*, 168–72).

from *The Book of Household Management* (1861)

## from CHAPTER I.

### *THE MISTRESS.*

AS WITH THE COMMANDER OF AN ARMY, or the leader of any enterprise, so is it with the mistress of a house. Her spirit will be seen through the whole establishment; and just in proportion as she performs her duties intelligently and thoroughly, so will her domestics follow in her path. . . . The author of "The Vicar of Wakefield" . . . says: "The modest virgin, the prudent wife, and the careful matron, are much more serviceable in life than petticoated philosophers, blustering heroines, or virago queens. She who makes her husband and her children happy, . . . is a much greater character than ladies described in romances. . . ."[1]

GOOD TEMPER SHOULD BE CULTIVATED by every mistress, as upon it the welfare of the household may be said to turn; indeed, its influence can hardly be over-estimated, as it has the effect of moulding the characters of those around her. . . . Gentleness . . . should pervade her conduct; for where such a spirit is habitually manifested, it not only delights her children, but makes her domestics attentive and respectful; her visitors are also pleased by it, and their happiness is increased. . . .

THE TREATMENT OF SERVANTS is of the highest possible moment, as well to the mistress as to the domestics themselves. On the head of the house the latter will naturally fix their attention; and if they perceive that the mistress's conduct is regulated by high and correct principles, they will not fail to respect her. If, also, a benevolent desire is shown to promote their comfort, at the same time that a steady performance of their duty is exacted, then their respect will not be unmingled with affection, and they will be still more solicitous to continue to deserve her favour. . . .

THE FOLLOWING TABLE OF THE AVERAGE YEARLY WAGES paid to domestics, with the various members of the household placed in the order in which they are usually ranked, will serve as a guide to regulate the expenditure of an establishment:—

[1]Oliver Goldsmith (1728/1730–74) published *The Vicar of Wakefield* in 1766. Beeton quotes (with slight variations) from Letter LXII in *The Citizen of the World* (1762), Goldsmith's fictional letters by a Chinese visitor to London.

|  | When not found in Livery. | When found in Livery.[2] |
|---|---|---|
| The House Steward | From £10 to £80 | — |
| The Valet | " 25 to 50[3] | From £20 to £30 |
| The Butler | " £25 to £50 | — |
| The Cook | " £20 to £40 | — |
| The Gardener | " £20 to £40 | — |
| The Footman | " £20 to £40 | " £15 to £25 |
| The Under Butler | " £15 to £30 | " £15 to £25 |
| The Coachman | — | " £20 to £35 |
| The Groom | " £15 to £30 | " £12 to £20 |
| The Under Footman | — | " £12 to £20 |
| The Page or Footboy | " £8 to £18 | " £6 to £14 |
| The Stableboy | " £6 to £12 | — |

|  | When no extra allowance is made for Tea, Sugar, and Beer. | When an extra allowance is made for Tea, Sugar, and Beer. |
|---|---|---|
| The Housekeeper | From £20 to £45 | From £18 to £40 |
| The Lady's-maid | " £12 to £25 | " £10 to £20 |
| The Head Nurse | " £15 to £30 | " £13 to £26 |
| The Cook | " £11 to £30 | " £12 to £26 |
| The Upper Housemaid | " £12 to £20 | " £10 to £17 |
| The Upper Laundry-maid | " £12 to £18 | " £10 to £15 |
| The Maid-of-all-work | " £9 to £14 | " £7-1/2 to £11 |
| The Under Housemaid | " £8 to £12 | " £6-1/2 to £10 |
| The Still-room Maid | " £9 to £14 | " £8 to £13 |
| The Nursemaid | " £8 to £12 | " £5 to £10 |
| The Under Laundry-maid | " £9 to £11 | " £8 to £12 |
| The Kitchen-maid | " £9 to £14 | " £8 to £12 |
| The Scullery-maid | " £5 to £9 | " £4 to £8. . . |

[2]*Found in livery:* uniforms provided for them. Some positions require no uniform; servants must be paid more if they are to provide their own uniforms or clothing. A stableboy like Heathcliff would have to clothe himself, and his income was about what it cost a governess for her laundry for a year.

[3]Beeton's tables abbreviate the "from £ to £" pattern in this way ("), but we have inserted the British pound sign after this for clarity.

All the domestics mentioned in the above table would enter into the establishment of a wealthy nobleman. The number of servants, of course, would become smaller in proportion to the lesser size of the establishment; and we may here enumerate a scale of servants suited to various incomes, commencing with—

> About £1,000 a year—A cook, upper housemaid, nurse maid, under housemaid, and a man servant.
> About £750 a year—A cook, housemaid, nursemaid, and footboy.
> About £500 a year—A cook, housemaid, and nursemaid.
> About £300 a year—A maid-of-all-work and nursemaid.
> About £200 or £150 a year—A maid-of-all-work (and girl occasionally). . . .

AFTER THIS GENERAL SUPERINTENDENCE of her servants, the mistress, if a mother of a young family, may devote herself to the instruction of some of its younger members, or to the examination of the state of their wardrobe, leaving the later portion of the morning for reading, or for some amusing recreation. . . .

Unless the means of the mistress be very circumscribed, and she be obliged to devote a great deal of her time to the making of her children's clothes, and other economical pursuits, it is right that she should give some time to the pleasures of literature, the innocent delights of the garden, and to the improvement of any special abilities for music, painting, and other elegant arts, which she may, happily, possess. . . .

In former times, when the bottle circulated freely amongst the guests, it was necessary for the ladies to retire earlier than they do at present, for the gentlemen of the company soon became unfit to conduct themselves with that decorum which is essential in the presence of ladies. Thanks, however, to the improvements in modern society, . . . delicacy of conduct towards the female sex has increased with the esteem in which they are now universally held, and thus, the very early withdrawing of the ladies from the dining-room is to be deprecated. . . .

# Regional and Popular

## Where Are the Brontës From?

The Brontë family produced two of the most renowned women writers, and *English* writers, of all time. But how English were the Brontës? Elizabeth Gaskell, like many after her, went out of her way to locate their genius in Yorkshire, a then remote region, while downplaying the family's Irish roots. Patrick Brontë, moreover, traced his descent to Scotland, whose premier writer, Sir Walter Scott, is widely acknowledged as an influence on the Brontës.[1] The published works seem uninvolved with the pressing Irish questions: home rule, Catholic civil rights, and the potato famine of the 1840s. Yet when a plaque was unveiled at Patrick Brontë's birthplace at Imdel in 1956, the Brontës' works were described as "a Yorkshire tune played on an Irish harp" (Chitham, *Irish Background*, 123).

Many have made the futile attempt to pin the origins of *Wuthering Heights* in certain locations. Emily Brontë tapped into rich scources: German and English Romanticism, Gothic novels, Latin classics, the folklore of the servants, and Patrick Brontë's stories of Ireland as well as her knowledge of Yorkshire, along with the shared reading and writing in the family.[2] This section illumi-

---

[1]They came from Irish-speaking South Down, but Patrick and his sister were said to have Scottish accents (Chitham, *Irish Background*, 42–43), while Charlotte's school-mate said she spoke with an Irish accent. Many lowland Scots migrated to Ulster beginning in 1607, encouraged by the Scottish King James I of England.

[2]See in particular Chitham, *Irish Background* and *Birth*; Delafield; Evans and Evans; Knoepflmacher; Orel; Pinion; Stoneman, *Wuthering*; Vogler.

nates a few of these genetic lines: Ireland and the story of Hugh Brunty; Yorkshire language and culture; ballads; and pilgrimages to Haworth.

## Ireland, Heathcliff, and the Brontës

Prejudice against the Irish in the century following Emily Brontë's death was reason enough to downplay the Brontës' "Celtic" origins and to highlight their propriety, Church of England orthodoxy, and Tory politics. The publication in 1893 of William Wright's *The Brontës in Ireland* helped to make the Brontës' Irish roots respectable. Cultural criticism today has opened fresh interest in Ireland's colonial relation to England. Since the twelfth century, the English had claimed rule over parts of Ireland, and from the sixteenth century, Protestant England increasingly sought political control and suppression of Gaelic language and Catholicism. A rebellion in 1641 led to a massacre of hundreds of thousands by the forces of the Puritan Oliver Cromwell. Such conflict continued; Patrick's younger brother William fought with the United Irishmen in the failed 1798 rebellion of Ulster Protestants (Chitham, *Irish Background*, 74). Absentee landlords and corrupt rent-collecting agents had depleted agriculture, while British economic restrictions and limited resources had handicapped industrial development, rendering Ireland vulnerable to the blight that destroyed the main source of food, the potato. Laborers often crossed the Irish Sea to Liverpool in search of seasonal farm or factory work. Emily Brontë's uncles Jamie and Hugh Brunty may have done so when they visited Haworth in about 1837 and 1845–49 (Chitham, *Irish Background*, 105–12).

Patrick Brontë acknowledged his Irish birth, corresponded with his Irish family, sent funds and gifts (including the 1853 edition of *Jane Eyre*), and visited Ireland at least once after his ordination. Not only was Patrick's novel *The Maid of Killarney* (1818) among the numerous "Irish" novels popular in England around the time of Emily's birth, but all his daughters' novels indirectly reflect themes and conventions of Irish fiction (Constable 109–34). *Wuthering Heights* particularly relates to a story in *Blackwood's Edinburgh Magazine*

(November 1840), "The Bridegroom of Barna," by Anglo-Irish writer
Bartholomew Simmons (1804–50) (Hoeveler 393–433).[1]

Elizabeth Gaskell related Patrick's version of his origins: "The
Rev. Patrick Brontë is a native of the County Down in Ireland. His
father Hugh Brontë, was left an orphan at an early age. He came
from the south to the north of the island, and settled in the parish of
Ahaderg, near Loughbrickland. There was some family tradition
that, humble as Hugh Brontë's circumstances were, he was the
descendant of an ancient family . . ." (LCB 34).

Gaskell's minimal information tantalized later investigators.
Patrick Brontë—Brunty or Prunty—was born at Ballynaskeagh,
eldest of ten children of a Protestant father, Hugh, and a Catholic
mother, Eilís (whose name suggests Ellis as well as Nelly). Hugh did
not actually come from the South of Ireland; he was born around
1755, possibly the son of poet and storyteller Pádraig Ó Pronntaigh
(c. 1705–63, anglicized as "Patrick O'Prunty"), who thrived during
a revival of Irish literature (Constable 25–35). Raised by his uncle
Welsh in the Boyne valley, Hugh Brunty moved further north for
work and at the time of Patrick's birth ran a wheat-drying kiln in a
little cottage. In time, the family gained a comfortable living and
encouraged Patrick's ambitions as a young schoolmaster.

Hugh, a celebrated storyteller, was known to embellish family
legend. One of his young listeners, William McAllister, grew up to
be the tutor of William Wright, author of *The Brontës in Ireland*.
The core narrative might be one of those that Patrick enjoyed
repeating to his children, a version of Heathcliff's story.

## William Wright (1837–1899)

*Irish-born and bred Rev. William Wright, journalist and missionary,
had a life-long interest in folklore and archeology that meshed with his
amateur research into the Brontë legends in Ireland. Wright went to
Damascus in 1865 as a missionary to the Jews, a ten-year sojourn during which he met celebrated traveler Sir Richard Burton, learned the
local languages, and served as special correspondent to the* Pall Mall

[1] In Charlotte's second novel, *Shirley*, an Irish curate is caricatured, yet Charlotte married another, Arthur Bell Nicholls. On their honeymoon in Ireland she discovered that
the Nichollses were genteel (they did not visit the Bruntys; Barker, *Brontës*, 758–59).

Gazette. *He eventually published an account of his travels in 1895. From 1884 to 1895, he published articles on discoveries among the remains of the Hittite Empire. Once back in England, he became editorial superintendent of the British and Foreign Bible Society, a position he retained until his death. His controversial* The Brontës in Ireland *was an immediate sensation in 1893, reaching a third edition that year and provoking a rebuttal by J. Ramsden in* The Brontë Homeland *(1897), as well as by Angus M. MacKay, whose book is excerpted on pp. 407–9. Wright blended popular interest in the Brontës, enthusiasm for Ireland, temperance, and Presbyterianism.*

## from *The Brontës in Ireland: Or, Facts Stranger Than Fiction* (1893)

### from Chapter III: Grandfather Brontë's Early Home

Hugh Brontë . . . first makes his appearance as if he had stepped out of a Brontë novel. . . . Story-telling . . . was a hereditary gift in the Brontë family. . . . Hugh Brontë . . . belonged to a large family of brothers and sisters. . . . [His] early childhood was spent in a comfortable home.

Some time about the middle of the last century [i.e., around 1760] . . . the family was thrown into excitement by the arrival of an uncle and aunt of whom they had never heard. The children at first thought the new-comers very rude and common, and they did not like the uncle's swarthy complexion and dark glancing eyes. . . .

Hugh . . . about five or six years old . . . became a great favourite with the new-comers. . . . They bought him little things . . . and when they had completely won his heart they proposed to him that, as they had no children of their own, he should go home with them and be their son. . . .

Consent was given, and paradise, unguarded by cherubim or flaming sword, lay open before the child. He longed for the day when he might begin to spend his life among ponies and dogs, and ramble through orchards and among flowers, and fish for trout in the river Boyne, and be a great scholar. . . . The day, or rather the night, came soon enough—a night to be remembered. . . .

His father lifted him in his arms and carried him out into the darkness, and placed him gently between his uncle and aunt on a seat with a raised back, which was laid across a cart from side to side. Sitting aloft on the cross-seat . . . little Hugh Brontë, with heart full of childish anticipations, began his rough journey out into the big world.

## from Chapter IV: The Foundling and Foster-Friends

We must now leave little Hugh Brontë with his new friends until we have a fuller acquaintance with the uncle to whom he has been committed. Hugh Brontë's father, the great-great-grandfather of the novelists, used to live in a farm on the banks of the Boyne, somewhere above Drogheda. Besides being a farmer he was a cattle-dealer, and he often crossed from Drogheda to Liverpool to dispose of his cattle.

On one of his return journeys from Liverpool a strange child was found in a bundle in the hold. . . . It was very young, very black, very dirty, and almost without clothing of any kind. No one on board knew whence it had come, and no one seemed to care. . . . The child was thrown on the deck. Some one said, "Toss it overboard"; but no one would touch it, and its cries were distressing. From sheer pity Mrs. Brontë was obliged to succour the abandoned infant. . . . The Brontës even at that early period were of a golden hue, and they exceedingly disliked the swarthy infant; but "pity melts the heart to love," and Mrs. Brontë brought it up among her own children. . . . The little foundling . . . was supposed to be a Welsh child on account of its colour. It might doubtless have laid claim to a more Oriental descent, but . . . they called it "Welsh."

Little Welsh was a weak, delicate, and fretful thing, and being despised for his colour and origin, . . . he grew up morose, envious, and cunning. He used secretly to break the toys, destroy the flower-beds, kill the birds. . . . Though they seldom caught him in the monkeyish acts . . . they attributed all the mischief to him, and detested and punished him accordingly. . . .

He became a favourite with Mr. Brontë. . . . Old Brontë took Welsh with him to fairs and markets, instead of his own sons, . . . and found him of the greatest service. . . . He would mingle with the people from whom Brontë wished to purchase cattle, find out from their conversation . . . the lowest price they would be willing to take, and report to his master. . . . Brontë became a rich and prosperous dealer, and Welsh became indispensable to him, and followed him like his shadow by day, and at night . . . coiled up beside him like his dog; but the more Brontë became attached to Welsh the more his children despised and hated the interloper.

As time passed Brontë's affairs passed more and more into the hands of his assistant. . . . They were returning from Liverpool after selling the largest drove of cattle that had ever crossed the Channel, when suddenly Brontë died on board. Welsh, who was with him . . . , professed to know nothing of his master's money. . . .

The young Brontës . . . had been brought up in comparative luxury. . . . They were well educated, and had been a good deal in England; but they neither understood farming nor dealing. . . . In this emergency Welsh requested an interview with the brothers and sisters together. He declared that he had a proposal to make that would restore the fallen fortunes of the family. . . . Welsh appeared dressed up as he had never been seen before. He was arrayed in broadcloth, black and shiny as his well-greased hair, and in fine linen, white and glistening as his prominent teeth. . . .

When all were assembled he began at once in the grand cattle-dealer style to express sympathy . . . , and to declare that on one condition he would carry on the dealing, and supply the wants of the family. . . . The condition was that the youngest sister, Mary, should become his wife. The proposal was rejected with a great outburst of indignant scorn. Many hot and bitter words were exchanged; but as Welsh was leaving . . . he turned and said, "Mary shall yet be my wife, and I will scatter the rest of you like chaff from this house, which shall be my home." With these words he passed out into the darkness. . . .

The landlord of Brontë's farm was an "absentee." The estate was administered by an agent. He was the great man of the district—local magistrate, grand juror, and pasha in general. His real business was the collection of rent. . . . The business of the sub-agent was to act as buffer between the tenant and the "squire," as the agent was always called. The sub-agent was generally a man without heart, conscience, or bowels, selected from the basest of the people. . . . [Welsh] was the very man for the post of sub-agent. . . .

But Welsh, while serving the squire, and recouping himself off the tenants . . . never . . . forgot . . . the double purpose of getting hold of his late master's farm and with it the person of Mary Brontë. . . . The agent promised that the farm should be transferred to Welsh on payment of a certain sum in case the Brontës were unable to pay the rent; but the rent did not fall into arrears. . . .

Welsh, finding himself foiled in his short cut to his master's homestead . . . resolved to change his tactics, and turn his attention to the other object of his quest, Mary Brontë.

In the neighbourhood there lived a female sub-agent called Meg, as base and unprincipled as himself. . . . She was the *spey-woman*, who used to tell the fortunes of servant-girls and lure them to their destruction. . . . Welsh employed this vile harpy to be his go-between with Mary. She was to say that he loved her to distraction . . . that he was now passing rich, and in great favour. . . .

After a time Mary listened to the vile woman's tales. Welsh could not be so bad as they believed him to be! Flowers taken from the gardens of the tenants found their way in great profusion into Mary's room. Trinkets wrung from anguish-stricken tenants . . . were laid on Mary's dressing-table. . . . At length Mary agreed to meet Welsh in a lone plantation on the farm, in company with the harpy, that she might express to him her gratitude. . . . That meeting sealed Mary's fate. She felt she could never again look any decent man in the face, so she consented to marry Welsh. . . .

Thus the man Welsh, who afterwards assumed the name Brontë, carried out his purpose of possessing his late master's farm and with it the person of his youngest daughter.

His threat of vengeance was also carried out—mother, sisters, brothers were scattered abroad, and so effectively that I have not been able, after much searching, to find a single trace of them.

[Chapter V returns to Hugh, Patrick Brontë's father, confirming that Welsh and Mary Brontë, counterparts of Heathcliff and Isabella Linton, were the aunt and uncle who adopted him. "The house from which the Brontës had been driven was burnt to the ground, and all Welsh's ill-gotten riches perished" (32). Chapter VI narrates young Hugh's Dickensian experience of being carried away one night from his home with the now-impoverished, abusive Welsh and his wife; the journey to their home took four days.]

## from Chapter VI: A Fearful Journey

Seventy years after that night Hugh Brontë used to tell the story with great vividness, . . . and in repeating the narrative he scarcely ever forgot a sentence or varied a word. . . . [The story] was first told me by my old tutor, the Rev. William McAllister, and confirmed subsequently by several of his friends who were men of education and intelligence. . . . [Hugh] possessed the rare faculty of seeing as well as thinking what he was speaking of. He made his listeners see and feel as well as hear.

Mr. McAllister had heard most of the orators of his time, including O'Connell and Cooke and Chalmers, but no man ever touched or roused and thrilled him by the force of eloquence as old Hugh Brontë had done.

It may be questioned if any tale ever told by Hugh Brontë's granddaughters equaled those which he narrated. . . . The grandfather had few of the cultured literary touches of the novelists, but he was generally the hero of his own romances, and narrated them with a rugged pathos and ferocious energy which went straight to the heart, but cannot be transferred to paper. . . .

### from Chapter VII: A Miserable Home

Seizing his little nephew and ward firmly by the two shoulders, and looking fiercely in his face, Welsh informed him that his father was a mean and black-hearted scoundrel. Welsh . . . had agreed to make Hugh his heir. . . . Hugh's father had promised to pay Welsh a sum of £50; but the *spalpeen* and deceiver had only paid £5, and Hugh would have to work for his bread and go without education. . . .[1]

A tall, gaunt, half-naked savage, called Gallagher, . . . [a] sanctimonious individual[,] was the steward of Welsh's house. . . . He was the associate of Meg, and had aided her in the schemes which led to Mary Brontë becoming Welsh's wife. . . . Gallagher was the original from whom Emily Brontë drew her portrait of Joseph. . . . Joseph's hypocrisy is of the stern Protestant type, Gallagher's of the wily Catholic type. Joseph raked the Bible promises to himself. . . . Gallagher took "the Blessed Virgin and all the saints" into his service. . . . Joseph . . . is less hateful than the real Gallagher. . . .

### from Chapter XV: The Irish Raconteur, or Story-Teller

The Brontës were too proud to talk even to their most intimate friends of their Irish home, much less to expose the foibles of their immediate ancestors to phlegmatic English ears; but Patrick Brontë would not omit to tell his daughters the thrilling adventures of their ancestors; and the girls, having brooded over the incidents, reproduced them in variant forms, and in the sombre setting of their own surroundings.

[1] The child's only friend was a fierce, nearly wild dog, Keeper, who proved deeply loyal. Many have noted the connection to Emily Brontë's dog, Keeper.

PATRICK BRONTË'S BIRTHPLACE.

This frontispiece to Wright's *The Brontës' in Ireland*
is characteristic of picturesque images of Irish poverty.

The originals lived and died, acted and were acted upon in
Louth and Down; but on the steeps of *Wuthering Heights* they strut
again, speaking with the Yorkshire brogue and braced by the tonic
air of the northern downs.

# Yorkshire: Regionalism, Dialect, and Ballads

## *Regionalism*

You could take the Brontës' works out of the country—and translate, adapt, and critique them in many modes—but you couldn't
take the country out of them, or so it seemed: Gothic Yorkshire was
essential to their significance. Emily Brontë and her novel, as Charlotte was quick to insist, were "rustic all through" (p. 335). Readers, reviewers, critics, and biographers have invested in the idea of

the authentic regionalism of the Brontës and their works, an idea just next door to the Romantic idea of the sublime.

Yet as Charlotte observed, the actual surroundings of Haworth are more bleak than inspiring: the scenery "is not romantic; it is scarcely striking" (p. 321). Charlotte astutely recognized that Emily's passion for this landscape infused it with meaning. Aspiring readers ever since have attempted to submit to a Brontë-like trance in that landscape, heightening the exotic aura of a region within reach of modern Britain.

## Elizabeth Gaskell (1810–1865)

*Elizabeth Gaskell, who wrote terrific Gothic tales herself, added to the strangeness of Yorkshire through a blend of realist sociology and romance, with a bit of self-portraiture. Gaskell attributes regional characteristics, in the advanced approach of her day, to a range of causes from racial ancestry to climate to economics, religion, and politics. Her portrait of "the West Riding" attempts to authenticate the coarse characters in* Wuthering Heights *and other Brontë novels, thereby investing the region with poetic interest. Readers took her cue and started to come up to Yorkshire to see for themselves.*

## from *The Life of Charlotte Brontë* (1857)

### from Chapter II

For a right understanding of the life of my dear friend, Charlotte Brontë, it appears to me more necessary in her case than in most others, that the reader should be made acquainted with the peculiar forms of population and society . . . from which both her own and her sisters' first impressions of human life must have been received. . . .

Even an inhabitant of the neighbouring county of Lancaster is struck by the peculiar force of character which the Yorkshiremen display. This makes them interesting as a race;[1] while, at the same time, as individuals, the remarkable degree of self-sufficiency [is] . . .

[1]In the 1850s, *race* denoted "family," "descendants," "ethnic group," or "nation," with a less biological or physical connotation than it has today.

rather apt to repel a stranger. . . . Conscious of . . . the birthright of
the natives of the West Riding, each man relies upon himself. . . . He
comes . . . to over-esteem his own energy and power. He belongs to
that keen, yet short-sighted class, who consider suspicion . . . a sign
of wisdom. . . . Their accost is curt; their accent and tone of speech
blunt and harsh. Something of this may, probably, be attributed to
the freedom of mountain air and of isolated hill-side life; something
be derived from their rough Norse ancestry. They have a quick perception of character, and a keen sense of humour. . . . Their feelings
are not easily roused, but their duration is lasting. Hence there is
much close friendship and faithful service; and for a correct exempli-
fication . . . I need only refer the reader of "Wuthering Heights" to
the character of "Joseph."

From the same cause come also enduring grudges . . . bequeathed
from generation to generation. I remember Miss Brontë once telling
me that it was a saying round about Haworth, "Keep a stone in thy
pocket seven year; turn it, and keep it seven year longer, that it may
be ever ready to thine hand when thine enemy draws near." . . .

The roads were so notoriously bad, even up to the last thirty
years, that there was little communication between one village and
another; . . . and, in lonely houses on the distant hill-side, or by the
small magnates of secluded hamlets, crimes might be committed
almost unknown. . . . It must be remembered that in those days
there was no rural constabulary; and the few magistrates . . . generally related to one another, . . . inclined to . . . wink at faults too
much like their own. . . .

Isolated as the hill villages may be, they are in the world, compared with the loneliness of the grey ancestral houses . . . in the
dense hollows of the moors. . . . The land has often been held by
one family since the days of the Tudors; the owners are, in fact, the
remains of the old yeomanry—small squires, who are rapidly
becoming extinct. . . . Either the possessor falls into idle, drinking
habits, and so is obliged eventually to sell his property: or he finds,
if more shrewd and adventurous, that the "beck" running down the
mountain-side, or the minerals beneath his feet, can be turned into
a new source of wealth; and . . . he turns manufacturer, or digs for
coal, or quarries for stone. . . .

A singular account was recently given me of a landowner . . .
whose house bore marks of handsome antiquity, as if his forefathers

had been for a long time people of consideration. My informant was struck with the appearance of the place, and proposed to . . . take a nearer inspection. The reply was, "Yo'd better not; he'd threap yo' down th' loan.[2] He's let fly at some folk's legs, and let shot lodge in 'em afore now, for going too near to his house." . . .

## Dialect

As the ballad revival and Sir Walter Scott's hugely popular novels made clear, readers took to the aura of dialect speech. Elizabeth Gaskell enjoys reproducing the Yorkshire speech for which Emily Brontë's ear was pitch-perfect. Far from marks of provincial ignorance, archaic speech could evoke indigenous strength and ancient tradition. Scholars studied dialects as links to high cultural heritage—including the King James translation of the Bible and Shakespeare. The patterns Richard Blakeborough features in the North Riding would be related to the Brontës' West Riding.[1]

### Richard Blakeborough (1850–1918)

*Richard Blakeborough, resident of Stockton-on-Tees in the North Riding, produced books on folklore in 1898 and 1907, a raft of contributions to antiquarian and dialect journals, and regular columns on folklore for such regional newspapers as the* Leeds Mercury. *Working from handwritten notes of field research, Blakeborough was devoted to oral culture. On the title page of his major work,* Wit, Character, Folklore and Customs of the North Riding of Yorkshire *(1898), he identifies himself as "Society Humorist," and an advertisement at the back shows that he can be booked for "Humorous Recitals of the Original Character Sketches in the Yorkshire Dialect" in drawing rooms or for "Literary Societies, Concerts & Bazaars, &c."*

---

[2]Whip you down the road.

[1]The large county of Yorkshire was divided into Thrydings (from Norse for "thirds").

from *Wit, Character, Folklore and Customs of the North Riding of Yorkshire* (1898)

## CHAPTER XVI

### A FEW SIMPLE HINTS ON THE GRAMMAR OF THE FOLK-SPEECH

#### THE ARTICLE.

There is no variation in the usage of the indefinite article, save that it still retains its place before participles and the adjectives *few*, *many*, and *great many*.

Ex.—"He started a calling o' ma, an' Ah started a genning at him, an' then wa set ti wark a lethering yan anuther."

Educated people do not nowadays say, "I sat a sipping of my tea, and a smiling at the kettle singing on the hob." . . . And to those who know as little of their Shakespeare as they do of their Bibles, such speech is put down to ignorance . . . when in point of fact they are listening to an echo of that old-time speech . . . long before their great grandmothers were born, and used by really quite respectable people; e.g.—

"As he was yet *a* coming" (Luke ix. 42).
"I go *a* fishing" (John xxi.3). . . .
"His greatness is yet *a* ripening" (*Henry VIII*).
"There is some ill *a* brewing towards my rest" (*Merchant of Venice*, Act ii. Sc. 5). . . .

The definite article, as mentioned elsewhere, is "t'." To this rule there are very few exceptions. Before certain letters it is almost inaudible; nevertheless, it is always there. . . . I know many people who arc fluent speakers of the dialect, but who read it, even when in printed form, with the greatest difficulty; others who can read fairly well, but so far as understanding the dialect when spoken, might as well listen to a batch of Chocktaw Indians. . . .

Take, for instance, a few words which the other day I heard a woman shout across a village street to her daughter. Firstly, as they sounded when uttered, then the same as they would be written, and thirdly, the translation.

*As spoken.* Teggattenlaadsitwinner.
*As written.* T' egg 'at t' 'en laad's i' t' winner.[1]
*Standard English.* The egg (that) the hen laid is in the window.

---

[1]"Window" is commonly pronounced *winder, winner, and windther*. [RB's note.]

## GENDER.

The same as in standard English, with this slight deviation: many things which are neuter are spoken of as being of the feminine gender. . . . A man speaking of his watch said, "It's yan ov t' best 'at Ah ivver 'ed; sha's a good un," i.e. "It is one of the best that I ever had; she is a good one." . . .

### from THE VERB.

| SINGULAR. | PLURAL. | |
|---|---|---|
| Ah is, *or* Ah's. *I am,* &c. | Wă ⎫ | ⎧ Wa're, *we are.* |
| Thoo is, *or* Thoo's. | Yă ⎬ are, *or* | ⎨ Ya're. |
| He, Sha, *or* it is. | Thă ⎭ | ⎩ Thă're. . . . |

Observe *is* and *be* generally take the place of *are* and *am.*

*Q.* "Is ta gahin' wiv uz²?" i.e. "Are you going with me?"

*A.* "Neea, Ah's nut," or "Neea, Ah isn't," i.e. "No, I is not" (I am not).

*Nobbut,* as a sign of the conditional mood, is quite as general as *if.*

*Q.* "Will ta cum?" Will you come?

*A.* "Nobbut it be owt leyke, an' nobbut I git deean;" i.e. "If it be anything like" (as to weather), "and if only I finish my work." . . .

The rules which were once accepted may have been laid aside in favour of others; but the country people move slowly—their speech is that of their grandparents. . . . They know nothing of the new order of things. And again, they keep very good company.

Examples:—

"I have already *chose* my officer."

*Othello,* Act i. Sc. 1.

"Methought this staff, mine office badge in court, was *broke* in twain."—*Henry VI, Part II,* Act i. Sc. 2. . . .

I can well understand those who know little of the various sources through which the standard English of to-day has come down to us, considering such words as those contained in the following list as being vulgar—*backerly, balk, belly-wark, botch, cant, chaamer, clag, cleg, drukken, flacker, flit, fra, lake, lang, leck, lig, lop,*

---

²"Uz," "us," is often used for "me." [RB's note.]

*lown, luke, mirk, neeaze, owerwelt, raun, roke, rud, scraffle, shive, snite, steg, stob, stower, sump, theeak, thrave, till,* &c. Though some words in the list may be new to the reader, they are in common usage amongst our people. And what is much more to their credit, every one of them were doing duty hundreds of years ago. . . . [I]n many cases the pronounciation is identical with that of their Danish relations. . . .

### Excerpt from "Glossary"

Can. *v.* May. "Can" is commonly used for "may."
> Ex. Q. *Can I smoke here?* Ans. *No, you caan't,* i.e., "No, you may not."

Canker, *v.* To rust.
Cankery, *adj.* Cross, rotten.
Cannily, *adv.* Wisely, with subtilty, nicely.
Canny, *adj.* Pleasing, judicious, skilful, considerable as to number.
> Ex.—*Sha's a canny lass,* i.e., "pleasing." *Thoo fraam'd varra cannily wiv him, i.e.* "You set to work very judiciously with him." *He did it varra cannily,* i.e. "He did it very skilfully." *Whya, ther wur a cannyish few an 'em.* i.e. "Why, there were a considerable number."

Cant, *v.* To raise one end.
Canty, *adj.* Full of spirits, lively.
Cap, *v.* To fix a piece of leather over the toe of a boot; to surprise, bewilder, excel.
> Ex.—*Ah nivver war sae capped i' mah leyfe,* i.e. "I never was so surprised in my life." *Yon caps 'em all,* i.e. "That one over there excels them all."

## *Ballads*

Ballads, which had migrated from Northern European and Celtic traditions through Irish, Scottish, and English versions, seem expressive of irrepressible traditions in *Wuthering Heights*; Nelly is their main source. She is singing "Fairy Annie's Wedding" when Lockwood returns to Wuthering Heights, possibly related to two "Fair Annie" ballads (Chitham, *A Life,* 200):[1] In "Fair

---

[1]Anna or Ania is an Irish goddess (Chitham, *Irish Background*, 130). On ballads in *Wuthering Heights,* see also Smith; Simpson; Stewart.

Annie" or "Fair Margaret and Sweet William," the fair woman loses her beloved to a wealthier match, and her beau dies of grief when he discovers her dead. And when nursing the motherless Hareton, Nelly hums a bit of the Danish ballad "The Ghaist's Warning," from Sir Walter Scott's *The Lady of the Lake* (Scott 243–46).

Just as ballads enrich the thematic density of Emily's novel, so do traces of fairy tales and other folk superstition, from the fairy cave and elf-bolts to the effect of feathers on the dying. Folklore in *Wuthering Heights* is a mixture of oral and literary tradition, fairy tales, and superstition. Young Catherine handles ballads as drawing-room literature to distract the peevish Linton, and she teases Hareton for his uncouth performance of "Chevy Chase."[2] Hints for the doomed, posthumous desire of Catherine and Heathcliff seem to lie in "Sweet William's Ghost" (Child 2.145–48). In the ballad, the ghost of Margaret's lover comes to her door, begging her to give him her "faith and troth." Finally she agrees to go with him.

> Now she has kilted her robes of green
>     A piece below her knee,
> And a' the live-lang winter night
>     The dead corps followed she.
>
> "Is there any room at your head, Willy,        45
>     Or any room at your feet?
> Or any room at your side, Willy,
>     Wherein that I may creep?"
>
> "There's no room at my head, Margaret,
>     There's no room at my feet;        50
> There's no room at my side, Margaret,
>     My coffin's made so meet."

But when the cock crows at dawn, the ghost vanishes. With the loss of her "true love Willy," she "stretch'd her soft limbs, and died."

---

[2]A border ballad, celebrated by Ben Jonson and Sir Philip Sidney, imagining a 15th-c. battle provoked when the English Earl Percy goes hunting in the Scottish Earl Douglas's land in the Cheviot Hills; published in Thomas Percy's *Reliques* of 1765.

## Anonymous

> *No one can identify the author or date—or even the country of origin—of most ballads and folk or fairy tales (the date given here is of a printed collection). The varying lyrics and melodies relay swift, violent action of incest, revenge, fate, return from the dead, and other elements of Gothic fiction. Brontë's readers would have been familiar with Thomas Percy's* Reliques *and with Walter Scott's collections of border ballads ("The Ghaist's Warning" appeared in "Notes to Canto IV" in Scott's* The Lady of the Lake*). According to Scott, "The mythology of one period . . . pass[es] into the romance of the next century, and that into the nursery-tale of the subsequent ages," while readily transferring between countries (253–54).*

## "The Ghaist's Warning" (1812)

### Translated from the Danish Koempe Viser, p. 721[1] . . .

1. Child Dyring has ridden him up under öe[2]
   *And O gin I were young!*
   There he has wedded sae fair a may.
   *I' the greenwood it lists me to ride.*

2. Thegither they liv'd for seven lang year,                    5
   *And O gin I were young!*
   And they seven bairns hae gotten in fere.
   *I' the greenwood it lists me to ride.*

3. Sae Death's come there intill that stead,
   *And O gin I were young!*                                     10
   And that winsun lily flower is dead.
   *I' the greenwood it lists me to ride.*

---

[1]Walter Scott's note, in "Notes to Canto the Fourth" in *The Lady of the Lake*. He borrowed with permission the translation by Robert Jamieson (1772–1844) found in *Popular Ballads and Songs* (1806). The *Kaempe viser* (ed. Peder Syv, Copenhagen, 1695) was a volume of Danish heroic ballads; Jamieson was a pioneer in recognizing links between Scandinavian and English folklore.

[2]"The original expression has been preserved," Scott writes in a note, because it is an untranslatable "standard Danish ballad phrase," without clear relevance or meaning—like the refrains.

4. That swain he has ridden him up under öe
   *And O gin I were young!*
   And syne he has married anither may.                          15
   *I' the greenwood it lists me to ride.*

5. He's married a may, and he's fessen her hame;
   *And O gin I were young!*
   But she was a grim and laidly dame.
   *I' the greenwood it lists me to ride.*                       20

6. Whan into the eastell court drave she,
   *And O gin I were young!*
   The seven bairns stuid wi' the tear in their ee.
   *I' the greenwood it lists me to ride.*

7. Nor ale nor mead to the bairnies she gave:                     25
   *And O gin I were young!*
   "But hunger and hate frae me ye's have."
   *I' the greenwood it lists me to ride. . . .*

9. She took frae them the groff wax light;
   *And O gin I were young!*
   Says, "Now ye sall ligg i' the mark a' night!"                35
   *I' the greenwood it lists me to ride.*

10. 'Twas lang i' the night, and the bairnies grat;
    *And O gin I were young!*
    Their mither she under the mools heard that;
    *I' the greenwood it lists me to ride. . . .*                40

12. That wife can stand up at our lord's knee,                    45
    *And O gin I were young!*
    And "may I gang and my bairnies see?"
    *I' the greenwood it lists me to ride.*

13. She prigged sae sair, and she prigged sae lang,
    *And O gin I were young!*                                     50
    That he at the last gae her leave to gang.
    *I' the greenwood it lists me to ride. . . .*

16. Whan near to the dwalling she can gang,
    *And O gin I were young!*
  The dogs they wow'd till the lift it rang.
    *I' the greenwood it lists me to ride.*

17. When she cam till the eastell yett,           65
    *And O gin I were young!*
  Her eldest dochter stood thereat.
    *I' the greenwood it lists me to ride. . . .*

19. "Forsooth ye're a woman baith fair and fine;
    *And O gin I were young!*
  But ye are nae dear mither mine."          75
    *I' the greenwood it lists me to ride.*

20. "Och! how should I be fine or fair?
    *And O gin I were young!*
  My cheek it is pale, and the ground's my lair."
    *I' the greenwood it lists me to ride. . . .*   80

23. Whan she cam till the chalmer in,          •  90
    *And O gin I were young!*
  Down the bairn's cheeks, the tears did rin.
    *I' the greenwood it lists me to ride. . . .*

25. Till her eldest docther syne said she,
    *And O gin I were young!*
  "Ye bid Child Dyring come here to me."
    *I' the greenwood it lists me to ride.*   100

26. Whan he cam to the chalmer in,
    *And O gin I were young!*
  Wi' angry mood she said to him:
    *I' the greenwood it lists me to ride.*

27. "I left ye routh o' ale and bread;          105
    *And O gin I were young!*
  My bairnies quail for hunger and need.
    *I' the greenwood it lists me to ride. . . .*

29. "I left ye sae mony a groff wax light;
    *And O gin I were young!*
   My bairnies ligg i' the mark a' night.                    115
    *I' the greenwood it lists me to ride.*

30. "Gin aft I come back to visit thee,
    *And O gin I were young!*
   Wae, dowy, and weary thy luck sall be."
    *I' the greenwood it lists me to ride. . . .*            120

32. Ay whan they heard the dog nirr and bell,               125
    *And O gin I were young!*
   Sae gae they the bairnies bread and ale.
    *I' the greenwood it lists me to ride. . . .*

34. Ay whan the little dog yowl'd wi' fear
    *And O gin I were young!*
   They shook at the thought that the dead was near.         135
    *I' the greenwood it lists me to ride.*
    [Or: *Fair words sae mony a heart they cheer.*]

### Prose Translation of "The Ghost's Warning"

1. The young gentle knight Dyring has ridden up to a certain place, and there he has married a fair maid.

Refrain: *Oh how I would be young again!*
    *I long to go riding in the greenwood.*

2. They lived together for seven long years and had seven children together.

3. So Death has come there to that place, and that charming lily flower is dead.

4. That swain, he has ridden up to a certain place, and then he has married another maid.

[Note: "swain": a servant to a knight; a man of low degree]

5. He's married a maid, and he's fetched her home, but she was a grim and ugly woman.

6. When she drove into the eastern courtyard, the seven children stood with tears in their eyes.

7. She gave no ale or mead to the children: "You'll get nothing but hunger and hate from me." . . .

9. She took from them the great [gross or large] wax candle, saying, "Now you shall lie in the murk all night!"

10. It was late in the night, and the children wept; their mother under the soil heard it. . . .

12. That wife was able to approach the Lord, and standing at his knee, she asked, "May I go and see my children?"

13. She entreated so sorely and she entreated so long that he at last gave her leave to go. . . .

16. When she got near to the dwelling, the dogs howled till the sky rang.

17. When she came to the eastern gate, her eldest daughter was standing there. . . .

19. "Truly you're a beautiful, fine woman, but you are no dear mother of mine."

20. "Och! how should I be fine or beautiful? My cheek is pale, and my lair is in the ground." . . .

23. When she came into the chamber, the tears ran down the children's cheeks. . . .

25. Then she said to her eldest daughter, "Go ask Child Dyring to come here to me."

26. When he came into the chamber, she spoke to him angrily:

27. "I left you plenty of ale and bread; my children are dying of hunger and want. . . .

29. "I left you so many a great wax candle; my children lie in the dark all night.

30. "When I start coming back often to visit thee, thy fate shall be full of woe, sorrow, and weariness." . . .

32. From that time, when they heard the dog snarl and bark, they gave the children bread and ale. . . .

34. From that time, when the little dog yowled with fear, they shook at the thought that the dead was near.

## *Pilgrims to Haworth*

In the 1850s, fans and tourists began to arrive in Haworth to sample the sights and souvenirs associated with Charlotte Brontë. When Patrick died in 1861, the new incumbent clergyman was more intent on expunging the Brontës than keeping the flame. This did not deter many devotees; by the 1890s, the visit to Haworth was a well-rehearsed rite. In many respects the tour follows the same script a century later, in spite of the effects of the automobile and the Internet.

### Matthew Arnold (1822–1888)

*Matthew Arnold, poet and critic, is perhaps best known today for a much-anthologized poem, "Dover Beach" (composed around 1851) and for his impact on academic literary criticism. He had visited Haworth in 1852 as government Inspector of Schools (appointed 1851; Chief Inspector in 1884). His elegy for Charlotte Brontë, who died March 31, 1855, mistakenly places the sisters in the churchyard (Anne Brontë was buried at Scarborough, and Emily and the others were buried in the church itself).[1] The first stanzas recall meeting Charlotte Brontë and Harriet Martineau at the home of Wordsworth's son-in-law, Edward Quillinan, in the Lake District in 1850 and praise the living Martineau. The speaker's focus on Charlotte, along with his awe for the ineffable Emily and his quiet tenderness for Anne, foretell the relative reputations of the sisters for decades to come. The Epilogue, however, seems to give Emily and* Wuthering Heights *the last word.*

[1]When Gaskell explained their actual burial site, Arnold wryly replied that it "put the finishing touch to . . . the fortunes of that ill-fated family that they should even be placed after death in the wrong, uncongenial spot" (June 1, 1855, letter cited in Allott and Allott, 422).

## from "Haworth Churchyard, April 1855" (1877)[2]

Where, behind Keighley, the road                                   55
Up to the heart of the moors
Between heath-clad showery hills
Runs, and colliers' carts
Poach[3] the deep ways coming down,
And a rough, grimed race have their homes              60
There on its slope is built
The moorland town. But the church
Stands on the crest of the hill,
Lonely and bleak; at its side
The parsonage-house and the graves.                       65

Strew with laurel the grave
Of the early-dying! Alas,
Early she goes on the path
To the silent country, and leaves
Half her laurels unwon,                                            70
Dying too soon! —yet green
Laurels she had, and a course
Short, but redoubled by fame.

And not friendless, and not
Only with strangers to meet,                                     75
Faces ungreeting and cold,
Thou, O mourned one, to-day
Enterest the house of the grave!
Those of thy blood, whom thou lov'dst,
Have preceded thee—young,                                    80
Loving, a sisterly band;
Some in art, some in gift
Inferior—all in fame.
They, like friends, shall receive

[2]First published in *Fraser's Magazine*, May 1855. Revised and reprinted in 1877. See Allott and Allott (422–30).

[3]Rare regional sense of *poach*, to thrust a foot, stick, or other object into something; to probe.

This comer, greet her with joy;                                    85
Welcome the sister, the friend;
Hear with delight of thy fame!

Round thee they lie—the grass
Blows from their graves to thy own!
She, whose genius, though not                                      90
Puissant like thine, was yet
Sweet and graceful;[4] and she
(How shall I sing her?) whose soul
Knew no fellow for might,
Passion, vehemence, grief,                                         95
Daring, since Byron died,
That world-famed son of fire—she, who sank
Baffled, unknown, self-consumed;
Whose too bold dying song
Stirred, like a clarion-blast, my soul.[5] . . .                  100

Sleep, O cluster of friends,
Sleep!—or only when May,
Brought by the west-wind, returns
Back to your native heaths,                                        115
And the plover is heard on the moors,
Yearly awake to behold
The opening summer, the sky,
The shining moorland—to hear
The drowsy bee, as of old,                                         120
Hum o'er the thyme, the grouse
Call from the heather in bloom!
Sleep, or only for this
Break your united repose!

[4]Anne Brontë, the sister whose gift *and* fame were inferior to Charlotte's (lines 80–83).

[5]In 1855, *stirred* was *shook,* and in 1881 Arnold restored it. In 1877, Arnold added a note: "See the last verses by Emily Brontë in *Poems by Currer, Ellis, and Acton Bell.*" Arnold refers to "No coward soul is mine" (see pp. 328–29), which actually first appeared in the 1850 edition of *Wuthering Heights*, with Charlotte's mistaken claim that it was Emily's last work. Eleven lines elegizing Branwell are omitted here.

Epilogue
So I sang; but the Muse,                                    125
Shaking her head, took the harp—
Stern interrupted my strain,
Angrily smote on the chords.

April showers
Rush o'er the Yorkshire moors.                              130
Stormy, through driving mist,
Loom the blurred hills; the rain
Lashes the newly-made grave.

Unquiet souls!
—In the dark fermentation of earth,                         135
In the never idle workshop of nature,
In the eternal movement,
Ye shall find yourselves again!

## Claude Meeker (1861–1929)

*Claude Meeker, a journalist from Ohio then serving as United States Consul in Bradford near Haworth, published "Haworth; Home of the Brontës" in a Cincinnati paper, and it was reprinted as Part II of the new* Transactions *of the Brontë Society in 1895. Meeker embeds accurate observation and some misconceptions within the flowery expressions of journalism and literary pilgrimage of the day. His article shows that Brontë worship at that time was spurred on by Americans and focused largely on Charlotte. When reprinted in the* Transactions, *it had fourteen illustrations, including portraits of the Brontës and some who knew them, Emily's drawing of Keeper, and images from the Black Bull Inn. "Birthplace of the Brontë Sisters. Thornton" is reproduced here.*

## from "Haworth; Home of the Brontës" (1895)

The fact that the Brontë country is not on the route of the tourists, is off the main line of travel, and almost free from the hurrying men with the red guide books,[1] may lend an additional interest to the

[1] Karl Baedeker's publishing house, founded in 1827, sold popular guidebooks—recognized by their red covers—for tourism around the world.

BIRTHPLACE OF THE BRONTË SISTERS. THORNTON.

Engraving by Arthur North [?], from Meeker, "Haworth; Home of the Brontës."

statement that a large sprinkling of the pilgrims to the Brontë shrine are Americans. . . . Americans have assisted Yorkshire and all England . . . to a more just appreciation of the Brontës and their works.

If the reader cares to see a picturesque and charming country and to enter into the romance and sentiment of the occasion, let him take an hour or two in midsummer and drive the ten or twelve miles. . . . The country is hilly or mountainous. . . . In the air there is the scent of new mown hay. . . . One can kill two birds with one stone by passing through Thornton. Here the Brontë sisters were born. . . . The birth-place dwelling still stands, but its glory has departed. The front room is now a butcher's shop. . . .

Though a spur of the Midland railway now connects Haworth to the outer world, it has not taken from it its indescribable charm of extreme rusticity. . . . New blood is seldom introduced to old Haworth. The advent of many factory operatives . . . [has] not robbed its people of their pristine Yorkshire vigor of speech, sturdiness of form and slowness of action. The river Worth . . . was a crystal beck in Charlotte Brontë's time. . . . Now it rushes past the railway station, its waters of an inky blackness from the refuse of mills and dyeworks, and with an odour of chemicals. . . . The church looms up . . . a beacon light leading you to the spot where the fated Brontë family lived, loved, sorrowed, and died. . . .

The history of the "Black Bull" seems interwoven with that of the village and church. . . . The present proprietor . . . remembers "old man Brontë" well. The people of the inn conduct visitors to the bar parlour . . . and there point out the chair in which Branwell Brontë used to sit. . . . It was in his own corner, with this chair as a throne, that Branwell Brontë, as oracle of the village, held forth. . . .

Only the tower of the Church now remains intact otherwise the church has been . . . rebuilt. . . . There is an American memorial to Charlotte Brontë in Haworth Church however. . . . The sexton's wife, who shows visitors through the church, stops before this window with a reverential expression . . . : "This window was presented by a rich American gentleman, on the condition that his name should never be known. . . ." [The late George W. Childs] the Philadelphia philanthropist accepted the responsibility. . . . His statue to Shakespeare at Stratford-on-Avon and the statue of Cowper at Westminster Abbey, have made his name known and honoured in England. . . .

Many wander through the churchyard groping among the old slabs searching for the tombs of Tabitha Aykroyd, who died in 1855, aged eighty-four, and Martha Brown, servants of the Brontë family, both of whom acquired reflected greatness. . . . One may wander out of the churchyard straight upon the moor. . . .

A mile or two out is a waterfall, a miniature Niagara, and here it was Charlotte would often come to enjoy sweet solitude and to think. . . .

Dr. Wright's work maintains that their power of narrative was inherited . . . from their story-telling grandfather, old Hugh Brontë, and that their marvellous tales are his vivid stories. . . . [A]n authority . . . advanced the proposition that the moorlands gave to the sisters' work the distinctive character. . . . Describing Charlotte's love for the moors Emily Brontë makes her say: "I dreamt once that I was in heaven, but it did not seem to be my home, and I broke my heart with weeping to come back . . . on the top of Wuthering Heights. . . ."[2]

None of the sisters seemed to thrive when away from her mountain home. Emily especially pined and drooped. . . . It will always remain a mystery how these girls, reared in a mountain hamlet, with a graveyard at the front door, with . . . barren moors on every side, with neighbours of the roughest type, cut off from most of the refinements of civilization . . . could write and speak and think as they did. . . .

I am not a hero nor heroine worshipper, but there were traits of character in this remarkable family of wild moor flowers calculated to attract the attention of any investigator. They were themselves like their favourite plant. The moor flower is short lived. . . . The Brontë society has been formed for the purpose of keeping alive the memory of these famous Yorkshire authoresses, to emulate their virtues and to encourage others. A museum will be established at Haworth, for which interesting relics have already been contributed. . . .

## Virginia Woolf (1882–1941)

*Virginia Woolf, one of the leading novelists of the twentieth century, grew up in London literary circles that had welcomed Charlotte Brontë during her brief fame. Woolf's father, Leslie Stephen, wrote the biography of Charlotte Brontë for the* Dictionary of National Biography *(1886); its publisher, George Smith, belonged to the house that had published Charlotte. Woolf wrote many essays and reviews, including* "Jane Eyre *and* Wuthering Heights" *(1916), which shows greater appreciation for Emily. The following short article, the first piece of Woolf's writing to be accepted, was published anonymously in* The Guardian *on December 21, 1904. Woolf still shares a Victorian preference for Charlotte over Emily.*

## "Haworth, November 1904" (1904)

I do not know whether pilgrimages to the shrines of famous men ought not to be condemned as sentimental journeys. . . . The curiosity

---

[2]Meeker mistakenly regards Catherine Earnshaw as a portrait of Charlotte Brontë.

is only legitimate when the house of a great writer or the country in which it is set adds something to our understanding of his books. This justification you have for a pilgrimage to the home and country of Charlotte Brontë and her sisters.

The *Life*, by Mrs Gaskell, gives you the impression that Haworth and the Brontës are somehow inextricably mixed. Haworth expresses the Brontës; the Brontës express Haworth. . . . How far surroundings radically affect people's minds, it is not for me to ask. . . . A real northern snowstorm had been doing the honours of the moors. It was rash to wait fine weather, and it was also cowardly. I understand that the sun very seldom shone on the Brontë family. . . . We certainly passed through a very cheerful land, which might be likened to a vast wedding cake, of which the icing was slightly undulating. . . .

Our excitement as we neared Haworth had in it an element of suspense that was really painful, as though we were to meet some long-separated friend, who might have changed in the interval—so clear an image of Haworth had we from print and picture. At a certain point we entered the valley, up both sides of which the village climbs, and right on the hill-top, looking down over its parish, we saw the famous oblong tower of the church. This marked the shrine at which we were to do homage.

. . . Haworth did certainly strike one not exactly as gloomy, but, what is worse for artistic purposes, as dingy and commonplace. . . . The museum is certainly rather a pallid and inanimate collection of objects. An effort ought to be made to keep things out of these mausoleums, but the choice often lies between them and destruction, so that we must be grateful for the care which has preserved much that is, under any circumstances, of deep interest. Here are many autograph letters, pencil drawings, and other documents. But the most touching case—so touching that one hardly feels reverent in one's gaze—is that which contains the little personal relics, the dresses and shoes of the dead woman. The natural fate of such things is to die before the body that wore them, and because these . . . have survived, Charlotte Brontë the woman comes to life, and one forgets the chiefly memorable fact that she was a great writer. Her shoes and her thin muslin dress have outlived her. One other object gives a thrill; the little oak stool which Emily carried with her on her solitary moorland tramps, and on which she sat, if not to write, as they say, to think what was probably better than her writing.

. . . [T]hat remarkable churchyard remains. The old edition of the *Life* had on its title-page a little print which struck the keynote of the book; it seemed to be all graves—gravestones stood ranked all round; you walked on a pavement lettered with dead names; the graves had solemnly invaded the garden of the parsonage itself, which was as a little oasis of life in the midst of the dead. This is no exaggeration of the artist's, as we found: the stones seem to start out of the ground at you in tall, upright lines, like an army of silent soldiers. . . . There is nothing remarkable in a mid-Victorian parsonage, though tenanted by genius, and the only room which awakens curiosity is the kitchen, now used as an ante-room, in which the girls tramped as they conceived their work.[1] One other spot has a certain grim interest—the oblong recess beside the staircase into which Emily drove her bulldog during the famous fight, and pinned him while she pommelled him. . . . It was due to the courtesy of the present incumbent that we were allowed to inspect it; in his place I should often feel inclined to exorcise the three famous ghosts.

## Shifting Literary Honors and the Beaten Track

By the 1920s, Emily Brontë had deposed her sister Charlotte as the supreme Brontë; she could be portrayed as the virgin oracle of austere truths, and the horrific scenes and harsh language of the novel were no longer so offensive. In 1927, Isabel C. Clarke (~1880–1951), a prolific Catholic novelist, had notable success with her novelized literary biographies, beginning with *Haworth Parsonage: A Picture of the Brontë Family* (1927). Inventing a love between Emily and curate William Weightman, Clarke rhapsodizes: "On visiting Haworth parsonage to-day, it is the frail and lovely ghost of Emily Brontë that haunts you." Clarke depicts family scenes.

> You see her going across to Branwell's room and extinguishing the flames of his burning bed with her frail pale hands. . . . you see her, spent with disease, toiling up the steep flight of stairs . . . , while her hollow cough echoes eerily. . . .
> And it is Emily . . . upon whom Fame would fain lay her brightest crown to-day. . . . She stands alone and apart,

[1]The Brontës paced back and forth as they worked on their novels in the dining room, not the kitchen. The "print" in the *Life* is Gaskell's (see p. 301).

not only above Charlotte and Anne, but above all her English sisters of the pen. . . . (286–87)

"Sisters of the pen" have necessarily gazed up at the Brontës as rare women to rank high in literary traditions. Emily Dickinson wrote several poems in tribute to the English women writers—"All overgrown by cunning moss" (148) ends "Oh what an afternoon for Heaven / When 'Brontë' entered there"—but Dickinson is thinking of Charlotte, the one whose fame made it across the Atlantic in her lifetime.[1] When Virginia Woolf made her pilgrimage to Haworth in 1904, Charlotte was the most haunting presence. But the later American poet Sylvia Plath (1932–63) perceived Haworth to be haunted primarily by Emily Brontë, as Clarke did in 1927. Plath's poem, simply titled "Wuthering Heights," envisions a pastoral nightmare, a threshold of the underworld. "There is no life higher than the grasstops / Or the hearts of sheep." Like Heathcliff's vengeance, "the wind / Pours by like destiny, bending / Everything in one direction." Ellis Bell's attraction to nature is deadly: "If I pay the roots of the heather / Too close attention, they will invite me / To whiten my bones among them."

Haworth graveyard readily suggests the "unquiet souls" of *Wuthering Heights*. Muriel Spark (1918–2006), a bestselling Scottish novelist, collected her writings on the Brontës, revealing a distinct preference for Emily and *Wuthering Heights*; one piece is called "My Favourite Villain: Heathcliff." She printed a transcript of a BBC TV recording, "At Emily Brontë's Grave, Haworth, April 1961."

> For many years I was intensely occupied by Emily Brontë— almost haunted. . . . It's as if she had consciously laid out the plot of her life in a play called *Emily Brontë*. . . . A fortnight ago when I went to Haworth, I seemed to fall under a spell. . . . Life, death and eternity—these are Emily's great themes, and the scene is set brooding here on her doorstep. . . . She often wrote of graves and tombstones. . . . I tried to take a short-cut among the tombs, but I got lost in a sea of stones . . . a bit frightening in an enjoyable sort of way." (314–15)

---

[1] Emily Dickinson asked to have Emily Brontë's poem, "No Coward Soul," read at her funeral (Hoeveler 306).

Since 1928, the Brontë Parsonage Museum has exhibited a more impressive collection than Virginia Woolf could have seen in 1904. The Black Bull is still enticing pilgrims, not far from the graveyard and the Villette Coffee House. A 1947 guidebook indicates that there was a Brontë Cinema in Victoria Road (Preston 7). Advertisements in a 1979 guidebook invite tourists to visit the Brontë Tapestries studio at Ponden Hall "(reputedly Thrushcross Grange . . .)"; to shop at the Brontë Tweed Mill Shop; "Make a meal of Brontë Country" at Haworth Old Hall; or revel in all the "Haunts of the Brontës" (Mitchell). Websites offer multiple gateways to Brontë Country; we list some prominent ones (see pp. 413–15).

Even as they all sought fame, the Brontës might well be turning over in their graves at this version of it. Arthur Bell Nicholls would be appalled, having sought to suppress Charlotte's correspondence and to discourage the Brontë mania. Even so, as Gaskell and Woolf suggest, to experience the environment of Haworth and the moors is to feel the pulse of *Wuthering Heights* and the other Brontë writings.

# Critical and Artful

The nineteenth-century reception of Emily Brontë's novel falls into two broad phases: initial recognition of raw power with uncertainty as to the author's identity or propriety, followed by the growing conviction that Emily Brontë was one of the transcendent geniuses of European literature and superior to Charlotte. With modernist rejection of Victorian culture and exploration of myth, the unconscious, and primitive desires, interest in *Wuthering Heights* flourished, although biographical focus on the author diminished. During the twentieth century, critical approaches to *Wuthering Heights* diversified, with renewed interest in Charlotte's as well as Emily's works since the post-1960s rise of both Victorian studies and feminist studies of women writers.[1]

Whatever the novel's shocking or profound spirit, it was first thought to be badly constructed with its multiple narrators and shifting times and tones. However, after C. P. Sanger's essay in 1926 and others that followed came a growing critical consensus that *Wuthering Heights* is one of the most ingeniously formed novels of all time, from the weather to the law. As much as any novel in the world, *Wuthering Heights* is a model of calibrated storytelling art, satisfying the student and theorist of narrative technique.

[1]See, e.g., Allott, *Critical Heritage*; Bloom, *Emily Brontë*; Brick; Ohmann; Peterson; Stoneman, *Wuthering Heights*; Vogler; Winnifrith, *Critical Essays*.

# Reviews of *Wuthering Heights,* 1848–1851

There were a dozen or more reviews or notices of the 1847 edition of *Wuthering Heights* and *Agnes Grey*. In 1850, Charlotte Brontë claimed, "Critics failed to do them justice" (p. 332). The standard view has been that *Wuthering Heights* was panned. The reviewer in *The New Monthly Magazine* (82 [January 1848]: 140) said Ellis Bell's novel should have been called "Withering Heights" as "the mind and body . . . instinctively shrink" from this "misanthropist's heaven." Yet a number of the reviews did recognize the author's powers. The criticisms influenced both the later writings of the Brontës and the way the surviving sister presented the public face of the novelists. By 1850 and 1851, critics were engaging with *Wuthering Heights* with respect and some awareness of the Bell family, but still with some confusion of the writers' identities; Charlotte corresponded with both George Henry Lewes and Sydney Dobell concerning their opinions.

Reviews and articles usually appeared anonymously or pseudonymously at this period, yet it was often possible to discover who wrote a review. Scholars have reconstructed the authors of most of the reviews of the Brontës' novels. The following reviews first appeared anonymously, other than Peck's, which was signed "G. W. P."

### Anonymous

*This review of the English edition published by Newby was among the clippings kept in Emily Brontë's desk. Douglas Jerrold (1803–57), dramatist and journalist, friend and father-in-law of Henry Mayhew (see pp. 341–43), edited this short-lived newspaper during 1846–48.*

from *Douglas Jerrold's Weekly Newspaper* 79 (Jan. 15, 1848): 77

**Wuthering Heights and Agnes Grey. By Ellis and Acton Bell.**

"Wuthering Heights" is a strange sort of book,—baffling all regular criticism; yet, it is impossible to begin and not finish it; and quite as impossible to lay it aside afterwards and say nothing about it. In the midst of the reader's perplexity the ideas predominant in his mind concerning this book are likely to be—brutal cruelty, and semi-savage love. What may be the moral which the author wishes the reader to deduce from his work, it is difficult to say. . . . There seems to us great power in this book but a purposeless power. . . . We are quite confident that the writer of "Wuthering Heights" wants but the practised skill to make a great artist; perhaps, a great dramatic artist. His qualities are, at present, excessive; a far more promising fault, let it be remembered, than if they were deficient. He may tone down, whereas the weak and inefficient writer, however carefully he may write by rule and line, will never work up his productions to the point of beauty in art. In "Wuthering Heights," the reader is shocked, disgusted, almost sickened by details of cruelty, inhumanity, and the most diabolical hate and vengeance, and anon come passages of powerful testimony to the supreme power of love—even over demons in the human form. The women in the book are of a strange fiendish-angelic nature, tantalizing, and terrible, and the men are indescribable out of the book itself. . . .

We strongly recommend all our readers who love novelty to get this story, for we can promise them that they never have read anything like it before. . . . [W]e must leave it to our readers to decide what sort of a book it is.

### Anonymous

*Like the previous review, this one of Newby's first edition of* Wuthering Heights *and* Agnes Grey *was saved in Emily's writing desk. The* Atlas *was a weekly journal of news and literature published in London from 1826 to 1862. It begins with speculation on the number and gender of the author(s) Currer, Acton, and Ellis Bell.*

### from *Atlas* (January 22, 1848): 59

*Wuthering Heights* is a strange, inartistic story. There are evidences in every chapter of a sort of rugged power—an unconscious strength. . . . The general effect is inexpressibly painful. We know of nothing in the whole range of our fictitious literature which presents such shocking pictures of the worst forms of humanity. . . . It . . . is a *sprawling* story, . . . though one presiding evil genius sheds a grim shadow over the whole. . . .

The book sadly wants relief. A few glimpses of sunshine would have increased the reality of the picture. . . . There is not in the entire *dramatis personae* a single character which is not utterly hateful or thoroughly contemptible. . . . Even the female characters excite something of loathing and much of contempt. Beautiful and loveable in their childhood, they all . . . "turn out badly." . . .

[An excerpt follows of Catherine's dying scene with Heathcliff; see pp. 143–46.]

This is at least forcible writing; but, to estimate it aright, the reader must . . . not fancy himself in a London mansion; but . . . far from the haunts of civilised men. . . .

*Jane Eyre* and *Wuthering Heights* are not things to be forgotten. The work of Currer Bell is a great performance; that of Ellis Bell is only a promise, but it is a colossal one.

## G. W. Peck (1817–1859)

*George Washington Peck, an American critic and one-time law clerk, wrote frequently for* The American Review. *This Whig New York monthly strove to establish itself as a national review of politics and literature, 1844–52. The reviewer's censure of Brontë's coarseness fits with what little is known of Peck, who savaged the novels of Herman Melville (author of* Moby-Dick*) and drank himself to an early death.*

### from *The American Review* 7:6 (June 1848): 572–86

### from "Wuthering Heights"

The book is original; it is powerful; full of suggestiveness. But still it is *coarse.* . . . The whole tone of the style of the book smacks of lowness. It would indicate that the writer was not accustomed to the society of gentlemen, and was not afraid, indeed, rather gloried, in showing it. . . . A person may be unmannered from want of delicacy of perception, or cultivation, or ill-mannered intentionally. The author of Wuthering Heights is both. . . .

It is evident that the author has suffered, not disappointment in love, but some great mortification of pride. Possibly his position in society has given him manners that have prevented him from associating with those among whom he feels he has intellect enough to be classed, and he is thus in reality the misanthropist he claims to be. Very likely he may be a young person who has spent his life, until within a few years, in some isolated town in the North of England. . . .

The influence which this book cannot but have upon manners, must be bad. For the coarseness extends farther than the mere style; it extends *all through*; and the crude style and rude expressions are too much in keeping with the necessary situations. It deals constantly in exaggerated extremes of passion. . . .

Could Mrs. Linton, after Heathcliff's return, desire his presence without being conscious that her feelings towards him were such as his presence would only render more intolerable, unless, as the author leaves us no room to suppose, she meant to be untrue to her husband? . . . There is in these characters an absence of all that natural desire which should accompany love. They are abstract and bodiless. Their love is feline; it is tigerish. . . .

Yet with all this faultiness, Wuthering Heights is, undoubtedly, a work of many singular merits. In the first place it is not a novel which deals with the shows of society, the surfaces and conventionalities of life. . . . It lifts the veil and shows boldly the dark side of our depraved nature. . . . It goes into the under-current of passion, and the rapid hold it has taken of the public shows how much truth there is hidden under its coarse extravagance. . . .

Nothing like it has ever been written before; it is to be hoped that in respect of its faults, for the sake of good manners, nothing will be hereafter. Let it stand by itself, a coarse, original, powerful book,—one that does not give us true characters, but horridly striking and effective ones. It will live a short and brilliant life, and then die and be forgotten. . . . Poor Cathy's ghost will not walk the earth forever; and the insane Heathcliff will soon rest quietly in his coveted repose.

## E. P. Whipple (1819–1886)

The North American Review, *begun in Boston in 1815 to rival the British literary quarterlies, is the oldest literary journal in the United States; after a hiatus, it continues today. Edwin Percy Whipple is known today as an arbiter of classic American literature. Edgar Allan Poe deemed Whipple to be possibly the best American critic but reproached him for his low estimation of* Jane Eyre. *This review signals that the Bells were taken very seriously in the 1848 season, but it labels "Acton Bell" the author of* Wuthering Heights *and in turn of* Jane Eyre.

### from *North American Review* 67 (October 1848): 354–70

### from "Novels of the Season"

Not many months ago, the New England States were visited by a distressing mental epidemic, passing under the name of the "Jane Eyre fever." . . .

. . . [T]he publishers of *Jane Eyre* announced *Wuthering Heights*, by the same author. When it came, it was purchased and read with universal eagerness; but, alas! it created disappointment almost as universal. It was a panacea for all the sufferers under the epidemic. . . .

The family mind is strikingly peculiar, giving a strong impression of unity, but it is still male and female. From the masculine tone of *Jane Eyre*, it might pass altogether as the composition of a man, were it not for some unconscious feminine peculiarities, . . . [In *Jane Eyre*] there are also scenes of passion, so hot, emphatic, and condensed in expression, and so sternly masculine in feeling, that we are almost sure we observe the mind of the author of *Wuthering Heights* at work. . . .

The truth is, that the whole firm of Bell & Co. seem to have a sense of the depravity of human nature peculiarly their own. . . .

Acton Bell [is] the author of *Wuthering Heights, The Tenant of Wildfell Hall*, and, if we mistake not, of certain offensive but powerful portions of *Jane Eyre*. Acton, when left altogether to his own imaginations, seems to take a morose satisfaction in developing a full and complete science of human brutality. In *Wuthering Heights* he has succeeded in reaching the summit of this laudable ambition.... Heathcote [*sic*] ... is a deformed monster.... [Acton Bell's] attempt at originality does not stop with the conception of Heathcote, but he aims further to exhibit the action of the sentiment of love on the nature of the being whom his morbid imagination has created. This is by far the ablest and most subtle portion of his labors, and indicates that strong hold upon the elements of character, and that decision of . . . delineation of . . . emotion, which distinguish the mind of the whole family. For all practical purposes, however, the power evinced in *Wuthering Heights* is power thrown away. Nightmares and dreams, through which devils dance and wolves howl, make bad novels. . . .

### George Henry Lewes (1817–1878)

*George Henry Lewes, English author and critic, is best known today as the partner of the novelist George Eliot (Marian Evans). He wrote in a range of genres, from biography to psychology and biology. Lewes contributed a positive review of* Jane Eyre *to Fraser's in 1847, and he corresponded with Charlotte Brontë as she wrote her second and third novels. He and Thornton Leigh Hunt founded the Radical weekly* The Leader *in 1850; Lewes was editor until 1854. This review concerns the 1850 edition with Charlotte's "Biographical Notice."*

### from *The Leader* 1 (December 28, 1850): 953

Critics, we are told, failed to do them justice. But to judge from the extracts given of articles in the *Britannia* and *Atlas*,[1] the critics were excessively indulgent, and we take it the public was most recalcitrant, and would *not* be amused with these strange wild pictures . . . , though painted with unmistakeable power. . . .

Curious enough it is to read *Wuthering Heights* and *The Tenant of Wildfell Hall*, and remember that the writers were two retiring, solitary, consumptive girls! Books, coarse even for men . . . turn out to be the productions of two girls . . . filling their loneliness with quiet studies, and writing these books from a sense of duty. . . .

[1]Unsigned review, *Britannia* (January 15, 1848): 42–43; review in *Atlas*, presented on p. 400. Both were among the five reviews that Emily saved as clippings.

The power, indeed, is wonderful. Heathcliff, devil though he may be, is drawn with a sort of dusky splendour which fascinates, and we feel the truth of his burning and impassioned love for Catherine, and of her inextinguishable love for him. It was a happy thought to make her love the kind, weak, elegant Edgar, and yet without lessening her passion for Heathcliff. . . . although she is ashamed of her early playmate she loves him with a passionate abandonment which sets culture, education, the world, at defiance. It is in the treatment of this subject that Ellis Bell shows real mastery, and it shows more genius, in the highest sense of the word, than you will find in a thousand novels. . . .

## Sydney Dobell (1824–1874)

*The critic Sydney Dobell published an article, "Currer Bell," in* Palladium *(September 1850): 161–75, declaring "Currer Bell is a woman," and deeming* Wuthering Heights *an earlier and "ruder" work by Currer. Charlotte wrote to thank Dobell for his "late justice" to Emily and sent him a copy of the 1850 edition of* Wuthering Heights *and* Agnes Grey *with the "Biographical Notice" that clearly distinguishes the three novelists. Dobell reviewed that edition in* Eclectic Review, *a London monthly of indeed eclectic educational, missionary, and reforming aims published from 1805 to 1868.*

### from *Eclectic Review* 1 (February 1, 1851): 222–27

We purpose dealing rather with the Biographical Notice prefixed to this volume, . . . whereas the *Fictions* it prefaces are already somewhat known to the public. Not that we shall wholly omit to record our judgment, more particularly on "Wuthering Heights"; . . .

It appears to us impossible to read [*Jane Eyre* and *Shirley*] without feeling that their excellences and faults . . . all betoken the authorship of a lady. In their perusal, we are in the company of an intelligent, free-spoken, and hearty woman, who feels deeply, can describe with power, has seen some of the rougher sides of life. . . .

That either of the works now before us should be attributed to the same writer as "Jane Eyre" and "Shirley," is one of the strangest blunders of criticism with which we ever met. . . . But we may now dispense with conjecture, for one of the sisterhood has kindly withdrawn the curtain, and invited us to look upon the *terra incognita* about which we have been contending. . . .

"Jane Eyre" was instantaneously popular; but not so the productions of Ellis and Acton Bell. We are not surprised at this. The successful work was attractive as well as talented, while "Wuthering Heights"—we know little of "Agnes Grey"—is one of the most repellent books we ever read. With all its talent—and it has much—we cannot imagine its being read through from any fascination in the tale itself. The powers it displays are not only premature, but are misdirected. . . .

As the characters of the tale are unattractive, so the chief incidents are sadly wanting in probability. . . . and have, therefore, but little more power to move our sympathies than the romances of the middle ages, or the ghost stories which made our granddames tremble.

# Early Criticism

The Brontës rose to prominence during a period of expanding literary journalism, amateur literary collecting and author worship, and nascent professional scholarship. The puzzle of Emily Brontë—"the sphynx of literature," as Angus MacKay calls her—was particularly rich material. New magazines such as *The Bookman* published volleys between critics and biographers. Theories abounded, such as that Branwell wrote *Wuthering Heights* or was the model for Heathcliff. Sources were ferreted out and proclaimed. The hundred years after Emily Brontë's death were a heyday of biographical criticism, and at first Charlotte was supreme. The legend of Emily Brontë, regarded as comparable to Shakespeare or Milton, was shaped at the end of the nineteenth century.

### Algernon Charles Swinburne (1837–1909)

*Although Algernon Charles Swinburne's life spanned the Victorian period, as poet and critic he was often scandalously at odds with the age. He was close to the Pre-Raphaelite painters and poets, and in the 1870s and 1880s was one of the very few to praise* Wuthering Heights *and to esteem Emily Brontë as superior to Charlotte and comparable to Shakespeare. This poetic reading of the novel was a review (*Athenaeum *[June 16, 1883]; reprinted in* Miscellanies *[1886, 269–70]) of the first biography of Emily Brontë, by the venturesome poet Mary Robinson (1883). Swinburne responds to Robinson's presentation of Emily's sympathy and support for Branwell.*

## from "Emily Brontë" (1883)

From the first we breathe the fresh dark air of tragic passion and presage; and to the last the changing wind and flying sunlight are in keeping with the stormy promise. . . . There is no monotony, there is no repetition, but there is no discord. This is the first and last necessity . . . for a poem worthy of the name; and this it is that distinguishes the hand of Emily from the hand of Charlotte Brontë. . . . The sweet and noble genius of Mrs Gaskell did not enable her to see far into so strange and sublime a problem [Emily's character]; but . . . Miss Robinson has been interested and attracted where Mrs Gaskell was scared and perplexed. . . .

Those who believe that Heathcliff was called into existence by the accident that his creator had witnessed the agonies of a violent weakling in love and in disgrace might believe that Shakespeare wrote *King Lear* because he had witnessed the bad effects of parental indulgence. . . .

Twice or thrice especially the details of deliberate or passionate brutality in Heathcliff's treatment of his victims make the reader feel for a moment as though he were reading a police report. . . . But the pervading atmosphere of the book is so high and healthy. . . . The love which devours life itself, which devastates the present and desolates the future with unquenchable and raging fire, has nothing less pure in it than flame or sunlight. . . . As was the author's life, so is her book in all things: troubled and taintless. . . . It may be true that not many will ever take it to their hearts: it is certain that those who do like it will like nothing very much better in the whole world of poetry or prose.

## Angus M. MacKay (~1853–1907)

*Far from well known today, Rev. Angus M. MacKay "was Rector of Holy Trinity Church, Dean Bridge, Edinburgh, when he died, aged*

*54, on New Year's Day, 1907," according to Clement Shorter.[1] He is
the author of* The Churchman's Introduction to the Old Testament
*(1901), along with other publications on faith and two books of
poetry. His point-by-point refutation of William Wright appeared in
1895 as an article in the* Westminster Review, *a respected liberal
quarterly. Part II of the book, "A Crop of Brontë Myths," shreds
Wright's claim that "the plot of* Wuthering Heights *was founded on
family history, and that the other Brontë novels had likewise an Irish
origin." The "applause" for Wright's book suggests that the "literary
world" has gone mad.*

## from *The Brontës: Fact and Fiction* (1897)

### from I. Fresh Light on Brontë Biography

The recent publication of Mr. [Clement] Shorter's admirable work,
*Charlotte Brontë and her Circle* [1896], has quickened the interest
which is everywhere felt in Brontë biography. . . . The doings and
sufferings of the shy, depressed, awkward girls at the bare parsonage or in the fashionable Pensionnat will continue to have a strange
attraction for all students of literary genius. . . .

The author of *Wuthering Heights* still remains, what she has
ever been, the sphinx of literature. . . . The mystery enshrouding
her is, indeed, partially accounted for when we learn how
almost absolutely impenetrable was the reserve in which this
lonely soul clothed herself. . . . Emily was one of those self-
centred natures which "will not abide our question."[2] As her
genius was "rare" in the felicitous sense in which that word is
applied to Ben Jonson.[3] . . . [i]t might be said of her, almost more
truly than of Milton:

[1]Shorter, *Immortal Memories* (1907); www.gutenberg.org/files/21869/21869-h/21869-
h.htm#footnote31 (accessed September 1, 2007). See the London *Times* obituary
(Friday, January 4, 1907; p. 1; issue 38221; col A).

[2]Matthew Arnold's sonnet, "Shakespeare" (1849), begins: "Others abide our question. Thou art free. / We ask and ask—Thou smilest and art still, / Out-topping
knowledge." Arnold compares Shakespeare to a mountain; mortals can't see its summit above the clouds.

[3]Ben Jonson (1572–1637), playwright, is buried in Westminster Abbey with a stone
inscribed "O Rare Ben Jonson."

"Her soul was like a star, and dwelt apart."[4]

Her genius may be compared to a mountain peak, whose bold contour compels attention yet forbids approach. . . . To this proud isolation of spirit is partly due the strong originality which places her in a rank above her sister, and explains why those who have appreciated her—from Sydney Dobell to Mr. Swinburne—have been fit, if few. . . .

## Mary A. Ward [Mrs. Humphry Ward] (1851–1920)

*Mary Augusta Ward, niece of Matthew Arnold, was a successful novelist, one of the most eminent British women of letters in her day. She pioneered serious consideration of the Brontës' literary influences and their relation to European culture. Ward notes "technical faultiness" and "romantic inequalities" of the novels, more in Emily's than Charlotte's, yet "Emily's genius was the greater of the two."*

## from "Introduction," *Wuthering Heights*, Haworth Edition (1900)

While for an earlier generation of critics, "Wuthering Heights" was, as a rule, matter for denunciation . . . it was again a poet [after Matthew Arnold]—Sydney Dobell in the "Palladium"—who, almost alone, had the courage to understand. . . .

Those among us of a later generation . . . can well remember that while Charlotte Brontë was a name of magic . . . "Wuthering Heights," if we read it at all, was read in hate, and with a prior sense of repulsion. . . .

But for us, fifty years later, . . . "Wuthering Heights" lives as great imagination, of which we must take . . . the bad with the good. . . . It holds a typical[1] and representative place in the English literature of the century. . . .

---

[4]William Wordsworth's sonnet "Milton" (1802) calls on the creator of *Paradise Lost* to restore England's self-sustaining "inward happiness": "Thy soul was like a star, and dwelt apart." John Milton (1608–74) begins Book VII of *Paradise Lost* on the theme of the poet's isolation and need for inspiration in "evil days" and asks his Muse to bring him discerning readers: "Still govern thou my song, / Urania, and fit audience find, though few" (ll. 26, 30–31).

---

[1]As an epitome or prototype (not commonplace).

Emily Brontë, like her sister, inherited Celtic blood, together with a stern and stoical tradition of daily life. She was a wayward, imaginative girl, physically delicate, brought up in loneliness and poverty, amid a harsh yet noble landscape of hill, moor and stream. . . . It was, indeed, by the reading of "Blackwood" in its days of most influence and vigour, and later, of "Fraser" . . . that the Brontë household was mainly kept in touch with the current literature, the criticism, poetry, and fiction. . . . So much for the influences of youth. There can be no question that they were "romantic" influences, and it can easily be shown that among them were many kindling sparks . . . of German poetry and fiction. . . .

In 1842 she and Charlotte journeyed to Brussels. . . . While Charlotte . . . was carried . . . into that profounder appreciation of the French Romantic spirit and method . . . Emily set herself against Brussels, against M. Héger, and against the French models. . . . She read a good deal of German fiction, and especially Hoffmann's tales.[2] . . .

Emily is pure mind and passion; . . . no one . . . can guess at the small likes and dislikes . . . of the artist who wrote it. She has the highest power—which was typically Shakespeare's power . . . — the power which gives life, intensest life, to the creatures of the imagination. . . .

As to the "exaltation of the Self," its claims, sensibilities and passions, in defiance of all social law and duty, there is no more vivid expression of it throughout Romantic literature than is contained in the conversation between the elder Catherine and Nelly Dean before Catherine marries Edgar Linton. And the violent, clashing egotisms of Heathcliff and Catherine . . . before Catherine's death, are as it were an epitome of . . . a whole phase of European feeling. . . .

## May Sinclair (1863–1946)

*Prominent British feminist and student of psychology, Greek, and philosophy, Mary (May) Amelia St Clair Sinclair published novels well received in Britain and the United States. Her work on the Brontës*

[2]E. T. A. Hoffmann (1776–1822), German Romantic author renowned for his tales of horror and the uncanny.

*yielded introductions to the Everyman Library editions (1907–14); her own novel,* The Three Sisters *(1914); and* The Three Brontës. *Sinclair celebrates Emily as a pagan mystic transcending civilized artifice, the major influence on Charlotte. Sinclair also adds momentum to the study of the Gondal cycle.*

## from *The Three Brontës* (1912)

*Wuthering Heights* was the fruit of a divine freedom. . . . It is not possible that Charlotte, of all people, should have read *Wuthering Heights* without a shock of enlightenment; that she should not have compared it with her own bloodless work; . . . Emily had dared to be herself; *she* had not been afraid of her own passion; . . . And Charlotte, I think, said to herself, "That is what I ought to have done." . . . These three Brontës, adoring each other, were intolerant of any other influence; and the strongest spirit, which was Emily's, prevailed. . . .

Around the figure of Emily Brontë there is none of that clamour and confusion [that surround Charlotte]. She stands apart in an enduring silence, and guards for ever her secret and her mystery. . . . And yet, . . . we see Emily Brontë more clearly than we can ever hope to see Charlotte now. . . . You see her tall and slender, in her rough clothes, tramping the moors with the form and the step of a virile adolescent. . . . You see her head carried high and crowned with its long, dark hair, coiled simply, caught up with a comb. You see her face, honey-pale, her slightly high, slightly aquiline nose; her beautiful eyes, dark-grey, luminous; . . . one moment alert, intent, and the next, inaccessibly remote. . . .

. . . No secret thing belonging to this disastrous family is sacred. . . . Some awful worshipper of Emily Brontë, . . . who will some day make up some story of some love-affair, some passion kindred to Catherine Earnshaw's. . . .

. . . Life . . . treated her worse than it treated Charlotte. She had none of the things that, after all, Charlotte had; neither praise nor fame in her lifetime; nor friendship, nor love, nor vision of love. . . . You cannot surprise her in any piteous gesture of desire or regret. . . . Charlotte's was not by any means "a chainless soul." . . .

I am reminded that one event she neither accepted nor endured. She fought death. Her spirit lifted the pathetic, febrile struggle of weakness with corruption, and turned it to a splendid, Titanic, and unearthly combat.

And yet it was in her life rather than her death that she was splendid. There is something shocking and repellent in her last defiance. It shrieks discord with the endurance and acceptance . . . that was the secret of her genius and of her life. . . .

[*Wuthering Heights*] belongs to no school; it follows no tendency. . . . It is not "Realism," it is not "Romance." . . . There is nothing in it you can seize and name. You will not find in it support for any creed or theory. . . . Emily Brontë . . . reveals a point of view above good and evil. Hers is an attitude of tolerance . . . too lucid and too high for pity. . . .

## Virginia Woolf (1882–1941)

*The London literary circles of novelist and critic Virginia Woolf descended from some who knew Charlotte Brontë in her period of fame: William Makepeace Thackeray; the Brontë publisher George Smith; the Arnold family. Woolf absorbs the views of Mary Ward, May Sinclair, and others who exalted Emily's austere genius over Charlotte's mature social engagement. This piece, suggesting Woolf's own literary aspirations as a novelist, appeared first as an article in the London* Times Literary Supplement *on April 13, 1916.*

### from "*Jane Eyre* and *Wuthering Heights*" (1916)

[B]oth Emily and Charlotte are always invoking the help of nature. They both feel the need of some more powerful symbol of the vast and slumbering passions. . . . Their storms, their moors, their lovely spaces of summer weather are not ornaments applied to decorate a dull page or display the writer's powers of observation—they carry on the emotion and light up the meaning of the book.

The meaning of a book, which lies so often apart from what happens and what is said . . . is necessarily hard to grasp. Especially this is so when, like the Brontës, the writer is poetic. . . . *Wuthering Heights* is a more difficult book to understand than *Jane Eyre*, because Emily was a greater poet than Charlotte. . . . [T]here is no "I" in *Wuthering Heights*. . . . The impulse which urged [Emily] to create was not her own suffering. . . . She looked out upon a world cleft into gigantic disorder and felt within her the power to unite it in a book. That gigantic ambition is to be felt throughout the novel. . . . It is this suggestion of power underlying the apparitions of human nature and lifting them up into the presence of greatness that gives the book its huge stature among other novels. But it was not enough for Emily Brontë to write a few lyrics, to utter a cry, to express a creed. In her poems she did this once and for all, and her poems will perhaps outlast her novel. But she was novelist as well as poet. She must take upon herself a more laborious and a more ungrateful task. She must face the fact of other existences, grapple with the mechanism of external things, build up, in recognisable shape, farms and houses and report the speeches of men and women who existed independently of herself. . . . The life at the farm with all its absurdities and its improbability is laid open to us. We are given every opportunity of comparing Wuthering Heights with a real farm. . . . Heathcliff . . . is impossible we say, but nevertheless no boy in literature has a more vivid existence than his. So it is with the two Catherines; never could women feel as they do or act in their manner, we say. All the same, they are the most lovable women in English fiction. . . . Hers, then, is the rarest of all powers. She could free life from its dependence on facts; with a few touches indicate the spirit of a face so that it needs no body; by speaking of the moor make the wind blow and the thunder roar.

# Sites and Resources on the Brontës

## *Exhibits*

### *Brontë Homeland Interpretive Centre*

Talks and tours in County Down, Ireland, along Brontë Homeland Drive; includes Patrick's birthplace.

Websites:
www.discovernorthernireland.com/product.aspx?ProductID=2857
and www.banbridge.gov.uk

Address: Church Hill Road, Drumballyroney, Rathfriland, County Down, Northern Ireland, BT32 5LX

Email: tic@banbridge.gov.uk • Phone: (028) 4062 3322

*Brontë Parsonage Museum and Brontë Society*

Scholars' library; daily self-guided tours of parsonage and museum; exhibits, workshops, and lectures; museum shop.

Websites: www.bronte.org.uk and www.bronte.info

Address: Haworth, Keighley, West Yorkshire, BD22 8DR, UK

Email: info@bronte.org.uk • Phone: 01535 642323

*The Brontë Way*

A 43-mile footpath from Oakwell Hall to Gawthorpe Hall.

Website: www.bronte-country.com/bronte-way.html

The Brontë Birthplace

Websites: www.brontebirthplace.org.uk/html/visit.htm and www.haworth-village.org.uk/brontes/thornton/thornton.asp

Address: 72/74 Market Street, Thornton, Bradford, BD13 3HF, West Yorkshire

Note: The site was put up for auction June 25, 2007. It reputedly sold to a London investor for £180,000.

Haworth Village

Websites: http://haworth.yorks.com/ and www.haworth-village.org.uk/brontes/

Ponden Hall (associated with Thrushcross Grange)

Website: www.pondenhall.co.uk/

*Westminster Abbey*

Poets' Corner features a memorial to the Brontë sisters.

Website: www.westminster-abbey.org/

Address: The Chapter Office, 20 Dean's Yard, London, SW1P 3PA, UK

Email: info@westminster-abbey.org • Phone: +44 (0) 20 7222 5152

## Selected Websites

Barker, Juliet. "Brontë, Emily Jane (1818–1848)." In *Oxford Dictionary of National Biography*. Oxford University Press, 2004. www.oxforddnb.com/view/article/3524.

Birmingham, Meredith. "The Bronte Family." December 16, 2006. www.brontefamily.org/.

"The Brontës of Haworth." www.thebrontes.com/.

Falk, Cecilia. "The Brontë Sisters." February 20, 2006. www2.sbbs.se/hp/cfalk/bronteng.htm.

Leary, Patrick. Victorian Research Web. October 2006. www./victorianresearch.org/.

————. VICTORIA: The Electronic Conference for Victorian Studies. [Archived discussion list.] 1993–2007. http://victorianresearch.org/discussion.html#vic.

Matsuoka, Mitsuharu. The Bronte Sisters Web. July 28, 2006. www.lang.nagoya-u.ac.jp/~matsuoka/Bronte.html.

————. "A Hyper-concordance to the Works of the Brontë Sisters." The Victorian Literary Studies Archive. July 6, 2004. http://victorian.lang.nagoya-u.ac.jp/concordance/bronte/.

The Victorian Web: Literature, History, and Culture in the Age of Victoria. University Scholars Program. "Emily Brontë (1818–48): An Overview." November 25, 2004. www.victorianweb.org/authors/bronte/ebronte/ ebronteov.html.

# Adaptations and Translations

## Performances

### Operas

Floyd, Carlisle. *Wuthering Heights*. Santa Fe Opera. 1958.

Hermann, Bernard.[1] *Wuthering Heights*. 1951. First staged: Portland Opera, 1982.

---

[1]Hermann (1911–75) was an Academy Award–winning film composer (*Citizen Kane*; *Psycho*) and wrote the score for *Jane Eyre* (dir. Robert Stevenson, with Orson Welles and Joan Fontaine, 1944).

## Ballets

Belarbi, Kader, chor. *Wuthering Heights*. Comp. Philippe Hersant. Paris Opera Ballet, 2002; 2005.

Kalleghan, Jane, chor. *Wuthering Heights*. Comp. Kate Bush. Cork City Ballet Company, 2007.

Nixon, David, chor. *Wuthering Heights*. Comp. Claude-Michel Schönberg. Northern Ballet Theatre (UK), 2002; Sadler's Wells, London, 2003.[2]

Weir, Natalie, chor. *Wuthering Heights*. Queensland Ballet, Brisbane, Australia, 2006.

## Stage Plays

Boyd, John, adapt. *Wuthering Heights*. Lyric Theatre, Belfast, Ireland, 1988.

Clifford, Jane, adapt. *Wuthering Heights*. Dir. Sue Dunderdale. York Theatre Royal, June 2–23, 2007.

Fenoglio, Beppe. *La Voca Nella Tempesta*. Einaudi, Turin, Italy, 1974.

Gaskill, William, adapt. and dir. *Wuthering Heights*. Royal Academy of Dramatic Arts, London, 2006.

Johanson, Robert. *Wuthering Heights: A Play*. Paper Mill Playhouse, Millburn, New Jersey, 1999. Woodstock: Dramatic Pub., 2000.

McCaffery, Michael, adapt. and dir. *Wuthering Heights*. Theatre Royal, London, 2006.

Thornton, Jane, adapt. *Wuthering Heights*. Dir. Mark Oldknow. Tight Fit Theatre, Wycombe, Buckinghamshire, England, 2006.

Vance, Charles, adapt. *Wuthering Heights*. London: French, 1990 [published]. Dir. Liz Bradley. Free Rain Theatre, Canberra, Australia, 2006. Dir. Sacha Walker. Woodhouse Players, London, 2006.

## Music Theatre

Dick, Paul, comp. *Wuthering Heights: A Romantic Musical*. Theatre Five, New York, 2006.

---

[2]See www.northernballettheatre.co.uk/wutheringheights.html.

Taylor, Bernard J., comp. *Wuthering Heights*. [Recorded 1992; first performed 1994.]

**Radio Plays**

Eckhardt, Agnes, adapt. "*Wuthering Heights*." *NBC University of the Air World's Great Novels*. 4 episodes. NBC. January 2–23, 1948. Phyllis Merrill Papers, New York Public Library, box 37, folder 1.

MacArthur, Charles, adapt. *Wuthering Heights*. Textron Theatre. CBS. 1945. Wladimir Selinsky Scripts, New York Public Library, box 1, folder 13.

**Sound Recordings**

Bush, Kate. "Wuthering Heights." Song. *The Kick Inside*. Rhapsody, 1978.

———. "Wuthering Heights." Music video. Dir. Keef [dir. Keith Macmillan, prod. John Weaver], 1978. [A remake is also widely available on the Internet.]

*Eternally Free: Brontë Poetry Set to Music*. Philip Henderson, comp. Readings by Geraldine Robertson-Brown. Gumption. "The Arts." 2005. www.useyourgumption.com/arts.htm.

*Wuthering Heights*. Abridged audiocassette. Cond. and comp. by Don Heckman. Perf. Claire Bloom and James Mason. Caedmon, 1978.

## *Film/Television Adaptations*

Bramble, A. V., dir. *Wuthering Heights*. Perf. Ann Trevor and Milton Rosmer. Ideal, 1920.

Buñuel, Luis, dir. *Wuthering Heights* [*Abismos de Pasión*]. Perf. Irasema Dilián and Jorge Mistral. Plexus, 1954.

Cartier, Rudolph, dir. *BBC Sunday Night Theatre: Wuthering Heights*. Perf. Richard Todd and Yvonne Mitchell. BBC, 1953.

———, dir. *Wuthering Heights*. Perf. Keith Michell and Claire Bloom. BBC, 1962.

Fuest, Robert, dir. *Wuthering Heights*. Perf. Anna Calder-Marshal and Timothy Dalton. AIP, 1970.

Hammond, Peter, dir. *Wuthering Heights*. Perf. Kay Adshead and Ken Hutchison. BBC, 1978.

Jacoby, Lois, adapt. *Wuthering Heights*. Dir. Paul Nickell. Perf. Charlton Heston. Studio One. CBS, 1950. Matinee Theatre. NBC, 1957. [Scripts, designs in Studio One Production Files of Worthington Miner, New York Public Library, box 19, folders 1, 4.]

Kosminsky, Peter, dir. *Emily Brontë's Wuthering Heights*. Perf. Juliette Binoche and Ralph Fiennes. Paramount, 1992.

Krishnamma, Suri, dir. *Wuthering Heights, CA*. Perf. Erika Christensen and Mike Vogel. MTV, 2003.

O'Ferrall, George More, dir. *Wuthering Heights*. Perf. Katharine Blake and Kieron Moore. BBC, 1948.

Rivette, Jacques, dir. *Wuthering Heights* [*Hurlevent*]. Perf. Fabienne Babe and Lucas Belvaux. AMLF, 1985.

Sasdy, Peter, dir. *Wuthering Heights*. Perf. Ian McShane and Angela Scoular. BBC, 1967.

"The Semaphore Version of 'Wuthering Heights.'" Perf. Michael Palin. *Monty Python's Flying Circus*. BBC, 1971.

Siguion-Reyna, Carlos. *Hihintayin Kita Sa Langit*. Perf. Richard Gomez and Dawn Zulueta. Reynafilms, 1991. [Remade: Tuviera, Mike. *The Promise*. Perf. Richard Gutierrez and Angel Locsin. GMA, 2007.]

Skynner, David, dir. *Wuthering Heights*. Perf. Orla Brady and Robert Cavanah. Masterpiece Theatre, 1998.

Wyler, William, dir. *Wuthering Heights*. Perf. Merle Oberon and Laurence Olivier. United Artists, 1939.

Yoshishige, Yoshida, dir. *Wuthering Heights* [*Arashi ga oka*]. Perf. Yusaku Matsuda and Yûko Tanaka. 1988.


## Some Translations

### Arabic

Muhsin, Fādil Habīb, 'Abd al-Haqq, Ahmad Muhammad, Dhikrá 'Abd al-Rahmān Hasan, and Muná Fathī Sālim, trans. *Murtafa 'aī Wudhiriñgh*. Beirut, Lebanon: al Maktabah al-Hadīthah, 2002.

## Chinese

Phillips, Brian, and Annie Bourneuf, trans. *Hu xiao shan zhuang* = *Wuthering Heights*. Tianjin Shi: Tianjin ke ji fan yi chu ban gong si, 2003.

Shiqiu, Liang. *Ci hen mian mian*. Shanghai: Zheng yan chu ban she, 1946.

West, Clare, and Bing Zhao. *Hu xiao shan zhuang* = *Wuthering Heights*. Beijing: Wai yu jiao xue yu yan jiu chu ban she, 1997.

## Czech

Simková, Bozena, trans. *Bourlivé Výsiny: Román*. Prague: Pokrok, 1912. Praze: Jan Laichter, 1946.

## Danish

Bodelsen, C. A., trans. *Stormfulde Højder*. Copenhagen: Gyldendal, 1928.

## Finnish

*Humiseva harju*. 1927. Porvoo: W. Söderström, 1952.

## French

Delebecque, Frédéric, trans. *Les Hauts de Hurle-Vent*. Paris: Nouvelle Librarie Nationale, 1925.

Drover, M., trans. *Les Hauts des Quatre-Vents*. Paris: Albin Michel, 1934.

Jean, Dominique, Michel Fuchs, and Annie Regourd, trans. *Wuthering Heights et Autres Romans, 1847–1848*. 3 vols. Bibliothèque de la Pléiade. Paris: Gallimard, 2002.

Lacassin, Francis, trans. *Wuthering Heights. Brontë: Oeuvres*. 3 vols. Paris: Robert Laffont, 1990.

Leyris, Pierre, trans. *Wuthering Heights*. Paris: Pauvert, 1972.

Monod, Sylvère, trans. *Hurlemont*. Paris: Garnier Frères, 1963.

Wyzewa, Théodore de, trans. *Un Amant*. Paris: Perrin, 1892.

## German

Gisela, Etzel, trans. *Der Sturmheidhof*. Leipzig: Julius Zeitler, 1908.

Rambach, Grete, trans. *Die Sturmhöhe: Roman*. Leipzig, 1938. Frankfurt am Main: Insel-Verl, 2001.

von Sonheimer, Gladys. *Liebe und Hass auf Wuthering Heights: Roman.* Zurich: Verlag der Arche, 1945.
*Wuthering Heights and Agnes Grey.* Leipzig: Tauchnitz, 1851.
*Wutherings-höhe.* Grimma and Leipzig: Verlags-Comptoir, 1851.

**(Modern) Greek**
Alexiou, Georgias, trans. *Ho Pyrgos Tōn Kataigidōn: Anemodarmena Hypsē.* [Athens]: Ekdoseis Vivliothēkē gia Holous, 19—.
*O Pyrgos Tōn Kataigidōn: Anemodarmena Yōē* [s.l.]: Ekdoseis Bibliothēkē Gai Oloue, 1960.

**Hebrew**
Yi.frah, Yiśra'el, trans. *Anḳat Gevahim.* Kefar Monash, Israel: 'Ofarim, 2007.

**Hindi**
Prasad, Brajkishore. *Jhañjhā bhavana.* New Delhi: Sāhitya Akādemī, 1999.

**Hungarian**
*Uvöltő Szelek.* Budapest: Magyar Helikon, 1971.

**Irish**
O'Ciosáin, Seán, trans. *Árda Wuthering.* Dublin: Oifig Díolta Foillseacháin, 1933.

**Italian**
Bianchi, Mariagrazia Oddera, trans. *Cime Tempestose.* Rome: Newton Compton Editori, 1997.
Binetti, Rosina, trans. *Cime Tempestose.* Milan: Treves, 1934; Garzanti, 1942.
*La Tempestosa: Romanzo.* Milan: ["La Grafica Moderna"], 1926.

**Japanese**
Nakaoka, Hiroshi. *Wuthering Heights.* Tokyo: Gogaku Shunjusha, 1972. [Abridged, illus., with sound cassette.]
Yamato, Yasuo, trans. *Arashigaoka.* Tokyo: Shintensha, 1946.

**Korean**
An, Tong-min, trans. *P'okp'ung ŭi oňdŏk.* Seoul: Pŏmusa, 1985.

Yi, Chang-sŏng, trans. *P'okp'ung ŭi oňdŏk: Pomulsŏm*. Seoul: Hagwŏnsa, 1972. [With R. L. Stevenson's *Treasure Island*.]

**Persian**
*Wātirīng Haītz*. Tehran: Bungāh-i Tarjumih va-Nashr-i Kitāb, 1976.

**Polish**
Sujkowska, Janina, trans. *Wichrowe Wzgórza*. Warsaw: Czytelnik, 1976.

**Portuguese**
Chaves, Ana Maria, trans. *O Alto dos Vendavais*. Lisbon: Dom Quixote, 2001.
Mendes, Oscar, and Victor Civita, trans. *O Morro dos Ventos Uivantes*. São Paulo: Abril Cultural, 1979.

**Romanian**
Polihroniade, Mary, trans. *La răscruce de vânturi*. Bucharest: Fundația pentru literatură si arta "Regele Carol II," 1937.
Stahl, Henriette Yvonne. *La răscruce de vînturi*. Bucharest: Garamond, 1991.

**Russian**
*Grozovoĭ Pereval*. Moskow: EKSMO-Press, 2000. [With *Agnes Grey*.]
*Grozovoĭ Pereval*. Moskow: Khudozhestvennaia literatura, 1990. [With Brontë's poems.]
Volpin, Nadezhda, trans. *Wuthering Heights*. Moscow: Belles Lettres, 1956.

**Spanish**
Ferrero, Miguel Perez, trans. *Cumbres Borrascosas*. Barcelona: Planeta, 1997.
Montoliu, C., trans. *Cumbres Borracosas*. Madrid: Atenea, 1921.

**Swedish**
Werin, Ada, trans. *Blåst*. Stockholm: Norstedt, 1927.

**Turkish**
Bergin, Azize. *Uğultulu Tepeler*. İstanbul: Alfa, 2004.
Öncül, Naciye, trans. *Rüzgârlı Bayır*. İstanbul: Basimevi, 1946; Can Yayınları, 2000.

## Some Sequels, Pendants, and Biographical Fiction

The following novels feature Emily Brontë or her characters, including prequels and sequels.

Banks, Lynne Reid. *Dark Quartet: The Story of the Brontës*. New York: Delacorte, 1976.

Barnard, Robert. *The Case of the Missing Brontë*. Boston, MA: G. K. Hall, 1983.

Brindley, Louise. *In the Shadow of the Brontës*. New York: St. Martin's, 1983.

Caine, Jeffrey. *Heathcliff*. New York: Knopf, 1978.

Clarke, Pauline. *The Return of the Twelves*. New York: Coward-McCann, 1963. [A boy finds the wooden soldiers that inspired the Brontë juvenilia.]

Condé, Maryse. *Windward Heights*. Trans. Richard Philcox. New York: Soho, 1998. [*La Migration des curs*, 1995; set in Guadaloupe, Cuba, and Dominica.]

Cornish, Dorothy Helen. *These Were the Brontës*. New York: Macmillan, 1940.

Davies, Stevie. *Four Dreamers and Emily*. New York: St. Martin's, 1997. [An Emily Brontë conference brings four women, including a 60-year-old virgin, together.]

Gardam, Jane. *The Summer After the Funeral*. New York: Macmillan, 1973. [A teenage girl believes she reincarnates Emily Brontë.]

Haire-Sargeant, Lin. *H.—: The Story of Heathcliff's Journey Back to Wuthering Heights*. New York: Pocket, 1992. Also as *Heathcliff: The Return to Wuthering Heights*. New York: Century, 1992.

Hughes, Glynn. *Brontë*. New York: St. Martin's, 1996.

L'Estrange, Anna [pseud.]. *Return to Wuthering Heights*. Los Angeles: Pinnacle, 1977. London: Corgi, 1978.

Roberts, Michele. *The Mistressclass*. London: Little, Brown; New York: Henry Holt, 2003. [On the Brontës.]

Sinclair, May. *The Three Sisters*. London: Hutchinson; New York: Macmillan, 1914.

Thornton Cook, E. *They Lived: A Brontë Novel.* London: Murray; New York: Scribner's, 1935.

Urquhart, Jane. *Changing Heaven.* Toronto: McClelland & Stewart, 1990.

Vandever, Jennifer. *The Brontë Project: A Novel of Passion, Desire, and Good PR.* New York: Shaye Aerheart, 2005.

Wallace, Kathleen. *Immortal Wheat; a Personal Interpretation. . . .* New York: Putnam, 1951. [On the Brontës.]

Wheatcroft, John. *Catherine: Her Book.* New York: Cornwall, 1983.

White, Hilda. *Wild Decembers: A Biographical Portrait of the Brontës.* New York: Dutton, 1957.

# Further Reading

Note: The following selective lists present resources in Brontë studies, both in earlier periods and recently.

- The first section indicates some sources designed for the student along with influential biographical studies. Editions of *Wuthering Heights* are listed by the editor's last name. Many sources cited in this edition appear here; critical studies since 1995 appear in the third section.
- The second section samples publications since 1855 for the general reader or tourist who is interested in the Brontës and their locations.
- The third section selects noteworthy publications on *Wuthering Heights* published since 1995 (some cited in this edition). In general, we have omitted publications that connect Emily Brontë and *Wuthering Heights* to other writers and works, to aspects of literary convention and literary history, or to adaptations (many may be found in a search in the *MLA Bibliography*). A standard resource is the journal *Transactions of the Brontë Society*, renamed *Brontë Studies* in 2002 (indexed at the Brontë Society and Brontë Parsonage Museum Web site, www.bronte.info). Students and teachers would also find it useful to consult *Approaches to Teaching Emily Brontë's* Wuthering Heights (Lonoff and Hasseler), which addresses a range of topics in addition to pedagogy.

## General Resources and Biographical Studies

Alexander, Christine, and Jane Sellars, eds. *The Art of the Brontës*. Cambridge, UK: Cambridge UP, 1995, 100–28.

Allott, Kenneth, and Miriam Allott, eds. *The Poems of Matthew Arnold*. New York: Longman, 1979.

Allott, Miriam, ed. *The Brontës: The Critical Heritage*. London: Routledge and Kegan Paul, 1974.

————. *Emily Brontë:* Wuthering Heights, *A Casebook.* Rev. ed. London: Macmillan, 1992.

Armstrong, Nancy. "Emily Brontë In and Out of Her Time." *Genre* 15 (1982): 243–64.

Barker, Juliet. *The Brontës.* London: Weidenfeld, 1994.

————. *The Brontës: A Life in Letters.* 1997. New York: Overlook, 2002.

Bloom, Harold. *Emily Brontë's* Wuthering Heights. New York: Chelsea House, 1996.

————, ed. *The Brontës.* New York: Chelsea House, 2000.

Booth, Alison. *How to Make It as a Woman: Collective Biographical History from Victoria to the Present.* Chicago: U Chicago P, 2004.

Brick, Allan R. "Lewes's Review of *Wuthering Heights*." *Nineteenth-Century Fiction* 14 (March 1960): 355–59.

Brontë Society, The. *The Brontë Society Annual Report 2006.* Haworth: The Brontë Society, 2006.

Burnett, John, ed. *Useful Toil: Autobiographies of Working People from the 1820s to the 1920s.* London: Allen Lane, 1974.

Cecil, David. "Emily Brontë." *Early Victorian Novelists.* London: Constable, 1934, 147–59.

Child, Francis James, ed. *English and Scottish Ballads.* Boston, MA: Little, Brown, 1857. Rpt. University of Michigan, *Making of America Books,* http://quod.lib.umich.edu/ (accessed August 13, 2007).

Chitham, Edward. *The Brontës' Irish Background.* London: Macmillan, 1986.

————. *A Life of Emily Brontë.* Oxford: Basil Blackwell, 1987.

————. *The Birth of* Wuthering Heights: *Emily Brontë at Work.* London: Macmillan, 1998.

Chitham, Edward, and Tom Winnifrith, eds. *Brontë Facts and Brontë Problems.* London: Macmillan, 1983.

Cracknell, Kenneth, and Susan J. White. *An Introduction to World Methodism.* Cambridge, UK: Cambridge UP, 2005.

Daley, A. Stuart. "The Moons and Almanacs of *Wuthering Heights*." *Huntington Library Quarterly* 37 (1974): 337–53.

Davenport, Basil, ed. *Wuthering Heights* by Emily Brontë. New York: Dodd, Mead, 1945.

Davies, Stevie. *Emily Brontë.* New York: Harvester, 1988.

Delafield, E. M., ed. *The Brontës: Their Lives Recorded by Their Contemporaries.* London: Hogarth, 1935.

Dunn, Richard J., ed. *Wuthering Heights* by Emily Brontë, 4th ed. New York: Norton, 2003.

Eagleton, Terry. "*Wuthering Heights.*" In *Myths of Power: A Marxist Study of the Brontës.* London: Macmillan, 1975, 97–121.

Eastlake, Charles L. *Hints on Household Taste in Furniture, Upholstery, and Other Details.* 1868. 4th ed. London: Longmans, Green, 1878. Rpt. New York: Dover, 1986.

Evans, Barbara, and Gareth Lloyd Evans. *The Scribner Companion to the Brontës.* New York: Scribner's, 1982.

Frank, Katherine. *Chainless Soul: A Life of Emily Brontë.* Boston, MA: Houghton, 1990.

Gaskell, Elizabeth. *The Life of Charlotte Brontë.* 1857. Oxford: Oxford UP, 1996.

Gérin, Winifred. *Emily Brontë: A Biography.* Oxford: Clarendon, 1971.

Gilbert, Sandra, and Susan Gubar. "Looking Oppositely: Emily Brontë's Bible of Hell." In *The Madwoman in the Attic: The Woman Writer and the Nineteenth-Century Imagination.* New Haven, CT: Yale UP, 1979, 248–308.

Glen, Heather, ed. *The Cambridge Companion to the Brontës.* Cambridge, UK: Cambridge UP, 2002.

Hatfield, C. W., ed. *The Complete Poems of Emily Jane Brontë.* 1941. New York: Columbia UP, 1995.

Holbrook, David. Wuthering Heights: *A Drama of Being.* Sheffield: Academic Press, 1997.

Homans, Margaret. "The Name of the Mother in *Wuthering Heights.*" In *Bearing the Word: Language and Female Experience in Nineteenth-Century Women's Writing.* Chicago: U of Chicago P, 1989, 68–99.

Hunter, Paul. *Before Novels: The Cultural Contexts of Eighteenth-Century English Fiction.* New York: Norton, 1990.

Jacobs, Carol. "*Wuthering Heights*: At the Threshold of Interpretation." In *Uncontainable Romanticism: Shelley, Brontë, Kleist.* Baltimore, MD: Johns Hopkins UP, 1989.

Kavanaugh, James. *Emily Brontë.* Oxford: Blackwell, 1985.

Knoepflmacher, U. C. Wuthering Heights: *A Study.* Athens, OH: Ohio UP, 1989.

Leavis, Q. D. "A Fresh Approach to *Wuthering Heights.*" In, *Lectures in America*, F. R. Leavis and Q. D. Leavis. London: Chatto and Windus, 1969, 85–138.

Lock, John, and Canon W. T. Dixon. *A Man of Sorrow: The Life, Letters and Times of Rev. Patrick Brontë 1777–1861.* 1965. London: Hodgkins, 1979.

Lonoff, Sue, ed. and trans. *The Belgian Essays: Charlotte Brontë and Emily Brontë.* New Haven, CT: Yale UP, 1996.

Marsden, Hilda, and Ian Jack, eds. *Wuthering Heights* by Emily Brontë. Oxford: Clarendon, 1976.

Mathison, John K. "Nelly Dean and the Power of *Wuthering Heights*." *Nineteenth Century Fiction* 11 (1956): 106–29.

McCarthy, Terence. "The Incompetent Narrator of *Wuthering Heights*." *Modern Language Quarterly* 42 (1981): 48–64.

Mellor, Anne. *Romanticism and Gender*. New York: Routledge, 1993.

Miller, J. Hillis. "*Wuthering Heights*: Repetition and the 'Uncanny.'" In *Fiction and Repetition: Seven English Novels*. Cambridge, MA: Harvard UP, 1982, 42–72.

Morgan, Edward Charles. "Emily Brontë." In *The Great Victorians*, ed. H. J. Massingham. London: Nicholson and Watson, 1932, 63–79.

Newman, Beth. "'The Situation of the Looker-On:' Gender Narration and Gaze in *Wuthering Heights*." *PMLA* 105 (1990): 1029–41.

Ohmann, Carol. "Emily Brontë in the Hands of Male Critics." *College English* 32 (May 1971): 906–13.

Orel, Harold, ed. *The Brontës: Interviews and Recollections*. London: Macmillan, 1997.

Peterson, Linda H., ed. *Wuthering Heights* by Emily Brontë, 2nd ed. Case Studies in Contemporary Criticism. New York: Bedford/St. Martin's, 2003.

Pinion, F. B. *A Brontë Companion: Literary Assessment, Background, and Reference*. New York: Harper and Row/Barnes and Noble, 1975.

Pykett, Lyn. *Emily Brontë*. Savage: Barnes, 1989.

Ratchford, Fannie Elizabeth. *The Brontës' Web of Childhood*. New York: Columbia UP, 1941.

———. *Gondal's Queen: A Novel in Verse by Emily Jane Brontë*. Austin, TX: U Texas P, 1955.

Roper, Derek, ed., with Edward Chitham. *The Poems of Emily Brontë*. Oxford: Clarendon Press, 1995.

Rosen, Andrew. "Emily Davies and the Women's Movement, 1862–1867." *The Journal of British Studies* 19 (Autumn 1979): 101–21.

Rybczynski, Witold. *Home: A Short History of an Idea*. 1986. New York: Penguin, 1987.

Sanger, Charles Percy. "The Structure of *Wuthering Heights*." In *Wuthering Heights, an Authoritative Text with Essays in Criticism*, ed. William M. Sale Jr. and Richard J. Dunn, 3rd ed. New York: Norton, 1990.

Scott, Walter. *The Lady of the Lake*. Baltimore, MD: Cushing, 1812.

Shannon, Edgar F. "Lockwood's Dreams and the Exegesis of *Wuthering Heights*." *Nineteenth-Century Fiction* 14 (1959): 95–109.

Shorter, Clement. *The Brontës: Life and Letters*. 2 vols. 1908. New York: Haskell, 1969.

Simpson, Jacqueline. "The Function of Folklore in *Jane Eyre* and *Wuthering Heights.*" *Folklore* 85 (Spring 1974): 47–61.

Spark, Muriel. *The Essence of the Brontës: A Compilation with Essays.* London: Peter Owen, 1993.

Stephens, W. B. *Education, Literacy and Society, 1830–1870: The Geography of Diversity in Provincial England.* Manchester, UK: Manchester UP, 1987.

Stoneman, Patsy. "Feminist Criticism of *Wuthering Heights.*" *Critical Survey* 4 (1992): 147–53.

———. *Brontë Transformations: The Cultural Dissemination of* Jane Eyre *and* Wuthering Heights. London: Prentice Hall Harvester Wheatsheaf, 1996.

———, ed. *Wuthering Heights* [Essays, Articles, Reviews]. New York: Columbia UP, 1998.

Thompson, E. P. *The Making of the English Working Class.* New York: Viking, 1963.

Tosh, John. *A Man's Place: Masculinity and the Middle-Class Home in Victorian England.* New Haven, CT: Yale, 1999.

Twycross-Martin, H. S. "Ellis, Sarah (1799–1872)." In *Oxford Dictionary of National Biography*, ed. H. C. G. Matthew and Brian Harrison. Oxford: OUP, 2004. http://www.oxforddnb.com/view/article/8711 (accessed September 11, 2007).

Van Ghent, Dorothy. "On *Wuthering Heights.*" In *The English Novel: Form and Function.* New York: Rinehart, 1953, 153–70.

Vogler, Thomas A., ed. *Twentieth-Century Interpretations of* Wuthering Heights. Englewood Cliffs, NJ: Prentice Hall, 1968.

Williams, Meg Harris. *A Strange Way of Killing: The Poetic Structure of* Wuthering Heights. Worcester: Clunie, 1987.

Williams, Rachel. "Reader, I Visited Him: Screen Roles Boost Tourism by £2bn." *The Guardian* (August 27, 2007). http://film.guardian. co.uk/news/story/0,,2156888,00.html (accessed September 3, 2007).

Winnifrith, Thomas J. "Branwell Brontë and Ponden Hall." In *Brontë Facts and Brontë Problems*, ed. Edward Chitham and Thomas J. Winnifrith, London: Macmillan, 1983, 77–83.

———. "Charlotte and Emily Bronte: A Study in the Rise and Fall of Literary Reputations." *The Yearbook of English Studies* 26 (1996): 14–24.

———, ed. *Critical Essays on Emily Brontë.* New York: Hall, 1997.

Woolf, Virginia. *A Room of One's Own.* 1929. New York: Harcourt, 1981.

Yeager, Patricia. "Violence in the Sitting Room: *Wuthering Heights* and the Woman's Novel." *Genre* 21 (1988): 203–29.

## Popular Reception and Travels to Brontë Country

Bentley, Phyllis. *The Brontës and Their World*. New York: Viking, 1969.

Chadwick, Esther. *In the Footsteps of the Brontës*. London: Pitman, 1914.

Clarke, Isabel C. *Haworth Parsonage: A Picture of the Brontë Family*. London: Hutchinson, 1927.

Dickinson, Emily. *The Complete Poems of Emily Dickinson*, ed. Thomas H. Johnson. Boston, MA: Little, Brown, 1960.

Hubbard, Elbert. *Little Journeys to the Homes of Famous Women*. 1897. New York: Putnam's, 1901.

Kellett, Jocelyn, and Donald Hopewell. *The Brontë Parsonage*. Haworth, UK: Brontë Society, 1978.

Lancashire County Planning Department and Standing Conference of South Pennine Authorities. *The Brontë Way*. Four illustrated and annotated walking tour maps. n. p. 1998.

Lemon, Charles. *A Centenary History of the Brontë Society*. Haworth, UK: The Brontë Society, 1993.

———, ed. *Early Visitors to Haworth: From Ellen Nussey to Virginia Woolf*. Haworth, UK: Brontë Society, 1996.

Miller, Lucasta. *The Brontë Myth*. 2001. New York: Knopf, 2003.

Mitchell, W. R. *Haworth and the Brontës: A Visitor's Guide*. Clapham, Lancaster, UK: Dalesman, 1979.

Nussey, Ellen. "Reminiscences of Charlotte Brontë." *Scribner's Monthly* 2:1 (May 1871): 18–31. Rpt. Cornell University, *Making of America*, 2005, http://cdl.library.cornell.edu/cgi-bin/moa/ (accessed August 10, 2007).

Plath, Sylvia. *Collected Poems*, ed. Ted Hughes. London: Faber, 1961.

Pollard, Arthur. *The Landscape of the Brontës*. Exeter: Webb and Bower, 1988.

Preston, A. H., ed. *Brochure and Guide to Haworth*. Haworth, UK: Parker, 1947.

Spark, Muriel. "At Emily Brontë's Grave, Haworth, April 1961." *The Essence of the Brontës*. London: Peter Owen, 1993, 314–16.

Turner, Whiteley. *A Spring-time Saunter: Round and About Brontë Land*. Halifax: Halifax Courier, 1913.

Watson, Nicola J. "Haworth." *The Literary Tourist: Readers and Places in Romantic and Victorian Britain*. Houndmills, UK: Palgrave Macmillan, 2006, 106–27.

## Selected Criticism Since 1995

Beaumont, Matthew. "Heathcliff's Great Hunger: The Cannibal Other in *Wuthering Heights*." *Journal of Victorian Culture* 9 (2004): 137–63.

Burns, Bonnie. "Nostalgia, Apostrophe, *Wuthering Heights*: The Queer Destiny of Heterosexuality." *Nineteenth-Century Feminisms* 1 (Fall–Winter 1999): 81–94.

Campbell, Ian. "The Brontës and Power." *Brontë Studies: The Journal of the Brontë Society* 30:1 (February 2005): 1–6.

Constable, Kathleen. *A Stranger within the Gates: Charlotte Brontë and Victorian Irishness*. Lanham, MD: UP of America, 2000.

Cook, Simon. "'The Ever-Shifting Kaleidoscope of the Imagination': Modern Illustrations to the Brontës." *Brontë Studies* 31 (2006): 7–22.

Cottom, Daniel. "I Think; Therefore, I Am Heathcliff." *ELH* 70:4 (Winter 2003): 1067–88.

Daley, A. Stuart. "A Revised Chronology of *Wuthering Heights*." *Brontë Society Transactions* 21 (1995): 169–73.

Duckett, R. J., ed. *The Brontës and Education*. Haworth, UK: Brontë Society, 2005.

Eagleton, Terry. *Heathcliff and the Great Hunger: Studies in Irish Culture*. London: Verso, 1995.

Geerken, Ingrid. "'The Dead Are Not Annihilated': Mortal Regret in *Wuthering Heights*." *Journal of Narrative Theory* 34 (2004): 373–406.

Gezari, Janet. "Fathoming 'Remembrance': Emily Brontë in Context." *ELH* 66:4 (Winter 1999): 965–84.

Gorsky, Susan Rubinow. "'I'll Cry Myself Sick': Illness in *Wuthering Heights*." *Literature and Medicine* 18:2 (Fall 1999): 173–91.

Haire-Sargeant, Lin. "Sympathy for the Devil: The Problem of Heathcliff in Film Versions of *Wuthering Heights*." In *Nineteenth-Century Women at the Movies: Adapting Classic Women's Fiction to Film*, ed. Barbara Tepa Lupack. Bowling Green, OH: Bowling Green State UP, 1999, 167–91.

Heywood, Christopher. "Introduction." In *Wuthering Heights*. New York: Broadview, 2002, 18–90.

Hoeveler, Diane Long, ed. *Wuthering Heights* by Emily Brontë. Boston: Houghton Mifflin, 2002.

Kreilkamp, Ivan. "Petted Things: *Wuthering Heights* and the Animal." *Yale Journal of Criticism: Interpretation in the Humanities* 18:1 (Spring 2005): 87–110.

Levy, Eric P. "The Psychology of Loneliness in *Wuthering Heights*." *Studies in the Novel* 28:2 (Summer 1996): 158–77.

Lonoff, Sue, and Terri A. Hasseler, eds. *Approaches to Teaching Emily Brontë's* Wuthering Heights. Approaches to Teaching World Literature 89. New York: MLA, 2006.

Marsden, Simon. "Imagination, Materiality and the Act of Writing in Emily Brontë's Diary Papers." *Nineteenth-Century Contexts* 28 (2006): 35–47.

———. "'Vain Are the Thousand Creeds': *Wuthering Heights*, the Bible and Liberal Protestantism." *Literature and Theology* 20 (2006): 236–50.

Mason, Emma. "The Clue to the Brontës?: Methodism and *Wuthering Heights*." In *Biblical Religion and the Novel, 1700–2000*, ed. Mark Knight and Thomas Woodman. Burlington, VT: Ashgate, 2006, 69–77.

Massé, Michelle A. "'He's More Myself Than I Am': Narcissism and Gender in *Wuthering Heights*." In *Psychoanalyses/Feminisms*, ed. Peter L. Rudnytsky and Andrew M. Gordon. Albany, NY: State U of New York P, 2000, 135–53.

Meyer, Susan. "'Your Father Was Emperor of China and Your Mother an Indian Queen': Reverse Imperialism in *Wuthering Heights*." In *Imperialism at Home: Race and Victorian Women's Fiction*. Ithaca, NY: Cornell UP, 1996, 96–125.

Nussbaum, Martha. "*Wuthering Heights*: The Romantic Ascent." *Philosophy and Literature* 20:2 (October1996): 362–82.

Smith, Sheila. "'At Once Strong and Eerie': The Supernatural in *Wuthering Heights* and Its Debt to the Traditional Ballad." *Review of English Studies* 172 (November 1997): 515–17.

Steinitz, Rebecca. "Diaries and Displacement in *Wuthering Heights*." *Studies in the Novel* 32:4 (Winter 2000): 407–19.

Stewart, Susan. "The Ballad in *Wuthering Heights*." *Representations* 86 (Spring 2004): 175–97.

Thormählen, Marianne. "The Brontë Pseudonyms: A Woman's Image—The Writer and Her Public." *English Studies* (1994): 246–55. July 20, 1992. www.victorianweb.org/authors/bronte/cbronte/thormahlen.html (accessed September 11, 2007).

———. *The Brontës and Education*. Cambridge: Cambridge UP, 2007.

Tytler, Graeme. "'Nelly, I Am Heathcliff!': The Problem of 'Identification' in *Wuthering Heights*." *Midwest Quarterly* 47 (2006): 167–81.

Vine, Steve. "Crypts of Identity: The Refusal of Mourning in *Wuthering Heights*." *English: The Journal of the English Association* 48:192 (Autumn 1999): 169–86.

Von Sneidern, Maja-Lisa. "*Wuthering Heights* and the Liverpool Slave Trade." *ELH* 62:1 (Spring 1995): 171–96.